A HISTORY OF POSTWAR JAPAN

A HISTORY OF POSTWAR JAPAN

Recovery, Prosperity, and Transformation

Simon Avenell

University of Hawai‘i Press
Honolulu

Printed in the United States of America

First printed, 2025

Library of Congress Cataloging-in-Publication Data

Names: Avenell, Simon author
Title: A history of postwar Japan : recovery, prosperity, and transformation / Simon Avenell.
Other titles: Recovery, prosperity, and transformation
Description: Honolulu : University of Hawai'i Press, [2025] | Includes bibliographical references and index.
Identifiers: LCCN 2024059271 (print) | LCCN 2024059272 (ebook) | ISBN 9780824898687 hardback | ISBN 9780824898694 trade paperback | ISBN 9780824898953 epub | ISBN 9780824898960 kindle edition | ISBN 9780824898946 pdf
Subjects: LCSH: Japan—History—1945– | Japan—Economic conditions—1945– | Japan—Politics and government—1945– | Japan—Social conditions—1945–
Classification: LCC DS889 .A985 2025 (print) | LCC DS889 (ebook) | DDC 952.04—dc23/eng/20250319
LC record available at https://lccn.loc.gov/2024059271
LC ebook record available at https://lccn.loc.gov/2024059272

Cover art: Taxis, buses and streetcars pass in front of the Nihon Gekijo Theater in Tokyo's Yurakucho in 1967. In the background, a new 0 series bullet train can be seen. Photograph courtesy of MeijiShowa/Afloimages.

University of Hawai'i Press books are printed on acid-free paper and meet the guidelines for permanence and durability of the Council on Library Resources.

Contents

List of Figures and Tables

List of Tables

Acknowledgments and Conventions

A comprehensive history like this book depends greatly on the productive outputs of hundreds of scholars over many years. I want to sincerely thank all of them. Without their work, this book would not have been possible. I thank the East Asian librarians at the Australian National University, who sourced a wide array of materials necessary for this project. I also thank the City of Sapporo and the National Research Institute for Earth Science and Disaster Resilience for granting permission to reproduce images. Thank you to the two reviewers who suggested important additions to better round out the coverage of the book. I am eternally grateful to Masako Ikeda at the University of Hawai‘i Press for her enthusiasm and her assistance with this project. I thank Helen Overmyer for her careful and thorough copyediting of the manuscript. A generous subvention from the University of Hawai‘i Press covered the cost for the many images in the book. I believe their addition makes for a far richer reading experience. Finally, I thank my wife for her unwavering support, advice, and companionship.

A brief word on conventions. Names are written in East Asian order, with family name preceding given names (e.g., Hiratsuka Raichō, Park Chung-hee, Xi Jinping) except for people who use Western name order. Long vowels are indicated by macrons (e.g., Honshū, Ōhira), except for words commonly used in English like "Tokyo" and "Osaka."

Abbreviations

AFC	Asian Financial Crisis
BLL	Buraku Liberation League
CAO	Cabinet Office
CDP	Constitutional Democratic Party
CEO	chief executive officer
CGP	Clean Government Party
CIA	Central Intelligence Agency
CS	Cabinet Secretariat
DBJ	Development Bank of Japan
DLP	Democratic Liberal Party
DP	Democratic Party
DPJ	Democratic Party of Japan
DSP	Democratic Socialist Party
EEOL	Equal Employment Opportunity Law
EPA	Economic Planning Agency
ESS	Economic and Scientific Section (of SCAP)
FAO	Food and Agriculture Organization of the United Nations
FDI	foreign direct investment
FEC	Far Eastern Commission
FILP	Fiscal Investment and Loan Program
G2	Assistant Chief of Staff or General Staff Section, Intelligence (of SCAP)
G5	Group of 5
GATT	General Agreement on Tariffs and Trade
GDP	gross domestic product
GFC	Global Financial Crisis
GHQ	General Headquarters (of SCAP)

GNP	gross national product (national income)
GS	Government Section (of SCAP)
IAEA	International Atomic Energy Agency
IRAA	Imperial Rule Assistance Association
JCG	Japan Coast Guard
JCP	Japanese Communist Party
JDP	Japan Democratic Party
JLP	Japan Liberal Party
JNP	Japan New Party
JNR	Japan National Railways
JP	Japan Post
JPP	Japan Progressive Party
JRP	Japan Renewal Party
JSP	Japan Socialist Party
LDP	Liberal Democratic Party
LNG	liquid natural gas
LP	Liberal Party
LWDO	Law for Worker Dispatch Operations
MHA	Ministry of Home Affairs
MHLW	Ministry of Health, Labour and Welfare
MITI	Ministry of International Trade and Industry
MOE	Ministry of Education
MOF	Ministry of Finance
MOFA	Ministry of Foreign Affairs
MOL	Ministry of Labor
NFP	New Frontier Party
NGO	nongovernmental organization
NHK	Nippon Hōsō Kyōkai
NLA	National Land Agency
NLC	New Liberal Club
NPA	National Police Agency
NPO	nonprofit organization
NPR	National Police Reserve
NPS	New Party Sakigake

NSF	National Safety Forces
NSO	National Strategy Office
NTT	Nippon Telegraph and Telephone Corporation
OAPEC	Organization of Arab Petroleum Exporting Countries
ODA	Official Development Assistance
OECD	Organisation for Economic Co-operation and Development
OPEC	Organization of the Petroleum Exporting Countries
PARC	Policy Affairs Research Council
PNP	People's New Party
POWs	prisoners of war
PR	proportional representation
PRC	People's Republic of China
RP	Reform Party
SCAP	Supreme Commander for the Allied Powers
SDF	Self-Defense Force
SDFR	Socialist Democratic Federation
SDP	Social Democratic Party
SII	Structural Impediments Initiative
SMD	single-member district
STDs	sexually transmitted diseases
TEPCO	Tokyo Electric Power Company
UN	United Nations
UNCED	United Nations Conference on Environment and Development
US	United States
USSR	Union of Soviet Socialist Republics
VER	voluntary export restraint

Introduction

Understanding Postwar Japan

This book recounts the history of Japan from its defeat in the Asia-Pacific War in 1945 through the early decades of the twenty-first century. Historians have referred to this period as Japan's postwar era, distinguishing it from the preceding years defined by colonial empire and militarism. Japan's postwar era has been characterized by striking economic transformation, the consolidation and continuity of liberal democracy, profound demographic changes, and the endurance of a far-reaching security and economic relationship with the United States of America. If 1868—the year of Japan's historic Meiji Restoration—is considered as a tentative beginning of Japanese modern history, then the postwar era accounts for over half of this more than 150-year period. As readers will discover, however, the historical narrative in this book does not start on August 15, 1945, but, rather, it begins by tracing the deeper historical continuities wrought by Japan's full-scale engagement with the West and Western-style modernity from the mid-nineteenth century onward. Short of total obliteration, there is really no such thing as a clear or perfect break in the history of human societies, and Japan is no exception here—despite the disjuncture of 1945. Accordingly, the postwar experience needs to be anchored in this longer historical journey. At the same time, this book also attempts to present the history of Japan's postwar era as a coherent and identifiable phase in the country's modern period. So, in this sense, it is also the history of a Japan somewhat different from what it had been before 1945.

In this introductory chapter I provide a broad overview of the major themes and issues in postwar Japanese history described in greater detail in subsequent chapters. It is worth noting at the outset that the notion of an identifiable and coherent phase of Japanese history called the "postwar era" is an interpretive intervention on the part of historians like me. As I discuss below, the "postwar era" is a period marker that others have vigorously challenged and even proposed legitimate alternatives to. For some conservative politicians, so stifling is the idea of the "postwar" that they have even called on the Japanese people to break free from the "postwar regime" once and for all. Nonetheless, in this introduction and in the naming and very structure of this book, I will attempt to make a case for the validity of the postwar era as a useful way to understand Japan's recent history while, at the same time, incorporating the insights of other possible chronologies of the past century or so. Readers interested primarily in the narrative might at this point proceed to chapter 1, but I encourage those interested in a discussion of the broader conceptualizations, themes, and dynamics of postwar Japanese history to first consider the ideas outlined below.

Given that historical periodizations are inherently artificial in the sense of being made by humans rather than occurring naturally, one might begin by considering the fundamental character of postwar Japan. To make the task more manageable, this can be meaningfully divided into three questions concerning the *why,* the *what,* and the *how* of the postwar era. First, *why*—some eighty years after the end of the Asia-Pacific War—might the period name "postwar" still be valid when the term is not systematically used in the historiography of most other nations? Second, disregarding the period name "postwar," *what* distinguishing characteristics and processes make it possible to treat this era from August 1945 onward as a coherent historical period? And third, based on these characteristics and processes, *how* might the postwar era be meaningfully chronologized both internally and alongside other historical phases in Japan? There is another matter relating to the postwar era that is addressed in the epilogue: Has the postwar era finished and, if so, based on what objective phenomena? Or, if the postwar era is yet to end, what must happen to produce that end?

The *Why* of Postwar Japanese History

Consider first the term "postwar," which has become the standard nomenclature for describing the period from 1945 onward in Japan. Despite numerous declarations about the "end of the postwar era" over the years, the term has proved remarkably durable and, if anything, its usage has increased over time. Those familiar with historical periodizations for other nations will recognize the unique usage of the term in the case of Japan. While the Japanese word *sengo* literally translates as "postwar," in practice its usage is more akin to "present-day" or "contemporary" history and quite different from terms like the German *Nachkriegszeit* (postwar period), which refers to the immediate years after Germany's defeat in war.[1] So why has this period name "postwar" sunk such deep roots in Japan, when it has been relegated to past history elsewhere?

For some, the postwar idea continues to be relevant primarily because Japan has yet to fully resolve historical issues with neighboring countries stemming from the Asia-Pacific War.[2] Ongoing frictions between Japan and countries such as South Korea over historical interpretations, apologies, and forms of compensation to victims have made the Asia-Pacific War a live and ongoing issue, arguably stranding Japan in a permanent postwar limbo. From this perspective, it is the persistent weight of history that makes the postwar idea relevant today and encourages conservatives to demand its immediate rejection.

But, while such unresolved pasts are certainly a factor, the very symbolism of the "postwar" idea has also underpinned its longevity. Historians point to the existence of a uniquely post-1945 mentality or "psychology" among the Japanese that has helped them to put a "difficult past behind" and establish a new set of goals to "aspire to."[3] Writing some thirty years ago, the historian Carol Gluck observed how the postwar era came to be associated with what she called the "founding myth of postwar Japan."[4] Origins of the myth can be traced to the conspiracy thesis developed by prosecutors at the International Military Tribunal for the Far East (the Tokyo War Crimes Tribunal) begun in 1946. The central focus of that tribunal was on Prime Minister Tōjō Hideki and a handful of political and military leaders who were accused and convicted of having conspired to draw Japan into a war against America and its allies. Among the numerous negative outcomes of this trial was a sense among many Japanese that they had been victims of their leaders during the war rather than complicit participants. Many easily concluded that the tribunal and its verdicts essentially severed ties with this dark past, opening up a bright new future for the nation. In this way, the myth of postwar Japan encompassed a popular sense of a "radical discontinuity" in which "history stopped and began anew with the defeat in 1945."[5] With this disjuncture, war was "severed" from peace, "the prewar from the postwar," and "the imperial state from the democratic society."[6]

Importantly, the myth of postwar Japan underwrote a new post-1945 mentality among the Japanese people based on a "contentment with the status quo" of democracy, peace, and affluence.[7] The preeminent historian of postwar Japan, Narita Ryūichi, argues that the "postwar" became so natural for the Japanese that they developed a "postwar identity" based on an "unconscious affirmation of 'current' conditions." This entrenched identity meant that the Japanese would never make any genuine attempt at "active transformation" throughout this era, preferring a status quo that sidestepped the past.[8]

Thus, the very labeling of the period after 1945 as the "postwar era" implicitly generates a number of complications in terms of the symbolism that the postwar idea invokes, as well as the other histories that it obscures. Indeed, once set in place, historical periodizations can become "intellectual straitjackets" that "tyrannize our understanding" of "the beginning, middle, and ending of things."[9]

One of the most obvious problems with the postwar idea is how it simplifies a more complicated timeline. For example, factually speaking, the postwar era did not begin on August 15, 1945, because military exchanges with Soviet forces continued on Sakhalin Island and the Kurile Islands (Chishima Rettō in Japanese) to the north. Moreover, it was not the emperor's broadcast of August 15 but the signing of the surrender documents in September 1945 that brought the war to an official end. The fact that countries such as the USSR (Union of Soviet Socialist Republics or "Soviet Union") (later Russia) have never signed a peace treaty with Japan only further complicates the term "postwar."

The strong connotation of historical rupture in the postwar idea also tends to obscure important continuities across the war divide. Scholars have produced much research connecting developments in the postwar era directly to the prewar and wartime years.[10] Andrew Gordon, for instance, points to a "transwar phase of history" stretching from the 1920s to the mid-1950s.[11] He sees continuities in terms of the centrality of rural life and agriculture, family composition and gender roles, patterns of work, and ruling structures. Only from the late 1950s does Gordon posit the emergence of a truly "postwar condition."[12] From a slightly different perspective, others identify the formation of a "total war system" in 1940s Japan that, in many ways, continued to operate under the Allied Occupation of Japan from 1945 to 1952.[13] For example, policies for agricultural reform under the Japanese wartime regime had attempted to break the stranglehold of landlords over tenants, thereby producing more owner farmers who would be incentivized to produce more rice.[14] Although the subsequent Allied Occupation had very different objectives, its land reforms more or less continued and expanded the earlier wartime policies aimed at dismantling such vested interests.[15] Proponents of the 1940s total war system thesis thus argue that it is better to treat wartime policies in areas such as labor-management relations, governmental interventions in the economy, and agricultural reforms on a "single continuum." Herein, the Occupation reforms represent merely a "contemporization" of the wartime system.[16]

Another radically different way of traversing Japanese history across the war divide has been to utilize imperial reign—specifically, the reign of the Shōwa Emperor, Hirohito, from 1926 to 1989.[17] This division is similar to the above transwar perspectives in that it downplays the discontinuity of 1945, but it is not without its problems. For example, while the death of Hirohito in 1989 roughly coincided with several other endings to produce a seeming moment of historical transition (see chap. 6), there was nothing particularly historic about 1926 when Hirohito assumed the throne. So, just as the postwar era does not appear to have a definitive end, the Shōwa era does not have a historically convincing beginning. Moreover, popular invocations of the Shōwa era in contemporary Japan are often attached to a nostalgia for the culture of the postwar portion of that era. Nowhere is this more evident than in the "two Hirohitos": the pre-1945 military leader versus the more affable image of the post-1945 people's emperor in a business suit.[18] In one way or another, these transwar perspectives counsel us not to overemphasize the disjuncture of 1945, instead recognizing the continuities linking postwar Japan to the prewar and wartime years—an approach adopted in this book.

Apart from masking transwar continuities, it is important to recognize how the idea of "Postwar Japan" (with a capital "P") can easily invoke a static or uniform understanding of this era, smoothing out lived realities, unexamined pasts, and historic changes over time. As the chapters of this book reveal, the postwar era has been one of enormous transformation in all spheres of human activity and human-nature interactions. Some even argue that the postwar idea "erroneously ties the Japan of today to the Japan of eighty years ago" with "the implication that the similarities . . . are more important than the changes."[19] Others contest the very notion that Japan after 1945 has even been postwar.[20] Beginning with the Korean War (1950–1953), continuing through the Vietnam War (1965–1974), and later the Iraq War (2003), they argue that "Japan has been an active participant in various wars since 1945," while not becoming directly involved in combat.[21] This is a provocative perspective indeed and cautions us to be wary of too easily designating postwar Japan an era of stasis and absolute pacifism after the earlier stage of militarism. The historical terrain has been far more jagged.

To genuinely capture the realities of the era, it is necessary to be attentive to the "fractures and discords concealed beneath a seamless 'national history.'"[22] For instance, what might be learned about the postwar era by traversing the complex topography of its ethnic, spatial, and other borders? Could it be that the "postwar here is not the same as the postwar there"—be this for minorities, women, the precariat, Okinawans, Ainu, and other marginalized groups?[23] The chapters in this book attempt to employ this perspective of unevenness by incorporating the experiences of such groups. Indeed, attentiveness to the ethnic, spatial, and other limitations inherent in the postwar idea can also help us to see post-1945 Japan as a postimperial space.

Given these problems of naming, should postwar Japan be called something else—"Japan since 1945," "contemporary Japan," or even "postimperial Japan"—or does the term "postwar" still have some usefulness today? The fact that Japanese still use the term, while certainly not validating its suitability as a period name, certainly confirms its enduring place in the national imaginary. For all its blind spots, obfuscations, and limitations, I use "postwar" in this book because—for now, at least—I believe that it continues to capture the essence of an era and its mentalities better than other appellations like "contemporary."

The *What* of Postwar Japanese History

Putting aside the problem of naming, the next task becomes one of identifying the characteristics, processes, and phenomena that make the years after 1945 a meaningful historical era—in other words, the *what* of postwar Japanese history. At least ten features that have given this era its own unique historical character can be identified.

Postimperial Japan. To begin with, defeat in war involved the almost-immediate loss of an empire stretching across large areas of East Asia and the Pacific. This was a loss of historic proportions, and the empire's relatively painless demise under American patronage bequeathed thorny problems for postwar generations. In a sense, the postimperial condition made Japan after August 1945 fundamentally different from anything it had been before—especially since the late nineteenth century—thus giving the new era its own distinctive hue.

Demilitarized Japan. Along with empire, the Japanese military was systematically disarmed and dismantled, and its role as a political actor ended. The new constitution of 1947 ensured that postwar Japan would not have a military, although American prodding and creative constitutional interpretation facilitated the establishment of the Self-Defense Forces (SDF) in 1954. Importantly, the removal of the military from politics opened a space for actors such as national bureaucrats to exert even greater influence over government in the postwar era. As the years progressed after 1945, Japanese leaders and people were intermittently faced with quandaries over national defense, security alliances, and international engagement growing out of a legal framework prohibiting the existence of an official military. Such quandaries were new because prior to 1945 the military had always been a legally legitimate state institution.

Democratized Japan. While progressive democratic movements and liberal thought had figured prominently in Japan before 1945, the state consistently utilized the Meiji legal-institutional framework to stifle their influence. Democracy in prewar Japan regularly had its wings clipped, if not forcefully broken. In contrast, the Allied Occupation reforms meant that the postwar era would be based on a new institutional architecture in which freedoms of assembly, organization, speech, and political participation were guaranteed. This consolidation of democracy in the constitution and state institutions established a new playing field for politics in the postwar era. The new institutional architecture also fueled the growth of a civil society, now liberated from the shackles of prewar and wartime suppression. In response, the enemies of democracy in the postwar era fashioned new weapons to pursue their agendas, but now there were greater limits on what they could do and how they could do it.

The American embrace. Japan's postwar era is distinguished by the evolution of a new relationship with the United States based on a form of subordinate independence. As discussed in chapter 1, America had been a major influence on Japanese history since the mid-nineteenth century, but the postwar years witnessed a fundamental recalibration and intensification of the relationship. The United States became Japan's national security blanket and a decisive influence on foreign policy-making, a powerful force in social and cultural developments, and a market by which Japan could resurrect its economy. Although the relationship experienced highs and lows, and while it was subject to staunch criticism at times, Japanese leaders and citizens never seriously considered pulling back from the American embrace, whether politically, economically, intellectually, or culturally.

One-party conservative rule. Going hand in glove with this American embrace was the dominance of one-party conservative rule in the postwar era. Apart from two occasions—one in the mid-1990s, the other from 2009 to 2012—the Liberal Democratic Party (LDP) governed continuously from its formation in 1955. This dominance gave postwar Japanese politics and democracy their own distinct flavor—predictable, but hardly optimal in the eyes of many LDP critics. The reverse side of this LDP dominance was the gradual decline of opposition parties, whose fleeting moments of triumph were overshadowed by decades of virtual irrelevance.

Economic transformation. While national politics in the postwar era has been characterized by long-term continuity, the Japanese economy and society have been spaces of often-astounding renovation and evolution, as well as obstinate stagnation. Throughout the postwar era, the Japanese economy experienced profound sectoral transformations from the primary to the secondary and, ultimately, the tertiary sector. Manufacturing industries in the secondary sector such as shipbuilding, petrochemicals, automobiles, electronics, and semiconductors paved the way for this sectoral transformation. From the late 1950s until the early 1970s, the economy experienced double-digit growth, and it continued to grow solidly—if not as impressively—until the late 1980s, different from many other industrialized economies worldwide. By the late 1960s, Japan had become the second largest capitalist economy in the world and was quickly establishing itself as an advanced technological and economic superpower.

But the story was not only one of upwards and outwards. Yet another defining feature of the postwar Japanese economy has been the prolonged struggle of policy-makers to accomplish fundamental reform following a financial and real estate bubble collapse in the early 1990s. The Japanese economy faced many challenges in the prewar years such as the recessionary conditions after World War I and, later, the Great Depression. But the challenge of structurally reforming a highly advanced economy in the late twentieth century was something new, especially in the face of historic demographic and public finance challenges.

Social homogenization. Economic change in postwar Japan was accompanied by significant social transformations that traced their roots to the prewar years but became even more pronounced from around the late 1950s onward. Growing affluence stimulated the spread of a mass consumer culture among both urban and rural inhabitants, many of whom began to view themselves as "middle class." This middle-class consciousness found expression in political, social, educational, and economic institutions and "was articulated over the postwar decades in discourses of culture, class, cohort, and life cycle."[24] It was a consciousness that had some basis in fact because incomes rose over time. Furthermore, modes of employment and patterns of consumption also tended to promote a certain homogenization in the lifeways of postwar Japanese.

At the same time, middle-class consciousness also had the effect of obscuring distinctions and forms of discrimination based on gender, ethnicity, education, employment, and geographical location—which greatly limited the life choices of many. Indeed, under the shadow of homogenization, disparity remained a part of the system, becoming far more visible in recent decades.

Demographic transformation. The other standout characteristic of postwar Japan has been demographic transformation and, like economic change, it is a theme that runs through this book from beginning to end. The origins of many of these demographic trends trace to the pre-1945 years, but developments after 1945 (and especially after the mid-1950s) were of a different scale altogether. In the period from the mid-1950s to the early 1970s, Japan was transformed from a largely rural society into an urbanized one. Many who remained in the countryside no longer farmed full time, and farming was often left to wives and elderly parents while men went to work in regional cities and large metropolises. Japanese life expectancy increased impressively, thanks to rising affluence and excellent health care. At the same time, the total fertility rate began to decline noticeably in the mid-1970s with families of two or fewer children becoming the norm. The combined effect of aging and low fertility developed into a demographic transformation of historic proportions. It presented policymakers with a new and challenging set of problems relating to government revenues and expenditures. The condition was new in both Japanese and world history.

Japan in the world. No longer a military power in its own right, Japan in the postwar era witnessed not only the construction of a new relationship with the United States but also the forging of a new way of engaging with the world more generally, especially with East Asia. Economically, this new engagement unfolded through export-intensive industries such as ships, steel, electronics, and automobiles; outward foreign direct investment (FDI); a growing presence in global capital markets; and, more recently, the emergence of the country's culture industries and inbound tourism. In terms of Japan's region—Northeast Asia and Southeast Asia—the postwar era represented one of growing economic interdependence. Japan relied on markets throughout the region to sell its products while simultaneously sourcing raw materials and energy and utilizing the region for much of its FDI. While this was the case in the past, now such activity occurred without the levers of colonialism and militarism. The ongoing legacy of unresolved historical issues stemming from the Asia-Pacific War also shaped Japan's postwar relationship with the outside world and, especially, its region. These problems included controversies over Japanese transgressions in its former colonies; fallout from its aggressive militarism; and territorial disputes with the Soviet Union (later Russia), South Korea, the People's Republic of China (PRC), and Taiwan.

The environmental challenge. While pre-1945 Japan was no stranger to environmental crises—including the environmental destruction wrought by war—the postwar era stands out as one of multifaceted and ever-intensifying environmental challenges and crises. As the chapters in this book show, the underbelly of Japan's postwar economic recovery and growth was environmental degradation and pollution of historic proportions. The country managed to overcome this crisis, but its growing economic footprint worldwide—especially in Asia—continued to enmesh Japan in environmental issues. Like other nations, in recent decades the Japanese have been forced to face looming global environmental challenges such as climate change. In this volatile environmental context, decisions about the economy, consumption, energy, and intergenerational responsibility have moved to the forefront of social and political debate.

The *How* of Postwar Japanese History

With these key characteristics in mind, *how* then might the postwar era be subdivided into more easily-digestible subphases, and what important watersheds can help us identify the shift from one phase to another? To borrow a term from biology and linguistics, the question here is about the "morphology" of Japan's postwar era—its form, structure, and interactions.[25] A challenge faced in subdividing a stretch of historical time like the postwar era is that different domains of activity—political, economic, social, cultural, and environmental—do not necessarily overlap in a seamless way and neither do their respective watersheds. Changes in one domain, such as the economy, may induce environmental, cultural, or social transformations but with a time lag, making it difficult to neatly subdivide. This task is only further complicated when attempting to align domestic and international developments. It is thus up to historians to determine which domains "deserve highest priority in compartmentalizing the past."[26]

This book divides the postwar era into six broad phases based on shifts in both politics and the economy that, in turn, had broad social, cultural, and environmental implications:

Phase one, *Occupation and Recovery* (1945–1947), was characterized by the desolation and destruction of defeat, the loss of colonial empire, the demoralization of foreign occupation, the implementation of democratic reform, and the revival of progressive politics.

Phase two, *The Age of Politics* (1948–1960), involved the shift in Occupation policies accompanying the onset of the Cold War, the formation of the long-ruling LDP, the signing of the San Francisco Peace Treaty and the United States (US)-Japan Security Treaty, the proliferation of civic protest in the form of peace movements and anti-US military base movements, and the emergence of Japan's so-called postwar developmental state at the helm of a growing economy. This age of politics reached its crescendo with the massive protests opposing the renewal of the US-Japan Security Treaty in 1960.

Phase three, *The Age of the Economy* (1960–1973), witnessed a shift in political emphasis from the divisive politics of national security and alliances to the objective of economic growth, symbolized by the new prime minister, Ikeda Hayato, and his income-doubling economic policy. From this time, many more Japanese began to enjoy the spoils of affluence as their lives became increasingly standardized into the system of mass production and mass consumption. Contentious politics did not disappear, however. On the contrary, the LDP and its allies faced challenges from radical students, antiwar protesters, and opponents of industrial pollution. After several "miraculous" spurts of double-digit economic growth, this age of the economy came to an end in the early 1970s with the collapse of the Bretton Woods system in 1971 (ending the halcyon days of a low yen), and the first Oil Shock of 1973 (marking the end of cheap energy).

Phase four, *Japan, The Economic Superpower* (1970s–1980s), encompassed Japan's comparatively speedy and successful recovery after the first and second Oil Shocks and its subsequent emergence as a full-fledged global economic superpower. Within politics, a new breed of politicians like Tanaka Kakuei emerged. These political actors were intent on securing some of the spoils of affluence for their respective constituencies and, in some views, they injected a form of pluralism into Japan's bureaucrat-directed developmental state. But they also intensified money politics, pork-barreling, and corruption. While inequality persisted, many Japanese began to revel in their affluence, so much so that, by the mid-1980s, the country entered a frenetic economic bubble precipitated by American pressure to appreciate the yen. As prices for real estate and securities soared, it seemed to many that Japan had truly become "Number One."

Phase five, during the 1990s, was *The Era of Unravelling*. The death of Emperor Hirohito and the collapse of the Cold War framework in Europe helped to foster a sense of ending among Japanese in the late 1980s. But the really shocking blows came in the early 1990s when price bubbles in the stock and real estate markets unceremoniously burst, plunging the country into a period of melancholy and lost direction. Natural disasters, shocking youth crimes, acts of terror on the subways, and a challenging labor market only added to the sense of hopelessness in what would come to be known as the "lost decade." At the same time, Asia—including the PRC—came back onto the Japanese radar screen as never before in the postwar era, in terms of growing economic interdependence and cultural exchange and also in connection to unresolved legacies from the Asia-Pacific War.

Phase six, *Japan in the New Millennium* (2001–present), witnessed the rise of new, populist political entrepreneurs with their own unique proposals to restore vitality to the nation. For the maverick LDP politician Koizumi Jun'ichirō, this involved a frontal attack on the LDP and a strong dose of neoliberal reform. For the short-lived government of the Democratic Party of Japan (DPJ), reform was about redistribution and social welfare, while for the LDP nationalist, Abe Shinzō, it involved constitutional reform and an elixir of "Abenomics." But none of these approaches could solve the fundamental demographic, economic, and public policy challenges facing the country. Such problems were only further exacerbated by a massive earthquake and tsunami in March 2011 that resulted in a nuclear power plant meltdown of historic proportions. If the country were to abandon nuclear power, where would it turn for reliable energy in an age of decarbonization?

Coupled with these domestic challenges, the new millennium presented Japan with troubling geopolitical challenges, most notably the rise of the PRC as a global military and economic power but also threats from North Korea and a belligerent Russia under President Vladimir Putin. The country's second postwar summer Olympic Games scheduled for 2020 were viewed by many as a chance for Japan to turn the corner on its decades of struggle, but the event unfortunately coincided with the global COVID-19 pandemic, resulting in a one-year postponement and an event held under tight pandemic restrictions. With a new emperor on the throne from 2019, Japanese political, business, and intellectual elites groped for solutions to the demographic, geopolitical, and economic challenges facing the country, while ordinary Japanese did their best to survive in conditions of growing precarity and uncertainty.

Here, then, is the historical terrain of the postwar era to be traversed in subsequent chapters. But before setting out on this postwar journey, preparations must be made by tracing the historical legacy of Japan before 1945, which I explore in the following chapter.

CHAPTER ONE

Japan Before 1945

The Revolutionary Meiji Era

August 15, 1945 is conventionally understood as the beginning of Japan's postwar era. This date marks the moment when Hirohito officially announced the country's surrender in the Asia-Pacific War. With this historic announcement, Japan's age of colonial empire and militarist expansionism abruptly ended, opening the way for a new era of peace, democracy, and stability. Of course, despite a strong desire among many Japanese to imagine this new age of "Peace and Democracy" as entirely divorced from the tainted prewar and wartime years, from a historical perspective, there were important legacies and continuities connecting Japan before August 15, 1945, to that after. Hence, any journey through Japan's postwar history must necessarily begin by excavating these manifold connections to the country's past.

Developments from the mid-nineteenth century, especially the 1920s, 1930s, and early 1940s, continued to echo in the social, political, and economic institutions of postwar Japan. Dating back even further, the country's remarkable Meiji era (1868–1912) reverberated in the mentalities of postwar Japanese. Leaders and ordinary people alike shared a collective memory of the country's amazing remodeling from an isolated and vulnerable agrarian nation into a global power. Most abhorred the militarist outcome that modernization appeared to have produced, but collective memory of the Meiji era made it possible for postwar Japanese to believe that the country might once again be radically rebuilt and refashioned—this time as a liberal democracy reborn from the charred ruins of militarism and defeat.

In this search for the historical roots of postwar Japan, the Meiji era thus emerges as a critical historical juncture. Japan's abrupt entry into the rough and tumble of international politics in the mid-nineteenth century, while not unexpected by the country's samurai leaders, nonetheless triggered political turmoil and ultimately the collapse of a slowly decaying semifeudal system. After Commodore Matthew Perry of the US Navy arrived in Japan with his flotilla of steam-powered black ships in July 1853, the Japanese shogun of the ruling Tokugawa domain was compelled to make concessions to the Western powers, opening the country to foreign trade and engagement more extensively than in the previous two-and-a-half centuries. Japan was by no means a closed country, having had extensive trade and cultural engagements with its Asian neighbors and some restricted contact with Westerners through the island of Dejima in Nagasaki. But, throughout the Tokugawa era (1603–1868), external relations were strictly regulated by the shogunal government in Edo (renamed Tokyo in 1868), which exerted a degree of control over the two-to-three-hundred semiautonomous domains across the country.

The arrival of the Americans and their demands for access to ports and resources threw an already-troubled domestic system into turmoil. Unable to resist Commodore Perry's gunboat diplomacy, fearful of colonization, and desperate to avoid the sorry fate of Qing Dynasty China, throughout the 1850s, the Tokugawa authorities relented to a series of treaties that infringed on the country's sovereignty by affording the Western powers control over Japanese tariffs, granting extraterritoriality (effectively legal immunity for foreigners in Japan), and opening access to ports and inland areas of the archipelago previously closed off. Relenting to these treaties was a bitter pill to swallow for the Tokugawa rulers but deemed necessary to avoid colonization while buying time for the country to build up national strength. The program to eliminate these so-called unequal treaties would dominate Japanese diplomacy and national politics until their final revision in the early twentieth century. Importantly, the institutions—political, economic, and social—established in

Figure 1.1. Depiction of Commodore Matthew C. Perry's visit to Kanagawa in 1854. Lithograph by Wilhelm Hein (Wikimedia Commons).

pursuing this objective would strike deep roots, some surviving in recognizable form across the chasm of war defeat in 1945.

Being a late developer meant that Japan entered international society in an age of high imperialism. As the Western powers encroached, astute leaders and perceptive intellectuals slowly recognized that the country faced an ultimatum: Japan must either adopt the stratagems and technologies of the great powers or be left vulnerable to Western geostrategic incursions or even colonization. This sense of threat and vulnerability infused the subsequent drive for Western-style modernity with a combination of desperation and fervor. It would motivate the Japanese to build the institutions of a Western-style polity, economy, and society at astonishing speed, forging a collective memory of national achievement at a time of crisis—similar in ways to the national reconstruction required after war defeat in 1945.

Throughout the 1850s and 1860s, recalcitrant domains located mainly in southwestern Japan, together with bands of revolutionary masterless samurai (*rōnin*), began to mobilize against the Tokugawa shogunate, which they felt could no longer manage international or domestic matters. Early on, these antishogunal forces drew on xenophobic sentiment tied closely to an emergent nationalist patriotism toward the Japanese emperor, who reemerged as a powerful political symbol after hundreds of years as a cloistered ceremonial figure in the ancient capital of Kyoto. Quixotically believing that their warrior spirit and imperial loyalty would be enough to expel the Western threat, some of the samurai patriots initially pursued a campaign of terror against the Western "barbarians." But, faced with the overwhelming military superiority of the foreigners, the antishogunal forces gradually recalibrated their political program from one of expulsion by violence to one of realistic engagement and thoroughgoing nation building. Key turning points came in 1863 and 1864 when the domains of Satsuma and Chōshū, which would lead the revolutionary movement against the shogunate, suffered humiliating military bombardments by the Westerners. Hereafter, the antishogunal patriots realized that the only realistic way forward would be through a program of national renovation based on intensive learning from the materially superior West, together with fundamental reform of antiquated domestic institutions.

The Tokugawa shogunate finally collapsed in 1868 following a short series of military engagements, after which the emperor was "restored" to power by the loyalist antishogunal forces. The new regime was ostensibly ruled by the sixteen-year-old Meiji emperor, who only assumed the throne in 1866. But, in reality, it was controlled by an oligarchy of former samurai from the victorious antishogunal domains. On assuming power, these oligarchs announced an ambitious program of reform, which is succinctly encapsulated in two key slogans of the time: "civilization and enlightenment" and "enrich the nation, strengthen the military." The Charter Oath, promulgated by the young emperor in April 1868, set out before the nation the five pledges of the new regime: the establishment of deliberative assemblies to involve the public in decision-making; the involvement of all strata of society in the affairs of state; the abolition of restrictions on occupation among the people; the abandonment of superstitions of the past and the embrace of the rational laws of nature; and the seeking of knowledge worldwide for national strengthening.

With this oath in place, Meiji nation building began apace. Old status hierarchies were eliminated, notably with the abolishment of the samurai class and their hereditary annual stipends. To ease the brunt of this sudden social demotion, a peerage system was created giving some former samurai elites an entitled social position and appointments as officials in the new system of prefectures nationwide. For samurai at the lower ranks, however, the outlook was not so bright. Stripped of their hereditary stipends, these samurai faced the grim reality of carving out a living on their own. In another rebuke to this former samurai class, in 1873, the oligarch Yamagata Aritomo, who was committed to strengthening Japan militarily, established a compulsory national conscription system for all males over twenty years of age. This was a controversial decision that would feed into the rise of political contention in the coming years.

To shore up government finances, in the same year, the new regime converted the land tax system to a uniform annual payment of 3 percent of the value of land holdings, much to the chagrin of landowners and the sharecroppers beholden to them. As they built up defenses and finances, the oligarchs also promoted learning and education. In 1872, a school system based on the French model was established with four years of compulsory education for all children six years and older. Although compulsory schooling faced resistance early on among the majority agricultural population, the education system proved crucial in realizing almost universal literacy and numeracy in the Meiji era, not to mention serving as a powerful state tool for the inculcation of patriotic values.

The Meiji leaders dove headlong into learning about the West, setting out on an eighteen-month fact-finding mission to the United States and Europe in 1871 led by the court noble Iwakura Tomomi. Along with (unsuccessfully) lobbying Western statesmen for revision of the unequal treaties, the few dozen members of the mission carefully studied all kinds of Western institutions, including parliaments, bureaucracies, legal systems, post offices, foundries, and hospitals. Undoubtedly a function of their relative youth, members of the mission, while astonished, were not overwhelmed by what they saw, returning to Japan convinced that their country—with collective effort and single-mindedness—could attain the heights of Western modernity.

Members of the mission like the restoration hero Ōkubo Toshimichi thereafter threw themselves headlong into promoting industrial development. Under Ōkubo's leadership, the state imported foreign technologies, employed thousands of foreign experts, and established model factories. While many of these initiatives had mixed results, they undoubtedly provided much of the technology, raw knowledge, and exemplars needed by private enterprise, which developed first in textile manufacturing and thereafter in heavy industry. Key in all these endeavors, it must be emphasized, was the role of the state. Through its elite bureaucracy established in the Meiji period, the state continued to be heavily involved in shaping economic development in the country well into the postwar era. Indeed, the national bureaucracy was one of the few institutions left relatively unscathed by the sweeping reforms led by the United States after 1945.

A Political Society

The oligarchs' program of massive political, economic, and social transformation was neither painless nor accepted with placid resignation. By unleashing new forces and aspirations, by striking at the heart of hereditary privilege, and by promising to build a freer and more mobile society, the oligarchs planted the seeds of an extremely complex polity. Opening up to the West, moreover, not only involved importing industrial and military technology; it also exposed Japanese people to new ideas about liberty and rights, in turn feeding into rising expectations for political participation and influence. The dissolution of the samurai class proved critical in unlocking this new sphere of political consciousness and activity in Japan, but so too did universal male conscription, compulsory education, and financial reform, all of which provoked the ire of farmers, silk producers, and others on the land.

Figure 1.2. Saigō Takamori (1828–1877), a leading figure in the Meiji Restoration and later a rebel against the new Meiji regime. National Diet Library.

When Saigō Takamori—another hero of the Meiji Restoration—proposed an invasion of Korea using former samurai in the early 1870s, he was rebuked by fellow oligarchs and abruptly quit the government. The oligarchs well understood the necessity for expansionism and brute force in an age of empire, but they felt that Japan was still too weak to pursue this path so soon after the restoration. The disgruntled Saigō and his followers subsequently mobilized an abortive rebellion against the government, which ended with Saigō's dramatic suicide in 1877. But antagonism to the new regime among former samurai did not end there, with others like Itagaki Taisuke channeling their frustrations into political activism. Throughout the 1870s, Itagaki and others pressured the oligarchs to honor their commitments in the Charter Oath, petitioning the government to establish a popularly elected assembly. Joined by a cadre of disaffected agriculturalists and others frustrated with the Meiji government's policies, into the 1880s Itagaki's League for the Establishment of a National Assembly began to advocate widely for a constitutional government that would institutionalize what they called "freedom and popular rights." Members of the league authored constitutional drafts and held rallies across the nation.

Figure 1.3. Itagaki Taisuke (1837–1919), a leading figure in the Meiji-era Freedom and Popular Rights Movement. National Diet Library.

The oligarchs were not averse to this demand for a constitution and national assembly because they knew that all so-called civilized nations possessed these accoutrements. But they also wanted to ensure that their power would not be compromised in a constitutional system. With these considerations in mind, in 1881, the government issued an imperial rescript promising to establish a national Diet in 1890. The Meiji Constitution, promulgated by the emperor in February 1889 ahead of the opening of the Diet, became an institutional expression of these competing pressures for popular representation and oligarchic power. The Diet consisted of a lower House of Representatives comprising members elected by a very restricted franchise of male voters qualified by wealth. It was checked by an upper House of Peers and a cabinet, military, and judiciary all appointed by, and only answerable to, the sovereign emperor. Along with most men, women were totally excluded from the franchise (and would be until after 1945) and their political involvement was further circumscribed by the Public Order Police Law of 1900, which forbade female participation in political rallies (until the 1920s), and the

Meiji Civil Code, which placed women under the authority of the male head of household.

Within this constitutional order, the oligarchs hoped to demonstrate to the world Japan's advanced civilization while retaining their exclusive influence as ministers of the cabinet and as privileged advisors to the emperor. But over time, the Diet and its political parties became more influential in national political debate and the oligarchs came under increasing pressure. As the oligarchs and their successors died off, the national bureaucracies began to command more and more power, although interministerial rivalry meant that the state did not always speak with one voice. Despite extremely circumscribed powers, the political parties skillfully utilized the lower house's power of budgetary veto to constantly pressure the oligarchs and the bureaucracy to restrain spending on the military and empire building and to reduce taxes. So influential did the parties become that, in 1900, the eminent oligarch Itō Hirobumi, who led the drafting of the Meiji Constitution, became president of the newly established Rikken Seiyūkai party, which the oligarchs hoped to use as a progovernment party in the Diet. Importantly, in 1918, the Rikken Seiyūkai would form the first genuinely party-led cabinet under the prime ministership of Hara Takashi. Prior to this, cabinets had been mostly "transcendental"—in other words, comprised of ministers who were not elected members of the lower house. The rising influence of the parties and their acceptance—if reluctant—by the oligarchs and state officials thus evidences the evolution of a more diverse political sphere in Japan by the beginning of the twentieth century. Interestingly, the historical lineage of the conservative LDP so dominant in post-1945 politics can be traced back to Itagaki's Liberal Party (1881) and Ōkuma Shigenobu's Rikken Kaishintō (1882) of the Meiji era.

Ordinary people, inspired by the influx of Western ideas of liberalism and rights, also became more politically active. By the early decades of the twentieth century, workers, tenant farmers, and other groups were collectively organizing around political and economic issues, sometimes violently, as with the Hibiya Riot in Tokyo following the Russo-Japanese War of 1904–1905. Upset that Japan would not receive an indemnity from the defeated Russians, rioters destroyed property and set buildings alight. Ordinary people exerted their influence over politics again in the so-called Taishō Political Crisis of 1912–1913. The crisis arose when the army minister resigned in protest over government funding and the military thereafter refused to provide a replacement as required under the law, precipitating the resignation of the cabinet. Angered at the apparent influence of the military over the government, a popular movement arose among lower house politicians, journalists, intellectuals, and citizens for the "protection of constitutional government." Determined to ignore this outside agitation, the oligarchs installed another of their number—Katsura Tarō—as prime minister, but his attempts to muster support in the Diet and to utilize the authority of the emperor invoked public outrage and riots across Japan. Katsura subsequently resigned, only to be replaced by another prime minister handpicked by the oligarchs.

This crisis made it patently clear to the oligarchs that the political parties could not be ignored and neither could the potentially violent energy of the people. Nowhere was this made clearer than in August 1918 when a protest over rising rice prices initiated by women in Toyama Prefecture sparked similar "rice riots" across the country. In response, the cabinet of Prime Minister Terauchi Masatake dispatched the police and military to quell the disturbances, but the popular backlash to this heavy-handed approach forced the cabinet to resign, opening the way for political parties to increase their influence.

Beginning in 1918 with the cabinet of Hara Takashi—popularly known as the "commoner prime minister"—party cabinets dominated politics until 1932 (with the exception of a few years in the early 1920s). Indeed, the early decades of the twentieth century arguably marked the high point of democracy in prewar Japan and are often referred to as the era of "Taishō Democracy" or "Imperial Democracy."[1] Alongside the political parties, throughout these decades new social movements formed to press their agendas. In 1912, the Christian journalist Suzuki Bunji and a handful of colleagues established the Friendship Society (Yūaikai) labor union. By the 1920s, the organization—now renamed the Japan Federation of Labor (Sōdōmei) and boasting around thirty thousand members nationwide—was pushing for an eight-hour workday and universal male suffrage. In 1920, some five thousand workers belonging to the organization attended the first May Day rally in Japan while, in 1921, around thirty-five thousand members participated in a labor dispute at the Kawasaki Mitsubishi shipbuilding yard. In 1922, yet another Christian activist, Kagawa Toyohiko, formed the Japan Farmers Union, which advocated for exploited tenant farmers and helped stimulate a wave of tenancy disputes against powerful landowners. In the same year, Saikō Mankichi and others from Japan's discriminated outcast Burakumin class formed the National Levelers Society, which pushed for genuine equality. The society's founding declaration of 1922 represents one of the earliest expressions of human rights consciousness in modern Japanese history.

Women also organized throughout the 1910s and 1920s. In 1911, Hiratsuka Raichō and others formed the Japanese Bluestocking Society, which through its literary magazine, *Seitō* (Bluestocking), advocated for women's liberation. Together with Ichikawa Fusae and others, in 1920, Hiratsuka formed the New Women's Association, which successfully lobbied the government for revision of the Public Order Police Law prohibiting women's participation in political rallies. Socialism and communism also made their appearance in Japan in these decades, although they would suffer from severe state suppression. In 1901, Abe Isoo, Katayama Sen, Kōtoku Shūsui, and others established the Social Democratic Party, but it was banned by authorities on the day of its establishment. The party boasted a progressive platform based on human equality, demilitarization, substantive social welfare, and equality in political participation. Socialists tried to organize again in 1906, forming the Japan Socialist Party, but it, too, was banned in 1907, followed by a further crackdown on socialists and anarchists falsely accused of plotting to assassinate the emperor in 1910. In 1922, Sakai Toshihiko, Yamakawa Hitoshi, and six others furtively established the Japanese Communist Party (JCP) and, even more than the socialists, were forced to operate in the shadows. A high point of this social activism came in 1925 when the government, under pressure from a powerful social movement, finally granted universal male suffrage.

Liberal scholars such as Minobe Tatsukichi and Yoshino Sakuzō offered theoretical backing for these expressions of Taishō Democracy. In somewhat tortured logic, Minobe's famed "emperor organ theory" posited that the emperor was but an "organ of the state" under the Meiji Constitution and not a sacred divinity, while Yoshino's "people as base" (*minponshugi*) proposed that democracy was possible within the structure of imperial sovereignty. Although the Americans and others involved in the post-1945 occupation—and even some Japanese—would later narrate a story of how the United States "bestowed" democracy upon Japan, these developments in the 1910s and 1920s remind us that postwar Japanese democracy also drew on domestic roots in political parties and social movements.

Figure 1.4. Hiratsuka Raichō (1886–1971), writer and advocate for women's liberation in modern Japan. National Diet Library.

At the same time, Taishō Democracy proved to be a fragile construction, unable to strike deep roots in Japan's prewar political institutions for several reasons. First, political parties constantly struggled for popular legitimacy. Incessant scandals involving bribery, pork-barreling, and cozy relations with powerful business conglomerates (zaibatsu) led to a popular view of the parties as largely self-interested and intrinsically corrupt. In what has been termed the "politics of compromise," the prominent parties became incestuously intertwined with the state and, when in power, they pursued conservative pro-state policies often aimed at stifling social energies.[2] Politicians were often beholden to the specialist knowledge of bureaucrats, who commonly left the public service to join politics—a practice that would continue into the postwar era. The most prominent example of pro-state political party conservatism came in 1925. In late April, just a few short weeks before enacting universal male suffrage legislation, the Imperial Diet passed the infamous Peace Preservation Law, which became a powerful tool for the suppression of speech, organizing, and protest. Such laws reveal the parties' preference for power within the system over and above independence or democratic integrity.

Second, the military was always fundamentally antagonistic to political parties and pluralism more generally, viewing the parties—like big business—as parasites on the sacred national body. In the 1930s, this antipathy would stimulate young officers to wage a campaign of violent terror against political and business leaders, opening the way for the eventual absorption of the parties into the total war state of the 1940s. Third, international developments would also take their toll on Taishō Democracy, particularly the post–World War I recession, the global economic depression from 1929, and military adventurism on the Asian continent in the early 1930s. Finally, the constitutional reality of imperial sovereignty always remained as an unbreachable barrier to the institutionalization of democracy in the prewar years.

Given these contending energies, groups, and institutions, the years from 1905 to 1932 in Japan have been described as an era of "imperial democracy" to emphasize the "contradictions" within a "movement for change that was broadly based and profound."[3] Over time this imperial democracy became a "structure and ideology of rule intended to cope with change" but crises from the late 1920s exposed contradictions in this system that would only be solved by a disastrous turn to fascism.[4]

Transformations in the Economy and Society

Just as the state would proactively attempt to shape economic development in postwar Japan, the Meiji government pursued a range of policies to promote industrial development, such as importing technology and foreign advisors, establishing state-owned mines and model factories, educating the populace, shaping a modern banking and financial system, and putting in place the transportation, communications, and regulatory infrastructure necessary for economic growth. Faced with depleted state coffers after quelling Saigō's rebellion in 1877, throughout the 1880s the government began to sell off its often-unprofitable interests in mines, chemicals, shipbuilding, and textiles to private companies, usually at greatly discounted prices. In turn, this privatization stimulated the growth of industries utilizing the latest Western technology. Industrialists like Mitsui Takayoshi, Iwasaki Yatarō (Mitsubishi), Yasuda Zenjirō, and Sumitomo Tomoito with close connections to oligarchs were among the greatest beneficiaries of this wave of privatization. They built the massive conglomerates—the zaibatsu—that dominated the Japanese economy prior to 1945 and reemerged again in the postwar in a modified form.

The textile industry, centered on cotton spinning in the Osaka region, led the shift to mechanized production in 1880s Japan. The Osaka Cotton Spinning Company established by the Meiji entrepreneur and banker Shibusawa Eiichi in 1882 was among the earliest and most successful of such operations, utilizing the latest steam-powered spinning machines from Great Britain and running on two shifts per day thanks to electric lighting on the factory floor. Operating these spinning machines was a cadre of young girls from the countryside, who often labored twelve hours or more a day and lived highly regimented lives in company dormitories under the intrusive eye of management. Thanks to the new machinery and the efforts of these women, by the late 1890s, Japan had become a net exporter of

Figure 1.5. The Tōyō Cotton Spinning Company (1914), established by Shibusawa Eiichi as the Osaka Cotton Spinning Company in 1882. National Diet Library.

cotton. The silk industry followed a similar trajectory with the diffusion of mechanized silk reeling and growing demand from countries like the United States. So successful was the industry that, by the early twentieth century, Japan had overtaken China to become the largest exporter of silk thread in the world.

Heavy industry developed later than light industry and was dominated early on by steel production and related sectors such as shipbuilding, railways, and armaments. State-owned enterprises proved critical in introducing new technology and providing models for the private sector. The establishment in 1897 of the government-owned and run Yahata Steel Works, which utilized German blast furnace technology, represented a critical early step on the pathway to heavy industrialization. When operations began at the works in 1901, it produced some 53 percent of pig iron and 82 percent of steel stock in Japan, figures that climbed to 73 and 95 percent, respectively, by 1911, making it the largest operation in the Far East. Railway construction also expanded greatly with the passing of the Railway Construction Act of 1892. This act provided for railway connections through prefectural capitals, army division headquarters, and naval ports. Private rail companies proliferated from the late 1890s, greatly outstripping state-owned operations until 1906 when the government passed the Railway Nationalization Law to bring most railways under its control for national security reasons.

Although shipbuilding traced its roots back to the late Tokugawa era, the establishment of the Nagasaki Shipbuilding Bureau by the Ministry of Public Works in 1871 elevated the industry to one of strategic importance. In 1884, the government engaged the Mitsubishi zaibatsu to operate the plant and, in 1887, it sold the operation to the zaibatsu at just 40 percent of the total capital outlay. The expansion of heavy industry thus greatly benefited the emergent zaibatsu, such as Mitsubishi, Mitsui, and Sumitomo, around the turn of the century. These industrial giants would continue to grow thereafter thanks to the vagaries of business cycles, political favors, intermittent wars, and international developments.[5]

World War I was a great boon for the Japanese economy, fundamentally transforming the country's industrial structure. Engulfed in their internecine struggle, the Europeans withdrew from Asian markets, opening the way for Japan to rapidly increase its exports of textiles and other products. Japanese munitions manufacturers lifted production to fill new orders from Europe, while cotton fabric and silk thread producers scrambled to meet demand from Asia and the United States. Japanese marine transport companies, shipbuilders, and steel makers reaped immense profits thanks to the global shortage of ships due to the war. In 1913, Japan's five shipbuilders only produced around fifty-one thousand tons per year but, by 1918, fifty-seven companies were producing over six hundred thousand tons annually.[6] The termination of trade with Germany—Japan's enemy at the time—also allowed for stunning growth in the chemical manufacturing industries, such as pharmaceuticals, dyes, and fertilizers. Although textiles still dominated manufacturing, pioneering companies also began to produce consumer appliances like radios. Reports proliferated on Japan's nouveau riche or *narikin* who made their fortunes in shipbuilding, the stock market, steel, chemicals, cotton, and silk.

Throughout the war years, exports outstripped imports, transforming Japan from a debtor to creditor nation in short time. The sectoral composition of the Japanese economy was also transformed. As figure 1.6 reveals, whereas agriculture and manufacturing each contributed around 45 percent to national production in 1914, by 1919 manufacturing accounted for 57 percent while agriculture had decreased to 35 percent.[7] The growth of manufacturing also promoted the diffusion of electrical power, fueled at this time by hydroelectric generation. Throughout the war years, electricity overtook steam as the primary energy source for industry.

The transforming economy also precipitated changes in Japanese society and culture, especially in the big cities of Tokyo and Osaka but also in regional towns and sometimes farming villages. In the 1880s, electric lights began to replace oil and gas lamps in public areas, and in 1895, the first electric streetcars commenced operations in Kyoto City, soon spreading elsewhere thanks to private investment. The first decade of the twentieth century witnessed several notable appearances: public telephones in 1900, the Mitsukoshi Drapery Store—Japan's first modern department store—in 1904, Japan's first domestically produced gasoline-powered automobile in 1907, and the construction of Japan's first apartment building (made of wood) in 1910.

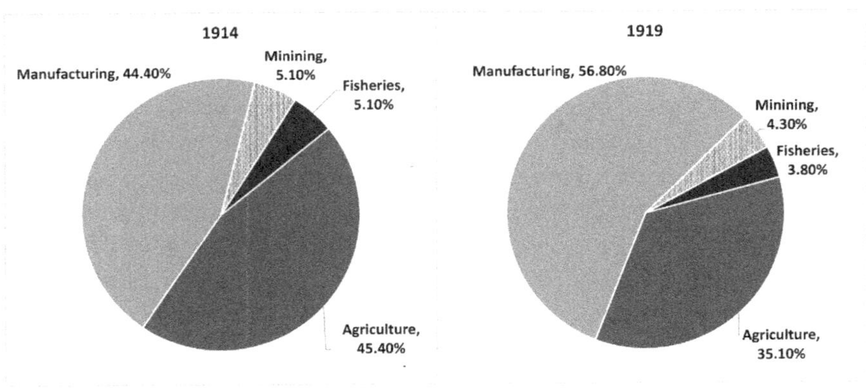

Source: Hokazono, *Nihonshi A*, 106.

Figure 1.6. Composition of Industry in Japan before and after World War I

Blue- and white-collar workers in the cities helped to create a new urban culture, invigorated by a vibrant realm of newspapers, magazines, radio, and cinema. The most affluent of these urbanites directed their desires toward Western-influenced fashions in clothing, cuisine, and housing. Ambitious young men aspired to become urban "salarymen"—the highly paid white-collar workers who commuted to their offices wearing splendid Western-style suits, embellished with stylish fedoras, pocket watches, and briefcases. Working women also became part of the new urban landscape, particularly around the time of World War I. Relegated to supporting the core of salarymen and paid over 50 percent less, these urban women worked as receptionists, typists, hairdressers, and famed "busgirls" (conductors) on the busy urban transport networks. A government survey of women's most desired jobs in 1920 offers a fascinating insight into the aspirations of women at the time. The most desirable profession was musician, followed in order by childcare worker, typist, artist, teacher, doctor, journalist, and nurse.[8] Outside of work, these "modern girls" were the avant-garde of fashion in 1920s Japan with their bob haircuts, flamboyant Western clothing, and uninhibited lifestyles. As a popular melody of the time went, "I'm a Ginza modern girl, when the sun goes down, I walk the treelined streets with my short skirt and bob cut and, like a Western girl, I search for love."

Figure 1.7. A busgirl (conductor) in Tokyo, 1934. Photograph by Ishikawa Kōyō (Wikimedia Commons).

Figure 1.8. Modern girls in 1928 dressed in beach pajama style. Photograph by Kageyama Kōyō (Wikimedia Commons).

Along with such cultural pursuits, the rising urban middle class aspired to new levels of domestic comfort epitomized in the so-called cultural dwellings or modern houses constructed in suburbs around the urban centers. A combination of both Western- and Japanese-style architecture, these houses boasted gas, running water, and electric lights.

Important as they were, however, urbanization and urban culture in early twentieth-century Japan must be kept in perspective. At least half the population continued to live a largely unchanged rural existence and would do so until the great urban migrations beginning in the mid- to late-1950s. The growth of rural tenancy into the war years also meant that life for many on the land became harder and poverty more widespread. Even in the cities, people were stratified, with the zaibatsu families and large landowners in a world of their own; the white-collar employees enjoying relatively affluent lives; a larger group of blue-collar workers, small factory owners, and retailers living comfortable but hardly luxuriant existences; and a lower rung of new arrivals from the countryside who eked out precarious livings as servants, retail workers, or factory hands.

After the economic boom times of World War I, the Japanese economy faced an extended period of economic malaise. Expansion during the war years exerted upward pressure on wages and other costs, making Japanese products more expensive internationally. Coupled with the return of the Europeans to markets abandoned during wartime, Japan now faced a reversal in its terms of trade as imports began to outstrip exports. Throughout the decade, the economy continued to perform poorly, mired in a state of protracted recession. Matters were made worse by the Great Kantō Earthquake in Tokyo and surrounds in September 1923. Over one hundred thousand died, many in fires, while businesses and infrastructure were flattened. The aftermath of the temblor witnessed horrific massacres of Koreans, Chinese, labor unionists, and anarchists by mobs of vigilantes and police who falsely accused such groups of poisoning water wells and other misdeeds.

In 1927, the country faced another financial crisis when many banks were forced to honor promissory notes defaulted on by their bankrupt clients. The government of Tanaka Giichi subsequently bailed out major institutions, like the Bank of Taiwan, by offering urgent loans for them to pay debtors, but many smaller banks failed. In the resulting disorder, the zaibatsu grew stronger as their banks swallowed up the assets of these failed financial institutions.

In 1929, the economy faced two further blows. In an attempt to revive the stagnant economy by lowering domestic prices, raising productivity, and fostering exports, the Hamaguchi Cabinet tightened the money supply, cut government expenditures, and returned Japan to the gold standard. But, just as these policies were beginning to bite, the Great Depression struck. Exports like silk plummeted as demand from the United States and elsewhere evaporated. Businesses failed, unemployment became rampant, and the countryside—now inundated with returnees from the city—was devastated. Only from 1931 with the policies of finance minister Takahashi Korekiyo did the economy begin to turn in a positive direction. Anticipating the pump-priming theories later advocated by John Maynard Keynes, Takahashi took Japan off the gold standard and implemented a bold policy of countercyclical government spending aimed at jumpstarting the economy out of recession. These policies proved remarkably effective, with Japan emerging from the

Figure 1.9. The Minami Ōta area of Yokohama after the Great Kantō Earthquake, 1923. Disaster Information Library, NIED.

depression earlier than other economies. But Takahashi's policies had just as profound effects in the longer term for the economy and society. Much government spending was directed to the military which, in the view of some, "eased Japan toward war."[9] True or not, thereafter the military budget continued to increase.

The economy also further transitioned from light to heavy industry, especially in steel, ships, machinery, and automobiles. The established zaibatsu like Mitsubishi and Mitsui benefited greatly from the new economic spending policies, but they were joined—indeed challenged—now by a new generation of zaibatsu in chemicals and heavy industries. In chemicals, companies such as Japan Chisso Fertilizer Corporation and Shōwa Denkō rose to prominence, while familiar names like Hitachi emerged in the electrical and mining sectors, and Toyota and Nissan in automobiles. These structural transformations of the economy were supported and partially directed by the economic ministries' so-called industrial policy, which would feed into mobilization for total war and continue into postwar economic policymaking for recovery and high-speed growth.

Japan in the World

The campaign to abolish the unequal treaties dominated Japan's interactions with the Western powers until the early twentieth century, when they were finally eliminated. This experience of subservience taught the Japanese important lessons about how strong nations projected their power internationally. Striving to become an "equal" of the West often meant replicating the West and, in an age of empire, this implied the need to expand. Although the evolution of Japan's colonial empire was by no means preordained, the country's arrival on the international scene at this particular historical juncture and the threats to national sovereignty it faced under the treaties undoubtedly planted the seeds of empire building as a means to national independence in the minds of Japanese leaders. In the coming years they would wholeheartedly embrace the creation of colonies in Taiwan, Korea, and elsewhere and, under the growing influence of the military beginning in the 1930s, they would pursue a ruthless war of aggression in China, Southeast Asia, and the Pacific. As subsequent chapters reveal, the legacies of this evolution in Japan's international posture continued to haunt Japan's relations with its Asian and Pacific neighbors throughout the post–World War II era.

Beginning with the Iwakura Mission of 1871, the oligarchs made numerous attempts to renegotiate the unequal treaties with little success, causing much consternation among the Japanese people. Incidents like the sinking of the British merchant ship *The Normanton* in 1886 further inflamed this sentiment after it was learned that the British crew had boarded lifeboats, leaving the Japanese crew members to drown.

Such blatant racism convinced the oligarchs, and all Japanese, that to achieve treaty renegotiation the country must establish its credentials as a "great" and "civilized" power. In international society of the late nineteenth century this demanded not only strength at home but, just as importantly, the projection of national power abroad through empire building. The nearby Korean peninsula, Okinawa, Hokkaidō, and Taiwan emerged as the obvious initial targets in this program of expansion, particularly because proximity afforded these regions an enhanced geopolitical and national security significance for Japan from the very outset.

Japan's emergence as an imperial power also had a more regional intent: namely, breaking apart the old Sinocentric order of tributary states in East Asia, already buckling under pressure from the Western powers. The Japanese had begun to challenge this order during the Tokugawa era, when the Satsuma domain managed to exert a degree of influence over the Kingdom of Ryūkyū, formally a tributary state of China. Despite signing a treaty of amity with the Qing rulers soon after the restoration, in 1871, the Japanese used the murder of a Ryūkyūan crew shipwrecked in Taiwan in the same year as a pretext to exert more influence over the small trading kingdom, which was finally absorbed into Japan as Okinawa Prefecture in 1879. In the north, in 1875, the Meiji regime concluded a treaty with Russia to settle territorial boundaries. Thereafter, the great expanses of Hokkaidō were utilized to resettle former samurai as farmer-soldiers—in the process, decimating the indigenous Ainu culture.

But it was the Korean peninsula that most occupied Japanese leaders' attention. Indeed, the fraught relationship with this neighbor is central to understanding the development of Japan's colonial empire. The Meiji government set about reconfiguring Japan's relationship with Korea almost from its inception, chipping away at the Chinese tributary order in East Asia. In 1868 and again in 1872, unsuccessful missions were sent to Korea to negotiate new arrangements and, in 1873, Saigō Takamori and others proposed a punitive expedition against the Koreans for not recognizing the new regime. Although the oligarchs rejected Saigō's plan, they well understood the geopolitical significance of Korea. When the Koreans bombed a Japanese ship "surveying" near the island of Kanghwa in 1876, the oligarchs used the opportunity to force the Joseon Court to sign a treaty with essentially the same unequal provisions as their own treaties with the West.

The oligarch Yamagata Aritomo clearly articulated the strategic significance of Korea for the Meiji regime in a speech delivered at the first Imperial Diet in 1890. He called for military strengthening to protect, first, Japan's "line of sovereignty," which meant the country's national borders, and second, Japan's "line of interest," which at that time referred to Korea. Given its proximity to the archipelago, the peninsula was depicted as a geographical "dagger" pointing at the heart of Japan. In other words, left unattended, it could become a staging ground for threats to national security by regional powers like Russia. Conversely, in Japanese hands, the peninsula could provide resources and territory and perhaps even an entry point for expansion onto the Asian continent.

Motivated by such perspectives, from the 1880s onward, Japan became more and more involved in Korean politics both officially and via a growing cadre of unofficial right-wing Japanese activists operating on the peninsula. These interventions would eventually bring Japan into open conflict with China, which still hoped to exert its traditional political hegemony over Korea. As early as 1881, Japan sent a group to assist Emperor Gwangmu in his modernizing efforts. The Japanese party consisted of enlisted military men and a ragtag of outsiders—many right-wing nationalists such as the former samurai Ōi Kentarō—who wanted to eliminate Chinese influence once and for all. Japanese involvement began to escalate with the so-called Imo Incident of 1882, when soldiers and poverty-stricken citizens mounted a revolt against Japanese-led modernization, attacking the Japanese legation and attempting to murder government leaders and Queen Min. The Chinese government sent in troops, who managed to quell the rebellion. But their decision to stay on after the revolt led to rising tensions with Japan, which demanded an indemnity and the right to station troops to protect its legation. An abortive coup d'état by the Japanese-educated Kim Ok-kyun in 1884—the Gapsin Coup—was again quelled by Chinese forces, but the resulting anti-Japanese backlash among Koreans resulted in the murder of numerous Japanese military men and residents. Pressured by calls for war at home, Japanese leaders negotiated an uneasy truce in the Tientsin Convention of 1885, under which both countries agreed to withdraw their troops and provide advance warning prior to any future dispatches.

After a nine-year truce, matters reached a head with the Donghak Peasant Rebellion of 1894, when impoverished farmers and others rebelled against the government and foreign intervention. Once again, the Korean authorities sought assistance from the Chinese who sent close to thirty thousand troops to quell the rebellion. Although the Qing leaders claimed to have informed the Japanese of this deployment ahead of time in line with the Tientsin Convention, Japan denied such notification, duly sending in its own troops to "protect" Japanese interests. The outcome in 1894 was war with China after the Japanese seized the Korean palace and installed a pro-Japanese government. The ensuing land and sea battles resulted in total victory for Japan in April 1895.

The outcomes of the war for Japan were mixed. Positively, it marked an important step in the elimination of the unequal treaties and a concomitant rise in national prestige vis-à-vis the West, where a Chinese victory had been anticipated. On the eve of the war in 1894, Japan signed the Anglo-Japanese Treaty of Commerce and Navigation, which removed British extraterritoriality in Japan and restored some tariff autonomy. This change in British policy reflected its growing concerns about the Russian threat in the region. The Treaty of Shimonoseki signed by Qing China and the Empire of Japan after the conflict proved bittersweet for the Japanese. The Chinese agreed to pay a massive indemnity—over four times Japan's annual budget—which was promptly injected into militarization and heavy industries such as shipbuilding and steel. Japan also gained territories: the island of Taiwan, the Pescadores Islands, the Liaodong Peninsula, four ports along the Yangtze River, and railroad and building concessions in Manchuria. But Japanese gratification with these outcomes suffered a cruel blow when Russia—with the support of France and Germany—forced Japan to relinquish the strategically important Liaodong Peninsula. Unable to resist this Tripartite Intervention of 1895, the Japanese relented, but the intervention remained a painful lesson in barefaced international realpolitik and formed the roots of a future conflict with Russia who was now focused on challenging Japanese supremacy in Korea. As the German chancellor Otto von Bismarck had told the Japanese some years earlier, in matters international, "might meant right," and the sooner small powers like Japan understood this, the better their chance of survival.

The Russo-Japanese War of 1904–1905 came after a decade of brewing tensions between Japan and other Western powers in East Asia. After both Russia and Japan contributed to the international force mobilized to subdue the Boxer Rebellion in Beijing in 1900, Russia refused to announce a schedule for the withdrawal of some one hundred thousand troops located in Manchuria. Fearing this intrusion, in 1902, the British concluded the Anglo-Japanese Alliance, which recognized Japan's interests in Korea and stipulated mutual support in the event of a conflict. While some like Itō Hirobumi advocated conciliation with the Russians, hawkish opinion at home supported a more muscular policy in Korea and northern China. Shortly before the official Japanese declaration of war in February 1904, the Imperial Japanese Navy launched a surprise attack on Russian vessels at Port Arthur. Thereafter, the Japanese registered some land and naval victories, but by 1905 the conflict was at a stalemate with victory possible on either side. The Japanese found themselves out of weaponry and money, while the Russians faced revolutionary troubles at home. After a stunning victory over the Russian Baltic Fleet at the Battle of Tsushima in May 1905, the Russians capitulated—much to the relief of Japan's leaders.

Like the Treaty of Shimonoseki, the Treaty of Portsmouth had both positive and negative outcomes for Japan. Negatively, the Russians refused to pay an indemnity, leaving the Japanese government coffers exceedingly depleted and sparking popular riots. But Japan gained control of the southern portion of Sakhalin

Island—known as Karafuto in Japanese—and, most importantly, protectorate status over Korea.

In the wake of these turn-of-the-century wars Japan was thus able to consolidate its budding colonial empire. Following the First Japan-Korea Convention of 1904 allowing Japan to send official advisors to Korea, in 1905, the Japanese—with the blessing of the Americans and British—forced a second convention, the Korea Protectorate Treaty, which stripped the Koreans of control over foreign affairs and allowed the stationing of Itō Hirobumi as resident general in Seoul. After the Koreans unsuccessfully appealed for the annulment of this treaty at the Second Hague Peace Conference of 1907, the incensed Japanese forced the Korean monarch to abdicate and imposed a new convention giving Japan total control over politics and military affairs. When Itō Hirobumi was assassinated by a Korean resistance leader in Harbin in 1909, the Japanese had had enough. In 1910, the Koreans were forced to sign the Korean Annexation Treaty, which established a government general in Kanjō (Seoul), now renamed Keijō. The governor general, Terauchi Masatake, promptly dispatched military police to suppress popular resistance and ordered a land survey that effectively stripped many farmers of their holdings, causing deep animosity toward the Japanese colonizers.

As discussed, World War I was a boon for the Japanese economy, stimulating a fundamental sectoral transformation and positive balance of trade. Diplomatically, Japan used the European confrontation to exert pressure on China, notably with its Twenty-One Demands of 1915. After intervention from the United States and the United Kingdom, Japan withdrew the most extreme of these demands, but the Chinese—represented by Yuan Shikai—yielded to Japanese control over German possessions in Micronesia and rights over German holdings in Shandong Province. Importantly, the Chinese also granted the Japanese ninety-nine-year leases in Lushun and Dalian, which were important gateways to the resource-rich reserves of northern China. But the Chinese and Korean people did not accept such incursions with feeble acquiescence. In the March First Movement of 1919, millions of Koreans joined rallies in support of independence, which were brutally suppressed by Japanese armed forces. In the same year, students, laborers, and ordinary Chinese citizens united in the so-called May Fourth Movement to protest territorial concessions granted to Japan under the 1919 Treaty of Versailles.

With its foothold on the Asian continent established, Japan entered a period of largely cooperative diplomacy until the late 1920s. The Treaty of Versailles confirmed Japan's rights over former German possessions and granted it a seat at the League of Nations (although the Japanese were infuriated when the Western powers refused to include a racial equality clause in the organization's founding charter). Through treaties such as the Washington Naval Treaty of 1922 and the London

Naval Treaty of 1930, Japan agreed with the four other major powers—the United States, the United Kingdom, France, and Italy—to limit naval construction to prevent a global arms race. Under the moderate foreign minister, Shidehara Kijūrō, who would serve as prime minister in the early postwar, Japan signed the Soviet-Japan Basic Treaty in 1925, which settled territorial issues between the two nations.

But cooperative diplomacy masked numerous tricky foreign policy dilemmas facing Japan in the 1920s. First was the issue of how to approach China. Should Japan cooperate with the Western powers or pursue a unilateral, interventionist policy on the continent, potentially alienating the United States and other countries that were increasingly concerned with Japan's incursions in northern China? Second, should Japan cooperate with the Republic of China under Sun Yat-sen and later Chiang Kai-shek or should it broker deals with local warlords to safeguard its northern interests? Third, how should Japan approach the Soviet Union? Despite signing a treaty in 1925, it was not clear whether appeasement, containment, or a more confrontational approach was appropriate. And finally, the vexing issue of Western racism toward Japan continued to color its relations with the West. The growth of a "yellow peril" discourse in the West, the denial of an anti-racism stance at the League of Nations, and anti-Japanese sentiment and laws in America all tended to undermine the rhetoric of cooperative diplomacy while emboldening the extremist right at home.

Military Adventurism and War in China

Reckless actions by the Japanese army in China in the late 1920s and early 1930s set the country on a path to unrestrained militarism. In 1928, junior officers of the Kwantung Army arbitrarily exploded a train at Huanggutun Railway Station, killing the warlord Zhang Zuolin, whose expansionist ambitions in northern China and cozy relationship with America and Britain threatened Japanese supremacy in the region. In the fallout, Prime Minister Tanaka Giichi and his cabinet were forced to resign when Emperor Hirohito expressed dissatisfaction with the government's poor management of the problem. The army, however, emerged unscathed, emboldened now to pursue its stratagems in China essentially unconstrained. Matters deteriorated further in September 1931, when Kwantung Army officers once again deliberately blew up a portion of the South Manchurian Railway near Mukden (Shenyang), falsely attributing the act to Chinese insurgents. Flouting government orders to deescalate matters, the Kwantung Army used the Mukden Incident as a pretext to extend its tentacles in the region. In 1932, the army installed Puyi—the last emperor of the Qing Dynasty—as chief executive of the newly created puppet state of Manchukuo. With this, the army had secured Japan's so-called lifeline of

Manchuria and Inner Mongolia. Idealists in the military imagined Manchukuo as a revolutionary experiment in statecraft—a nation where community and loyalty would eclipse the selfishness of the business and politics that they so despised in contemporary Japan. Realities on the ground belied this glossy idealism. The Lytton Commission dispatched by the League of Nations bluntly concluded in its 1933 report that Manchukuo was not born from the spontaneous will of the people. In turn, the league reconfirmed the sovereign rights of China in the region and ordered Japanese forces to withdraw immediately. Backed into a corner, the Japanese dug in their heels, dramatically withdrawing from the League of Nations in 1933. With this, the era of Japanese cooperative diplomacy was over, and hereafter the military began its steady ascent.

The 1930s was a tumultuous era of intensifying military violence and political suppression, as young officers and right-wing extremists vented their frustrations over international, political, and economic developments. Naval officers were deeply angered by the government's meek acceptance of the London Naval Treaty (1930), and they abhorred diplomats' "toothless" cooperative diplomacy. Military men—many of rural origin—viewed the zaibatsu tycoons and the politicians as self-interested miscreants who greedily lined their pockets at the expense of poor country folk. The formation of the Soviet Union also deeply concerned the military and, combined with the growth of unionism among workers in Japan, intensified their fears about the infiltration of communism.

The violence began in 1930, when a rightist youth shot Prime Minister Hamaguchi. This was followed in 1931 by an abortive coup d'état by army officers. In the politically charged atmosphere after the Mukden Incident, the far-right League of Blood murdered a former finance minister and a zaibatsu head, while young naval officers stormed the prime minister's residence, shooting Inukai Tsuyoshi to death. This assassination marked the end of party cabinets in prewar Japan and the death of Taishō Democracy. Compounding this political upheaval, the great outpouring of sympathy for the naval officers responsible for the assassination resulted in light sentences and encouraged further military lawlessness. Within the armed forces two factions emerged: an Imperial Way Faction of younger officers determined to destroy capitalism and the Meiji institutional order, and a Control Faction of older elites who preferred to pursue military control and mobilization for war within the existing state framework. This factional rivalry was resolved in 1936 when Imperial Way adherents mounted an abortive Shōwa Restoration, assassinating political leaders and occupying central Tokyo. The plot only ended when an incensed Emperor Hirohito ordered the insurgents to surrender. But the damage had been done. The Control Faction of the army swooped on the opportunity to extend its power over politics and force increased military expenditure.

Figure 1.10. Rebel troops returning to their barracks after the failed February 26, 1936, coup d'état. Photographer unknown (Wikimedia Commons).

Isolated from international society, in September 1937 Japan sought solidarity in the Tripartite Pact with Germany and Italy. Just months earlier in July, the country launched a full-scale war in China following a skirmish with Chinese troops at the Marco Polo Bridge near Beijing. Although no official declaration of war was ever made, the Japanese persisted with this unwinnable quagmire in China for eight years, along the way slaughtering millions and committing horrific atrocities in Nanjing and in gruesome biological and chemical weapons experiments conducted on Chinese victims by the army's infamous Unit 731 in Harbin. The government attempted to justify this Japanese aggression by declaring a "new order" in East Asia in 1938. The world, it was argued, had divided into Anglo-American and Soviet-Communist blocs. Accordingly, it was Japan's historic mission to "liberate" East Asia through the creation of an autarkic bloc in the region. Military leaders attempted to take this new order a step further in 1940, with the declaration of a Greater East Asia Co-Prosperity Sphere, encompassing both East and Southeast Asia. This sphere was touted by political and military leaders and intellectuals of all political hues as a revolutionary vehicle for the economic and political liberation of Asian people from the West. But, in practice, it served as no more than an ideological subterfuge for Japan's brutal military expansionism. The horrific legacies of this duplicitous "historic mission" of "liberation" in Asia would continue to complicate and sour Japan's relations with its neighbors throughout the postwar era.

As Japan's leaders constructed a new order abroad, they pursued a similar new order at home. Individuals and groups considered to be antagonistic to the nation's historic mission were targeted for repression. Religions such as the Jehovah's Witnesses, Ōmoto-kyō, and Tenri-kyō were hounded by state surveillance and their activities were severely limited by regulations like the Religious Organizations Law of 1939. Intellectuals came under attack for their "dangerous" ideas. In 1935, Professor Minobe Tatsukichi's widely accepted emperor organ theory was condemned by rightists for insulting the monarch. Minobe was forced to resign from the House of Peers and his book banned. In the wake of the Marco Polo Bridge Incident in 1937, Tokyo Imperial University economist, Yanaihara Tadao, had to step down after publishing an essay defending the right of citizens to criticize the government. Two years later, yet another professor from the university, Kawai Eijirō, suffered a similar fate after he criticized fascism. Suppression escalated further in 1938, when Ōuchi Hyōe and other prominent economists were incarcerated under the Peace Preservation Law for mobilizing a people's front opposed to the war in China. In the face of this persecution, many intellectuals and leftist activists began to openly recant their political beliefs and embrace Japan's "historic" mission in Asia.

Along with suppression, the state also proactively mobilized society and economy through campaigns and regulations. Following Prime Minister Konoe Fumimaro's launch of the National Spiritual Mobilization Movement in 1937, laws and ordinances were enacted for national mobilization (1938), a national service draft (1939), and price regulation (1939). Labor unions were organized into Patriotic Industrial Service Federations, while farmers and landlords came under rice price and rental rate controls via the Ministry of Agriculture. Interestingly, state intervention in labor and agriculture at this time laid the roots of practices and processes seen again in the postwar era. For example, workers benefited from the implementation of seniority wage systems, while tenant and owner-cultivators benefited from government purchases of their rice at a premium. Tenants also benefited from an expansion in the government program to assist them in purchasing their plots.

Drawing on the Nazi model, in 1940, Prime Minister Konoe began the New Order Movement, which aimed to unite all the political parties under the newly established Imperial Rule Assistance Association (IRAA). The IRAA was subsequently extended to include civil society groups nationwide, but it never reached the same level of integration and control as the National Socialist Party in Germany. The New Order Movement also extended to unions, now subsumed into the Japan Industrial Promotion Association. In 1941, all elementary schools were nationalized and curriculum further modified to inculcate imperial loyalty and patriotism. The Important Industries Law of the same year enabled the government to establish control associations in critical industries headed by zaibatsu heads and bureaucrats.

The New Order also stretched out into the colonies, where imperial subjects faced even greater demands to "Japanize" (*kōminka*) through clothing, language, compulsory shrine visits, and other practices. As the war with China (and later the Western Allies) intensified, colonial subjects were drafted into the Japanese military or forced to work in factories and mines, where many perished. Young women—euphemistically called "comfort women"—were unwittingly and forcibly mobilized into an organized system of military prostitution servicing Japanese forces throughout Asia and the Pacific.

Total War and Total Defeat

Tensions with the Western Allies increased after 1940, when the Japanese army sent troops into French-controlled Indochina and, almost simultaneously, forced the British to close the Burma Route that the Allies were using to support Chiang Kai-shek's forces. Last-minute negotiations with the Americans throughout the summer and fall of 1941 proved futile, as the Japanese doggedly refused US demands to withdraw their troops from both China and Indochina. The military's call for a decisive strike on the United States was further strengthened in August 1941 when the Americans decided to cut off oil supplies to Japan, adding to a series of earlier embargoes on other resources.

On December 8, 1941, the Japanese government—now under the prime ministership of General Tōjō Hideki—crossed the point of no return when the army invaded the Malay Peninsula and the navy mounted a surprise attack on the US naval base at Pearl Harbor in Hawai'i. The United States, Great Britain, and their allies immediately declared war on the Empire of Japan, precipitating the commencement of the Asia-Pacific War.

Following their successful campaigns in Indochina, Malaysia, and Pearl Harbor, Japanese forces quickly occupied the British possessions of Hong Kong and Singapore, American-controlled Guam and Luzon, and eventually much of Southeast Asia and the western Pacific. But the tide of the war turned quickly. By the middle of 1942, the Imperial Japanese Navy was on the defensive, having suffered catastrophic defeats in battles at the Coral Sea and Midway. After losing control of Guadalcanal in 1942, the Japanese Empire began its rapid demise, as Japanese forces suffered one disastrous defeat after another on Pacific-island strongholds. With the Allied occupation of Saipan in July 1944, the main islands of Japan were now within range of American B29 bombers, leaving the Tōjō Cabinet with no choice but to resign.

From 1944 to mid-1945, the Allies unleashed incessant air raids, first on strategic targets such as ports, airfields, and factories but later indiscriminately on the large metropolises of Tokyo, Osaka, Nagoya, and elsewhere. Incendiary bombing on Tokyo claimed over one hundred thousand lives, with similar destruction in around fifty other cities across the archipelago. The populations of big cities dwindled, as initially children and then adults began to retreat to the countryside. In one of the bloodiest campaigns of the war, in April 1945, the Allies landed on Okinawa. Lacking reinforcements, the Japanese army forced Okinawan civilians to fight and, when defeat seemed certain, convinced many to commit group suicide rather than be captured by the enemy. Okinawans accused of being spies were ruthlessly executed.

In February 1945, President Franklin D. Roosevelt, Prime Minister Winston Churchill, and Soviet leader Joseph Stalin met in Yalta, on the Crimean Peninsula, to determine the arrangements for post-defeat Germany. At this meeting, Stalin secretly agreed to declare war on Japan following Germany's defeat—abrogating the Soviet-Japan Neutrality Pact of 1941. This meeting was followed in July 1945 by the Potsdam Declaration, signed by the United States, Great Britain, and China. The declaration demanded the immediate "unconditional surrender of all Japanese armed forces"; otherwise Japan faced "prompt and utter destruction."

Figure 1.11. The Yalta Conference (Churchill, Roosevelt, Stalin), February 1945. US Government photographer (Wikimedia Commons).

Demoralized by destructive air raids, some elites began advocating for surrender, with former prime minister Konoe petitioning the emperor to surrender in February 1945 and the Suzuki Kantarō Cabinet negotiating for an end with the Allies via the Soviet Union. But Emperor Hirohito remained unconvinced in early 1945, and fanatics within the military were unwilling to accept unconditional surrender lest this despoil the sacred national polity. Army leaders continued to push for a final ground war on the main islands. Only after the Soviet declaration of war on August 8 and the horrific atomic bombings of Hiroshima on August 6 and Nagasaki on August 9 did Emperor Hirohito finally relent, ordering unconditional acceptance of the conditions of the Potsdam Declaration on August 14, 1945. With this order, Japan's war against the Allies was over and its colonial empire defunct.

Historical Legacies for the Postwar Era

As subsequent chapters reveal, the historical experience charted above has continued to weigh heavily in the political, economic, and social institutions of postwar Japan. While other nations like Germany or those on the victorious Allied side largely abandoned the term "postwar" a few years after war's end, the Japanese have continued to utilize it to describe the era from mid-1945 onward. The term's ongoing currency speaks to how the notion of the "postwar" has encapsulated a distinctive national imaginary in Japan, with "post" representing the widespread desire for renewal and rupture from the past and "war" signifying history's enduring shadows and legacies.

Accordingly, while subsequent chapters will reveal a postwar Japan transformed, they will also speak to continuities. The Japanese state, as this chapter showed, was a critical actor in economic development, and its role in shaping the economy through industrial policy would emerge once again in the postwar era. Although partially dissolved, the zaibatsu similarly endured—if in a different organizational form—dominating the postwar Japanese economy, especially during the era of high-speed economic growth. The aspirations and initiatives of Taishō Democracy, although stifled in the 1930s, would also reemerge in the postwar era through a vibrant realm of civic movements. Political parties on both the left and right would reorganize from the ashes of defeat, reviving traditions and legacies stretching back to the 1920s and even earlier. Social, cultural, and demographic trends prior to 1945, wrought by structural changes in the economy, urbanization, Westernization, and mobilization for total war, would also reemerge in the postwar era thanks to the reforms of the American-led occupation and high-speed economic growth. The postwar era would also be one of lingering "postimperiality," as the Japanese were faced with the legacies of colonial empire and military aggression that had left a trail of destruction and human misery throughout the Asia-Pacific region. And, finally, the Japanese people's own sense of betrayal and victimization by their state would also deeply shape postwar politics, external relations, and national identity. In all these ways, the postwar era would unfold as one of striking transformation under the persistent shadow of a palpable and often-troubling past.

CHAPTER TWO

Occupation and Recovery, 1945–1947

War Endings and Continuities

At twelve noon on August 15, 1945, Japanese people nationwide gathered around their radios for an unprecedented broadcast by Emperor Hirohito. Although prerecorded on a scratchy phonograph record and broadcast over damaged telecommunications infrastructure, it was the first time most people had heard the emperor's voice, so all knew that something of great import was being announced. In the most archaic language barely understandable to many Japanese, Hirohito advised that he had ordered the government to accept the provisions of the Potsdam Declaration. In a masterpiece of understatement, he lamented that the war had "developed not necessarily to Japan's advantage" despite the best efforts of the people. The enemy's use of "a new and most cruel bomb" meant that continuing to fight would not only "result in an ultimate collapse and obliteration of the Japanese nation" but would also "lead to the total extinction of human civilization." Hirohito could only express his "deepest sense of regret" to the "allied nations of East Asia" who had "consistently cooperated with the Empire towards the emancipation" of the region. In a striking denial of history, the emperor explained how he had declared war on America and Britain out of a "sincere desire to ensure Japan's self-preservation and the stabilization of East Asia," and in no way was the intention "either to infringe upon the sovereignty of other nations or to embark upon territorial aggrandizement." Nonetheless, to "pave the way for a grand peace for all the generations to come," Hirohito told his war-weary subjects that now they must "endure the unendurable" and "suffer" what was "unsufferable." Although the words "defeat" and "surrender" were strikingly absent from the emperor's ambiguous and rather disingenuous address, the implications were clear to all: the war was over and now Japan faced an uncertain future at the hands of the enemy.[1]

Hirohito's historic announcement of war's end, while spiritually demoralizing for many, was hardly unexpected. For months, the main islands had been battered by wave after wave of Allied aerial bombardment. The atomic bomb dropped on Hiroshima on August 6 killed 140,000 people almost instantly while, in Nagasaki, the more powerful plutonium bomb of August 9 obliterated 70,000 lives. Survivors

Figure 2.1. People gather in the Umeda district of Osaka to listen to Emperor Hirohito's surrender radio broadcast on August 15, 1945. Courtesy of The Asahi Shimbun Company.

lived with the health effects of radiation exposure and endured forms of social discrimination. Allied air raids deploying conventional bombs also wreaked havoc. Strategic targets were the initial focus, but indiscriminate firebombing of cities became the norm throughout 1944 and 1945. Apart from cities of cultural importance like Kyoto and Kanazawa, most of Japan's urban areas were targeted. Allied strategic bombing sorties from mid-1944 until defeat battered some ninety cities across the archipelago, of which twenty lost over 50 percent of their built structures. *Yakinohara* or "burnt fields" became the generic description for these apocalyptic landscapes. Among the worst instances was the Tokyo air raid of March 9–10, 1945, which killed over one hundred thousand and wounded some forty thousand others. Over seven hundred thousand buildings were destroyed in the capital, whose population had dwindled from around 6.7 million in 1940 to 2.8 million in 1945, as many fled to the relative safety of the countryside. A similar pattern of destruction and depopulation unfolded in other cities like Osaka, Nagoya, Yokohama, and Kobe. Although numbers vary, up to 3.1 million Japanese—around 4.4 percent of the population—died in the war years from 1937 to 1945. Countless civilians and Allied combatants throughout East Asia and the Pacific also perished during the conflict, leaving deep wounds in the relationship between Japan and these countries. China alone lost as many as ten million lives.

With defeat, the Japanese Empire was dissolved, and Japan reverted almost to its pre-1895 borders (with the exception of the Kurile Islands, occupied by the Soviet Union in the closing days of the war). In the face of such human loss, humiliation, and destruction at home, many Japanese could not help feeling like victims of their government and of the Allies. To an extent this was certainly true, but the

Figure 2.2. Hiroshima after the atomic bomb. The Hiroshima Prefectural Industrial Promotion Hall (the Atomic Bomb Dome) is visible in the background (1945). US National Archives.

Figure 2.3. A family tills a wheat crop on the burnt-out ruins in Tokyo's central Kanda district in January 1946. According to the *Asahi shinbun*, urbanites used agricultural methods learned from farmers during their evacuation to the countryside in the latter stages of the war. Many families also kept a goat for protein. Courtesy of The Asahi Shimbun Company.

popular sense of victimization also made it difficult for many—but not all—Japanese to recognize how their colonial and military misadventures had victimized others and how they individually might be complicit.

Although August 15, 1945 subsequently became the iconic moment of defeat and the nativity of the postwar era in popular memory, the reality is that people experienced this transition from war to postwar very differently. People in Okinawa suffered their own tragic war's end some months earlier. Moreover, hostilities did not completely cease with Hirohito's surrender broadcast, continuing in Thailand and the Philippines for a day or two longer and, on Palau and in New Guinea, until early September. Following the Soviet declaration of war on August 8, combat continued against Soviet forces in Manchuria until August 18 and in Hokkaido and nearby Karafuto (today the southern half of Sakhalin) until August 22.

The repatriation of 3.1 million military personnel and close to 3.2 million civilians from around the Asia-Pacific region (table 2.1) stretched well beyond August 15. Allied forces managed Japanese military repatriations under the conditions of the Potsdam Declaration, completing this process—with a few important exceptions—by late 1945. Civilians, however, had to find their own routes home. Faced with diminished transportation and food supplies, the Japanese government initially advised civilians abroad to remain on site. But holding strong was simply not a choice for these expatriates who now faced hostile locals intent on revenge. For the over 1.5 million settlers in the defunct state of Manchukuo, all that remained was to abandon their assets and desperately flee from the advancing Soviet forces. In the resulting chaos, some seventy thousand settlers lost their lives, including youth mobilized by the military to resist the Soviet army. Once alerted to this situation, from December 1945 the Americans began to offer logistical support for civilian repatriation, which was eventually extended to Japanese citizens in all regions of the former empire in March 1946.

As Japanese citizens scrambled to return home, another reverse process was unfolding among the country's former colonial subjects. Some had been conscripted or recruited into the military, but thousands of others were forcibly brought to Japan to work in factories or mines, where many had perished. Based on agreements made under the Cairo Declaration of the United States, the United Kingdom, and the Republic of China in late 1943, all Koreans and Chinese in the Japanese military were to be returned to their countries of origin once demobilized. The Americans outlined their approach in SCAPIN-224 (Supreme Commander for the Allied Powers Index Number) of November 1945, which provided for the repatriation of "non-Japanese" individuals—including Okinawans—throughout 1946 and 1947.[2] The Japanese government, not wanting the "burden" of these former subjects, offered its enthusiastic support. By 1946, around 1.4 million had returned to Korea

Table 2.1 Numbers of Military and Nonmilitary Repatriates by Region

	Military and Civilian Employees	Civilians	Responsible Force
Total	**3,107,411**	**3,189,835**	
USSR	453,787	19,179	USSR
Manchuria	41,916	1,003,609	USSR
Dalian	10,917	215,037	USSR
Chishima / Karafuto	16,006	277,568	USSR
Korea (north)	25,391	297,194	USSR
Korea (south)	181,209	416,110	US
China	1,044,460	497,374	China
Taiwan	157,388	322,156	China
Hong Kong	14,285	5,062	UK
French Indochina	28,710	3,593	UK/China, etc.
The Philippines	108,912	24,211	US
Dutch East Indies	14,129	1,464	UK/Australia, etc.
Southeast Asia	655,330	56,177	UK
Australia	130,398	8,445	Australia
New Zealand	391	406	Australia
Hawai'i	3,349	310	US
Okinawa	57,364	12,052	US
Nearby islands	60,007	2,382	US
Pacific Ocean islands	103,462	27,506	US

Source: Maizuru Hikiage Kinenkan, "Hikiage no hajimari."

alone. Similar repatriations unfolded to Taiwan, mainland China, and northern Korea, by then under Soviet control.

Nonetheless, some six hundred thousand Koreans and many Taiwanese remained in Japan. These individuals were progressively stripped of citizenship rights and forced to register as foreigners. When Korean groups attempted to

Figure 2.4. Repatriates from the defunct colonies boarding a special train at Shinagawa Station in Tokyo to return to their hometowns (June 1946). Courtesy of The Asahi Shimbun Company.

establish ethnic Korean schools in 1948, the Ministry of Education issued a ban with support from the American occupiers, who cracked down on Korean protesters in Kobe City, arresting seventeen hundred and declaring a state of emergency. The tribulations of former colonial subjects did not end there. Some Taiwanese and Koreans who had served in the Japanese military were later tried as war criminals. Moreover, because they were not officially citizens, former colonial subjects did not qualify for military pensions.

Like former colonial subjects who remained in Japan, for thousands of Japanese still overseas, the war did not end for many years after August 15, 1945. For some, it never ended at all. Although six hundred thousand Japanese soldiers were repatriated from Southeast Asia at war's end, over 130,000 were forced to remain for another year. In May 1946, the British Command decided that it would detain these troops as "Japanese Surrendered Personnel," forcing them to engage in unpaid labor on reconstruction projects and agriculture in formerly occupied territories. The Americans opposed this initiative, but the British stood firm, determined to extract some retribution for the hellish treatment of Allied prisoners of war.

Japanese forces stranded in Soviet controlled areas such as Manchuria, Sakhalin, and northern Korea faced an even grimmer postwar journey. Soviet prisoners of war (POWs) were organized into work groups of around fifteen hundred and sent to labor camps across the expanse of Soviet territories, where they loaded cargo, dug mines, and logged forests. Living conditions in the camps were horrendous, with lice-infested quarters and constant outbreaks of typhoid and dysentery. Although the precise numbers remain unclear, there were over 570,000 of these so-called Siberian detainees. Up to fifty-five thousand died terrible deaths due to starvation, disease, cold weather, and violence. Many died as they tried to escape, summarily executed by Soviet guards. Negotiations between the Soviet and Japanese governments resulted in the return of most detainees from 1947 through 1950, although a small number—around one thousand—remained, marrying local women and beginning new lives. Some of the detainees became communists and committed to spreading the ideology on their return to Japan.

Apart from those captured by the Soviets, other Japanese troops were either abandoned or chose to remain in China, Vietnam, Indonesia, or the Philippines, where they became involved in independence struggles and civil wars, served as technicians, pursued new lives, or remained in hiding. Japanese were shocked in the early 1970s when Japanese soldiers—unaware the war had ended—were discovered hiding in the jungles of the Philippines, Indonesia, and Guam. Conversely, in 1958, a hunting group in Hokkaido was surprised to discover Liu Lianren, a Chinese national from Shandong Province, who had survived surreptitiously in the snowy wilderness for over thirteen years after escaping from a forced labor camp in 1944.

Along with unrepatriated military personnel, many Japanese civilians were simply unable to return home after the war. Thousands of children who were separated from their parents in the frenzied rush to escape from Manchuria were adopted into Chinese families. Young Japanese women who were left behind married local men. Life for these abandoned Japanese was complicated and demanding, as they faced malice and discrimination from locals for the transgressions of Japanese empire and militarism. As they struggled for acceptance, many also silently hoped to reconnect with their roots in Japan. In 1959, the Japanese government officially pronounced around thirteen thousand of these abandoned citizens as deceased, but official attempts to locate the abandoned citizens began anew with the resumption of diplomatic ties between Japan and the PRC in 1972. It was not until the 1980s and 1990s that some of the abandoned were able to visit Japan and reestablish family linkages.

Former colonial subjects faced similar abandonment after the war. Although most Japanese settlers were able to return from Karafuto after defeat, thousands of Koreans—considered Japanese imperial subjects during the war—were abandoned there and never able to return to Korea. The continued existence of such abandoned people across the former Japanese Empire was a constant reminder of how the war endured in palpable ways well beyond Japan's surrender to the Allies.

Society and Culture in the Ashes of Defeat

Hirohito's August 15 broadcast may have been ambiguous and misleading on many levels, but his entreaty to the Japanese people to "endure the unendurable" correctly portended the excruciating conditions that they would face in the aftermath of defeat. In certain ways, life quickly reverted to its prewar normality. Just days after defeat, cities began to switch on streetlights that were previously turned off to impede the Allied air raids. On August 20, the emperor issued a decree allowing all citizens to remove evening blackout curtains from their windows. Radio weather reports, suspended during the war lest they give the enemy a strategic advantage, were restored. Radio stations began to play music, and functioning cinemas started screening movies. For those with money and livable dwellings, it became possible to connect a private telephone service.[3]

But a far harsher reality accompanied this return to normality for most people. The economy at war's end was in tatters. Isolated from overseas markets and starved of resources, business and industry came to a virtual standstill. Domestic coal production nosedived due to fractured transportation networks, sporadic energy supplies, and thousands of colonial subjects abandoning mines to return to their home countries. Massive food shortages were exacerbated by the abysmal rice harvest in 1945—just 60 percent of a normal year and the worst since 1910.[4] The sudden loss of resource-rich colonies, like Manchukuo, also left the domestic economy at the whim of local conditions. Millions of soldiers and civilians returning from abroad only added to the early postwar turmoil. Unemployment skyrocketed, and the spike in demand for scarce daily necessities triggered hyperinflation. The government attempted to intervene in February 1946 by issuing a new yen and setting limits on deposit account withdrawals, but the inflation was unrelenting.

In 1946, the average food intake of Japanese stood at fourteen hundred kilocalories per day, just 70 percent of 1935 levels and close to half the caloric intake of Japanese today. Given that nutritional guidelines posit thirteen to fourteen hundred kilocalories per day as the bare minimum for an adult male to survive, the immediate threat to survival at this time is obvious. The situation was further aggravated by a government rationing system that only allocated one thousand kilocalories per citizen per day.[5] By 1946, some were even warning that there might be ten million deaths from starvation. Thankfully, this horror did not eventuate, but Tokyo metropolitan police records throughout late 1945 indicate hundreds of deaths from starvation in the capital.[6] Families were forced to spend up to 70 percent of their income on food alone in 1946–1947. At the request of the government, throughout 1946 the Americans imported supplies of flour, barley, and rice from the Philippines and elsewhere, but the food shortages persisted. In the face of these dire circumstances, urbanites desperate for sustenance boarded overcrowded "shopping trains" bound for agricultural areas, where they paid exorbitant prices or exchanged kimonos, family treasures, and other precious items for rice, oats, potatoes, pumpkins, and other fresh produce. As such activity violated the government's rationing system, shoppers often found themselves stripped of food purchases when police conducted confiscation raids on trains arriving in the cities.

People also turned to the illegal black markets that proliferated nationwide in response to the life-threatening food shortages. The first of these appeared in August 1945, with the opening of the "Blue Sky Market" in Tokyo's Shinjuku region. By late 1945, police estimated there to be some three thousand markets across the capital. Osaka, Nagoya, and other large cities followed a similar trend. Established beside train stations, the black markets were often controlled by Yakuza crime syndicates, Koreans, or Taiwanese, provoking animosity and racial discrimination among the Japanese, who had no choice but to obtain food and other necessities like winter clothing and heating fuel from hawkers. Price gouging was rampant, with rice costing 132 percent and sugar and sweet potatoes an astounding 250 percent of official prices.[7]

Although the total population of Tokyo in October 1945 stood at around 2.78 million, the number of registered ration recipients was 2.8 million—meaning that around twenty-four thousand ration recipients were unaccounted for. If a family member died, this was intentionally not reported, nor were miscarriages. There are even stories of family pets, such as cats, being registered for ration distributions with names like "Kimura Tamako."[8] Some highly principled individuals did try to follow the government rationing rules, but their stories mostly ended in tragedy. On October 11, 1945, for example, Tokyo District Court judge Yamaguchi Yoshitada died of malnutrition after consuming only his government rations. His will noted that "the Food Control Law is unjust but, since this is the law, citizens must obey it." Some two weeks later, Kameo Eijirō, a German-language teacher at the former Tokyo Higher School famous for his translations from German, similarly died of malnutrition after consuming only government rations.[9]

It was the weakest in society who suffered the greatest and sacrificed most at this time. Unimaginable hardship awaited discharged soldiers and civilians from the colonies on their return to Japan. Settlers returned home emptyhanded after having earlier abandoned everything to move to the colonies. With very few choices, they were now forced to move to isolated or unfertile regions like Konsengenya in Hokkaido; Sanrizuka in Chiba; Kamikuishiki in Yamanashi; Nasu in Tochigi; and Iitate, Namie, and Futaba in Fukushima.[10] The government tried to assist repatriated soldiers and civilians by implementing a large-scale agricultural land reclamation project for five years from 1946. Returning settlers from Manchukuo were given preferential treatment in the project. But the process was by no means seamless. Reclamation was a tortuous task and the quality of land differed greatly. Coupled with this, the reclamation project was complicated by land reforms unfolding under the Occupation.[11] Not until 1953 did military pensions recommence for former soldiers, while official subsidies and support for returned settlers only began with the passing of laws in 1956 and 1965. Former colonial subjects—now stripped of Japanese citizenship—did not qualify for any of these government initiatives.

Young women and their children also sacrificed a great deal in the early postwar years. Fearful that the arriving Allied Occupation forces might engage in indiscriminate rape, on August 21, 1945, the government established the innocuously-named "Recreation and Amusement Association" to provide sexual services for the occupying forces after they arrived. Of the estimated fifty thousand women recruited, many were prostitutes, geisha, waitresses, and hostesses, but others were unwittingly attracted by ambiguous newspaper advertisements sponsored by the government promising high pay, clothing, food, and lodging. On August 18, the government directed all prefectural governors to use local police forces to begin recruiting women who would provide sexual services "for the nation."[12] The American military was initially supportive of the system, but the operation was

Figure 2.5. So-called *panpan* are rounded up by US military police in Kokura City (Fukuoka Prefecture) for compulsory STD testing in 1948. Courtesy of The Asahi Shimbun Company.

terminated in January 1946 after criticisms from Christian chaplains and concerns about sexually transmitted diseases (STDs). But this official about-face did not bring an end to prostitution as a means of survival for many young women. By 1952, the government estimated that around seventy thousand women—known colloquially as *panpan*—were selling sex. Over time, red light districts developed around Allied military facilities. In response, local residents began to demand that these *panpan* be banned from public baths and their children excluded from playgrounds. The children born of liaisons between *panpan* and Allied soldiers were often abandoned after birth. Known as "mixed-blood orphans" (although they were not orphans), these children were placed in special facilities established by philanthropists. They faced double discrimination as the offspring of women considered to be of "loose morals" and for their "mixed-blood."[13]

Faced with these desperate times, Japanese intellectuals, writers, and creative artists attempted to make sense of Japan's descent into war, the meaning of its defeat, and the pathway toward a new democratic nation. In a 1946 essay entitled "Theory and Psychology of Ultra-Nationalism," the political thinker and Tokyo University professor, Maruyama Masao, explored what he viewed as the mental subservience of the Japanese to authority and the ways this psychological predisposition had assisted the descent into war. Around the same time, the historian, Ōtsuka Hisao, called on the Japanese to nurture a "modern human form" by expunging the premodern elements of their psyche in favor of a genuine individualism. Others like the legal sociologist, Takeyoshi Kawashima, analyzed the premodern aspects of social institutions, like the Japanese patrilineal family, in the hope of exposing and eradicating the remnants of feudalism. In one way or another, all of these modernist thinkers presented the West and Western modernity as ideals toward which Japan must now move. Filmmakers transmitted similar values to the masses, as in director Imai Tadashi's 1949 classic *Aoi sanmyaku* (The blue mountains), which idealized the American value of romantic love. Such ideas resonated seamlessly with the propaganda of the American-led Occupation.

Not all were spellbound by America, of course. Writing in 1948, the sinologist Takeuchi Yoshimi lionized China, which he argued had pursued its own independent—if agonized—pathway to modernity. In contrast, Takeuchi accused Japan of constantly mimicking the West in its relentless drive for modernity and thus never developing a genuine stance of national independence. Like good "honor students," the Japanese could mimic Westerners but, according to Takeuchi, they had never fashioned their own autonomous path. Marxists—now free to promote their ideas—enthusiastically joined this efflorescent intellectual discussion. Like the modernists, some Marxists blamed "feudalistic" and "premodern" flaws for Japanese militarism. They identified the Meiji Restoration as an incomplete revolution, which now must be properly concluded. Under the Allied Occupation this meant revolution with a small "r"—in other words, the construction of liberal democracy in Japan.

Intellectuals and literati like Tsurumi Shunsuke, Ōkuma Nobuyuki, and Ara Masato explored troubling questions of war responsibility head on. Why had they and other supposedly conscientious Japanese failed to resist, and why had so many people been so easily mobilized into the war effort? There were no easy answers here but, for some like Ōkuma, the starting point lay in a candid exposition of his own personal failings in the 1930s and 1940s. Tsurumi and members of his Institute for the Science of Thought extended this project into the realm of popular activism. They established various cultural and literary groups among ordinary people with the aim of helping the Japanese develop a strong sense of individual self-reliance resistant to the tentacles of the state. Others, like the novelist Dazai Osamu, moved in an entirely different direction, exploring sexual liberation and self-gratification (sometimes to the point of self-destruction) in the context of early postwar deprivation. Their so-called *kasutori* culture, named after the cheap rice wine they drank, spoke to a sense of melancholic resignation in the face of absolute destruction, coupled with a determination to live for the carnal pleasures of the here and now. Though such cultural and intellectual trends varied greatly, they all pointed to a desire for something new among a war-wearied people.

General Douglas MacArthur Arrives

On August 19, 1945, a Japanese delegation led by Deputy Chief of Staff of the Imperial Japanese Army General Kawabe Torashirō travelled to Manila to discuss the details of the coming Occupation with American military officials. Of most concern for the Japanese was the institutional structure of the Occupation. Would it operate by direct military rule or would the Americans work through the Japanese government? On returning to Japan, the diplomat Okazaki Katsuo, a member of the entourage, reported—to the great relief of all—that the Americans appeared to be leaning in the direction of indirect rule.

Ten days later, on August 30, General Douglas MacArthur of the US Army arrived at Atsugi Air Base south of Tokyo. Newly appointed as Supreme Commander for the Allied Powers (SCAP), MacArthur was a decorated hero of two world wars, a fastidious curator of his public image, and a man with presidential ambitions. With just a handful of military police and staff in tow, MacArthur emerged from the aircraft at Atsugi with his trademark sunglasses and custom-made oversized corn pipe. A photo of the time portrays a relaxed MacArthur, hands on hips, surveying the landscape, surrounded by senior army officers. This was not the general's first time in Japan, having travelled in the country when his father was serving as

Figure 2.6. General Douglas MacArthur arrives at Atsugi Air Base south of Tokyo on August 30, 1945. Naval History and Heritage Command.

governor general of the Philippines many years before. An avid reader of military history, he apparently had a great respect for Japanese military luminaries like General Tōgo Heihachirō, the naval hero responsible for defeating the Russian Pacific Fleet in 1905.[14] But now was not the time for respect. MacArthur was here to remake Japan.

On hearing of MacArthur's confident arrival in enemy territory essentially unprotected, the British wartime prime minister, Winston Churchill, declared "of all the amazing deeds of bravery of the war, I regard MacArthur's personal landing at Atsugi as the greatest of the lot."[15] Churchill's declaration was an overstatement because the Japanese were not resisting at all. But MacArthur's entrance was undoubtedly a masterpiece of political theatre. Indeed, throughout his tenure, MacArthur made sure to limit his public appearances and personal meetings to accentuate this aura of absolute supremacy. It was an aura underwritten by genuine power. In a memorandum of September 6 authorized by President Harry Truman, MacArthur was advised that he could "exercise authority" as he "deem[ed] proper to carry out [his] mission." "Our relations with Japan do not rest on a contractual basis," the memorandum explained, "but on an unconditional surrender. Since your authority is supreme, you will not entertain any question on the part of the Japanese as to its scope."[16] Importantly, this supreme authority would also extend over the other Allied countries involved in the Occupation of Japan, despite their futile attempts to occasionally advance different agendas.

The Asia-Pacific War officially ended with the signing of the documents of surrender on the deck of the *USS Missouri* in Tokyo Bay on September 2, 1945. Representatives from the United States and eight nations signed on the Allied side, while two signatories—foreign minister Shigemitsu Mamoru and military chief of staff Umezu Yoshijirō—signed for Japan. Initially, the Americans had intended to make the emperor sign the surrender documents because he was the sovereign. However, this plan was abandoned after some expressed concerns that humiliating the emperor publicly might provoke a backlash among the Japanese and impede the smooth implementation of the Occupation. Accordingly, Japanese representatives from the cabinet and the military were both required to sign because these branches of government were only responsible to the emperor under the Meiji Constitution. The Americans added to the drama of the moment by displaying the Stars and Stripes flown by Commodore Perry when he had come to open up Japan over ninety years earlier. Now the time had come to complete Perry's unfinished business.

MacArthur continued this theme in a radio broadcast later that day, likening himself to the great commodore. "We stand in Tokyo today reminiscent of our countryman, Commodore Perry, ninety-two years ago," MacArthur declared. "His [Perry's] purpose was to bring to Japan an era of enlightenment and progress by lifting the veil of isolation to the friendship, trade, and commerce of the world. But, alas, the knowledge thereby gained of western science was forged into an instrument of oppression and human enslavement. [. . .] We are committed by the Potsdam Declaration of principles to see that the Japanese people are liberated from this condition of slavery."[17]

Six days later, MacArthur relocated from the Hotel New Grand in Yokohama to the new General Headquarters (GHQ) of SCAP in the Daiichi Seimei Building, located near the Imperial Palace in central Tokyo. Among his first and most important actions was a meeting with Emperor Hirohito on September 27. Like MacArthur's arrival and the surrender ceremony, this meeting was another carefully staged affair. The emperor was required to travel by vehicle to GHQ for the meeting—not the reverse—leaving no doubt in Japanese minds as to who was now in charge. Records of this first of ten meetings indicate that Hirohito expressed a willingness to accept full responsibility both politicly and militarily for waging the war, apparently even stating that "you may hang me."[18] MacArthur later confessed that he had feared the emperor might use the meeting to plead his innocence and evade prosecution as a war criminal. But hearing Hirohito's humble acceptance of responsibility, the general was deeply moved, referring to him as a "great gentleman of

Figure 2.7. General Umezu Yoshijirō signs the Instrument of Surrender on behalf of Japanese Imperial General Headquarters on board the *USS Missouri,* September 2, 1945. Naval History and Heritage Command.

Japan."[19] Whether Hirohito did in fact agree to accept total responsibility is a point of debate among historians, but other details of the time suggest that the emperor was genuinely considering abdication. On the day after the American forces arrived in Japan, the emperor, aware of the Potsdam Declaration's call for punishing Japanese war criminals, asked Minister of the Interior Kido Kōichi if matters might be solved by Hirohito "alone taking responsibility."[20] But Kido managed to persuade the emperor otherwise. Although Hirohito did not know it at the time of his meeting with MacArthur, there was also growing support among American elites in favor of retaining the emperor as a political tool. MacArthur knew better than any other that the emperor could be a useful tool for gaining Japanese compliance. At the end of their first meeting, the two posed for a famous photo. In it, MacArthur again stands relaxed, hands on hips. To his left, the much smaller Hirohito stands stiffly with arms to his side. Nowhere was Japan's subordination to the United States more clearly expressed.

Figure 2.8. General Douglas MacArthur and Emperor Hirohito meet on September 27, 1945. Photograph by Gaetano Faillace (Wikimedia Commons).

The Nature, Objectives, and Organization of the Allied Occupation

The Occupation was generally well received by the Japanese people, most of whom were tired of wartime deprivation and destruction and the strict state controls. There were some sporadic instances of resistance by military radicals. On August 15, for instance, several militants forced their way into the emperor's palace in an attempt to stop the imperial surrender broadcast, but they were quickly detained. In a special radio broadcast on August 21, the newly appointed prime minister, Prince Higashikuni Naruhiko, convinced a group of army officers to abandon their plot for a coup d'état.[21] Meanwhile, a number of pilots at Atsugi Air Base who were reluctant to surrender their aircraft took off on August 21, only to return submissively two days later.[22] But such instances were rare indeed and, for the most part, the transition from war to occupation was a peaceful one. This transition was assisted by the Allied forces, who were only lightly armed and under strict orders to show the utmost respect for the

Japanese people and for important institutions—such as the emperor—and other sites of cultural significance, like shrines and temples.

Despite initial fears of rape and plunder, the Americans' provision of emergency food supplies and support for civilian repatriation tended to foster a popular image of benevolence. SCAP reinforced this image by maintaining strict control over the media. Although freedom of speech was restored under an October 4, 1945 directive (see later in this chapter), the Press Code issued just weeks earlier forbade any "destructive criticism" or reporting that might "invite mistrust or resentment" toward the occupying forces.[23] Censorship of the press, radio, and cinema meant that Allied crimes such as sexual offenses—which did occur—were either not reported or, if they were, only in the vaguest of terms. Details of the havoc wreaked by the atomic bombings of Hiroshima and Nagasaki were also extensively censored lest these provoke a popular backlash. Any material venerating Japan's "feudal" past was also prohibited, meaning that there would be no more movies glorifying the violent vendettas of samurai warriors or tales of revered war heroes. Nonetheless, SCAP censorship was never all embracing. At the grass roots, itinerant theatre groups continued performing outdoors or in ramshackle sheds, entertaining the masses with tear-jerking stories of valor from the country's past. Given the widespread sense of national failure, such entertainment provided a comforting escapism for many.

Another important reason for the broad acceptance of the Occupation connected to the ways its policies built on legacies from the prewar and wartime eras. SCAP was not beginning on barren ground in its drive for democratization. As noted in chapter 1, the era of Taishō Democracy witnessed the growth of a vibrant realm of social movements including labor unions, Buraku activism, socialists, anarchists, communists, and a women's suffrage campaign. During the same period, reformist bureaucrats had taken up the issue of land reform in response to rising tenant unrest. In early 1938, the government passed the Farmland Adjustment Law that restricted the ownership rights of landlords and strengthened the position of tenants—all with the aim of improving productivity. One outcome of such developments was the gradual weakening of vested interests, which had been protected under the Meiji state framework.[24] During the 1940s, the government went even further, directly paying tenants at a premium for their produce and making it easier for them to purchase their land. Importantly, many of the bureaucrats responsible for these initiatives survived the postwar purges, thus providing SCAP with willing assistants when it began its own land reform during the Occupation.

The Americans had been formulating plans for the Occupation of Japan from as early as 1942. As would be formally articulated in the Potsdam Declaration in June 1945, these plans envisaged a menu of demilitarization, the provision of basic human rights, and the establishment of American-style democracy based on government freely chosen by the people. The American occupiers wanted the process to be beneficial for Japan, different from the Treaty of Versailles, whose punitive aspects fed into the rise of National Socialism in Germany. Japan, they felt, needed to be supported to recover and reintegrate as a healthy liberal democracy. This ethos was reinforced by the prominence early on of Occupation officials with a New Deal vision for Japan. They believed that strong social, political, and economic policy interventions could bring about momentous change for the better. In this sense, the Occupation of Japan differed dramatically from historical occupations, which punished defeated nations but did not necessarily dismantle and reconstitute institutions like the military, the legal system, or landholdings.

By the same token, until around 1948, there was general agreement within SCAP that Japan should only be reconstructed as a small nation incapable of threatening the world again. As late as 1946, the Pauley Commission was advising President Truman that Japan's industrial assets should be shipped off as war reparations to victim nations and the country's standard of living be no higher than that of other nations of the region. As revealed later, this vision of a small Japan was short-lived.

Unlike postwar Germany, where the Allies implemented direct military government in clearly demarcated zones, the Occupation of Japan adopted a centralized, vertical structure of command (fig. 2.9). At the apex was the Far Eastern Commission (FEC), established in Washington, DC in December 1945 and consisting of eleven countries. It was charged with setting and overseeing Occupation policy. In theory, the FEC's decisions were to be communicated to the US government, which, in turn, would issue the directives for MacArthur to implement in Japan. But the right of veto among the big four powers and the necessity for majority decisions meant that the FEC often struggled to reach decisions, giving MacArthur broad authority to implement policies "deemed necessary to implement his mission."[25] On the ground in Tokyo, an Allied Council for Japan was established, comprising representatives from the United States, the USSR, the Republic of China, and one from the British Commonwealth. The council's role was to advise and consult with GHQ on matters of importance but, in practice, its influence appears to have been limited. Indeed, although an "Allied" Occupation in name, MacArthur and his staff were controlling the show.

SCAP itself consisted of four general and nine specialist sections, among which the Government Section (GS), the military intelligence staff under Major General Charles Willoughby (G2), and the Economic and Scientific Section (ESS) had great influence and often came into mutual conflict due to their differing perspectives. With so few fluent language speakers or individuals possessing practical knowledge about the country, direct military government, as in Germany, was deemed

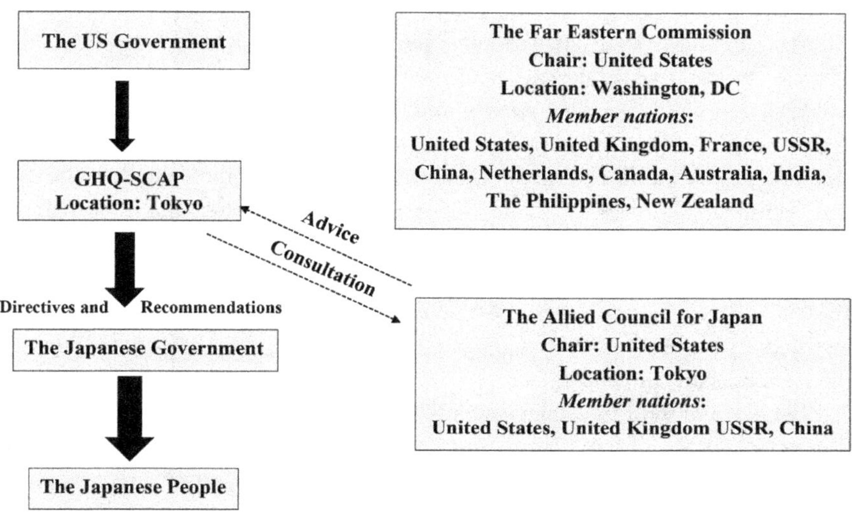

Source: Hokazono et al., *Nihonshi A*, p. 136.

Figure 2.9. Structure of the Allied Occupation of Japan

inappropriate. Instead, SCAP sections chose to work through the extant Japanese state apparatus of bureaucracies and the Diet, issuing orders and directives that were translated into Japanese and subsequently codified in laws and implemented by Japanese officials. SCAP frequently called on politicians to pass relevant laws in the Diet—the most important of which would be the new postwar constitution. Ironically, until the revision of the Meiji Constitution, the emperor's power of edict was yet another useful mechanism for implementing SCAP initiatives.

SCAP's indirect approach had its tradeoffs. Because Japanese officials were the ones ultimately responsible for translating and implementing SCAP directives, they had considerable discretion. Hence, how directives were worded in Japanese and how they played out in practice sometimes differed from SCAP's initial intent.

Demilitarization and Assigning War Responsibility

MacArthur received his orders for the Occupation in the form of two directives from Washington, DC. The first, approved by President Truman on September 6, 1945, and titled "Politico-Military Problems in the Far East: United States Initial Post-Defeat Policy Relating to Japan" (SWNCC [State-War-Navy Coordinating

Committee] 150/4), called for the "establishment of a peaceful and responsible government" to ensure that Japan would "not again become a menace to the United States or to the peace and security of the world." To this end, Japan's sovereignty would be limited to the main islands and "such minor outlying islands as may be determined," the country would be completely disarmed and demilitarized, and the Japanese people would be "encouraged to develop a desire for individual liberties" and "afforded opportunity to develop for themselves an economy" capable of meeting "peacetime requirements."[26] The second document, the "Basic Directive for Post-Surrender Military Government in Japan" (JCS [Joint Chiefs of Staff] 1380/15), dated November 3, 1945, offered MacArthur a more detailed set of instructions for reform, directing him to work through the "Emperor of Japan or the Japanese Government."[27]

The first and most pressing task for SCAP was demilitarization and demobilization, which proceeded in a surprisingly efficient and peaceful fashion under the direction of the Japanese government. One day after the emperor's surrender broadcast, the Imperial Headquarters ordered all Japanese forces to immediately cease combat, followed on August 17 by an edict from Hirohito directing naval and army forces to surrender their weapons and discontinue all forms of resistance. The demobilization process was a mammoth task, involving some 7.9 million members of the Japanese military, of whom around 3.5 million were located throughout the Asia-Pacific. The other half were on the home islands, armed and ready for the anticipated ground battle. Although hostilities did continue in some areas, by around mid-October the demobilization process was largely complete. The remaining army and naval organs—like the Ministry of the Army and Navy—were dismantled by the end of November.

A wave of purges followed the demilitarization process in line with Article 6 of the Potsdam Declaration, which called for the elimination of "those who . . . deceived and misled the people of Japan into embarking on world conquest." Under its directive "Removal and Exclusion of Undesirable Personnel from Public Office" (SCAPIN-550) of January 1946, SCAP identified seven categories of individuals liable for removal: (A) war criminals; (B) career military and naval personnel: special police and officials of the war ministries; (C) ultranationalists; (D) leaders of IRAA associations; (E) those involved in organizations financing and developing Japanese expansion; (F) governors of occupied territories; and (G) additional militarists and ultranationalists (e.g., journalists).[28] The first purge of 1945 was rather limited with just a few thousand removed from politics, business, private associations, education, and the media. Dissatisfied, SCAP's GS broadened the scope of liable individuals in a second purge of January 1947, resulting in the removal of over two hundred thousand from positions in business, the media, politics, and the public service by May of that year.[29] The great majority of the purged were of military origin, but the purges were also implemented in political and media circles. The incumbent government, under the Progressive Party of Shidehara Kijūrō, was rocked when 262 of its 274 Diet members were purged, while Liberal Party leader Hatoyama Ichirō's hopes of assuming the prime ministership in May 1946 were dashed when he too was purged. Leftist parties did not escape unscathed, with the Japan Socialist Party (JSP) losing eleven of its seventeen Diet members. Newspaper editorial boards and publishers of high-circulation magazines like *Bungei Shunjū* were also targeted due to their wartime support of Japanese militarism.

Nonetheless, with the shift in Occupation policy from around 1948, an astounding 80 percent of these individuals would be depurged by 1951. Moreover, SCAP's approach of indirect rule meant that the Japanese national bureaucracy could not be excessively disrupted, hence only a few thousand were purged. But there is no doubt that the purges opened the way for a new generation of leaders in business and government, in turn contributing to the Occupation's reformist agenda and injecting fresh energies into these sectors.

Along with purges, the Potsdam Declaration also required the Occupation to mete out "stern justice . . . to all war criminals, including those who have visited cruelties upon our prisoners." Beginning in September 1945, a handful of individuals, including wartime prime minister General Tōjō Hideki, were detained on suspicion of war crimes, followed later in the same year by the arrest of former minister of the interior Kido Kōichi and former prime minister Prince Konoe Fumimaro (although Konoe committed suicide by drinking potassium cyanide before he could be arrested). In a directive of late January 1946, SCAP set out the three broad classes of war criminals to be tried in the upcoming military tribunals. At the apex were the Class A criminals who comprised the military and other leaders charged with crimes against peace and crimes against humanity (new principles established in the Nuremberg Trials of Nazi war criminals) and conventional war crimes. Next came the Class B and Class C suspects charged with violations of international law and established war crimes, such as the murder and rape of civilians, maltreatment of POWs under the Geneva Convention, and the use of prohibited chemical weapons. Trials for the latter Class B and Class C suspects were conducted throughout East and Southeast Asia from late 1945 until early 1951 under the direction of the United States, the United Kingdom, the Netherlands, France, Australia, China, and the Philippines. Of the 5,700 tried, 984 received death sentences; 3,419 received prison sentences; and the remaining 1,279 were found not guilty or released for other reasons. These trials were not without their problems, often lacking competent interpreters and lawyers and the identities of culprits not always adequately verified.[30] Former colonial subjects from Korea and Taiwan forcefully drafted into the

Japanese military also found themselves dragged before these tribunals, among whom 321 received death sentences and many others prison terms. Compounding their agony, because these former subjects were no longer considered Japanese nationals, they and their families did not qualify for military pensions or compensation and the Japanese government offered no apology for their hardships.

The centerpiece of the tribunals was the International Military Tribunal for the Far East or, more simply, the Tokyo War Crimes Tribunal, which ran for two-and-a-half years from May 1946 until November 1948. The judicial panel consisted of eleven justices from the Allied nations of the United States, the United Kingdom, China, the Philippines, New Zealand, Canada, the Netherlands, Australia, the USSR, France, and India, with no representation from Japan. Among the one hundred or so detained on suspicion of Class A war crimes at Tokyo's Sugamo Prison, ultimately only twenty-eight were charged with the conspiracy of planning, starting, and carrying out a war of aggression resulting in "crimes against peace." The defendants also faced charges of "crimes against humanity" for offenses such as the massacre of innocent civilians. Among the indicted were many of the wartime leaders including Tōjō Hideki and Kido Kōichi, along with several other generals, admirals, and diplomats. The choice of twenty-eight defendants was somewhat arbitrary and produced absurd outcomes at times. For example, in late April 1946, just before the trials were to commence, Soviet prosecutors requested the inclusion of two further defendants, Umezu Yoshijirō and Shigemitsu Mamoru, but construction of the courtroom dock had ended, leaving no space for more defendants at this late stage. After negotiations, it was agreed that two others already indicted would arbitrarily be replaced by Umezu and Shigemitsu.

More disconcerting for many was the absence of Emperor Hirohito from the list of defendants, despite the war having been waged in his name. MacArthur and many other Japan experts, like former ambassador Joseph Grew, were convinced that dragging Hirohito before the tribunal would provoke popular dissent—if not violent resistance—in Japan, potentially stymieing the Occupation's reform initiatives. Except for a few on the left, popular sentiment within Japan also appears to have been leaning in the direction of absolving the emperor from any war responsibility. Conversely, Allied nations like Australia and Britain lobbied strongly to prosecute Hirohito due to the horrific treatment of Commonwealth POWs in Southeast Asia by the Japanese military during the war. Public opinion in the United States was also hostile toward the emperor: polls taken in 1946 revealed that only 7 percent approved of exonerating the emperor, with the overwhelming majority wanting his execution or imprisonment.[31] Faced with this animosity, MacArthur orchestrated an ingenious piece of political theatre in league with the Japanese government. On New Year's Day 1946, Hirohito issued the "Rescript on the Construction of a New Japan," a curious document written by SCAP and Japanese officials. In the rescript—which Hirohito insisted should begin with a reproduction of the Charter Oath issued by the new Meiji leaders almost eighty years earlier—Hirohito rejected the "false conception" that the emperor was "divine" or that the Japanese people were "superior" and "fated to rule the world."[32] MacArthur was apparently delighted with the rescript, which he hoped would both assuage hostility in America and dampen Allies' calls for Hirohito's war responsibility. The question over whether to indict the emperor seems to have been finally resolved in late January 1946, when MacArthur sent a communication to chief of staff of the US Army, Dwight Eisenhower, advising that, for the good of the Occupation and the prevention of a "communistic line" among the "mutilated masses," the emperor should not be classified as a war criminal. If he was indicted, MacArthur warned, a further one "million" troops and "several hundred thousand" more civil servants would be needed.[33] Interestingly, in this wire to Eisenhower, MacArthur referred to the emperor as "a symbol which united all Japanese"—a depiction that would later reappear in the postwar constitution (see later in this chapter).[34] Although indignant to the end, in early April 1946 the other Allied nations relented, notifying the US government through the FEC that no action was to be taken against the emperor as a war criminal.[35]

Figure 2.10. Emperor Hirohito raises his hat to children and elderly people who greet him during an inspection of a ruined school in Yokohama (February 20, 1946). Courtesy of The Asahi Shimbun Company.

Thereafter, the emperor underwent a stunning transformation, abandoning his military regalia for a conservative business suit topped with a fedora. From February 1946—with the blessing and encouragement of SCAP—Hirohito began to make national tours aimed at propagating his new image as a soft-spoken proponent of peace and democracy. His somewhat wooden interactions with ordinary Japanese prompted sardonic depictions of "Mr. Ah-so san" ("Mr. Oh, is that so?"), visiting factories, villages, farms, and townships in every prefecture except Okinawa.

With Hirohito "saved" and the list of twenty-eight defendants settled, the tribunal began its work. Although the prosecution consisted of lawyers from most of the Allied nations, proceedings were carefully controlled and orchestrated by the Americans under the watchful oversight of the chief prosecutor, Joseph Keenan, a Harvard Law graduate and veteran of World War I. Keenan and his team understood well that, in the context of the Occupation, the tribunal had as much political importance as it did legal. Their charge was to assign blame for the war—as per the Potsdam Declaration—yet, at the same time, insulate the emperor and reassure the Japanese people that their only mistake had been to trust a handful of warmongering leaders who led them into a foolish war of aggression. Accomplishing the latter would be quite simple, as it was easier for most Japanese to believe they had been victimized—first by their own government and later by the Allied air raids and atomic bombings. Insulating the emperor required more creative approaches, and involved active cooperation from the defendants, of whom Tōjō Hideki was the most important.

Tōjō had come under a degree of public criticism after a failed suicide attempt on learning of his impending arrest. If he had truly wanted to die, some sneered, then why shoot himself in the chest and not in the mouth, and why not take his life immediately on hearing the emperor's surrender? Ironically, it was Tōjō who had issued the so-called Battlefield Instructions of 1941 to Japanese forces, advising them to commit suicide rather than be taken captive.[36] But now, as the most high-profile defendant in the Tokyo tribunal, Tōjō emerged as a critical pawn for the Americans. Working through Japanese intermediaries and MacArthur's right-hand man Bonner Fellers, Tōjō was persuaded to take full responsibility for the war in his testimony in return for a guarantee of the emperor's safety and immunity from prosecution. Except for one gaffe during cross examination, Tōjō proved remarkably compliant. Under carefully orchestrated questioning from Keenan in early 1948, Tōjō stated that the High Command made the decision to go to war against the will of the emperor, whose "spirit of peace and friendship" did not fade to the very end.[37]

On November 12, 1948, the tribunal reached its verdict. Seven defendants, including Tōjō, received death sentences, sixteen received life sentences, one defendant twenty years, and another seven years in prison. Two died during proceedings and another was found mentally unfit. The executions were carried out six weeks

Figure 2.11. Defendants at the Tokyo War Crimes Tribunal, 1946. US Army.

later after failed attempts at appeal by the Japanese defense team. The remaining individuals arrested on suspicion of war crimes were freed without indictment or conviction by 1949—some of them, like Kishi Nobusuke, Sasagawa Ryōichi, and Kodama Yoshio, later playing influential roles in postwar politics. In 1978, the seven executed, the two who died during the trial, and the five who perished in prison were quietly enshrined as "martyrs for the nation" in the Yasukuni Shrine for Japan's war dead, planting the seeds of deep discontent that grew between Japan and its Asian neighbors thereafter.

Overall, the tribunal bequeathed an ambiguous historical legacy. First, the fact that the judges and prosecutors were only drawn from the Allied side gave the tribunal a strong flavor of victors' justice—in other words, retribution by the victors over the vanquished. The retroactive application of law also came under attack from the defense team and the Indian judge Radhabinod Pal, who wrote one of the dissenting opinions to the guilty verdicts. As both argued, in principle, only those who had violated established conventions of war should be tried, not those whose offenses did not exist in law when the relevant acts were committed. As Tōjō's lawyer Kiyose

Ichirō argued, until the Nuremberg Trials, wars of aggression and crimes against peace had not been illegal and waging war was a right of all nation-states. Japan, he asserted, had simply invoked its right of self-defense.[38]

A second problem of the trial was that while Japanese transgressions in Asia received some attention during proceedings, these were treated as largely peripheral to the crimes committed by Japanese forces against America and its allies. As a result, issues such as the Nanjing massacre of 1937, Japanese chemical and biological weapons testing on human subjects at its infamous Unit 731 in Harbin, wartime sexual violence and exploitation in the so-called comfort women system, and other atrocities throughout Asia were left largely unresolved. Third, as Japan was not considered to be at war with its former colonies of Korea and Taiwan, voices from these countries were not properly heard at the tribunal.

One outcome of the tribunal, then, was the formation of a "Pacific War view of history" among many Japanese, which tended to limit collective memory to the conflict between Japan and the United States, concealing transgressions in Asia and promoting a sense of Japanese victimization. The Americans played no small part in this process by arranging for individuals such as Tōjō to publicly bear the burden of war responsibility.

Rebuilding a Democratic Japan

Along with punishment and retribution, the Occupation of Japan also pursued a bold reformist agenda aimed at not only demilitarization but also the fundamental renovation of a society seen to be crippled by feudalistic and authoritarian institutions and attitudes. With a healthy dose of American-style democracy and New Deal liberalism, it was believed that Japan could be made into a compliant ally of the United States. Anticipating this coming deluge of reform, Japanese leaders initiated several preemptive reforms of their own just months after defeat. In December 1945, the House of Representatives Election Law was amended to recognize women's suffrage rights and set the voting age at twenty and the eligible age for elective office at twenty-five. Just five days later, the Diet passed the Labor Union Law—drafted by many of the same bureaucrats involved in labor issues in the prewar—thereby guaranteeing various rights such as organizing and collective bargaining. Governments under Prime Minister Higashikuni and later Shidehara Kijūrō also made initial attempts at land reform, yet another policy agenda carried over from the prewar and wartime. As early as August 1945, the Ministry of Agriculture prepared legislation requiring that all land over three hectares held by owners was to be redistributed to tenants. But this bill was subsequently diluted by the Shidehara Cabinet in the face of fierce opposition from landowners and fears that extensive disruptions to rural life might open the way for socialism and communism. Shidehara's watered-down Farmland Reform Law, passed by the Diet in late December, required land more than five hectares held by both resident and absentee landlords to be redistributed to tenants over a five-year period.

The first major reform initiated by SCAP was its civil rights directive (SCAPIN-93) of October 4, 1945, ordering the Japanese government to remove restrictions on political, civil, and religious freedoms, along with the immediate release of all political prisoners.[39] The directive required the repeal or revision of some fifteen draconian laws, including the Peace Preservation Law, the Protection and Surveillance Law for Thought Offenses, the Defense Security Law, and the Military Secrets Protection Law. Unwilling to accept such far-reaching reforms, the Higashikuni Cabinet resigned the following day, leaving the task to Shidehara Kijūrō, who took over as prime minister on October 9 and promptly released some three thousand political prisoners—including leaders of the JCP. MacArthur used his first meeting with Shidehara on October 11 to present the new prime minister with what would become known as the Five Major Reforms.[40] First, MacArthur directed Shidehara to immediately disband the Special Higher Police, responsible for investigating and arresting individuals suspected of "thought crimes" during the war. The general's reforms also called for the promotion of labor unionization, the liberation of women, the democratization of education, and the liberalization of the economy to remove cartels and other monopolistic structures. Implementing this grand slew of initiatives would fully engage both SCAP and Japanese officials in the coming years, although the emphasis and extent of reform would change over time.

Land reform was a top priority for SCAP, which, in a directive of December 9, 1945, emphasized the need to eradicate the "economic bondage" that had "enslaved the Japanese farmer to centuries of feudal oppression."[41] Unimpressed with the Japanese government's land reform legislation of late 1945, the following May, SCAP presented Japanese officials with its own more robust program of reform, paving the way for two pieces of sweeping legislation to pass the Diet in October. Under the SCAP-crafted reform, all tenanted land of absentee landlords, all tenanted land more than one hectare held by resident landlords (four hectares in Hokkaido), and all owner-cultivated land exceeding three hectares (twelve hectares in Hokkaido) was subject to compulsory purchase by the government and resale to tenants. Land Committees comprising tenants (50 percent), landlords (30 percent), and owner cultivators (20 percent) were elected in each locality to administer land transfers and to manage disputes. The process began in March 1947 and was completed by July 1950 with thoroughly transformative outcomes. Approximately 1.78 million hectares of land held by 2.52 million owners was redistributed among 4.2 million tenants. Whereas in 1938 around 47 percent of land was tenanted and

53 percent owner farmed, by 1950 an astounding 91 percent was now owner farmed and only 9 percent under tenant cultivation (fig. 2.12). The strata of so-called parasitic landlords disappeared almost overnight, replaced now by a massive class of small-plot cultivators. Conservatives who had initially wanted to shield the traditional landowners now expressed their delight over a countryside reborn as an "impregnable fortress" against communism. On the ground, the new owner cultivators were incentivized to raise productivity, in turn helping to address the food shortage crises of the early postwar period. Rising incomes in the countryside thanks to this productivity also fed into the consumption boom of the late 1950s

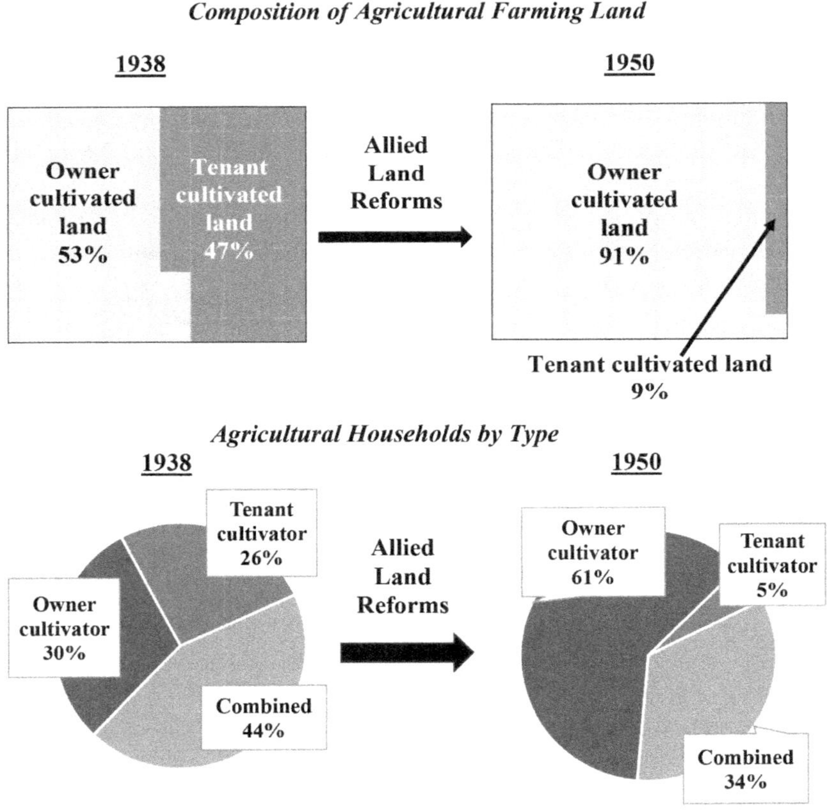

Source: Hokazono, *Nihonshi A*, 138.

Figure 2.12. Agricultural Farming Land and Households before and after the Land Reforms of the Allied Occupation.

and 1960s, as rural families began to indulge in the same consumer durables—washing machines, televisions, and so on—as their counterparts in the cities. Politically, this new class of owner cultivators also emerged as the critical electoral base for the conservatives, who would rule almost without interruption from the early 1950s onward.

While SCAP officers worked with Japanese officials to liberate Japan's "feudalistic" countryside, early on they also pursued a program of economic democratization centered on reigning in the financial and industrial power of the zaibatsu. At war's end, the big four zaibatsu alone (Mitsubishi, Mitsui, Sumitomo, Yasuda) accounted for close to 25 percent of the value of the Japanese economy. The ten largest zaibatsu together held 49 percent of paid-up capital in the heavy and chemical industries and 53 percent in financial services. Policymakers in Washington, DC appear to have felt—at least early on—that some measures must be taken to reform this situation, although it is important to note that there was never absolute agreement on just how deep or broad such reforms should be. "Japan hands" like prewar ambassador Joseph Grew argued that many within the zaibatsu had been opposed to the military and, hence, they should be maintained as a force for peace. Other elements in the US State Department argued that, since economic recovery would depend greatly on domestic demand, the zaibatsu should be dissolved to facilitate fairer distribution of wealth throughout society.[42]

The initial post-surrender policies on the zaibatsu were quite broad, simply directing MacArthur to dissolve the "large industrial and banking corporations"—a task he entrusted to Colonel Raymond Kramer, chief of SCAP's ESS. In November 1945, the ESS issued a directive to the Japanese government requiring the dissolution of the holding companies of the big four zaibatsu, the breakup of smaller conglomerates, and the liberation of subsidiary companies via elimination of corporate shareholdings and concurrent executive appointments.[43] The big four came in for particular attention because they were seen to have actively supported militarism, exploited people in conquered regions and in mines and factories within Japan, and stifled equitable income distribution. Following the directive of 1945, ESS established the Holding Company Liquidation Committee in August 1946 to oversee the process. By June 1947, the committee had dealt with eighty-three companies. Twenty-eight firms—including the big four—classified as zaibatsu headquarters or organizations effectively operating as such were dissolved and their shareholdings transferred to the committee. A further fifty-one entities deemed to be holding companies in critical industries were allowed to continue or incorporate as new entities, but only after relinquishing their shareholdings to the committee. The remaining four companies were completely dissolved. Fifty-six executives and upper managers from zaibatsu families in the ten largest conglomerates were forced to surrender their company positions indefinitely and to relinquish their shareholdings. Important for later corporate reorganization in Japan however, zaibatsu banks were exempted from these dissolution processes.

Building on this program, in April 1947, the Diet passed the Law Relating to Prohibition of Private Monopoly and Maintenance of Fair Trade—more simply, the Antimonopoly Law—with the aim of extending economic deconcentration into industries such as steel, paper, brewing, electrical, and transportation. Of the 325 companies targeted under the new law, however, only eleven were split up and seven others merely required to close factories or shut down subsidiaries.[44]

But by October 1947 when the Law for the Elimination of Excessive Concentration of Economic Power passed the Diet, enthusiasm for deconcentration was on the wane. Japanese conservatives worried increasingly about the rise of leftist forces domestically while policymakers in Washington, DC cast concerned eyes on deteriorating political conditions in the Far East. Within SCAP, officials in both the ESS and the G2 intelligence section argued—with ever-more influence—that further deconcentration would make Japan dependent on the United States and expose the country to communist infiltration. They found allies in American businessmen who wanted to recommence trade. Given this loss of impetus, the zaibatsu dissolution was thus arguably among the least successful in terms of thoroughness compared with other SCAP initiatives. Nonetheless, as noted earlier, the purging of zaibatsu families and other upper management undoubtedly opened the way for a new generation of businessmen, while the deconcentration in certain industries made it possible for new companies like Sony and Honda to emerge and thrive.

SCAP also demanded thoroughgoing reform of education, which was seen to have played a central role in inculcating ultranationalistic values during the war. The first step came with two October 1945 directives ordering the Japanese government to dismiss all teachers responsible for supporting ultranationalism and militarism during the war and all those potentially standing in the way of the Occupation reforms. The Ministry of Education (MOE) was charged with overseeing this process through the establishment of a Teacher Qualification Screening Panel. But, by the time the Japanese government passed the relevant legislation in May 1946, some 115,000 teachers and education officials had already voluntarily retired in anticipation of the coming purges. The new legislation and screening panel reviews resulted in the purging of close to 5,000 teachers by 1947.[45]

In September 1945, the MOE—without prompting from SCAP—directed prefectural governors to remove all war-related and ultranationalistic elements from school textbooks. The extreme shortages of paper and printing facilities left schools with no choice but to have students eliminate the pertinent sections by gluing on scrap paper, cutting out pages, or applying black ink (fig. 2.13)—leaving many

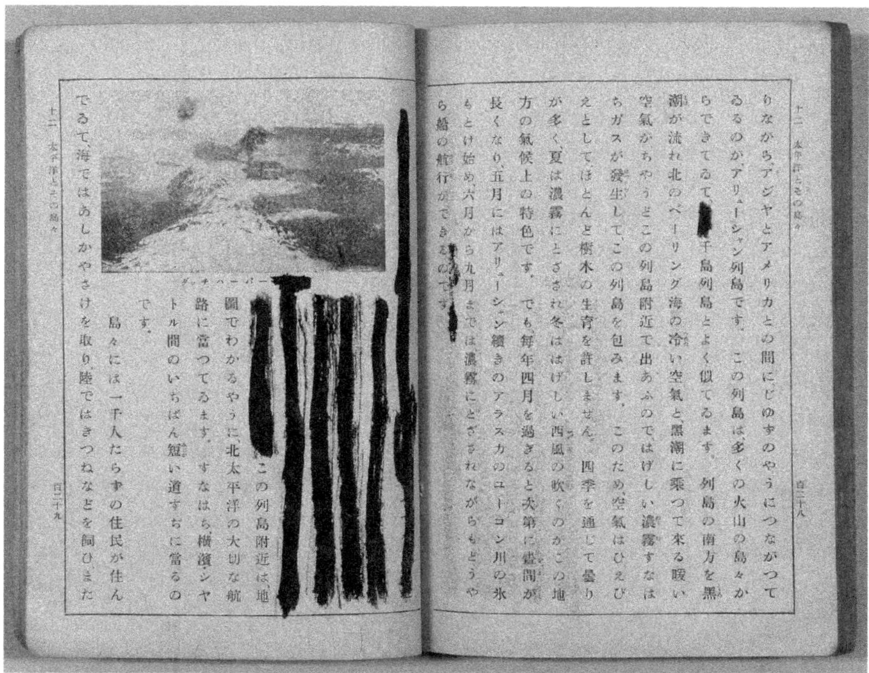

十二　太平洋とその島々

りながら、アジヤとアメリカとの間に、じゆずのやうにつながつてゐるのが、アリューシャン列島です。この列島は、多くの火山の島々からできてゐて、[blacked out]千島列島とよく似てゐます。列島の南方を黒潮が流れ北のベーリング海の冷い空氣と、黒潮に乘つて來る暖い空氣がちやうどこの列島附近で出あふので、はげしい濃霧すなはちガスが發生して、この列島を包みます。このため、空氣はひえびえとして、ほとんど樹木の生育を許しません。四季を通じて曇りが多く、夏は濃霧にとざされ冬ははげしい西風の吹くのがこの地方の氣候上の特色です。でも、毎年四月を過ぎると次第に晝間が長くなり、五月にはアリューシャン續きのアラスカのユーコン川の氷もとけ始め、六月から九月までは濃霧にとざされながらもどうやら船の航行ができるのです。

百二十八

十二　太平洋とその島々

ダッチハーバー

[blacked out] この列島附近は、地圖でわかるやうに、北太平洋の大切な航路に當つてゐます。すなはち、横濱・シヤトル間のいちばん短い道すぢに當るのです。

島々には一千人たらずの住民が住んでゐて、海ではあしかやさけを取り、陸ではきつねなどを飼ひ、また

百二十九

Figure 2.13. This geography textbook was used by a boy in Sapporo immediately after the war. The blackened-out part of the text contains details on Attu Island in the Aleutians, which was originally American territory but later occupied by the Japanese military from mid-1942 to around mid-1943. City of Sapporo.

students rightly confused over just what could be believed in the new postwar era. SCAP followed up with a December directive suspending Japanese history, geography, and morals courses until further notice and, early the following year, issued a more comprehensive set of guidelines for textbook deletions. Again, without SCAP prompting, the MOE ordered the removal of images of the emperor displayed in every school (and bowed before daily), along with copies of the Imperial Rescript on Education—a Confucian-inspired nationalistic tract all students had been required to memorize and regularly recite. After much pressure, the rescript was officially abrogated by the Diet in 1948. With the SCAP directive dismantling State Shintō in December 1945, the teaching of Shintō doctrine was banned, as too were school Shintō shrines and shrine excursions.

The overall structure and ethos of education also underwent significant transformation with the passing of three laws in 1947: the Basic Law on Education, the

School Education Law, and the Board of Education Law. These laws drew on the recommendations of the United States Education Mission to Japan by twenty-six American experts in March 1946. The Basic Law laid out the framework for postwar education based on the values of democracy, pacifism, equal educational opportunity, and gender equality, as enshrined in the new constitution (see later in this chapter) of the same year. Replacing the multitrack system of the prewar, which separated boys and girls, the new system was standardized into a 6-3-3-4(2) model: six years of elementary school, three years each for middle and high school, and four years for university or two for women's junior colleges. Elementary and middle school education became compulsory and free of charge under the new system. To sever the control of the central government over personnel, curriculum, and educational administration, powers formerly in the hands of centrally appointed prefectural governors or mayors were transferred to locally elected boards of education. Thanks to the reforms, the number of students advancing to high school increased dramatically, exceeding 50 percent by the late 1950s and 90 percent by the mid-1970s. The gender gap also narrowed, with more young women going on to high school and university, although for many years women were encouraged to undertake higher education in two-year junior colleges with the expectation that they would soon marry and leave the workforce.

The new postwar constitution was among the most important legacies of the US-led Occupation of Japan. Unlike education or economic reforms, which were later rolled back to an extent, the constitution remained unrevised despite conservatives' burning desire to do so. MacArthur was intimately involved in the constitutional reform process, consulting with Japanese leaders on the issue as early as October 1945. After the foreign ministers of the USSR, the United States, and Britain agreed in December 1945 to establish the FEC to oversee the Occupation, the constitutional reform issue became even more pressing for MacArthur. As GS chief and lawyer Brigadier Courtney Whitney warned MacArthur, the FEC would have authority to approve any constitutional changes, thus potentially taking the process out of SCAP's hands and imposing revisions anathema to American's vision for the country. Whitney suggested that if MacArthur could have a draft revision ready prior to the first meeting of the FEC in late February 1946, he could present it as a fait accompli.[46]

On the Japanese side, the primary concern was to ensure that any revision would maintain the core elements of the Meiji Constitution, especially the imperial institution and the emperor's sovereignty. Two groups of Japanese were initially involved in the revision process, one led by Prince Konoe Fumimaro, who served as minister of state in the short-lived Higashikuni Cabinet (August 17–October 9, 1945) and the other led by Shidehara Kijūrō, who assumed the prime ministership on October 9, 1945. After a meeting with MacArthur in early October, Konoe engaged the constitutional scholar Sasaki Sōichi from Kyoto University to work with him and a team in the Ministry of Home Affairs to produce a draft. But Konoe soon found himself out in the cold with the resignation of the Higashikuni Cabinet and its replacement by the Shidehara Cabinet in early October. Despite Shidehara's order that he abandon his revision initiative, Konoe resisted, renting a room in the resort town of Hakone south of Tokyo where he and Sasaki labored on a draft. But the two were forced to abandon their efforts in early December when SCAP, worried about undermining the new Shidehara administration, publicly declared that the prince had not been officially engaged in the revision process. Two weeks later SCAP announced Konoe's arrest and indictment in the Tokyo War Crimes Tribunal as a Class A war criminal, after which he promptly committed suicide.

With Konoe out of the way, Prime Minister Shidehara could now focus on preparing an official government draft. Shidehara met with MacArthur in early October, at which time the general emphasized that the revised constitution would need to incorporate liberal aspects such as human, political, and social rights, to which Shidehara appears to have agreed. Soon after, Shidehara established the Constitutional Issue Investigative Committee, chaired by legal scholar and minister of state, Matsumoto Jōji, and comprising constitutional law experts mostly from the University of Tokyo, like Minobe Tatsukichi, the architect of the prewar "emperor organ theory." The committee met in secret until early February 1946, submitting one of its two drafts to SCAP on the eighth day of that month. Thanks to a scoop by the *Mainichi shinbun*, on February 1, however, SCAP and the rest of Japan learned what was coming. The leaked draft—reproduced in its entirety on the newspaper's front page—revealed a document startlingly like the Meiji Constitution, with the emperor retained as sovereign and the Japanese people still his "subjects."

While the Matsumoto Committee worked on its draft, political parties and civic groups also labored conscientiously to produce their own drafts, which were widely circulated in the media and even submitted to SCAP for consideration. Apart from the JCP's draft of November 1945 placing sovereignty in the people, drafts by the other political parties—both left and right—were markedly conservative, retaining either imperial or state sovereignty and differing only in the amount of power afforded to the sovereign. Outside of politics, the Constitutional Research Group, formed by the statistician and social activist Takano Iwasaburō and six other intellectuals, produced an innovative draft that caught the attention of SCAP. Like the JCP, this group's draft placed sovereignty in the Japanese people and, while the imperial institution was retained, it relegated the emperor to performing rituals and heading national ceremonies.

Unbeknown to Shidehara and the Matsumoto Committee, after seeing the *Mainichi shinbun* report of February 1, MacArthur had decided that the only expedient option would be for the Americans to produce a draft themselves given the looming threat of the FEC. In a meeting on February 3, MacArthur ordered Courtney Whitney to form a group within the GS to prepare a draft constitution in a week. He provided Whitney with a short memorandum—the so-called MacArthur note—setting out the key principles to be incorporated in the draft. First, the imperial institution was to be maintained, with the emperor as head of state and his duties to be "exercised in accordance with the constitution and responsible to the basic will of the people." Second, the state's right to wage war was to be renounced as a means for settling disputes and "even for preserving its own security." Third, feudal structures, such as the peerage system, were to be abolished—except, of course, for the imperial institution. And fourth, a British-style budgetary system was to be adopted.[47] With these principles in hand, Whitney and twenty others from the GS began work on the draft. Although leaders of the group like Whitney, Deputy GS Chief Charles Kades, Commander Alfred R. Hussey, and Lieutenant Colonel Milo E. Rowell had legal training, other members did not, and none of the group had expertise in constitutional law. Among their number was a twenty-two-year-old woman named Beate Sirota, the daughter of Ukrainian-Jewish parents, who had fled Russia for Austria in the 1920s. The family ultimately ended up in Japan for work, where they remained as internees during the war. Sirota left Japan for college in the United States in the late 1930s and was naturalized in 1945, opening the way for her to participate in the Occupation and reunite with her parents. Her important contribution to the GS constitutional draft was to lobby hard for the inclusion of women's civil rights concerning marriage, divorce, and inheritance, which were duly included.

After a week of intensive drafting, on February 13, Whitney invited Foreign Minister Yoshida Shigeru, Matsumoto Jōji, and other Japanese officials for a meeting about the revision process. The Japanese group arrived expecting to discuss their draft, which had been submitted to SCAP just days earlier, and were rightly taken aback when presented with the American draft. Even more shocking for them was its content: popular sovereignty, a "symbolic" emperor, war renunciation, and a unicameral legislature. Reading the draft, Matsumoto complained that describing the emperor as a "symbol" was a "piece of literary prose" that had no place in a legal document. Moreover, he and his compatriots argued that popular sovereignty was fundamentally at odds with the mentality of the Japanese people.[48] But the Americans were unmoved by these objections, convinced—no doubt, correctly—that their draft would have broad public support. As Whitney warned Yoshida and the group: if the draft was not duly accepted by the cabinet and submitted to the

Diet for approval, SCAP would have no choice but to release it to the public, order the cabinet to resign, dissolve the Diet, and hold a general election.[49] Presented with this ultimatum, Prime Minister Shidehara had no option but to relent, all the more so because he feared—like MacArthur—that if the FEC stepped in with its republican visions for Japan, the very existence of the imperial institution might be in danger. In late February, Shidehara reported on these developments to Emperor Hirohito, who offered his consent for a document that, while guaranteeing the survival of the imperial institution, would also eliminate all of his political powers.

The draft was submitted to the Ninetieth Imperial Diet as an amendment to—rather than an abrogation of—the Meiji Constitution on June 20, 1946, becoming law on November 3, following debate and some minor (and not-so-minor) amendments in both houses. The new constitution came into effect on May 5, 1947. It contained several noteworthy features. First, to the chagrin of some Japanese conservatives, sovereign power was unequivocally placed in the hands of the people. Second, the emperor was retained, but now as the "symbol of the state and of the unity of the people." Historians are not certain how the GS group hit upon the term "symbol." As noted earlier, MacArthur used "symbol" to describe the role of the emperor in his correspondence with Eisenhower some months earlier. Richard Poole and George Nelson, charged with drafting the relevant articles on the emperor, referred to laws and scholarship surrounding the British monarchy. They appear to have been particularly influenced by the Statute of Westminster, whose preamble described the Crown as "the symbol of the free association of the members of the British Commonwealth of Nations." Nelson also recalled referring to Walter Bagehot's *The English Constitution* (1867), which used the term "symbol" when classifying the sovereign as having only formalistic power.[50] Shidehara and his colleagues were left infuriated by this terminology, but they had no choice but to consent as a quid pro quo for the survival of the imperial institution.

Third, in terms of the institutions of government, the new constitution made the cabinet responsible to the Diet, with the majority of ministers being elected officials and the prime minister always a member of the Diet. Although the initial American draft proposed a unicameral legislature, after discussion with the Japanese, the Americans consented to a bicameral system. Members of the lower House of Representatives would be elected on four-year terms and hold the weight of power, while members in the upper House of Councillors would be elected on staggered six-year cycles, with half of the seats up for election every three years. The upper house could delay or revise legislation from the lower house but could be overridden by two-thirds super-majority votes in the latter. The constitution also established an autonomous judiciary headed by the Supreme Court, which was afforded powers of constitutional review and judicial appointments.

Fourth, alongside these institutions, the constitution included an impressive array of rights such as freedoms of speech, association, and religion. Social and cultural rights to "minimum standards of wholesome and cultured living" were guaranteed under Article 25 and, thanks to the work of Beate Sirota and colleagues, women's rights were clearly articulated under Articles 14 and 24.

Fifth, among the most controversial aspects of the new constitution were its pacifist and war-renouncing elements, articulated in the Preamble but even more so in Article 9. As the Preamble notes, the Japanese people "desire peace for all time" and to "preserve" their "peace and security" will trust in the "justice and faith of the peace-loving peoples of the world." Article 9 consists of two paragraphs as follows:

> Aspiring sincerely to an international peace based on justice and order, the Japanese people forever renounce war as a sovereign right of the nation and the threat or use of force as means of settling international disputes.
>
> *In order to accomplish the aim of the preceding paragraph,* land, sea, and air forces, as well as other war potential, will never be maintained. The right of belligerency of the state will not be recognized.[51]

Like the "symbolic" emperor, the exact origins of this article are not entirely clear. MacArthur's note to Whitney of early October clearly specified that the constitution should renounce war, including self-defense, although this was not a position broadly accepted in Washington, DC or even among MacArthur's staff in SCAP. Charles Kades, one of the leaders of the GS constitutional steering committee, believed that requiring Japan to abandon its right of self-defense was "unrealistic" and "irrational," and he made sure this stipulation was not included in the original SCAP draft. Interestingly, too, given its later pacifist tilt, initially the JCP vehemently opposed the renouncing of war and abandonment of military forces, arguing that self-defense was the right of all nations. There are suggestions that it may have been Shidehara and other conservatives who first proposed the content of Article 9 to MacArthur in order to convince the Americans that Japan was now a peace-loving nation and hence the emperor should be retained.

Regardless of its origins, war renouncement found a place in Article 9 but not without important modification. During Diet deliberations, Liberal Party politician and later briefly prime minister, Ashida Hitoshi, proposed an important addition to the second paragraph of Article 9 (italicized). The inclusion of this phrase opened the way for subsequent Japanese governments to interpret Article 9 to mean that the country could not maintain a military for the purpose of war or settling international disputes, but this did not rule out maintaining forces for self-defense.

In this way, the Ashida clause opened the way for Japan to later establish its SDF. Given that the Americans did not oppose this amendment, and coupled with Kades dismissal of MacArthur's directive that Japan abandon its right of self-defense, it seems safe to conclude that there was general support on the US side for some kind of remilitarization in Japan for self-defense purposes. With the escalation of the Cold War thereafter, some American leaders would even express their regret at ever having included Article 9.

Accompanying the constitution, a series of laws were either amended or passed anew, resulting in transformational changes to numerous state and social institutions. Revisions to the Meiji Civil Code in late 1947 abolished the family system that was based on patriarchal household heads. Associated rights to inheritance and succession were also amended and gender equality among siblings and spouses clearly codified. Around the same time, the Criminal Code was amended to abolish offences relating to lèse-majesté, high treason, and adultery, despite strong opposition from conservative politicians. The Criminal Procedure Code was amended to include basic human rights, such as arrest warrants and the right to remain silent. Local government also underwent regulatory reform thanks to the newly passed Local Autonomy Law, which established elections for prefectural and municipal assemblies as well as governors and mayors. Local governments were granted greater taxing authority in the hope of extending their autonomy vis-à-vis the national government, although, as time would tell, financial dependence on the center persisted. Related to this new law, the infamous prewar Ministry of Home Affairs (MHA) was dismantled, with its finance powers moved to the Ministry of Finance, policing to the Public Security Agency (later the National Police Agency), and public works to the Construction Board (later the Ministry of Construction). Whitney and others viewed the dismantling of the MHA as critical for weeding out the system of wartime control based on "feudal totalitarianism." The MHA was one of the few state ministries to be so thoroughly dismantled by the Occupation, although it is worth noting that many bureaucrats from the ministry found positions in the newly created agencies and boards.

The new Police Law of December 1947 resulted in a short-lived decentralization of policing throughout Japan. Under the law, municipalities with populations over five thousand were required to establish their own independent police forces, while a national force was created to service less populated areas. Local administrations were not pleased with this system because of the burden on their finances. SCAP was also internally divided between the GS, which saw police decentralization as critical for democratization of the state, and G2 intelligence, which felt decentralization would compromise police investigations. MacArthur solved the dispute in favor of decentralization, although this system would only stay in place until 1954.

Finally, a National Public Service Law was passed, transforming bureaucrats from "imperial officials" to "servants of the public," fixing their salaries by rank, and specifying clear career paths. But this law did not significantly diminish the power and prestige of the national bureaucracies and, alongside the negligeable purges, meant that state officials could carry on without major interruption.

The Revival of Politics

The Japanese people responded enthusiastically to these reforms through political participation and activism. From late 1945, numerous political parties were either reconstituted after wartime suppression or established anew. On the conservative side of politics, in November 1945, Hatoyama Ichirō—a stalwart of the prewar Rikken Seiyūkai—assumed leadership of the newly established Japan Liberal Party (JLP), alongside eminent colleagues such as Ashida Hitoshi, Yoshida Shigeru, and Kōno Ichirō. Just days later, conservative politicians such as Machida Chūji and Shidehara Kijūrō formed the Japan Progressive Party (JPP), picking up the lineage of the Rikken Minseitō. Although many members of both parties would soon be temporarily purged from political life, the JLP and JPP thereafter served as important centers of gravity for the rebuilding of conservative politics in postwar Japan. Their members would constitute the backbone of the LDP on its formation in 1955.

The short-lived (December 1945–May 1946) Japan Cooperative Party occupied the center of politics, with its platform of democracy, cooperativism, and agricultural self-sufficiency, drawing on the philosophy of the prewar Christian activist Kagawa Toyohiko. On the left, the JSP formed as an amalgamation of prewar proletarian, workers, and socialist political parties together with reformist bureaucrats who entered politics. From the very outset, the JSP was riven by ideological and strategic differences between its left and right factions—reflected clearly in the party's wavering between the English translations of the party's name as "Social Democratic Party of Japan" and "Japan Socialist Party." These tensions would constantly hinder the JSP's ability to convince voters that it was capable of governing. Finally, with the release from prison of leaders such as Tokuda Kyūichi and Shiga Yoshio in October 1945 and the return of Nosaka Sanzō from exile in China in early 1946, the JCP—now legal—resumed operations. Until 1951, the JCP adopted a largely moderate platform, evident in Nosaka's call for the party to become a "lovable JCP," which meant cooperating with the Occupation authorities for democratization, the eradication of militarism, and the full implementation of the Potsdam Declaration.

The first general election for the House of Representatives in April 1946 attracted a voter turnout of 72 percent, with an electorate now well over double its prewar size thanks to the inclusion of women and citizens over twenty years of age

Figure 2.14. The first House of Representatives election after the war held on April 10, 1946. The photo shows a female voter exercising her right to vote for the first time. Courtesy of The Asahi Shimbun Company.

(growing from 14.6 to 36.9 million voters). The five parties discussed above, together with some three hundred other smaller parties, contested 466 seats in fifty-four large multimember electoral districts of two to fourteen seats. Over 80 percent of the winners were newly elected, including thirty-nine women who entered the Diet for the first time. No party won a majority, with the JLP claiming 140 seats, the JPP 94, the JSP 92, and the JCP its first ever Diet seat. MacArthur was overjoyed with the result, stating in the media that the result revealed how the Japanese people, by choosing a "middle way," were "not dominated by political ideologies on either the extreme left or right." Indeed "democracy," MacArthur effused, had taken its "first healthy step forward."[52]

After the election, Hatoyama of the JLP was poised to become prime minister in a conservative coalition government, but his purging by Occupation authorities opened the way for Yoshida Shigeru to take over as leader of the party and form the coalition in May 1946. Determined to stabilize the unsteady alliance, Yoshida called a general election in late 1947, which, to his great astonishment, resulted in the JSP securing the most—but not a majority of—seats (143) in the lower house. In May, JSP leader Katayama Tetsu became the first socialist prime minister in Japanese history in a collation with the conservative Democratic Party (DP) and the short-lived centrist Japan Cooperative Party. Katayama set about passing various progressive labor reform laws, revising the Civil and Penal Codes, and establishing the Economic Stabilization Bureau, which instituted a program of priority production focused on the revitalization of critical industries like coal and steel. But, as with the previous Yoshida administration, Katayama's government proved fragile, particularly due to opposition from within the ranks of his own JSP. In early 1948, the left wing of the JSP called on the Katayama cabinet to withdraw its budget from the Diet, leaving Katayama and his ministers no option but to resign. Resisting pressure from G2 intelligence, which was determined to crush socialist influence in politics, SCAP's liberal GS approved the appointment of Ashida Hitoshi of the DP as prime minister without holding another election. But, once again, the Ashida cabinet was short-lived, brought down by a scandal involving bribes paid by the Shōwa Denkō Corporation to leading government ministers and high-ranking bureaucrats. The scandal came to light thanks to intelligence intentionally made public by Charles Willoughby and the staff of G2, still fuming over the GS's approval of the supposedly "left-soft" Ashida as prime minister. Barely seven months in power, the Ashida cabinet fell in October 1948, opening the way for the return of Yoshida Shigeru and a noticeable shift in Occupation policy from the liberal agenda of GS to the economy-focused, conservative agenda of G2 and Washington, DC. Such was the turmoil of early postwar party politics.

Alongside this tumult within party politics in these early postwar years, labor and civic groups also began to exercise their new political rights and freedoms, picking up from the era of Taishō democracy. Early on, SCAP policy sought to foster labor activism, seeing it as an ideal vehicle for nurturing democracy. MacArthur issued his directive legalizing labor unions in October 1945, and in March 1946, a labor union law came into effect. Workers were quick to organize. By the end of 1945, some five hundred unions accounted for close to 381,000 members, and by 1946, the number had grown to almost 4.9 million members in 17,266 unions. The rate of unionization reached its postwar peak in 1949 at 55.8 percent or 6.65 million of the total 11.93 million workers (fig. 2.15). Both new and old unions led this surge in organization building and activism, including the left-wing National Congress of Industrial Unions (Sanbetsu) and the Japan Federation of Labor Unions (Sōdōmei), which traced its roots to the prewar Japan Federation of Labor (fig. 2.16).

Immediately after the war, the burning issue for workers and Japanese people more generally was obtaining enough food to survive in conditions of soaring inflation and food shortages. From war's end to early 1946, food prices more than doubled, provoking many ordinary citizens to take to the streets to express their frustrations. On May 14, 1946, groups in Tokyo held a "Give Us Rice" demonstration, marching from Setagaya ward to the Imperial Palace where they demanded to

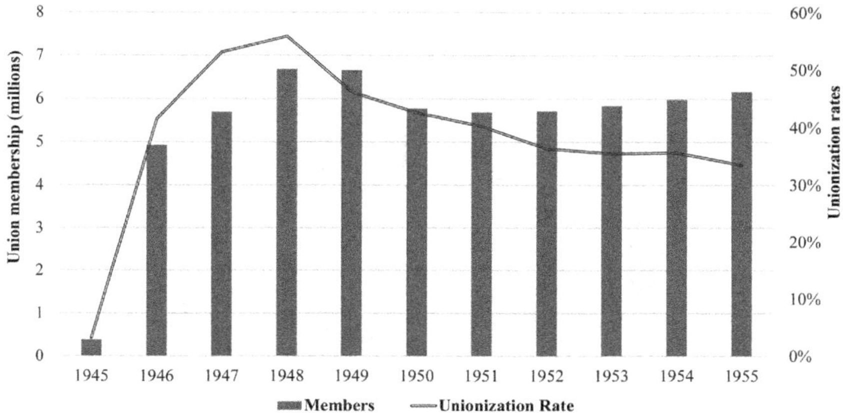

Sources: Sōmushō Tōkei Kyoku, "Rōdō Kumiai Shuruibetsu"; Nishikawa, "Rōdō Kumiai," 950.

Figure 2.15. Union Membership and Unionization Rates, 1945–1955

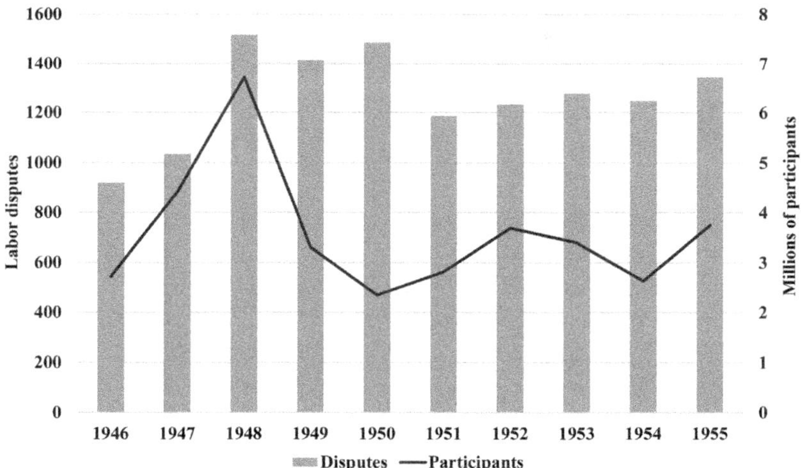

Source: Rōdō Seisaku Kenkyū-Kenshū Kikō, "Hayawakari Gurafu de miru Chōki Rōdō Tōkei."

Figure 2.16. Labor Disputes and Participants, 1946–1955

be shown the emperor's daily menu—an act that would have been suicidal just months earlier. Five days later, some 250,000 protestors, including union members, housewives, and small business owners, engaged in the so-called Food May Day rally, at which they demanded an increase in food rations. Gathering outside the

Figure 2.17. "Give Us Rice!" protesters gather outside the Imperial Palace demanding a meeting with the emperor on May 14, 1945. Courtesy of The Asahi Shimbun Company.

Imperial Palace again, protestors vented their frustrations toward the emperor, with one placard reading "Imperial Edict. The National Body has been defended and maintained. We [i.e., the emperor] can eat to our heart's content. The unfortunate people can starve to death. Signed under the Privy Seal."[53] Matsushima Matsutarō, the individual responsible for this placard, was promptly arrested for lèse-majesté but later released without conviction when this law was rescinded.

While many took to the streets and lambasted the previously "sacred" emperor, others adopted just as provocative actions within companies. In October 1945, for instance, editors at the *Yomiuri shinbun* ejected managers and declared that they and fellow workers would be taking over management of the company. Such "production control" struggles proliferated, with over one hundred actions involving seventy-five thousand workers in the early months of 1946. Similar actions took place at Japan National Railways (JNR) and shipbuilding companies, where laid-off workers assumed control of management to stop the closure of facilities. In late 1945, workers at the Keisei Electric Railway Company offered patrons three days of free rides when management refused a fivefold wage increase. Thereafter, they began to appropriate funds from ticket sales to pay the extra wages.[54]

Faced with worsening hyperinflation, in late 1946, Sanbetsu union leaders began planning for a general strike to be held on February 1, 1947. It was envisaged that the action would bring all public services and industrial operations to a stop. Union leaders hoped that the strike would concentrate the energies of workers after months of discrete mobilizations across a range of industries and public sector organizations.

The strike, however, never materialized, mainly because it exceeded the tolerance limits of MacArthur and others in SCAP, who were increasingly concerned about the influence of socialists and communists. Accordingly, on January 31, 1947, the eve of the strike, MacArthur issued a directive banning the action. He explained that SCAP could not allow "so deadly a social weapon" given the "impoverished and emaciated condition of Japan."[55] William Marquat, Head of the ESS, simultaneously summoned Ii Yashirō, head of the Joint Struggle Committee of the Government and Public Agencies Union, to his office and ordered that the strike be cancelled immediately because SCAP could not approve an action that so threatened the "stability of the

Figure 2.18. A broken Ii Yashirō announces the cancellation of the general strike on January 31, 1947. Courtesy of The Asahi Shimbun Company.

nation."[56] Left with no alternative, Ii asked Marquat for permission to make an announcement over the radio, which was granted. That evening a tearful Ii told listeners that there was "no choice other than to cancel the strike." Trying to put a positive spin on a crushing defeat, Ii concluded his announcement by saying that the struggle of workers involved two steps forward and one step back.[57]

By 1947, Japanese people from all walks of life had demonstrated their enthusiasm to take up the new rights granted under the constitution and the Occupation reforms. The political parties, while unstable, evidenced the emergence of a vigorous realm of institutional politics. To this extent, the early phase of democratic reform under the American-led Occupation can be considered a success. Accompanying such advances, however, was SCAP's willingness to both directly and indirectly intervene in political activism and party politics if either of these threatened the Americans' strategic vision for Japan. As the specter of the Cold War intensified in the coming years, this vision would continue to evolve (or even narrow, in the eyes of some), opening the way for an era of sustained conservative domination in the country.

CHAPTER THREE

The Age of Politics, 1948–1960

"Reversing Course": The Shift in Occupation Policy

The banned general strike of February 1947 was an ominous sign of shifting priorities among certain SCAP officials during the late 1940s, prompting some at the time and many later to speak of a so-called reverse course in these years, as emphasis shifted from democratization to economic reconstruction and the fortification of anti-communist conservative rule in Japan. The term "reverse course" (*gyaku kōsu*) first appeared as the title of a *Yomiuri shinbun* series in early November 1951, followed by an editorial in the same publication on November 15 titled "Reflecting on the 'Reverse Course.'" The editorial noted a "frighteningly strange phenomenon of retrogression" different from the "renovationist atmosphere of a few years earlier," and it pointed to the "revival" of "prewar things," such as the depurging of certain individuals earlier purged from public life for their wartime involvement.[1] Reverse course or not, Occupation policies shifted, political conditions for leftist parties and organizations became noticeably more hostile, and conservative forces gradually took the upper hand in politics from around 1948.

The reverse course traced its roots to planning among American policymakers prior to Japan's defeat. Joseph Grew, the former ambassador to Japan and deputy secretary of state at war's end, together with other Japan experts in Washington, believed that only modest reforms would be necessary in Japan, and that the postwar focus should be on economic reconstruction of a nation that had strayed off course. This could all be done, they argued, by removing the warmongers and restoring the moderate, levelheaded leaders from prewar politics, public administration, and business. This approach was implemented to an extent in the early years of the Occupation but was largely overshadowed by the strong emphasis on unfettered democratization under New Dealers in SCAP. But some American elites began to call for a shift in Occupation policy as the threat of the Soviet Union increased in Europe, as the nationalists lost ground to Mao's communists in China, and as leftist forces extended their influence in politics and labor unions within Japan. In January 1948, Kenneth Claiborne Royall, the last person to hold the position of secretary of war in the United States, delivered his so-called bulwark against communism speech in San Francisco. In the speech, Royall lionized Japan's prewar military and industrial elite, arguing that "their services would in many instances contribute to the economic recovery of Japan." He expressed particular concern about "steriliz[ing]" the "business ability of Japan" by dissolving the powerful zaibatsu.[2]

Royall's proposals soon found form in official American policy with the drafting of National Security Council Document 13/2 (NSC 13/2) by George Kennan, then policy planning chief in the State Department.[3] With respect to the economy, this document called for a focus on economic stability through strict management of government finances, controlling inflation, stemming labor militancy, and raising exports and production. In terms of the military, in principle, Kennan's document stayed faithful to demilitarization, endorsing "industrial disarmament" and "prohibition of the manufacture of the weapons of war." But it also recommended the reinforcing and re-equipping of the police force, including the coast guard. The document was subsequently communicated to MacArthur in December 1948, although the general had already been briefed on the policy by Kennan during his visit to Japan some months earlier. At their meeting, Kennan told MacArthur that it was necessary to revise the punitive policies toward Japan given developments in the Far East and Europe. Specifically, the purges of wartime collaborators were to cease, police decentralization reversed and policing functions strengthened, war crimes tribunals quickly wound up, economic recovery prioritized, and the various powers of SCAP returned to Japan with an eye to a peace settlement. The document marked a clear reorientation in Occupation policy and a shift in control from MacArthur and the New Dealers to Washington, DC and the more conservative ESS and G2 sections in SCAP. MacArthur himself appears to have been opposed to many of the recommendations, believing that they violated the fundamental principles of the Occupation aimed at rebuilding Japan as a peaceful nation. Nonetheless, he had no choice but to comply.

With the full cooperation of the Japanese government—first under Ashida Hitoshi and then Yoshida Shigeru—the recommendations of NSC 13/2 proceeded apace. Although many within the Truman administration had been concerned about the impact of economic deconcentration on political and social stability in Japan since the early days of the Occupation, the policy transformations of 1948 brought the dissolution of Japanese companies almost to a stop. Of the companies targeted by the Liquidation Commission, ultimately only sixteen were dissolved completely, a further twenty-six dissolved and restructured, eleven thoroughly reorganized, and thirty left intact—an approach that garnered support not only from Japanese officials and conservative politicians but also many on the left who feared the impact of job losses if industry was decimated. Importantly, the banks of the major zaibatsu were left largely intact, opening the way for later corporate reconcentration around them. In connection to labor, in 1948, the Diet passed legislation banning public sector employees' right to strike and bargain collectively. SCAP actively cracked down on contentious labor tactics, like factory takeovers, even mobilizing troops to quell a dispute at the Toho Motion Pictures Company in August 1948. In 1949, the Trade Union Law was revised, strengthening the power of employers in collective bargaining, cutting off wages for striking workers, requiring a thirty-day "cooling off" period before strikes in critical industries, and enhancing the powers of the minister of labor and prefectural governors in dispute resolution.

Purges of wartime collaborators were also rapidly wound up and a new series of "red purges" instituted to weed out alleged communist and socialist infiltration of public and private sector institutions. Under MacArthur and his successor Matthew Ridgeway, around 360,000 war conspirators were depurged, including politicians like Hatoyama Ichirō, Ishibashi Tanzan, and Kishi Nobusuke—all of whom would go on to serve as prime minister. In June 1950, MacArthur turned his attention to the left, ordering the Japanese government to purge twenty-four members of the JCP's central committee and seventeen from the editorial board of its official mouthpiece, *Akahata,* which was banned from publishing for thirty days. These crackdowns had a devastating effect on the JCP, whose membership declined from over one hundred thousand in early 1950 to around seventy thousand by year's end. After targeting the central organs of the JCP, the government turned its attention to alleged communist sympathizers in workplaces, schools, public corporations, and the media. Close to thirteen thousand people alleged to be communist party members or to have "red tendencies" were ousted from diverse industries such as the media, electronics, transportation, coal, steel, and mining, as well as the public sector. This crackdown provoked many in the formerly "lovable" JCP to go underground, where they pursued a program of violent insurrection in the early 1950s.

The other major aspect of the shift in Occupation policy was Japanese rearmament. Prime Minister Yoshida Shigeru had in mind a future in which Japan would prioritize economic growth over remilitarization under the protective shield of the United States—an approach that would later be termed the "Yoshida Doctrine." However, this doctrine became increasingly difficult to strictly maintain as the geopolitical map in East Asia transformed following the "loss" of China to the communists in 1949 and the outbreak of war on the Korean peninsula in June 1950. In secret negotiations for a security treaty with President Truman's envoy John Foster Dulles in early 1950, Yoshida and his finance minister Ikeda Hayato had repeatedly resisted American pressure for remilitarization, saying that the peace-loving Japanese people would never support it. Yoshida's only concession to Dulles was that Japan would eventually remilitarize but only in a staged process after the country had fully recovered economically.

MacArthur initially supported Yoshida, fearing the negative effects of Japanese militarization on stability in the Far East. But the outbreak of the Korean War forced him to swiftly change direction. With US forces deployed to the battlefront in Korea, in July 1950, MacArthur issued a directive to Yoshida ordering that Japan immediately establish a National Police Reserve (NPR) of seventy-five thousand recruits led by former officers of the Imperial Japanese Army and expand the Japan Coast Guard (JCG) by eight thousand. The NPR would be responsible for maintaining order domestically after the departure of US forces to Korea. As it was based on an Occupation directive, the NPR Ordinance came into force on August 10, 1950, without needing to pass through the Diet. The ordinance gave the prime minister power to call on the NPR at "times of special" need. Its ranks were to be filled by newly mobilized amateurs up to the age of thirty-five without military experience. With the promise of an above average salary together with food and lodging, the NPR proved enticing for many youth, and close to four hundred thousand applied for the seventy-five thousand slots. In the early stages, officials from the former Ministry of Home Affairs responsible for organizing the NPR made sure

Figure 3.1. Members of the National Police Reserve do morning exercises at the Sendai Haramachi Camp. Courtesy of The Asahi Shimbun Company.

that ex-military men were excluded from leadership positions. But subsequent depurging in October 1950 and throughout 1951—especially in August when all former military personnel of the rank colonel and below were depurged—opened the way for them to enlist, bolstering the reserve to around 110,000 by the end of that year. SCAP and the Yoshida government publicly described the NPR as a police force for maintaining order domestically and not an army, but critics were quick to point to the provision of US military training and logistical support, the stationing of NPR forces in military barracks, and the armaments it possessed as evidence of its military character. In fact, by early 1951, Yoshida was even arguing in the Diet that the Japanese Constitution allowed the country to maintain forces for self-defense—a position that opened a pathway for the transformation of the NPR into the Self-Defense Forces in 1954.

Although not revealed publicly until decades later, coast guard minesweepers were also deployed to Korean waters to clear up mines deposited by North Korea in the conflict, but these deployments ended abruptly when a vessel collided with a mine, killing one and injuring eighteen others. Behind the scenes, former Imperial Japanese Navy elites—buoyed by developments—began planning in secret for the reestablishment of the navy, even sharing a private proposal with the Americans on the Soviet Union as Japan's number one enemy.[4] Together, such developments evidence the noticeable shift in Occupation policy in the early 1950s, if not an absolute "reverse course."

The Korean War: A "Gift from the Gods"

Hand in hand with the above policies was a combined effort by the Americans and the Yoshida government to rein in the rampant hyperinflation wreaking havoc on the economy. In 1945, inflation stood at 365 percent, and the figure was still at 165 percent in 1948 despite various countermeasures. With a communist victory looming in China, Japan became even more important for the Americans as a bulwark against the likely future communist regime on the Asian mainland. To this end, economic recovery was seen as critical.

In December 1945, MacArthur relayed Washington's so-called Nine-Point Economic Stabilization Plan to Yoshida. The core aims of the plan were to control inflation and bring about currency stabilization, to promote exports through the setting of a fixed exchange rate, and to encourage a self-supporting Japanese economy. Specifically, the plan involved balancing the budget, strengthening tax collection, limiting investment to essential corporations, stabilizing wages, controlling prices, strengthening exchange rate management, raising efficiency in raw material allocation to support exports, increasing the production of raw materials and industrial finished goods, and improving distribution of the food supply.

To oversee implementation of this exacting austerity plan, President Truman appointed the Detroit banker, Joseph Dodge, who had experience with currency reforms in the western zones of occupied Germany. Soon after his arrival in Japan in February 1949, Dodge declared that the Japanese economy was walking on stilts—one stilt being American aid and the other government subsidies. If either of these stilts were removed, Dodge said, the economy would fall and break its neck, hence the urgent need to rehabilitate free enterprise and competition through comprehensive economic rationalization. Prime Minister Yoshida—himself a devout economic liberal—was overjoyed by this "Dodge Line" for reform, referring to the banker as a "god-sent messenger." Yoshida's cabinet announced that it would faithfully implement all elements of the plan—even in the face of opposition from Yoshida's own political allies who wanted tax cuts and increased government spending to satisfy their constituents.

Dodge immediately instituted stringent fiscal and monetary restraints to balance the budget, raised public utility charges, fixed the Japanese exchange rate at 360 yen to the dollar to stimulate exports, and ended emergency lending by the Reconstruction Finance Bank to siphon liquidity out of the economy. The impacts of these measures were instantaneous and severe. Inflation was certainly brought under control, but this resulted in a severe economic recession—called the "Dodge Recession" at the time—with countless bankruptcies among small and medium-sized enterprises. Faced with uncertainty about market conditions, industries like consumer appliance makers began to slash production and lay off workers in anticipation of decreasing demand, resulting in unemployment and more misery for many ordinary Japanese already faced with recession.

Job cuts were not limited to the private sector. Emboldened by the Dodge Line, in May 1949, the Yoshida administration passed the Law for the Total Number of Civil Servants, which allowed it to implement a drastic reduction in the number of public servants by 270,000. The JNR was hit particularly hard when its management, led by President Shimoyama Sadanori, undertook to dismiss close to one hundred thousand of the organization's six hundred thousand strong workforce. While constituting part of the overall austerity plan, the job cuts at JNR were also aimed at breaking the back of the militant National Railway Workers Union, Kokurō, which JNR management, the Yoshida administration, and SCAP all viewed as a hotbed of socialist and communist influence. Ignoring Kokurō's threats of direct action, Shimoyama announced the first round of thirty thousand dismissals on July 4, 1949, followed by the second round of sixty-three thousand just eight days later.

These provocative actions provoked several shocking incidents. Following his announcement of the first round of dismissals in early July, President Shimoyama disappeared after leaving his chauffeur-driven car to visit the upmarket Mitsukoshi department store in Tokyo's Nihonbashi area. The following day, his lifeless, mangled body was discovered beside the railway tracks close to Kitasenjū Station to the north of Tokyo. A subsequent autopsy was unable to determine whether the cause of death was suicide or murder. Three days after the second round of dismissals, an unmanned train mysteriously slammed into the platform of Mitaka station in Eastern Tokyo, killing six and injuring fourteen others. Eleven labor activists were arrested, but the court subsequently determined that there were no grounds for a conspiracy, assigning all guilt to a single individual, Takeuchi Keisuke. Adding to the tension of the moment, around a month later, on August 17, a train running on the Tōhoku Line derailed at Matsukawa in Fukushima Prefecture, killing the engineer and his two assistants. After the incident, police arrested twenty members of the JCP who belonged to Kokurō and worked at the nearby Toshiba Matsukawa factory. The labor union at the factory—from which five thousand workers had recently been laid off—was involved in a joint struggle with the Kokurō subdivision

Figure 3.2. Officials survey the damage after the Mitaka Incident in 1949. Courtesy of The Asahi Shimbun Company.

in Matsukawa, hence police accusations of a conspiracy in the derailment. In 1950, a judge found all of the defendants guilty and sentenced some to death, but the Supreme Court found all innocent in 1963 after extended appeals. Like Shimoyama's death and the Mitaka Incident, the Matsukawa incident was never solved, with some even suggesting that these incidents were carried out by the American Counter Intelligence Corps to undermine the legitimacy of communists in Japan.[5]

The Dodge Line neither strangled nor rescued Japan but greatly accelerated existing trends, such as lowering inflation and promoting economic growth.[6] The outbreak of the Korean War can be understood similarly, especially in terms of the ways it stimulated rapid growth in many important postwar industries and helped fortify aspects of the US-Japan relationship. Although many Japanese subsequently remembered the Korean War as one in which Japan had only indirect involvement, in reality, Japanese participation was multidimensional. To begin with, all US military bases on the main islands of Japan and in Okinawa were used by the American military for sorties, logistics, and supplies. After the outbreak of war, US Army divisions were stationed in Osaka, command of the Seventh Fleet relocated from the Philippines to Sasebo in Nagasaki Prefecture, and air force bombers stationed at bases around Honshū and Kyūshū. Around eight thousand Japanese were also directly involved in war-related operations, whether on the Korean peninsula or in surrounding waters. Of the twelve hundred involved in the minesweeping operations discussed earlier, most were former members of the Imperial Japanese Navy. General Willoughby, MacArthur's chief of intelligence during the conflict, also called on former Japanese military elites for tactical assistance thanks to their intricate knowledge of terrain on the Korean peninsula.[7] Around one to two thousand Japanese were deployed to Korea to engage in the repair of machinery, security operations, transportation, and the loading of arms and ammunition. Due to the secrecy of such involvements, the number of deaths and casualties among these Japanese participants remains uncertain, although research suggests around fifty-two were killed and a further 349 injured throughout the conflict.[8] Interestingly, a handful of Japanese sympathetic to North Korea joined the Chinese volunteer army in the war, while around six hundred Koreans residing in Japan fought alongside their South Korean counterparts, of whom around 135 either perished or went missing in action.[9]

Along with such direct support, Japan also served as the hub for rear support to the American-led war through transportation, rations provision, medical treatment for the injured, servicing of military equipment and bases, and so-called special procurements. Referred to as "blessed rain after the drought" of the Dodge Line, special procurements exceeded US$300 million per year in the first two years of the war and over US$400 million in the third (fig. 3.3).[10] The procurements represented an

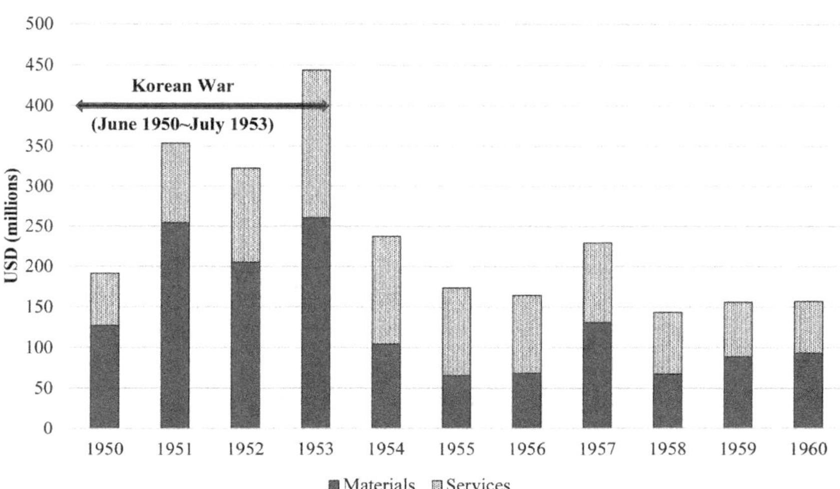

Source: Asai, "1950-nendai no Tokuju," 234.

Figure 3.3. Income from US Military Special Procurements, 1950–1960

important break with the existing procurement process under the Occupation. Herein SCAP had issued materiel requests to the Japanese government, which then took responsibility for procurement as part of the postwar reparations settlement.[11] Korean War special procurements, conversely, involved the US military placing orders directly with Japanese suppliers, resulting in a greater flow of money directly into the Japanese economy. Procurements were diverse, including cotton, blankets, wool, building materials, trucks, jute bags, barbed wire, blankets, toothbrushes, soap, cannon shells, steel materials, and most of the scrap iron available in Japan (table 3.1).

The special procurements proved to be a boon for the Japanese economy, with Yoshida referring to them as a "gift from the gods" just as Joseph Dodge had been. GDP growth in 1951 was 12 percent—much higher than the predicted range of 4.9 to 9.4 percent in the absence of the war. Thanks to the war, Japanese industrial production, real GDP, and personal consumption all reached prewar levels by 1951, while mining and manufacturing exceeded prewar levels. By 1952, per capita national income overtook its prewar highs. Certain industries such as automobiles and trucks made conspicuous gains. Prior to the Korean War, the Toyota Corporation sold only around three hundred trucks per year, but this number jumped to fifteen hundred per month throughout the conflict, pumping huge capital reserves into the company. The electronics maker Sony Corporation also benefited greatly. Before the war, its most successful device was a weighty sound recording device called "Densuke," but US special procurements resulted in massive orders for a diverse range of radio wave detectors.

Over the years of the war, procurements accounted for around 60 percent of Japan's exports, which increased almost threefold. With the influx of capital, the government encouraged industries such as steel and coal to engage in rationalization aimed at modernizing their industrial processes and equipment. The government assisted by injecting funds into the iron and steel industry, laying the foundations for its international competitiveness in the coming years. Industry also responded by increasing investment in plant and equipment. Apart from the economic benefits, the Korean War also spurred the ongoing transformation in US-Japan relations, with Japan shedding its image of a former "enemy" to an indispensable "ally" at the frontline of the Cold War. Indeed, it was against the backdrop of this tension in the Far East that a window of opportunity opened for the Japanese to finally broker a peace settlement, paving the way for the country's return to international society.

Table 3.1 Major Categories of US Military Special Procurement Contracts, 1950–1955 (US$ millions)

Ranking	*Materials*		*Services*	
1	Weapons	149	Building construction	108
2	Coal	104	Automobile repairs	83
3	Jute bags	34	Transport and storage	76
4	Automotive parts	31	Telecommunications	71
5	Cotton material	30	Machinery repairs	48

Source: Sasaki et al., *Sengoshi daijiten,* p. 611.

Returning to International Society Under US Hegemony

As discussed earlier, Yoshida Shigeru sent Finance Minister Ikeda Hayato to Washington, DC in April 1950, ostensibly for trade discussions but in reality to begin negotiations for a peace treaty. Yoshida entrusted Ikeda with a letter for Truman containing three main points: first, that Japan was not wedded to a comprehensive peace settlement and would be satisfied with a partial one comprising essentially America's allies in the anti-communist capitalist world; second, that US forces could remain in Japan after the peace settlement and the return of Japanese sovereignty; and third, that, if necessary, the Japanese government would orchestrate a way for the United States to keep its bases without appearing to have applied pressure on Japan. John Foster Dulles, in charge of the peace settlement process on the American side, was largely satisfied with these concessions, despite initially only being able to secure a vague Japanese commitment to rearmament sometime in the future. The outbreak of the Korean War and Japan's agreeing to establish the NPR in 1950 helped put such concerns to rest. For the defense establishment in America spooked by the prospect of nations falling like "dominos" to communism in the Far East, Yoshida's willingness to accept US bases in return for a peace settlement proved to be a deal clincher.

As public discussion over the peace settlement heated up in Japan throughout 1950, progressive forces began to push back against the Yoshida administration's approach, emphasizing several core concerns. First, they debated whether the peace settlement should be a comprehensive one including all countries, such as the USSR and the PRC, or if a partial settlement would suffice. Second, they wondered about the character of Japanese national security afterwards. Should the country pursue some form of armed or unarmed neutrality, or would Japan be better served sheltering under the shield of American military bases dotted across the archipelago? These issues proved divisive even among progressives. The JCP demanded a comprehensive settlement and argued that Japan should be armed yet neutral. The JSP literally split into two separate parties over the issue in October 1951, with the right wing supporting a partial settlement but no military alliance with the United States and the left wing rejecting both outcomes. The Peace Problems Symposium formed by progressive intellectuals like Maruyama Masao, Nanabara Shigeru, Tsuru Shigeto, and others was among the earliest to advocate strongly for a comprehensive settlement and unarmed neutrality. In a series of high-profile statements published in 1949 and 1950, the group proposed three (and then four) principles of peace for the country: a comprehensive peace settlement, unarmed neutrality, the withdrawal of US military bases, and opposition to remilitarization. Progressives, like University of Tokyo president Nanbara Shigeru, criticized conservatives' quid pro quo of a security treaty with the United States in return for a peace settlement as little more than "subordinate dependence" and yet another "unequal treaty." In response, Yoshida labelled Nanbara a "prostitute of learning" for his uncompromising demand for a comprehensive solution.[12] Public opinion leaned more in the direction of Yoshida's approach, with a

November 1949 survey by the *Mainichi shinbun* indicating those in support of a partial settlement at 42.5 percent and those favoring a comprehensive one at 33 percent. An *Asahi shinbun* survey exactly one year later—and following the outbreak of the Korean War in June—had those supporting a partial settlement at 45.6 percent and those supporting a comprehensive one at a measly 21.4 percent.[13]

While the Japanese argued among themselves, Dulles negotiated with Allied nations to support a partial peace treaty to be signed at a conference in San Francisco in early September 1951. Growing out of his experience at the Paris Peace Conference after the war in Europe in 1946, Dulles wanted their support for a lenient settlement that would not exact large reparations from the Japanese. Although Great Britain, Australia, the PRC, New Zealand, and Southeast Asian nations initially demanded a punitive settlement with extensive reparations, Dulles was able to bring them onboard—if reluctantly—with guarantees that America would ensure no revival of Japanese militarism.

Ultimately, fifty-two countries participated in the conference held at the War Memorial Opera House in San Francisco. India, Myanmar, and Yugoslavia refused to participate out of opposition to American control over the treaty process and their advocacy of Japanese nonalignment. Both the PRC and Chinese Taiwan were not invited because the Americans and British could not agree on which regime to recognize as the official government of China. South Korea was not invited because, as a recognized colony, it had never been at a state of war with Japan. The Soviets, Czechs, and Polish attended but refused to sign the treaty after all parties to the treaty declined to include a clause forbidding Japan from rearming.

With no opportunity for debate—merely a vote of support or nonsupport—forty-nine countries plus Japan signed the Treaty of Peace with Japan (also known as the San Francisco Peace Treaty) on September 8, 1951. The treaty was subsequently ratified by both houses of the Japanese Diet in October and November, respectively, coming into force on April 28, 1952. After the signing of the treaty, some in Japan—like Nanbara Shigeru—suggested that it would be timely for the emperor to abdicate, to which Hirohito himself appears to have been agreeable. But the emperor's aides would have nothing of this, modifying his speech delivered at the treaty promulgation ceremony at the Imperial Palace to remove any mention of abdication and war responsibility.[14]

Consistent with Dulles' designs, the content of the treaty was largely favorable to Japan. Under the treaty, Japan agreed to abandon all rights and claims against the Allies—including reparations for atomic bombing victims—as well as claims on Japanese assets left in neutral or Axis nations, which were to be used for compensation to Allied servicemen. The treaty specified that Japan must make reparations payments but, thanks to Dulles's preconference negotiations, the United

Figure 3.4. Yoshida Shigeru signs the Treaty of Peace with Japan in San Francisco on September 8, 1951. Courtesy of The Asahi Shimbun Company.

States and many other counties agreed to permanently abandon any such claims because of the potential damage to the fragile Japanese economy. The exceptions to this agreement, however, were certain nations in Southeast Asia that retained their right to claim reparations. With respect to territory, the Japanese agreed to the independence of Korea and to abandoning possession of the Pescadores Islands, Taiwan, the Kurile Islands, and Southern Karafuto to the north of Hokkaido. Okinawa and Ogasawara remained under US trusteeship, although the treaty was so worded that Japan implicitly retained residual sovereignty. The treaty also did very little to resolve issues of war responsibility, especially Japanese responsibility to individual victims of its colonial and military adventures. Only Article 11 of the treaty specified quite generally that Japan would accept all judgements of the Allied military tribunals. These unresolved reconciliation and compensation issues with individual victims would haunt Japan-Asia relations in the coming decades.

Japan officially regained its sovereignty when the treaty came into force in April 1952. But, as its critics had loudly pointed out, it was a conditional or subservient sovereignty due to the continued political influence and military presence of the United States. The treaty itself stipulated that all occupying forces must leave Japan ninety days after it came into effect, but it also allowed these forces to remain with the consent of the Japanese government. In fact, just hours after Yoshida signed the peace treaty, he signed another treaty, which would in many ways be far more influential on subsequent postwar Japanese history: namely, the Treaty of Mutual Cooperation and Security between the United States and Japan—or simply the Anpo Treaty, based on its Japanese title. As noted earlier, Yoshida had envisioned US forces staying on under a security alliance after the peace settlement, and he was not the only conservative with such an opinion. As early as 1947, Ashida Hitoshi and security experts had produced a plan on "post–peace settlement Japan" in which American military bases remained. The report was delivered to MacArthur but had no political traction at the time. Despite its claims to being mutual, the Anpo Treaty greatly favored US interests, while admittedly conforming to the Yoshida Doctrine of a mercantilist, largely nonmilitarized Japan under American military patronage. Specifically, the treaty allowed America to station some 260,000 troops on over twenty-eight hundred bases nationwide (most concentrated on US-administered Okinawa), with the provision for more bases in unspecified areas. The treaty stipulated that American forces could be deployed when Japan came under attack from the outside, but it placed no clear-cut obligation on the United States to defend Japan. The treaty also allowed for the deployment of US troops to quell domestic insurrection or riots at the request of the Japanese government, raising questions about the possible violation of national sovereignty. The United States was also permitted under the treaty to use its bases in Japan for actions in the Far East without prior consultation, as it had done during the Korean War. Here critics pointed to the ways the treaty might potentially make Japan a target in US military conflicts in the region. Moreover, the vagueness of the term "Far East" also raised questions about the very scope of the treaty. Such concerns were only exacerbated by the absence of any time limit on the instrument.[15]

The Anpo Treaty was further operationalized in February 1952 with the signing of the US-Japan Administrative Agreement. This document delineated the US right of command and its exclusive use of military bases, clarified Japan's responsibility to share costs, put servicemen under the dominion of US law for crimes committed in Japan, and gave the US military special powers, such as detaining Japanese citizens and demolishing buildings. Although the Japanese political left and right were opposed on almost everything, both agreed that the Anpo Treaty and its associated agreements greatly undermined Japanese independence and put the country at risk of attack in the thick of the Cold War. Indeed, such anxieties and frustrations lay the foundations of a massive political protest against the renewal of this treaty around the end of the decade.

With the two treaties in place in 1952, Japanese leaders were keen to reestablish Japan's position in the international community and to recalibrate the country's relationship with its neighbors. Throughout the 1950s Japan gained membership in the World Health Organization (May 1951), the International Labour Organization (June 1951), the Food and Agriculture Organization of the United Nations (FAO) (November 1951), the International Monetary Fund (May 1952), and the General Agreement on Tariffs and Trade (GATT) (June 1955). Membership of the United Nations (UN) would have to wait until the normalization of ties with the Soviet Union in 1956.

In 1952 Japan signed peace treaties with the Republic of China (Taiwan) and India and in 1954 with Burma (Myanmar). Reparations agreements were also reached with the Philippines, Indonesia, Burma, and South Vietnam, amounting to a total of around one billion US dollars in outlays by 1976. Rather than cash transfers, however, these reparations were mainly in the form of Official Development Assistance (ODA), such as construction projects and the provision of manufactured items. Importantly, the government used mostly Japanese companies for these reparations, thus contributing to economic recovery in heavy and other industries at home while providing Japanese industry with a foothold in the markets of Southeast Asia, where they would come to dominate in the ensuing decades. As Yoshida Shigeru later recalled, some may have seen this activity as reparations, but it was nothing other than investment for political and business elites.[16]

Japanese leaders also set about normalizing shattered bilateral relationships with neighboring countries—with varying levels of success. Rehabilitating relations with the Soviet Union was a central policy objective of Hatoyama Ichirō, who held the prime ministership from December 1954 to the end of 1956. Hatoyama sought Japanese membership in the UN, but this was only possible with Soviet support due to its veto power as a permanent member of the UN Security Council. Although a staunch anti-communist, Hatoyama believed that improved relations with the Soviets might be more advantageous for Japan in the event of a conflict between the superpowers. The death of Soviet leader Joseph Stalin in March 1953 and his replacement by Nikita Khrushchev in 1954 opened the way for détente between the USSR and Japan. Khrushchev appears to have felt that the absence of bilateral relations worked only to the advantage of the Americans and that if these relations were normalized, the Soviets might be able to exert more influence over Japanese leaders and the public—perhaps even convincing the country to resist America's embrace.

It was in this context that a Soviet representative in Japan with personal connections from the Occupation days approached Hatoyama in 1955 with a letter from Moscow raising the possibility of normalizing relations. Immediately receptive, Minister of Agriculture Kōno Ichirō made a visit to Moscow in the following year that opened the way for the signing of the Japan-USSR Fisheries Treaty. Building on this momentum, in July 1956, Foreign Minister Shigemitsu Mamoru visited Moscow to begin formal discussions for normalization. The main sticking point in negotiations was the unresolved territorial issue stemming from World War II. In the latter stages of the war, the Soviets had invaded the Kurile Islands, expelling all Japanese residents and claiming sovereignty. In the negotiations, Japan claimed sovereign rights over the four southernmost islands of Etorofu, Kunashiri, Shikotan, and Habomai and demanded their return. In response, the Soviets proposed returning only the smaller Habomai and Shikotan. Faced with the collapse of the talks, Hatoyama agreed to a Soviet promise that Habomai and Shikotan would be returned to Japan on the signing of a peace treaty sometime in the future (although this outcome has still not been realized at the writing of this book). Thanks to Hatoyama's compromise, however, relations were formally normalized in October 1956 with the signing of the Joint Declaration of Japan and the Soviet Union. The communiqué declared an end to the state of war between the two countries, the restoration of diplomatic ties, the release of Japanese detainees, the commencement of trade and fishing, a broad statement on the unresolved territorial issue, and—the biggest prize for Hatoyama—support for Japanese membership in the UN, which was realized by unanimous vote at the UN General Assembly in December 1956.

Relations with Japan's other neighbors in Northeast Asia remained complicated. Designs to normalize relations with the PRC were impeded because of Japan's recognition of the nationalist regime in Taiwan as the official government of China. This meant that trade remained one of the only points of connection between the PRC and Japan for many years—much to the frustration of many on both the left and the right, who saw China as a natural market and partner for Japan in the region. The Treaty of Peace between the Republic of China and Japan (also known as the Taipei Treaty) signed in April 1952 served as the formal symbol of Japan's estrangement from the PRC, leaving relations in limbo for two more decades.

With shared Cold War threats from the PRC and North Korea and a common ally in the United States, South Korea and Japan seemed to be natural partners. But the unresolved legacies of empire and various territorial disagreements meant that this relationship also remained strained throughout the 1950s and beyond. The South Koreans had hoped to participate in the San Francisco Peace Conference as one of the victor nations, but since the country was never at war with Japan, this request was refused by the Americans. Nonetheless, the Treaty of Peace with Japan did clearly specify that South Korea retained the right to claim reparations from Japan for the period of colonial rule. Negotiations for normalization with Japan began in early 1952 but were hampered by competing claims: the South Koreans demanded reparations for the thirty-eight years of Japanese colonial rule on the basis that the Annexation Treaty of 1910 was illegal, and the Japanese demanded the return of Japanese assets from this period. Another factor obstructing progress concerned territorial claims. In 1952, just prior to the beginning of normalization talks, President Syngman Rhee announced the so-called Rhee Line that unilaterally determined the international boundary between Japan and South Korea, including the island of Dokdo (Korean) or Takeshima (Japanese) within its waters. Thereafter, sovereignty of the island would remain in dispute and continue to confound negotiations. In 1953, tensions worsened when a Japanese fisherman was shot by the South Korean military and Japanese fishing vessels were periodically taken into custody for violating South Korean territorial waters. Relations were also strained by the Japanese side. Japanese officials involved in the normalization discussions repeatedly made offhand remarks claiming that colonization had been "good" for Korea, providing ports and railways and pouring money into the country. With each such gaffe, the negotiations would inevitably stall.

The incarceration of Korean nationals in Japan at the Ōmura Immigration Detention Center in Nagasaki also complicated negotiations. The detainees included Koreans who had been in Japan since before the war and, having been convicted of crimes, were slated for deportation. There were also some Koreans who had entered Japan after the war and had been apprehended for various crimes. The Japanese wished to deport these individuals to South Korea, which refused to accept them. When South Korea did finally agree to receive the detainees in 1958, the Japanese government now refused, citing human rights concerns—again resulting in cancellation of the normalization negotiations. To complicate matters further, beginning in 1959, the Japanese government supported an initiative for thousands of Korean residents of Japan to relocate to North Korea. Faced with these roadblocks, the bilateral relationship would not be normalized until 1965 and, even then, territorial issues and questions of historical responsibility would remain unresolved.

The San Francisco Peace Treaty and Japan's subsequent membership in international organizations throughout the 1950s marked the country's return to international society in this era. But the signing of the Anpo Treaty put Japan squarely in the Western camp and especially the tight embrace of the United States. Although relations with nations in the region were greatly improved through peace treaties and reparations agreements, Japan's complicated relations with the USSR, the PRC, and South Korea hinted at a challenging future as the country returned to the world stage in the wake of colonial empire, militarism, and seven years of American-led Occupation.

The Establishment of the 1955 System: Solidifying Conservative Rule

Along with Japan's return to international society, the other significant political development of the 1950s was the establishment of conservative political rule under the LDP. The LDP would hold the reins of power almost without interruption from 1955 onwards in the so-called 1955 System. Conservatives began to lay the foundations of this system after the Occupation ended in 1952 by continuing—and in many ways extending—the reverse course policies begun during the latter years of the Occupation.

In April 1951, President Truman suddenly dismissed MacArthur after he made public statements about the need to extend the Korean War into China and the possibility of using nuclear weapons in the conflict. On the day of his departure from Japan, over two hundred thousand people lined the streets with American flags in hand to bid the general farewell. Japanese newspapers published laudatory editorials on MacArthur's contribution to Japanese democracy, while the Diet passed a motion of gratitude. In terms of establishing the 1955 System, MacArthur's replacement, General Matthew Ridgway, provided Japanese conservatives with the freedom they needed to wind back many—although not all—of the Occupation-era reforms. Yoshida and his successors focused on controlling social protest and labor activism and revising aspects of education, policing, defense, and the constitution.

Following the violent "Bloody May Day" clashes between protesters and police outside the Imperial Palace just days after the signing of the San Francisco Peace Treaty in 1952, the Yoshida government passed the Subversive Activities Prevention Law and established the Public Security Intelligence Agency to conduct investigations under the new law. The labor movement came in for particular suppression with the 1953 prohibition of strikes in critical industries like coal and electricity generation. Education also experienced a significant recentralization in these years. Under the original Occupation reforms, local school boards of education were popularly elected, but a 1956 revision to the Boards of Education Law now gave prefectural governors the power to appoint board members. Two laws that were passed in 1954 forbade public school teachers from engaging in political demonstrations and rallies or encouraging students to participate, at the risk of strict disciplinary measures.

In a similar way, policing was recentralized. Under the initial Occupation reforms, policing was handled by local towns and villages alongside the National Rural Police Force. In 1954, however, these local policing forces were replaced by a single national force under the supervision of the National Police Agency (NPA). In turn, the NPA was administered by the National Public Safety Commission of the Japanese Cabinet. Because this commission was responsible for appointing police chiefs at the prefectural level, it effectively put control of policing in the hands of the central government.

Conservatives also continued the reconstitution of Japan's defense capabilities that were begun under MacArthur with the establishment of the NPR during the Korean War. In July 1952, the Security Agency was established to oversee the National Safety Forces (NSF) that succeeded the land and maritime NPR. Leadership of the new agency included numerous former Imperial Japanese Army colonels and Navy officials who had recently been depurged. As conservatives jostled for political control throughout 1953, Yoshida—now in a minority government—was forced to cooperate with the other conservative parties on policy issues like defense. In September of that year, the three main conservative parties (see later in this chapter) agreed that the Security Agency Law would be revised to enable the creation of a national self-defense force. Encouraged by these developments, in March 1954 America signed a Mutual Defense Assistance Agreement with Japan in which it agreed to provide armaments and to station troops in Japan in return for a Japanese commitment to rearm for defensive purposes. This agreement came on the back of a statement by Vice President Richard Nixon during a visit to Japan in 1953 in which he said that including Article 9 (the peace clause) in the constitution had been a "mistake."[17] With this agreement in place, the way was now open for the establishment of the SDF.

On July 1, 1954, the Defense Agency was established, replacing the National Security Agency. The new agency was placed under the strict civilian control of a minister and positioned as an external agency of the prime minister's and cabinet offices. The Maritime and Ground SDF carried over from their previous iterations as the NPR and NSF, while the Air Self-Defense Force was created anew. Careful not to provoke public concern, behind the scenes the US military provided support for the establishment, organization, training, and equipping of the new SDF. Questions over the constitutionality of the SDF arose almost immediately, although conservatives pushed back, arguing that the force only had defense capabilities and could not wage war. Although this interpretation may have had some validity at the outset, as the SDF grew in size and technical capability over the years, the argument that it was something less than a full-fledged military became more and more hollow.

Handling this ambiguity about the true nature of the SDF connected to another aim of conservatives as they lay the foundations for long-term hegemony: namely, constitutional revision. Both Yoshida and his successor Hatoyama tried to open a pathway to revision, with the former establishing a committee to investigate the issue in 1954 and the latter attempting to reform the electoral system to single member districts so conservatives could gain the numbers needed to initiate the revision process in the Diet. But neither Yoshida nor Hatoyama succeeded in what became a kind of holy grail for some conservatives throughout the postwar era. Looked at in the broad historical sweep of the Occupation reforms and subsequent backsteps, conservatives' inability to bring about constitutional revision is a reminder that the key institutions of postwar Japanese democracy—though challenged, compromised, and in some cases revised—had struck deep roots despite the conservative resurgence.

Toward the 1955 System

While Yoshida and the conservatives pushed forward with their revisionist agenda, they also jostled for power among themselves. Yoshida had managed to cling to the prime ministership since his return to power after the fall of the Ashida cabinet in 1948, but by the early 1950s his "one-man" show was attracting the ire of progressives and many conservatives alike.[18] SCAP's progressive GS did its best to prevent the "reactionary" Yoshida from returning to the prime ministership in 1948, but it was unsuccessful due to the failed economic policies of the previous socialist Katayama cabinet and its centrist successor the Ashida Hitoshi Democratic Party.[19]

On assuming the prime ministership for a second time in October 1948, Yoshida could only form a minority government. A motion of no confidence soon thereafter forced him to dissolve the Diet and call a general election. In the resulting election of January 1949, Yoshida's Democratic Liberal Party (DLP) scored an overwhelming victory, capturing 246 out of 466 seats in the House of Representatives. Voters punished the centrist parties and JSP for their economic mismanagement and corruption. Significantly, Yoshida used this electoral mandate to bring many of his bureaucratic colleagues into politics, including Ikeda Hayato, then an undersecretary in the powerful Ministry of Finance, and Satō Eisaku, an undersecretary in transportation. Both individuals would go on to serve as prime minister during the golden years of Japanese economic growth in the 1960s and early 1970s. Among Yoshida's legacies, the fortification of this pipeline between postwar conservatives and elite bureaucrats would prove crucial in shaping the postwar contours of Japan's so-called developmental state.[20] It also meant that highly politicized issues like constitutional revision would be pushed to the back of the conservative agenda for many decades.

But Yoshida's honeymoon revival in the late 1940s was short-lived. From around mid-1951, his political rivals made a comeback to politics after being depurged under the Occupation reverse course. Influential conservative heavyweights like Hatoyama Ichirō, Kōno Ichirō, Ishibashi Tanzan, and Kishi Nobusuke returned from the political wilderness eager to regain their foothold at the center of power. Many of these individuals were hostile to the Yoshida Doctrine with its tepid attitude toward rearmament and subservience to the United States. They wanted greater Japanese independence through revision of the American-imposed constitution and the rebuilding of Japan's military. Hatoyama Ichirō championed this opinion even after rejoining Yoshida's DLP, which he had hoped to assume leadership of based on a commitment from Yoshida when he was purged on the eve of becoming prime minister in 1946. Yoshida's refusal to keep his promise and relinquish the leadership, however, created a rift between the two that would ultimately contribute to Yoshida's downfall.

Apart from challenges from within his own party, Yoshida also faced attacks from conservatives in the newly established (1952) Reform Party (RP), which pushed a policy platform of "butter and guns"—in other words, social welfare and remilitarization.[21] The first signs of trouble for Yoshida came in the general election of October 1952 when his DLP—now renamed the Liberal Party (LP)—lost forty-five seats, although still clinging to a majority. Most worrying for conservatives in the newly sovereign Japan was the electoral gains of the JSP, divided into two parties though it may have been. In the 1949 election, the united JSP had claimed only forty-eight seats, but after the 1952 election, the left and right wings of the party claimed a combined total of 111 seats. Despite this growing threat from the left, Yoshida maintained his dictatorial and haughty demeanor. In February 1953, he caused an uproar in the Diet when he called a JSP member an "idiot" in response to insistent questioning. Yoshida subsequently offered a halfhearted apology but Hatoyama and others in the party swooped on the opportunity, joining with both JSP wings to pass a motion of no confidence that forced Yoshida to go to the polls barely six months after the previous election. The subsequent election of April 1953 saw Yoshida's Liberals lose their majority (reduced to 202 seats), compelled now to form a minority government with support from the rival RP.

To make matters worse, in early 1954, Yoshida's party was rocked by a bribery scandal. High-ranking government officials—including Yoshida's ex-bureaucrat protégé Satō Eisaku—were identified by the Tokyo Public Prosecutors' Office as having received bribes from shipbuilding companies in return for government subsidies. A warrant was subsequently issued to the House of Representatives for Satō's arrest, but Yoshida's minister of justice intervened at the last minute, using his right of command to postpone the arrest due to the need for Satō to participate in important legislative discussions. This would be the only time such extraordinary powers were invoked in the postwar era and the action was met with broad public condemnation of the Yoshida government. Satō was later exonerated as part of an amnesty granted when Japan joined the UN in 1956. But the incident proved fatal for Yoshida's political survival.

In November 1954, Hatoyama and colleagues bolted the party, and together with Kishi Nobusuke, the RP, and other Yoshida adversaries established the Japan

Democratic Party (JDP), which touted hawkish policies of a new constitution and rearmament. The following month, the JDP combined with the left and right factions of the JSP to pass yet another motion of no confidence in Yoshida. Backed into a corner, Yoshida contemplated calling yet another election but, under pressure from his own party members and business organizations, he indignantly relinquished the party leadership (although not his Diet seat), saying "if that's the case, then I'll quit and go enjoy some quiet reading in Ōiso" (his home south of Tokyo).[22]

The way was now open for Hatoyama's JDP to form a minority government with support from the two JSP wings on the proviso that he would call a swift general election. At a press conference in January 1955, Hatoyama announced a new policy direction for Japan, including efforts to normalize relations with the USSR and the PRC and constitutional revision to allow rearmament. As noted earlier, only the first of these objectives would be realized.

After the general election in February 1955, the JDP emerged as the largest party but without a majority. The Liberals, now under the leadership of Ogata Taketora, were punished by voters, wining only 112 seats—a drop of eighty-five. Conversely, the JSP and JCP were the big winners. Combined, the two wings of the JSP claimed 156 seats, which easily cleared the two-thirds required to block the Diet from initiating the constitutional revision process. The JCP also increased from eleven to twenty-two seats. This powerful showing at the polls confirmed the JSP's encouraging performance at the previous election and also served as an endorsement of the decision by leaders of the warring left and right factions to reunite after the election. For many in the party, the 1955 election not only confirmed widespread support for the proconstitutional, pacifist stance of the socialists. More inspiringly, it also suggested that a reunited JSP might even be able to win government soon. With the wind in their sails, in an October 1955 meeting in Tokyo, the left and right wings of the JSP formalized reunification, with Asanuma Jirō of the right faction as secretary general and Suzuki Masaburō of the left as chairman. Of course, unification did not mean the end of ideological and tactical cleavages in the party, which would continue to undermine JSP unity thereafter (the JSP would split again in 1960) and stain its public image. For its part, in July 1955, the JCP abandoned the strategy of violent insurrection—so-called far-left adventurism—adopting instead a strategy of peaceful revolution based on action within the confines of parliamentary politics.

The reunification of the JSP and strong performance of the JCP in 1955 provoked serious concern among business leaders, conservative politicians, and officials in Washington. As the key funders of the conservative parties, the major business organizations began to apply pressure for unification to counterbalance a rising left, which they feared would reignite radical unionism and disrupt business. They enticed conservative heavyweights in the JDP and LP with promises of generous funding in the event of a conservative unification. It also later came to light that Washington, DC, working through the Central Intelligence Agency (CIA), had funneled money into the conservative parties to facilitate unification and prevent a socialist government in Japan.

Members of the LP, RP, and JLP (a breakaway from the LP) had, in fact, been negotiating for unification since 1954, but quarrels over leadership and party-internal opposition hampered progress. Only with the reunification of the JSP and the strong showing by the left at the 1955 election did resistance to unification among conservatives begin to wane. In June 1955, Hatoyama and Ogata finally began discussions on unification. The defining moment came on November 15, 1955, when delegates at a joint LP and JDP conference at Chūō University Hall in Tokyo agreed to unite under the banner of the Liberal Democratic Party. Instead of a single president, the newly formed LDP had four acting presidential representatives: Hatoyama Ichirō and Miki Bukichi from the Democrats, and Ogata Taketora and Ōno Banboku from the Liberals. After the sudden death of Ōno in April 1956, Hatoyama became the party's first president.

The establishment of the LDP put the conservatives in an overwhelming position of power in both houses of the Diet: 297 seats compared to the JSP's 156 in the House of Representatives, and 118 seats in the House of Councillors compared to the JSP's 68. Although Japanese politics now ostensibly had a two-party system, the ratio of essentially two-to-one between the conservatives and progressives prompted some to describe the situation as a "one-and-a-half party system" or, even worse, a "pseudo two-party system."[23] In hindsight, we know that the LDP would remain in power throughout the postwar era with only two interruptions. Moreover, we also know that the JSP would slowly wither to a position of political insignificance. Historically, then, the dominance of the LDP is undeniable.

Nonetheless, at the time of its formation in 1955, the future of the LDP and Japanese politics more generally remained uncertain, and even the most optimistic of conservative pundits could not have predicted the LDP's subsequent ascendency. Furthermore, as noted below in this chapter and in the following chapters, the LDP faced challenges electorally due to demographic and socioeconomic changes and from emergent social energies. It was forced again and again to adapt—even compromise—its policy profile to retain power. This adaptability has undoubtedly been one of the reasons for its longevity. Nowhere is this more evident than the LDP's founding policy platform of constitutional revision. Resistance from both within and outside the LDP meant that, rather than pursuing constitutional revision, throughout most of the postwar era the party's policy line was characterized by, first, a focus on economic growth, and second, national security through dependence on the United States—both of which traced a lineage back to the Yoshida Doctrine. The electoral system based on midsized multimember districts also played a role in moving the LDP away from highly politicized, ideological issues, encouraging instead the development of party-internal factionalism, money politics (and associated corruption), and policies built around pork-barreling at the grassroots. In short, changing circumstances, issues, and incentives meant that single-party rule would not result in political stasis.

Challenging the 1955 System

The persistence of contentious politics despite the LDP's creation offers clear evidence that overwhelming Diet control did not amount to smooth sailing for the conservatives. On the contrary, the 1950s and beyond witnessed a range of civic movements and protests against key components of the 1955 System, especially the country's deep intertwinement with the United States. As noted in the previous chapter, organized labor became an important political force almost immediately after the war—so much so that, by 1947, MacArthur felt impelled to cancel the planned general strike. The attacks on labor continued in the Red Purge begun in the late 1940s and the various restrictions on political activities imposed on public employees and workers in critical industries. In 1955, the General Council of Trade Unions of Japan, or Sōhyō, began to coordinate unions across a range of industries and enterprises into a nationwide "spring offensive" aimed at increasing wages. Individual company unions witnessed internecine battles between moderate factions wanting to cooperate with management and those committed to disputative tactics. The zenith of this latter approach would come at the turn of the decade with the massive anti–Anpo Treaty protests and the struggle at the Miike coal mine.

School and university students also became politically active during this period. In the early postwar years, school students mobilized in democratization movements to oust principals and teachers who had enforced ultranationalistic practices during the war. In 1948, the All-Japan Federation of Student Self-Governing Associations, or Zengakuren, became the hub for university student mobilization nationwide. Early on, JCP members dominated Zengakuren, but the relationship between the two organizations wavered over time. The Red Purges of the late 1940s and early 1950s dealt a strong blow to Zengakuren and, in 1951, many joined with the JCP in its turn to rural guerilla warfare. This approach was an utter failure and, with the JCP's return to mainstream politics in 1955, the student movement also reverted to conventional activism. But, unlike the JCP and the labor movement, radical—sometimes dangerously violent—action lived on in the repertoire of student activism, rearing its head in the Anpo struggle of 1959–1960 and beyond.

Along with students and workers, newly enfranchised Japanese women also began to organize, building on women's movements from the prewar. In 1946, the leftist writer Miyamoto Yuriko and other elite women established the Women's Democratic Club to pursue peace and democracy in the wake of war while, in 1948, prewar women's activist Oku Mumeo and others established the Association of Consumer Organizations (Shufuren). Oku's association focused on peace, living costs, food safety, product quality, and taxes. In 1952, the National Federation of Women's Organizations (Chifuren) was established as a central coordinating hub for local women's organizations. Early on, Chifuren focused on antinuclear weapons activism but later expanded its mandate to consumer product surveys and the sale of low-priced cosmetics to members. Similarly, in 1955, two thousand women assembled in Tokyo to establish the Japanese Congress of Mothers following the American detonation of a hydrogen bomb at Bikini Atoll the previous year. The Congress pursued a pacifist, antinuclear weapons agenda from the standpoint of mothers, which, although later criticized by Japanese feminists, placed women at the leading edge of Cold War politics.

Throughout the 1950s, local communities mobilized to oppose American military facilities in their towns and villages. In July 1952, farmers and politicians united to resist the expansion of a US military facility in the town of Sunagawa in the east of Tokyo. Under the expansion, some fourteen households would lose all of their land and another forty households over 50 percent. Initially, locals conducted a signature campaign, lobbied Diet members, and submitted counterproposals to the base commander. Matters escalated in March 1954, when the government announced it had approved runway extensions on US military bases in Tachikawa (Sunagawa), Yokota, Niigata, Aichi, and elsewhere. With this, locals quickly formed the Alliance to Oppose Extension of the Sunagawa Base. Landowners renting properties to the US military refused to extend agreements, instead initiating court proceedings for immediate eviction. Unperturbed, in 1957 the government invoked special laws for land use and repossession and subsequently began surveying work on private lands to be incorporated in the expanded bases. In July 1957, around one thousand locals, together with supporters from labor unions and student groups, gathered outside the fence of the northern perimeter of the Sunagawa base. Government surveyors were protected by a squad of fifteen hundred police. In the ensuing melee, around three hundred protesters forcibly stormed the base, resulting in the arrest of 250, of whom seven were ultimately charged with illegal entry into restricted premises. In an unprecedented court decision in March 1959, Judge Itō Akio of the Tokyo District Court ruled that the presence of US military bases was indeed unconstitutional and, accordingly, dismissed all charges against the defendants. On appeal, however, the Supreme Court reversed Itō's verdict, affirming the constitutionality of American

Figure 3.5. Women of Sunagawa opposing the expansion of the US military base in their region join arms in solidarity and song behind the watchtower of the protest movement in October 1956. Courtesy of The Asahi Shimbun Company.

bases. In its decision, the court stated that it was not the place of the judiciary to rule on high-level political issues like the Security Treaty.[24]

A similar protest occurred in Uchinada, a village of around one thousand households located in Ishikawa Prefecture on the Sea of Japan. In September 1952, the government announced that sand dunes in the area had been selected for US artillery testing for the Korean War. Initially, the mayor and local assembly resolved to oppose any forcible land repossession, but they relented after the government pledged that the firing range would only be utilized for four months and compensation provided in the form of road repairs and new childcare facilities. But relations soured in 1953 when the government reversed its original decision, unilaterally extending the period of use. In response, local farmers and fishermen, together with prefectural workers, members of national unions, students, JCP and JSP members, and ordinary citizens, mobilized into an opposition movement under the slogan "money is for one year, land is forever."[25] Over time, however, local participants found their finances strained, with some eventually shifting to support the construction of a US military base in the region in hopes it would improve standards of living. Although the movement fractured, the devastated sand dunes were finally returned to the village with the end of US test firing in 1956.

Sunagawa and Uchinada are but two examples of the anti–military base struggles across Japan during the 1950s, with other incidents unfolding at the Negishi base in Yokohama, the Myōgisan training facility in Gunma, the Asamasan training grounds in Nagano, and the Mount Fuji foothills base. Military bases on Okinawa under US administrative control until 1972 also faced local opposition movements from as early as 1956. Apart from land struggles, the transgressions of US servicemen on and around US bases in Japan regularly provoked the fury of residents. In 1957, for example, Corporal Third Class William S. Girard shot and killed a Japanese woman who had entered the Sōmagahara military training grounds in Gunma Prefecture to collect ammunition shells. After the incident, the US military released a statement saying that, although Girard's action was "inappropriate," it was carried out in terms of the standard exercise of his duties, hence the Americans would claim first jurisdiction in any legal proceedings. After protestations from the Japanese government and the accompanying public uproar, the Americans allowed Girard to be tried in Japan on the proviso he would receive a light sentence. The corporal was subsequently found guilty of manslaughter, given a three-year suspended sentence, and allowed to return home to the United States with his Japanese wife.[26] Despite American reorganization of its bases and troop deployment following the incident, Girard's was but an early instance of crimes and violent acts committed by US servicemen against Japanese citizens living around US military facilities, especially on Okinawa.

The antinuclear bomb movement was yet another important manifestation of resistance to the 1955 System. In early March 1954, crew aboard the tuna fishing vessel *Dai-Go Fukuryū-maru* (Lucky Dragon No. 5), at work in the South Pacific, were exposed to radioactive fallout following a US hydrogen bomb test at Bikini Atoll. After returning to the port of Yaizu in Shizuoka Prefecture, the crew members fell ill with radiation sickness. One of their number, the radio operator Kuboyama Aikichi, eventually died. The incident provoked a kind of mass panic in Japan, with terms such as "ashes of death" (*shi no hai*) and "nuked tuna" entering the popular lexicon. Significantly, this incident sparked a nationwide movement against nuclear weapons, becoming a foundational moment in the postwar Japanese peace movement. Immediately following the war, peace movements—especially those relating to the atomic bombings of Hiroshima and Nagasaki—had been stifled by American censorship. But with the Occupation now over, citizens were freer to organize. In March 1954, the Yaizu Municipal Assembly in Shizuoka Prefecture

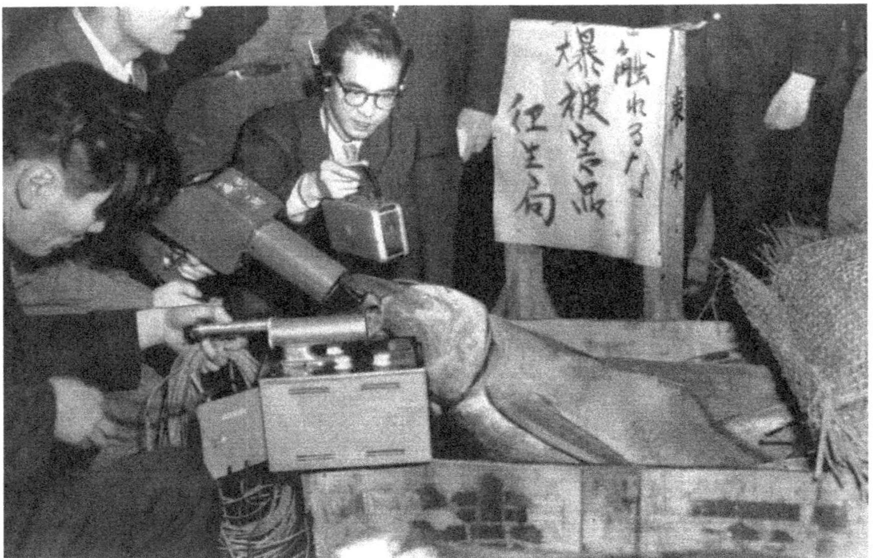

Figure 3.6. An official of the Tokyo Metropolitan Bureau of Public Health uses a Geiger counter to test the radioactivity of a tuna landed by the *Lucky Dragon No. 5,* whose crew and catch were exposed to radioactive fallout following the US military hydrogen bomb test at Bikini Atoll in 1954. Courtesy of The Asahi Shimbun Company.

passed a symbolic resolution banning the testing of atomic and hydrogen bombs. In May, an international relations scholar, Yasui Kaoru, together with his wife Tazuko, cultural groups, and women's organizations, formed the Suginami Council for the Movement Against Atomic and Hydrogen Bombs, which began a nationwide signature campaign opposing nuclear weapons testing. This was arguably the first national mass movement in postwar Japan, collecting over thirty-two million signatures. Building on these developments, the Japan Council against Atomic and Hydrogen Bombs, or Gensuikyō, was established in 1955, holding the first World Convention for the Prohibition of Atomic and Hydrogen Weapons in Hiroshima on August 8 of that year—the tenth anniversary of the Hiroshima bombing. Convention delegates traveled from as far away as the United States, Poland, Italy, and Ceylon (Sri Lanka), as well as from Asia-Pacific countries like Australia, Vietnam, Indonesia, Malaysia, and South Korea. Although Gensuikyō would split in the early 1960s over Cold War rivalries, it evidenced the power of popular energy with respect to contentious issues such as nuclear weapons. Moreover, alongside the other movements discussed above, it served as a check on the conservative hegemony sinking deep roots under the LDP government and the Anpo Treaty. As subsequent chapters reveal, workers, students, women, pacifists, and local communities continued to be a thorn in the side of Japan's conservative rulers.

Economy and Society: Transwar Continuities and Transformations in the 1950s

An Economy in Transition

The 1950s were an important period of transition economically, politically, culturally, and socially in Japan, as transwar institutions, practices, and ways of life were slowly remolded or replaced by the emergent postwar order. This sense of transition was no better expressed than in the phrase "it's no longer the postwar" (*mohaya sengo dewanai*), which appeared in the 1956 economic white paper of the Economic Planning Agency (EPA). Anticipating the massive capital investment boom among businesses in the coming years, the report concluded that it was "no longer the postwar" of Japan benefiting from America's economic patronage. The country was now "facing a different situation," "recovery-led growth" was "over," and "future growth" had to be supported by technological "modernization."[27] Some months before the release of this white paper, the literary scholar Nakano Yoshio published an essay of the same title—"It's No Longer the Postwar"—in which he focused not on the economy but the mentality of the people. Reflecting on the recent reunification of the conservative forces in the LDP (and especially the fact that around 30 percent of Hatoyama's cabinet were formerly purged individuals), Nakano called on readers to remain vigilant to the revival of reactionary forces. As he explained, moving forward was not simply a matter of "shedding the 'postwar mentality'" by relegating the war and its legacies to the past. At the same time, Nakano also asserted that it was appropriate now to treat the "wounds of defeat" less "emotionally" and more "thoughtfully" in order to build the future.[28]

This subtle intermingling of a lingering past, a fluid present, and an uncertain future in the EPA white paper and Nakano's essay neatly encapsulates the zeitgeist of 1950s Japan. The economy was certainly on the move by the mid-1950s, poised to enter an era of astounding growth, but this transformation would be overseen by state institutions with transwar lineages. With a few important exceptions, the Occupation left the national bureaucracy largely intact for pragmatic reasons. In relation to the economy, bureaucratic continuity in the Ministry of Finance and especially the Ministry of Commerce and Industry (the Ministry of International Trade and Industry [MITI] from 1949) meant that state officials would play an influential and perhaps decisive role in economic planning and policymaking.

Along with their wartime involvement in munitions and resource allocation, bureaucrats in MITI also drew on their experience guiding the short-lived Priority Production Program for the revival of the coal and steel industries in the early post-war era. On its establishment in 1949, MITI was entrusted with several critical tools for managing the economy. The Foreign Exchange and Foreign Trade Law gave MITI control over all foreign currency transactions as well as the certification of imports and exports. MITI also had oversight and approval powers for technology imports and joint ventures. Through the Development Bank of Japan (DBJ) established in 1951, MITI was able to implement the government's industrial policies, approving loans only for those industries targeted as critical for economic growth, such as steel, shipbuilding, and coal.

Capital for the DBJ was sourced from the Fiscal Investment and Loan Program (FILP), a specially created budget separate from the General Account and funded by the savings of small depositors held in the government-owned Japan Post Bank. Bureaucrats had exclusive control of the FILP throughout the years of high-speed growth. MITI also exerted influence over industry through deliberative councils comprising executives and academic experts. Here officials were able to school corporate elites in the latest practices in management, quality control, and labor efficiency. In terms of regulation, the revision of the Antimonopoly Law in 1953 gave MITI further discretion to permit cartels for the promotion of industrial rationalization, to allow price maintenance agreements in specified industries, and to approve mergers and shareholdings among companies. With these levers in hand, economic bureaucrats set about sculpting Japan's economic revival throughout the 1950s and beyond.

Along with bureaucratic leadership, other factors played into Japan's economic resurgence in the 1950s. US military special procurements during the Korean War had been vital, but Japan continued to benefit from US patronage thereafter with unrestricted access to US markets, a favorable exchange rate, and low defense spending thanks to the Anpo Treaty. The extended period of global economic growth under the Bretton Woods system and GATT, combined with relatively cheap energy costs, also meant that Japan would be embarking on its economic comeback at an extremely opportune moment globally.

In 1955, industrial output exceeded its maximum prewar levels, helping Japanese exports to increase (although they would not exceed imports until 1965). By the mid-1950s, shipbuilding was already a major export earner for Japan, increasing from 368,000 tons in 1950 to 1.9 million tons in 1960.[29] The steel industry was not far behind thanks to demand from shipbuilding, automobiles, and other manufactured goods. In 1950, the country produced 4.84 million tons of crude steel, which increased over fivefold to 22.14 million tons by 1960.[30] The growth of these industries, coupled with government support, encouraged technological innovation through importation of the latest technologies from the United States and Europe. Industries such as steel, shipbuilding, and chemicals benefited from automation and upscaling, while purchases of semiconductor technology provided opportunities for electronics makers like the Sony Corporation. MITI also facilitated development of the petrochemical industry by planning the construction of four large combines from 1955 to 1960. These combines mass produced synthetic fibers (polyester, polyacrylic, polypropylene), synthetic resins (vinyl chloride, urea resin, silicon), and synthetic rubber. They also produced unwanted outputs like industrial pollution—with devastating outcomes for the environment and local communities.

The Japanese automobile industry also began its meteoric rise in the 1950s, building on the special procurements of the Korean War. Early on, Japanese automakers depended on tie-ups with Western companies, producing vehicles under license for Renault (Hino) and Austin (Nissan). But, throughout the decade, they also began to manufacture domestically designed vehicles. In 1955, for example, Toyota released the Toyopet Crown, the first Japanese vehicle of recognized international quality. The company followed up in 1957 with the Toyota Corona, which would become a longtime best seller worldwide. Like the steel and shipbuilding industries, automakers like Toyota actively imported management techniques from the West, especially in quality control and just-in-time production methods.

But it is important to note that, at least in the 1950s, not all were convinced of Japan's potential as a passenger car exporter. Some government elites even argued that domestic production was unnecessary and that Japan should rely solely on imports. Although this stance was eventually rejected, the government's "National Car Plan" of 1955 concluded that the only way for Japan to compete against American automakers would be to produce a single domestic passenger car.[31] On this point too, Japanese automakers decided to tread a different path to bureaucratic elites—with astounding outcomes.

Mirroring the automobile and ship industries, production of home appliances such as washing machines, televisions, rice cookers, and vacuum cleaners skyrocketed during the 1950s thanks to surging domestic consumer demand and high tariffs on imported products. Television manufacturing was identified as a strategically important future export industry and led the way in the adoption of electronics technology.

The retail economy also experienced its own transformations during the 1950s, thanks to new products such as televisions. The result was a distribution revolution. Under old-style distribution, individual products moved from wholesale networks to thousands of sole proprietor outlets and a few department stores. But now producers of consumer durables, cosmetics, dairy products, and the like began to establish

Figure 3.7. Domestic passenger cars produced by various automobile manufacturers after World War II are displayed in front of the Imperial Palace in Central Tokyo. From the left: Ota PK, Toyopet Master, Toyopet Crown, Prince Sedan, and Datsun 110 (1955). Courtesy of The Asahi Shimbun Company.

direct distribution channels to small retailers and open their own retail outlets—effectively bypassing the wholesalers. Department stores and supermarkets also proliferated during the 1950s, challenging the entrenched mom-and-pop stores. Private railways like Hanshin, Tobu, Odakyu, and Toei built department stores at their terminuses, while large operations from the Osaka area like Daimaru, Sogo, and Hankyu entered the Tokyo market. Thanks to the gradual proliferation of electric refrigerators, consumers who had previously shopped daily now began to stock up at local supermarkets with their low prices, self-service, and massive selection. The first supermarket in Japan was reportedly the upmarket Kinokuniya store in Tokyo's Aoyama district in 1953. But the real takeoff came after the entrepreneur Nakauchi Isao established the first Daiei supermarket in Osaka in 1957. The concept proved a hit with housewife shoppers, and by 1959 there were around one thousand supermarkets nationwide. By the late 1960s, turnover at the supermarkets run by Daiei, Seiyū, Jasco, and others would be outstripping the once dominant department stores.

Behind these transformations in the economy lay an energy revolution during the 1950s. The relatively poor quality of Japanese coal, the difficulty of mining it, and ongoing labor strife in the industry encouraged a gradual shift to cheaper crude oil from the Middle East. Initially, the Japanese government's energy policy was focused on self-sufficiency. Herein, the coal industry was to be remodeled to make it competitive with imported energy substitutes like crude oil, in turn limiting the outflow of foreign reserves. Memories of the Allied oil embargo during the Asia-Pacific War deeply informed this perspective. But, throughout the decade, policy-makers were forced to concede that domestic coal could not compete with imported oil either on price or utility. The development of massive oil tankers—of which Japan was a leading producer—meant that oil prices continued to decrease. Moreover, the emergence of the petrochemical industry, particularly in the production of ethylene for use in metal fabrication, anesthetics, refrigerants, rubber, and plastics, made oil all the more appealing. Cheap imported oil also proved attractive to the new electric utilities, which were established nationwide in 1952 to provide generation and distribution. As a result, in the years 1955 to 1960, reliance on imported primary energy increased from 24 percent to 44.2 percent, coal use decreased from 49.2 percent to 41.5 percent, and consumption of oil increased from 20.2 percent to 37.7 percent.[32]

A Society in Transition

The 1950s also witnessed an efflorescence of culture as the Japanese looked to the future while reconsidering their recent tribulations. Writers began to examine Japan's war experience in novels such as Ōoka Shōhei's *Nobi* (*Fires on the Plain*) of 1951, which explored the mental devastation of a lone Japanese soldier in the Philippines during the war, and Yoshida Mitsuru's *Senkan Yamato no Saigo* (*Requiem for Battleship Yamato*), written in 1945 but not published until 1952 due to Occupation censorship. *Requiem* recounted Yoshida's direct experience of the tragic sinking of the massive battleship and death of most of the crew on its one-way mission to confront American forces near Okinawa in 1945. Intellectuals also began to reconsider the issue of war responsibility tackled in the early postwar years, only now some drew attention to questions of Japan's unresolved responsibility to Asia. In 1956, for instance, the philosopher and social commentator Tsurumi Shunsuke proposed the term "Fifteen-Year War" as an alternative to "Pacific War," which tended to obscure Japan's militarism in Asia due to its focus on the conflict with America.

Youth, women, and countryfolk organized a plethora of cultural circles and writing groups aimed at exploring daily life and fortifying democratic consciousness. Young men flooding back to the countryside from the battlefield formed democratic youth groups, which engaged in dance, theatre, and other cultural activities.[33] Progressive rural teachers encouraged their pupils to think about politics and democracy, most famously in the 1951 book, *Yamabiko gakkō* (Mountain echo school), edited by the Yamagata Prefecture middle-school teacher Muchaku Seikyō. This bestseller contained essays and woodcuttings by students, reflecting on their lives, aspirations, and frustrations in the new social, economic, and political realities of early 1950s Japan.[34] New lifestyle magazines such as *Ashi* (The reed) and *Jinsei techō* (Life notes) offered youth similar outlets for expressing their innermost hopes and anxieties and their strong desire for democratic self-cultivation. In factories, workers organized cultural circle movements, as in the Keihin industrial region of Tokyo and Yokohama where some seventy circles boasting five thousand members established the Convention of Tokyo Regional Literary Circles.[35]

Progressive academics intent on promoting popular democracy, like the sociologist Tsurumi Kazuko, organized so-called life composition circles among women factory workers to document their daily lives and consider their situation as blue-collar women on the peripheries of society. In some cases, these circles became politically active, as at the Omi Silk Yarn Spinning Company in 1954, where female workers involved in circle activities conducted a "human rights strike," demanding recognition of their labor union, opposing compulsory participation in religious rituals, seeking privacy for personal correspondence and personal belongings, and demanding freedom to marry.[36]

Together with such organized activities, other forms of leisure proliferated throughout the decade. Indicative of the transitional nature of the moment, traditional forms of leisure endured alongside the new pastimes of an emergent mass society. In the countryside, free time was often spent close to home in community and religious events. In the cities, children still played outdoors and frequented local book rental stores and candy shops. But the spread of mass communications and the new retail economy were simultaneously transforming the terrain of leisure. Popular music, radio, weekly magazines, and cinema captured the attention of the masses, with the 1950s representing a golden age for movie theatres and magazines alike. In 1954, cinema audiences gasped in fear at *Godzilla,* the story of a monster from the Jurassic period that attacks Tokyo after being disturbed by hydrogen bomb tests (like the one performed by the United States in Bikini Atoll). The film director, Kurosawa Akira, received international acclaim with his masterpiece, *The Seven Samurai,* in the same year. Teenage sensation Misora Hibari's songs dominated the airwaves with hits such as *Tokyo Kiddo* and *Ringo Oiwake.* As the decade progressed, television ownership soared (as detailed later in this chapter), heralding a move away from the collective leisure pursuits of the early 1950s in favor of more passive, individualized patterns of leisure. Some observers even began expressing concern about this mass society, as with the scholar Matsushita Keiichi who, in 1956, warned that this new social formation was eating away at the political consciousness of the masses, making them apathetic and prone to manipulation by technocrats. Given the massive protests of a few years hence, Matsushita was proven wrong, but his identification of a society undergoing rapid massification was right on target.

Figure 3.8. Muchaku Seikyō's *Yamabiko gakkō* (Mountain echo school). Seidōsha, 1951.

Figure 3.9. Promotional poster for the first *Godzilla* film in 1954. Toho Company Ltd.

The countryside was not immune to the changes unfolding during this transitional decade. Until around 1955, life in the countryside remained much as it had been during the prewar years. The influx of millions of returnees from the colonies and battlefields in 1945 boosted the rural population, which would remain relatively unchanged from war's end to the mid-1950s (although decreasing as a proportion of the absolute population). But from 1955 to 1960, the agricultural workforce began to decrease, as countryfolk—mainly youth—moved to the big cities in search of work. During this half decade, the rural workforce decreased by over two million. Interestingly, as the workforce was decreasing, from 1951 to 1960, agricultural output actually increased by some 14 percent, evidencing how rural labor productivity was on the rise. These productivity gains were made possible thanks to the use of fertilizers and pesticides, new seed varieties, and machinery.[37] Gains were made in almost all areas, including livestock, sericulture, rice cultivation, vegetables, and fruits. With more time on their hands and more opportunities to pursue, the number of part-time farmers with side employment also increased throughout the 1950s.

The other side of this story of gradual rural depopulation was the surge in urbanization in big cities like Tokyo, Osaka, and Nagoya, whose populations doubled in the 1950s, fed by the flow of rural migrants. The beginning of the so-called Jinmu economic boom in 1954 encouraged many rural youth and young families to move to the cities in search of an affluent lifestyle. Beginning in 1955, thousands of rural youth boarded trains bound for the industrial regions of Tokyo, Osaka, and Nagoya, where they took on jobs in large and small factories and retail stores. Despite their dreams, migration to the city was not always easy for these "golden eggs" (*kin no tamago*), as they were known. They tended to fill positions shunned by city dwellers and, as a result, changed jobs regularly, making life in the city quite challenging for many.

As urbanization intensified, a "donut pattern" began to emerge in the big metropolises, with the population of inner-city areas like Tokyo's Chiyoda ward decreasing, while in outer areas like Mitaka and Koganei it increased. A similar phenomenon unfolded in the prefectures of Saitama, Chiba, and Kanagawa, which served as suburban bedroom communities for the white-collar employees who squeezed onto overcrowded commuter trains bound for Tokyo on workdays.

Material culture began its transformation in the 1950s, fueled by the surging urban population. The once rice-based diet of the Japanese was now complemented by consumption of other staples such as bread and noodles. Protein consumption increased dramatically, especially animal proteins like meat, dairy, and eggs. Western imports featured more prominently in the Japanese diet, with consumption of chewing gum, cola, chocolate, butter, beer, and whiskey all proliferating. Processed and instant foods like canned sausages, instant ramen, and instant soup

Figure 3.10. A group initiation ceremony for junior high school graduates from Niigata Prefecture at the Sakura Shinmachi Shopping Center in Setagaya Ward, Tokyo, in March 1956. Local store owners hired fifty-three middle-school graduates from Niigata. In addition to the shop owners, female customers can also be seen (to the right) attending the ceremony. Courtesy of The Asahi Shimbun Company.

captured the attention of consumers as they strolled the aisles of supermarkets. The Nissin Corporation caused a craze in 1958 with the release of its Chikin Ramen, which, although relatively expensive, quickly became a best seller among consumers for its taste and convenience. Growing affluence also meant that, by the late 1950s, urbanites were spending up to 10 percent of their food expenses on dining out.[38]

Like diet, clothing and clothing practices transitioned in the 1950s. Polyester, for example, became very popular for business shirts and blouses due to its durability, washability, and ease of ironing.[39] Its spread reflected the growing popularity of Western-style clothing more generally. Of course, echoes of the past remained: in the 1950s women still spent over two hours daily on sewing (more and more on electric machines), and it was not until the end of the decade that mass-produced underwear began to replace hand-knitted cotton underwear.[40]

Increased consumption of consumer durables like televisions, rice cookers, and refrigerators is another striking feature of material culture in 1950s Japan. Throughout the decade, ordinary Japanese strove to save enough to buy the "three sacred treasures," a term borrowed from imperial myth. Rather than the emperor's mythic jewel, sword, and mirror, however, the treasures were now a black-and-white television, an electric washing machine, and an electric refrigerator. Indeed, 1953 became known as "year one of the home appliance age" (*denka gannen*), as the three sacred treasures were joined by automatic rice cookers, juicers, electric blankets, transistor radios, and tape recorders. When the national broadcaster, Nippon Hōsō Kyōkai (NHK), began television broadcasting in January 1953, the 140,000-yen price tag for a television proved out of reach for most Japanese. Instead, people gathered around televisions placed in shop windows, outside train stations, in cafes and restaurants, or even at the homes of wealthy neighbors, where they watched popular sports like baseball, sumo, and professional wrestling. But, as incomes increased and unit prices dropped, television sales surged. In 1956—the beginning of the television set boom—156,000 units were sold, climbing to 750,000 in 1957, 1.56 million in 1958, and 3.29 million in 1959. The completion of Tokyo Tower in 1958, which made possible the establishment of numerous commercial television stations, followed by the

Figure 3.11. People gather to watch a live TV broadcast of the 35th National High School Baseball Championship Tournament (Kōshien) in August 1953. Courtesy of The Asahi Shimbun Company.

royal wedding of Crown Prince Akihito and his commoner bride Shōda Michiko in 1959, provided yet another boost to television sales late in the decade.

Of course, not all was perfect in this emergent consumer paradise. Urbanization brought with it a range of undesirable problems such as environmental pollution and, most acutely, housing challenges. As the economy grew throughout the 1950s, wages naturally increased, but in the largest cities land prices skyrocketed, with the cost of residential land tripling in the years 1955 to 1960. These soaring land prices made the dream of home ownership impossible for many who were left with no choice but to rent. In turn, housing supply came under great pressure. In the last five years of the 1950s, the number of households renting jumped from 146,500 to 833,600.[41] Many families were forced to stay in cheap apartment blocks with a single Japanese-style room, a small closet, no bathroom, and a shared toilet. The more affluent were able to secure a public apartment in one of the *danchi,* the medium-rise complexes constructed by regional governments and the Japan Housing Corporation established in 1955. Located on outskirts of large metropolises or in surrounding prefectures, the *danchi* contained anywhere from one

Figure 3.12. An aerial photo of the massive Senriyama *danchi* in Osaka Prefecture. The *Asahi shinbun* reported that residents—*danchizoku*—tended to stay aloof from residents of surrounding communities, forming their own internal residents' associations (1958). Courtesy of The Asahi Shimbun Company.

thousand to three thousand apartments, each with around two bedrooms, a dining-kitchen area, toilet, and bathroom. *Danchi* residents—so-called *danchizoku* or the *danchi* tribe—were predominantly white-collar employees and more educated compared to those renting cheaper, privately-owned apartments.

As the 1950s drew to a close, Japanese conservatives boasted strong control over national politics even while the left, led by the united JSP, stood as a roadblock in the way of constitutional revision. Economic bureaucrats, together with business leaders and the conservatives, were intensely focused on making Japan into an international economic powerhouse, and their support for targeted industries like shipbuilding and steel seemed to be moving the economy in a positive direction. The daily lives of many Japanese also began to improve as the hardships of the wartime and early postwar slowly gave way to a brighter future of unconstrained consumption and increasing leisure. Rural youth flocked to the big cities in search of this better life. Urbanization, mass communications, mass culture, and rising affluence had the effect of reducing diversity in the direction of more standardized lifeways—a process that would only intensify thereafter.

Yet standardization did not mean an end to disparity and discrimination. Groups such as resident Koreans and Chinese, discriminated outcast (Burakumin) communities, and atomic bomb victims faced immense obstacles in a society where difference was becoming more difficult. The people of Okinawa were still under US military administration and local communities across the archipelago endured the inconvenience of living beside military bases. Disparities persisted between those working in large and small companies, the lesser and more-highly educated, the urban centers and the peripheries, and men and women.

Finally, by the end of the decade, the single-minded focus on economic growth was beginning to take its toll on the environment and human health, first apparent with the identification in 1956 of methylmercury poisoning among residents of Minamata Bay in southern Japan. Many of these problems would rise to the surface—sometimes in the form of fierce and violent protest—as the Japanese economic miracle unfolded throughout the 1960s.

CHAPTER FOUR

The Age of the Economy, 1960–1973

The Anpo Treaty Crisis and Miike Strike

When Hatoyama Ichirō retired from politics in 1956, Ishibashi Tanzan assumed the LDP presidency following a nail-biting contest with Kishi Nobusuke. Kishi had ranked first after the initial vote only to lose in the run-off to Ishibashi, now supported by the third-ranked candidate's faction. Different from both Hatoyama and Kishi, Ishibashi was a moderate on national security and constitutional matters, preferring to focus on the economy and full employment with his finance minister and Yoshida progeny, Ikeda Hayato. As the first postwar prime minister to have graduated from a private university and worked in journalism, Ishibashi was hailed by the media as a "people's prime minister." But his leadership was short-lived, coming to an end just nine weeks after it began due to pneumonia aggravated by the stresses of trying to hold together a cabinet comprising political and ideological rivals—notably Kishi, who served as deputy prime minister and minister for foreign affairs under Ishibashi.

With Ishibashi's exit, the way was now open for Kishi to step into the LDP leadership, heralding one of the most tumultuous chapters in postwar Japanese history. A graduate of the elite Tokyo Imperial University (later the University of Tokyo), Kishi cut his bureaucratic teeth as an official in the Ministry of Industry and Commerce during the 1930s, later working in occupied Manchuria, where he played a critical role in the development of Japan's puppet state, Manchukuo. During the war, Kishi served as deputy minister of munitions in the Tōjō cabinet, a role that resulted in his arrest by the Occupation authorities in 1945 on suspicion of Class A war crimes. Thanks to the shift in American priorities, Kishi's fortunes changed dramatically in 1948 when he and other detainees were released without trial, a day after the execution of the defendants found guilty in the Tokyo Tribunal. Depurged in 1952, Kishi quickly reentered politics, successfully running for the House of Representatives in the April 1953 election as a member of Yoshida's Liberal Party. After helping orchestrate the formation of the LDP in 1955, Kishi became secretary general of the party, setting his sights on the leadership, which he captured in February 1957 on Ishibashi's sudden retirement.

With Kishi's ascent, Ishibashi's economic approach gave way to the hawkish agenda earlier pursued by Hatoyama that was based on constitutional revision, rearmament, and the revival of nationalism. Starkly different from the economic liberalism of Yoshida, Kishi—thanks to his bureaucratic pedigree and experiences—saw a strong role for the state in the economy and society. Under his watch, both the National Health Insurance Law (1958) and the National Pension Law (1959) were passed, putting in place Japan's postwar welfare system. What worried many, however, was Kishi's designs for national security and remilitarization. Based on the First Defense Build Up Plan of 1957, shortly after assuming office, Kishi used the LDP's majority in the Diet to push through amendments to the two self-defense laws, which resulted in an increase of some ten thousand SDF personnel. As a staunch anti-communist, Kishi remained firmly committed to the US-Japan alliance, but he also wanted to remedy what he saw as Japan's subordination to America by reviving the imperial "grandeur" of the country's past. Kishi's confrontational and arrogant style only further aggravated his adversaries both within and beyond the LDP. Just months after assuming the party presidency, Kishi provoked controversy when he told a House of Councillors committee that the new constitution did not necessarily ban the possession of nuclear weapons for the country's self-defense.

But Kishi's most provocative act while in office was to undertake a revision of the Anpo Treaty as a first step toward his holy grail of constitutional revision and the restoration of genuine national independence. Kishi knew, of course, that such a move would likely provoke hostility and possibly even combative dissent from the left, so in 1957 and 1958 he moved to strengthen his position with several preemptive initiatives. To dent the influence of leftist educators, particularly those active in the peace movement, in 1957 the Kishi administration implemented a new performance evaluation system for teachers, rating them on a scale of A to E in terms of ability and attitude. Members of the militant Japan Teachers Union, Nikkyōsō, quickly mobilized in opposition to what they saw as a blatant LDP attempt to blunt opposition to its policies. Their movement drew support among intellectuals and activists across the nation who labeled the government's move as a revival of prewar thought control. Despite such protestations, however, the system was duly implemented.

Further fanning anti-Kishi sentiment, in late 1958 the government announced its intent to revise the Police Duties Performance Law, giving police enhanced powers to search citizens' possessions and premises without a warrant. Because the proposed revisions gave police the authority to act preemptively, opponents feared that the new powers would be utilized to stifle dissent and suppress unions and other mass movements. The weekly magazine *Shūkan myōjō* went even further, running an article titled "The fearsome police are back—the date-busting Police Duties

Law."[1] The article warned that the revisions would resurrect the prewar conditions when police regularly stopped youth and couples for arbitrary questioning.

Worried about the electoral blowback and opposed to Kishi's high-handed approach, Ikeda Hayato and Miki Takeo, both ministers in Kishi's cabinet, resigned in protest. Some sixty-five civic groups led by the labor organization Sōhyō, the JSP, and others formed the National Council Opposing Revision of the Police Duties Law, which engaged in a series of united actions across the nation involving millions of workers and ordinary citizens. Determined to proceed with the revisions, Kishi had the Diet session extended in November 1958 so he could ramrod the law through both houses. But this move backfired spectacularly as many more citizens were provoked to join the protests. Forced into a corner, Kishi and the LDP were left with no choice but to scrap the amendments.

Kishi may have lost the Police Duties Performance Law struggle, but he refused to let this stifle his drive for revision of the Anpo Treaty. Following intensive negotiations with the American government, in January 1960 Kishi travelled to Washington, DC—after fighting through protests trying to block his departure from Haneda Airport—where he signed the revised treaty with President Dwight Eisenhower. As discussed in chapter 3, the original Anpo Treaty signed in 1951 had arguably institutionalized Japan's subservient independence to its Pacific ally, especially in how it exempted US personnel from domestic laws, put no obligation on America to defend Japan, and allowed the United States to suppress domestic unrest if requested by the Japanese government. For their part, the Americans were open to treaty revision to the extent that this would buttress their anti-communist strategy of containing the PRC and the USSR. They wanted an increasingly affluent Japan to provide greater economic assistance to non-communist Asian nations, as well as for Japan to assume greater responsibility in mutual self-defense in the Pacific region. In this sense, Kishi's desire for a more balanced treaty corresponded nicely with American designs for greater Japanese load sharing under the agreement.

The revised treaty and associated agreements clarified these issues and arguably produced a more bilaterally balanced relationship than before. To begin with, the new treaty more clearly—although not categorically—specified America's duty to defend Japan under the rubric of collective self-defense, which required mutual military support if either side came under attack on Japanese soil. To this end, the Japanese promised to strengthen their SDF capability and to maintain financial and logistical support for US forces in Japan. Different from the earlier agreement, the Americans consented to "prior consultation" with the Japanese before making major adjustments to the stationing of military bases and facilities in Japan, as well as before deploying forces in Japan for operations in the Far East or beyond. This so-called Far East clause in the revised treaty caused a degree of consternation among opponents, as it seemed to imply that the US military could use any of its forces in Japan for conflicts in the Far East, leaving Japan vulnerable to attack in the event of a war in the region. The US also agreed to notify Japan before bringing in atomic weapons, which also brought the nuclear issue to public attention. Kishi and supporters of the revised Anpo Treaty pushed back against such apprehensions, arguing that the removal of US military powers to quell domestic dissent, the requirements for prior consultation, and the ability of either side to rescind the treaty after ten years (with twelve months' notice) made the agreement far more equitable and was to be welcomed in the national interest.

While many Japanese appear to have initially supported Kishi's aims to make the treaty more equal, as they learned about the new obligations, like the duty of mutual military self-defense, and as they considered the risks of Japan becoming embroiled in a US war—possibly nuclear—in the Far East, opinions began to shift. Kishi's aim of using the Anpo revision as a stepping stone to revise the constitution and remilitarize also ran against the grain of a deep-seated pacifist sentiment in the country. Opponents began mobilizing in opposition from as early as 1959, most notably in the National Council to Prevent Revision of the US-Japan Security Treaty formed in March of that year as an outgrowth of the earlier mobilizations against the Police Duties Performance Law. Member organizations of the council included the JSP, JCP, Sōhyō, and antiatomic weapons groups. The movement quickly spread nationwide, with branches in all prefectures by August 1959 and eventually over two thousand groups affiliating themselves with the struggle.

Beginning in April 1959, the National Council led a series of twenty-three united actions opposing the treaty renewal. Hundreds and thousands of people across the archipelago became involved. Other groups also began to organize, like the intellectuals who formed the Anpo Problem Research Group in July and the Group to Criticize the Anpo Treaty established in October by writers, commentators, filmmakers, performers, and other creative artists. In December 1959, the Peace Problems Symposium, which had actively opposed the initial treaty in the early 1950s, resumed activities, issuing a statement opposing the treaty renewal.

Not all was smooth sailing among treaty opponents, however. In September 1960, Nishio Suehiro and members of the JSP's right wing quit the party following disagreements over the JSP's strategy and its approach to the Anpo Treaty opposition. In turn, they formed the center-left Democratic Socialist Party (DSP). More broadly, opponents brought a mishmash of motives and agendas to the struggle—some wanting to defend democracy against the revival of prewar politicians like Kishi, others fearful of Japan becoming involved in another destructive war, and still others quixotically hoping for revolution.

The haughty Kishi was unperturbed by such civic rumblings and, in May 1960, after continued obstruction by the opposition parties following the introduction of the treaty for Diet approval in February, he determined to take decisive action. With thousands of protesters surrounding the Diet, just before midnight on the evening of May 19, Kishi ordered police to physically remove JSP and other opposition politicians who had been preventing the speaker of the lower house from leaving his office to proceed to the chamber. With his path cleared, the speaker called the lower house to order, after which a fifty-day extension to the regular Diet session was approved by attending LDP members. As the clock ticked past midnight to June 20, the speaker called a new session to order, at which time the treaty was passed by LDP politicians in the absence of the opposition parties and some LDP members who boycotted the vote in protest. Under Diet procedures, if a treaty was passed by the lower house, it would be automatically ratified thirty days later even if it had not passed the upper house. This "midnight coup d'état," as some called it, meant that the treaty would be automatically ratified on June 19 in time for a planned visit by President Eisenhower to celebrate the accomplishment.

Kishi was well aware that the treaty revision would be controversial. The Police Duties Performance Law protests had presaged the potential for conflict. But few could have anticipated the explosion of dissent following the events of May 19 and 20. Throughout May and June, millions of citizens—some belonging to organizations, others nonaligned—engaged in massive demonstrations around the Diet building and across Japan. On June 4, some five million came out onto the streets demanding the dissolution of the Diet and the resignation of the Kishi cabinet, while thirteen million signed a petition calling for immediate elections. Six days later, the American presidential secretary, James Haggarty—in Japan to discuss Eisenhower's visit—had to be rescued by a US military helicopter after his automobile was surrounded by enraged students and other protesters near Haneda Airport.

Intellectuals became vocal mouthpieces for the struggle. Writing in the monthly magazine *Sekai* in May 1960, the sociologist and critic, Shimizu Ikutarō, implored people to "go to the Diet now," while the Sinologist Takeuchi Yoshimi quit his position at Tokyo Metropolitan University in protest, saying that the struggle was quite simply one between "democracy" and "despotism." Many ordinary citizens, who had not previously been involved in political protest, felt impelled to join the struggle. The Voiceless Voices Group formed by the artist Kobayashi Tomi during the protests became a magnet for these "nonaligned citizens," including many housewives, small business owners, and white-collar workers, who did not belong to mainstream political or labor organizations. The group took its name from comments by Kishi at a press conference in June when he had said that he would not resign and that it was his duty to listen to the voices of the voiceless, like the people happily shopping in the Ginza area of Tokyo, those packing movie cinemas, or fans attending baseball games—all of whom were not part of the struggle.

Nonetheless, the protests continued to escalate, reaching a climax on June 15, when students and others broke through the police barricade and stormed the Diet precincts. In the ensuing clashes, a young female student activist from the University of Tokyo, Kanba Michiko, was trampled to death and around six hundred others were injured. The following day, Eisenhower's visit was formally cancelled and the tenor of public opinion began to shift. Major newspapers, which had been highly critical of Kishi, now questioned student violence and began calling for the "defense of parliamentary politics."

At midnight on June 19, the Anpo Treaty was automatically ratified, still not having passed through the upper house. An embattled Kishi released a statement

Figure 4.1. Students demonstrating against the renewal of the US-Japan Security Treaty force their way into the Diet premises through the south gate on June 15, 1960. The violent clash with riot squads resulted in numerous injuries and the death of a female student, Kanba Michiko. Courtesy of The Asahi Shimbun Company.

saying that his cabinet would resign once the revision process was finally settled—which happened on July 18. With Eisenhower's visit cancelled, the ratified documents were unobtrusively exchanged with American officials at the Japanese foreign minister's residence in late June, along with a Status of Forces Agreement that put administration of US military bases in American hands, exempted the US military from domestic taxes, and maintained extraterritoriality for US military personnel.

For Kishi and hawkish nationalists in the LDP, it was a pyrrhic victory. They had hoped the treaty would be the first step toward constitutional revision, remilitarization, and greater Japanese autonomy, but the outcome was remarkably different. Thereafter, the issue of constitutional revision would fade from political debate for many decades. The SDF would continue to grow, but it would never be recognized as a military in the formal sense, and the United States would maintain and even extend its influence over Japanese security and international relations. For all his desire to break the subservient independence of the Yoshida Doctrine, Kishi's arrogance and confrontational approach had arguably made it even stronger. The stage was now set for a shift from politically divisive issues to something almost everyone could agree on: economic growth.

Before turning to that discussion, however, one further upheaval of the time demands attention because its dénouement also helped lay the foundation for government policy and industrial development thereafter. This was the so-called Mitsui Miike coal mine strike of 1959 and 1960. The origins of this dispute lay in Japan's energy transition from coal to cheap oil from the Middle East, which resulted in the consecutive closure and downscaling of coal mines around the country at this time. In the summer of 1959, the Mitsui Corporation announced that 1,278 out of the fifteen thousand employees at the mine in northern Kyūshū were to be dismissed, including around three hundred activists in the union. The company hoped that removal of these workplace activists would break the back of a powerful union that had negotiated very favorable working conditions for miners and threatened to obstruct future rationalization. The ensuing strike lasted for 312 days and involved a company lockout, clashes between striking workers and members of a cooperative second union formed in March 1960, and the fatal stabbing of a union leader by organized crime thugs.

After failed attempts at governmental mediation, the dispute reached its climax in mid-1960 when workers occupied the mine's coal hoppers. In response, the company sent in ten thousand police to face off with twenty thousand armed protesters who had been preventing second union members from entering the premises to work. Faced with impending bloodshed, the striking union had no choice but to relent and accept the government mediation proposal in full, effectively resulting in defeat. Throughout the dispute, the striking workers were supported by Sōhyō,

Figure 4.2. Striking workers of the militant first union clash with members of the cooperative second union who attempted to forcibly enter the Mitsui Miike coal mine to begin working on March 28, 1960, after sixty-four days of lockout. Many on both sides were injured in the melee. Courtesy of The Asahi Shimbun Company.

the Japan Coal Miners Union, and student organizations like Zengakuren, while the Mitsui mine management received support from the business sector. This division led some to label the struggle as a decisive battle between Capital and Labor. It is certainly true that the victory of management over contentious unionists at Miike represented more than the growing pains of an energy transition from domestic coal to imported petroleum. It also signaled the wider decline of contentious labor activism in Japan. Both outcomes would deeply shape subsequent economic growth.

Income Doubling and Industrial Transformation

After the tumult of 1959 and 1960, the political sphere was primed for change, which came in the form of a new LDP prime minister, Ikeda Hayato, in July 1960. The Americans offered their support in 1961 when the newly elected president, John

F. Kennedy, appointed Edwin O. Reischauer—a Japanese history professor at Harvard University—as US ambassador to Japan. Reischauer was charged with helping to recalibrate America's public image in the country. Ikeda, as noted earlier, was a Yoshida progeny from the bureaucratic (LP) lineage of the LDP with impeccable economic credentials, having served as minister in one or other of the economic bureaucracies under Yoshida, Ishibashi, and Kishi. On assuming the prime ministership, Ikeda distanced himself from Kishi's confrontational style, declaring his intention to pursue a politics of "tolerance and perseverance" through cooperation with "friends" in the JSP, JCP, and DSP. Instead of contentious issues like national security or constitutional revision, Ikeda would pursue a low-posture agenda focused on economic growth, certainly because of his own expertise, but also as a shrewd political strategy to cultivate public support for a bruised LDP. Indeed, so associated with economic growth did Ikeda become, that the French president Charles de Gaulle supposedly labelled him a "transistor salesman" after their meeting in 1962.[2] The mass media noted this shift in priorities, announcing the end of the "season of politics" and beginning of the "season of the economy"—although subsequent civic and student activism in the decade would undermine a simplistic switch from politics to economics.[3]

The centerpiece of Ikeda's agenda was the National Income Doubling Plan, approved by his cabinet in December 1960. Under this plan, both national income (gross national product or GNP) and the average wage were forecast to double in ten years based on a projected annual average growth rate of 7.2 percent. The plan aimed for full employment, improvements in infrastructure, enhanced international economic competitiveness, technological innovation, and rising labor efficiency. Steel, shipbuilding, petrochemicals, and consumer durables like automobiles, electrical goods, and synthetic fibers were all identified as strategic industries, while agriculture was earmarked for supported rationalization and other "sunset" industries for gradual phasing out.

Although a refreshing change after the confrontational politics of Kishi, the Income Doubling Plan was by no means a hurried exercise in damage control, tracing its roots to discussions in the prime minister's powerful Economic Advisory Council during the Kishi administration. As minister of state and then minister of international trade and industry under Kishi, Ikeda began advocating early on for a "doubling of monthly salaries." The New Long-Term Economic Plan of December 1957 also included many elements of the later income-doubling initiative. Kishi's designs for treaty renewal and constitutional revision, however, overshadowed these economic aspirations throughout 1959 and early 1960.

On assuming office in July 1960, Ikeda quickly pushed the economy to the top of his policy agenda, rewording "salary doubling" to "income doubling" to encompass the core LDP constituencies of farmers and small- and medium-sized enterprises. A meeting with Bank of Japan governor, Shimomura Osamu, in September 1960 confirmed for Ikeda that an annual growth rate of 9 percent was entirely reasonable and, hence, the 7.2 percent of the plan almost guaranteed. In fact, the economy was already beginning to surge in the late 1950s, averaging over 8 percent growth in the four years from FY1956 and recording a stunning 11.2 percent growth in FY1959 alone. In hindsight, the growth projection in the plan was quite conservative.

State-led infrastructural development was a core element of the plan, which envisaged the evolution of a "Pacific belt" along the east coast of the archipelago, absorbing labor from agricultural regions and evenly dispersing industry. Under the First National Comprehensive Development Plan (Zensō) of August 1962, a system of "nodal development" around the four major industrial regions of Keihin (Tokyo), Chūkyō (Nagoya), Hanshin (Osaka), and Kitakyūshū (Kyūshū) was adopted. Fifteen municipalities were approved as New Industrial Cities following an intensive lobbying campaign by regional administrations, while a further six areas were designated as Special Industrial Improvement Zones. Government funds were made available to support the construction of large infrastructure projects like ports and petrochemical combines. The famed industrial policy of Japan's postwar developmental state arguably reached its zenith through the Income Doubling Plan and related plans like Zensō.

As discussed in chapter 3, in the early postwar era and stretching into the 1950s, MITI implemented industrial policy through formal tools like control over foreign exchange and the issuing of technology licenses. The Ministry of Finance (MOF) and Bank of Japan crafted policies aimed at encouraging businesses to utilize bank loans over stock equity for capital raising to foster a culture of long-term investment over short-term profit seeking. In turn, these financial policies encouraged large conglomerates to reorganize around powerful banks, which made lending decisions based on informal "window guidance" handed down by the MOF. Government economic strategies like the Income Doubling Plan, while merely forecasts, provided industry with a roadmap in terms of official thinking about the future, thus influencing investment decisions within firms.

So-called administrative guidance, in which economic bureaucracies issued nonbinding directives, notifications, and advice to firms and industries regarding their operations and behavior, became an influential tool in the implementation of the state's industrial policy. This guidance was backed up by protectionist policies, tax breaks, subsidies, and low interest loans for targeted growth industries. The system was knit together by networks of bureaucratic, political, and business elites, trained and socialized in the nation's top universities. Just as many national bureaucrats like Ikeda Hayato gravitated toward politics, so too did others transition from the bureaucracy into executive roles in financial institutions and other industries in a process colorfully known as *amakudari* or "descending from heaven" ("heaven" being the elite national public service). In this way, politics, business, and the national bureaucracy were tied together in a powerful and mutually reinforcing "iron triangle." Given the amazing growth rates, it is hardly surprising that Japan's developmental state looked to many like the perfect system for producing economic "miracles." Of course, as is usually the case, miraculous growth could not continue forever. Moreover, the farsighted decisions of elites often came at great human, social, and environmental costs.

In the short term, however, Ikeda's Income Doubling Plan was a roaring success. Confirming Governor Shimomura's predictions, from FY1960 to FY1965 real growth averaged over 9 percent and exceeded 11 percent for the 1960s overall. Nominal GNP and per capita gross domestic product (GDP) both doubled by FY1966, four years ahead of schedule. In 1968, Japanese national income outstripped the United Kingdom and West Germany, making its economy the third largest in the world after the United States and the USSR. Foreign observers began to wax lyrical about Japan. An article in the British publication, *The Economist,* applauded the country's economic "miracle" as early as 1962.[4]

At the same time, while the national economy proudly assumed its place alongside the global economic superpowers, per capita GDP in Japan ranked only twenty-fifth, just below Puerto Rico and only 30.9 percent that of the United States.[5] But no one could deny that things were getting better both individually and overall. The period from 1958 to 1970 witnessed three sustained phases of impressive economic growth: the Iwato boom (forty-two months, 1958–1961), the Olympics boom (twenty-four months, 1962–1964), and the Izanagi boom (fifty-seven months, 1965–1970) (fig. 4.3).

The transformation of Tokyo's cityscape in preparation for the 1964 Olympics and the opening of the first Shinkansen (bullet train) line in the same year served as potent physical manifestations of the unfolding economic miracle. The Tokyo Olympics—the first in Asia—ran from October 10 to 24, with 5,541 competitors from ninety-three countries. The PRC, North Korea, and Indonesia did not participate, and China's detonation of an atomic bomb during the games along with the buildup of American troops in South Vietnam cast a shadow over the event. Nonetheless, for the Japanese people, the Olympics signified the country's peaceful return to international society after the destruction of war, occupation, and recovery. Those lucky enough to obtain tickets filled the majestic Olympic venues, while many others replaced their black-and-white televisions with the latest color models. Although there had been public rumblings over the cost of holding the event, medal-winning performances by Japanese athletes aroused a kind of

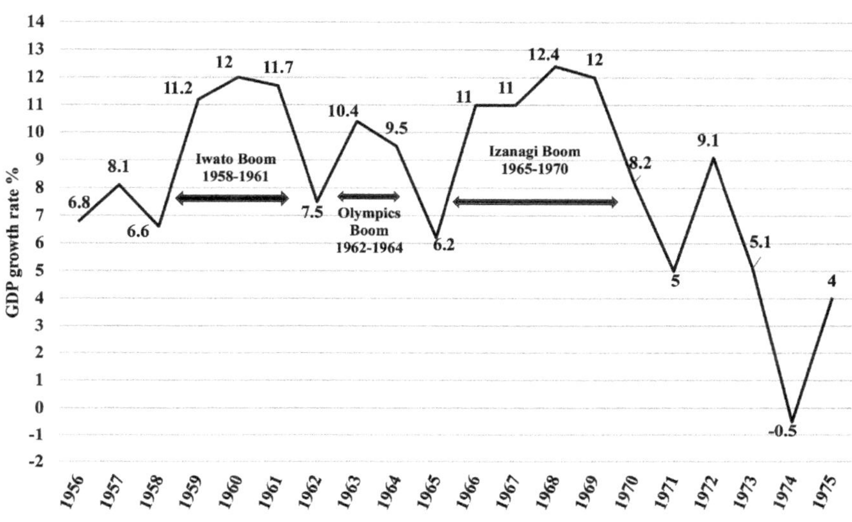

Source: Naikakufu Keizai Shakai Sōgō Kenkyūjo, "Kokumin Keizai Keisan (GDP Tōkei)."

Figure 4.3. Annual Growth of Real GDP of Japan, 1956–1975

Olympic fever across the country. Television ratings soared into the mid-eightieth percentile for the women's volleyball final in which the smaller Japanese—known as the "Witches of the Orient" for their superhuman ability—triumphed over their intimidating Soviet rivals to capture the gold medal. Sociologists at the time noted a significant change in Japanese national consciousness thanks to the Olympics: prior to the games, there had been a great reticence toward national symbols, but now many more citizens seemed to have lost their antipathy toward the flag and national anthem.[6]

The government, firmly on the path of national income doubling, used the event as an opportunity for social and economic renovation in Tokyo and beyond. Leading into the games, the government instituted various social campaigns aimed at ensuring the country would project an image of technological and cultural modernity equal to the West. Residents of Tokyo and elsewhere were encouraged to participate in urban cleaning initiatives and movements for personal hygiene and physical fitness. The Tokyo Bureau of Sanitation issued millions of plastic buckets to citizens for trash collection by a shiny new fleet of waste collection trucks. Teachers exhorted students to become involved through comparisons with great cities like New York where there was "not a single piece of trash on the ground."[7] Local municipalities did their part, issuing ordinances restricting the use of billboards

Figure 4.4. The Japanese team enters the National Stadium at the opening ceremony of the Tokyo Olympic Games on October 10, 1964. Courtesy of The Asahi Shimbun Company.

and the pasting of handbills and posters. Red light districts also were subjected to closer official oversight.

As officials worked to improve individual behavior, the Tokyo cityscape was transforming before residents' eyes. The completion of the Tokyo Tower in 1958—proudly nine meters higher than the Eiffel Tower—was an early sign of things to come. Prior to the Olympics, grand hotels like the Okura and Otani opened for business. In 1968, the thirty-six-story Kasumigaseki Building, Japan's first modern skyscraper, opened in central Tokyo. The nation's transport infrastructure was also upgraded. In 1960, only 32 percent of Japan's roads were improved, but this figure stood at 59 percent by 1965 and it had reached 84 percent by 1970. Construction began on the Tokyo Metropolitan Expressway in 1960. By 1964, a 33-kilometer loop had been completed connecting Haneda Airport, central Tokyo, and Shinjuku and Shibuya on the west of the city. The construction process proved quite disruptive with around ten thousand areas excavated and over fifty thousand people forced to relocate.[8] National expressways also opened throughout the decade. In 1963 and 1968, respectively, sections of the Meishin (Nagoya-Kobe) and Tōmei

(Tokyo-Nagoya) expressways opened, funded by the World Bank and designed by the mastermind of the West German Autobahn. Thanks to this investment, Japan had the most improved roads of any industrialized nation as a proportion of national land area by the 1970s.[9] Automobile registrations increased accordingly, jumping from around 1.9 million vehicles in 1965 to 6.8 million by 1970.

Rail infrastructure was not ignored in the rush to build new roads. The Marunouchi, Hibiya, and Asakusa subways and the monorail connecting Haneda Airport to Hamamatsuchō in central Tokyo were all completed in time for the games. Most impressive of all was the opening of the Shinkansen line between Tokyo and Osaka on October 1—a mere ten days before the Olympics' opening ceremony and around one-and-a-half years ahead of schedule. The brainchild of JNR chairman, Sogō Shinji, the Shinkansen was a massive—and predictably controversial— project, with many questioning its necessity at a time when rail construction was declining globally in favor of road transport. Nonetheless, Sogō refused to give up on his dream for high-speed rail. Cabinet approval eventually came in 1958—thanks to support from Minister of Finance Satō Eisaku—on the

Figure 4.5. Japan National Railways President Ishida Reisuke officially opens the Tōkaidō Shinkansen line connecting Tokyo and Osaka at Tokyo Station on October 1, 1964. Courtesy of The Asahi Shimbun Company.

proviso that the project be partly funded by a loan from the World Bank to insulate it from the whims of domestic politics. The Shinkansen used cutting-edge aerodynamic technology from aircraft design, highly efficient carriage motors, an automatic electronic control mechanism, seamless wide-gauge long rails, and steel-reinforced concrete sleepers—all of which combined to make the journey between Tokyo and Osaka possible in just over four hours.[10] By tying together the big three east coast cities of Tokyo, Nagoya, and Osaka, the Shinkansen effectively created a new "megalopolis," while further concentrating economic, cultural, and political power in the capital.[11]

Ikeda's Income Doubling Plan also further encouraged the transformation of industry begun during the 1950s. The manufacturing industry continued its historic advance with an increase in the relative weight of value-added production in heavy and petrochemical processes like metals manufacturing, shipbuilding, chemicals, and machinery (fig. 4.6). Conversely, the manufacture of textiles decreased dramatically, replaced now by production of consumer durables like automobiles and home appliances, which began to earn export income for the country while satiating voracious domestic demand (fig. 4.7).

Companies facilitated economic growth through intensive investment in new technologies from abroad and by expanding capital investment more generally; it was this capital investment combined with domestic demand that made income doubling possible. In the 1960s, technology was responsible for up to 45 percent of

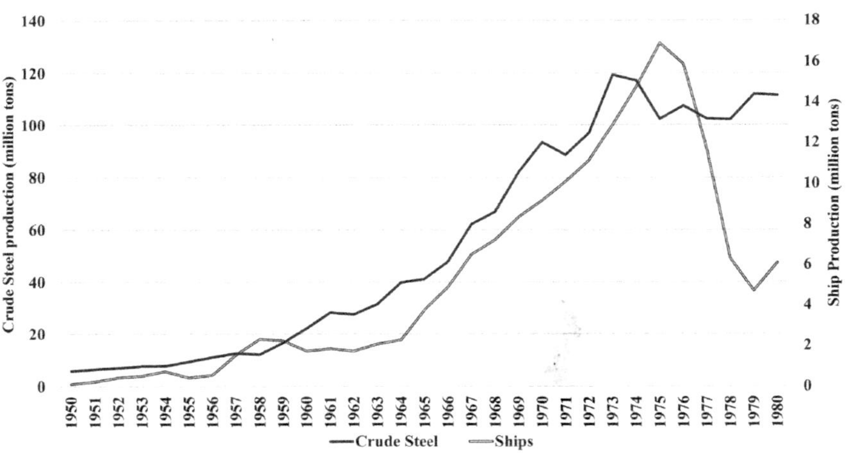

Sources: Yasutomi, "Nihon Tekkōgyō," 51; Yoshiki, "Sengo Kenzō," 172.

Figure 4.6. Annual Production of Crude Steel and Ships in Japan, 1950–1980

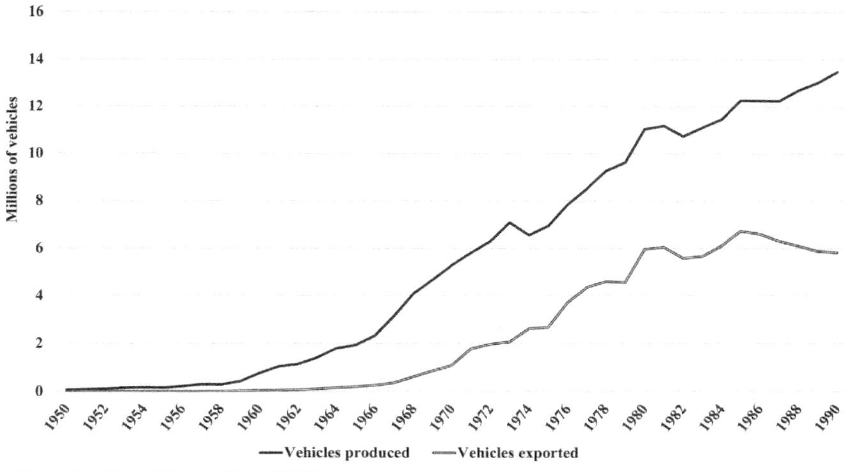

Source: Ono, "Sengo Nihon no Jidōsha," 70, 73.

Figure 4.7. Japanese Vehicle Production and Exports, 1950–1990

Japanese growth.[12] In 1962 alone, fixed capital constituted 34.4 percent of GNP in Japan compared with around 16 percent in the United States and the United Kingdom, 19.6 percent in France, and 25.3 percent in West Germany.[13] Technological improvements meant production costs decreased, resulting in a drop in the unit price of finished goods. Technological advances in the steel industry meant better quality sheet metal at lower costs, which, in turn, connected to price reductions in consumer durables like automobiles and appliances. The profits from the increased demand were subsequently reinvested in better machinery and technology—a kind of virtuous cycle that the 1960 government economic white paper described as "investment inviting investment."[14] So successful was this process that, by the end of the decade, many Japanese corporations were technologically self-sufficient and able to conduct research and development in house.[15]

This massive investment in technology and plant and equipment required a similarly impressive level of financing. As noted earlier, a feature of the Japanese economy at the time was the overwhelming reliance of industry on debt financing—in other words, bank loans—over equity raising. During the era of high-speed economic growth, around 80 to 90 percent of financing for large corporations came from bank lending, and debt-equity ratios were commonly around 75:25.[16] Corporations utilized both private banks and former public financial institutions like the Industrial Bank of Japan for capital sourcing. The banks benefited from high savings rates by ordinary depositors, a monetary policy aimed at low interest rates, and a system of "overloans" in which banks were able to loan above their deposit holdings thanks to the injection of funds (i.e., credit) from the Bank of Japan. The six largest banks were Mitsui, Mitsubishi, Sumitomo, Fuji, Daiichi (later Daiichi Kangyo), and Sanwa. Because of their role as primary capital finance providers, over time the banks came to play a role similar to the holding companies of the prewar zaibatsu, albeit through relations of debt rather than equity. What emerged in the postwar era was a new kind of business formation known in Japanese as a keiretsu. The keiretsu were usually centered on a main bank surrounded by an insurance company, a trust bank, manufacturing operations, a trading company, and often a private railway and retail operations.[17] The core bank exerted influence over other members of the keiretsu via loans, but other connections formed across the group through cross-shareholdings, regularized business dealings, and intragroup management. Moreover, thanks to the overloan system and window guidance, the MOF and Bank of Japan were able to influence the lending priorities of keiretsu banks, hence providing another mechanism for Japan's developmental state to shape economic development at the level of the firm. Within the keiretsu, so-called general trading companies (*sōgō shōsha*) managed exports and imports and formulated and implemented foreign investment projects for their groups. At their height, trading companies like Mitsui Bussan, Mitsubishi Shōji, Sumitomo, Itō Chū, Marubeni, and Nisshō-Iwai managed close to 50 percent of Japan's external trade. Under the trading companies, FDI—while still modest—increased almost sixfold between 1965 and 1970.

Located in the shadows of these massive postwar conglomerates—yet nonetheless just as important for economic growth—was the sphere of small- and medium-sized enterprises. In 1965, 83 percent of companies in Japan employed less than one thousand workers and 53 percent less than one hundred.[18] The government supported this sphere by passing several laws in 1963 aimed at raising productivity. The benefits of economic growth in the 1950s and 1960s trickled down to these subcontractors for large industry and, over time, some moved beyond subcontractor status to become internationally recognized brands in their own right. Growth also facilitated gradual improvements in technology, management, and productivity in these firms. Existence was far more uncertain for small- and medium-size enterprises when compared with the conglomerates, as it also was for workers in these operations. The subcontracting system allowed large industry to easily scale back subcontracting during business downturns simply by cancelling or decreasing orders. For the subcontractors and their employees, however, this could mean bankruptcy and unemployment. To be sure, conditions for small- and medium-sized enterprises were much better than in the prewar period, but their precarious position is a reminder that the "miracle" also involved precarity and vulnerability for many.

Income doubling and economic transformation in the 1960s also accelerated Japan's energy transition—signified most graphically in the Miike dispute. In 1960, oil represented just over 35 percent of Japan's primary energy supply and coal around 38 percent, but oil was supplying around 70 percent and coal only 21 percent by 1970.[19] Importantly, too, almost all (95 percent) of this oil was imported from the Middle East and Southeast Asia, making the Japanese economy extremely vulnerable to price variations for energy on the global market. While oil was cheap and plentiful, things were fine, and the economy benefited. But this situation could—and indeed would—be upset if international conditions changed.

The shift to imported oil was also about more than energy supply. Crude oil was the foundation of the petrochemical industry, which helped facilitate the economic miracle. Massive petrochemical complexes were constructed in Yokkaichi, Kawasaki, and elsewhere around the archipelago. Oil also became a part of daily life as kerosine heaters—first introduced in the mid-1950s as cooking stoves—proved wildly popular among consumers for their ease of use and ash-free operation compared with charcoal. Kerosine sales skyrocketed from 930,000 kiloliters in 1960 to 8.96 million by 1969.[20] Coupled with the diffusion of plastics, oil thus became a core foundation of business and daily life in income-doubling Japan.

Standardization, Transformation, Disparity

In public opinion surveys on daily life conducted annually by the Cabinet Office during the 1960s, over 90 percent of respondents consistently indicated their subjective social status as "middle class," with over 50 percent placing themselves in the "middle of the middle."[21] The fact that most people identified with the middle class in Japan is hardly surprising as this tends to be the case in most industrialized nations and even in developing countries.[22] Nonetheless, media pundits and political entrepreneurs seized on these results, proclaiming the transformation of Japan from a war-destroyed country of farmers into an "entirely middle-class nation" (*ichioku sōchūryū*). Such observations were not incorrect, although they tended to overstate the transformation in popular consciousness: even as Japanese incomes doubled throughout the decade, the number of people indicating their social status as middle class did not really increase dramatically (it was already over 90 percent), nor was there much change into the 1970s.[23]

But the rise of this discourse on middle-class consciousness is interesting from a historical perspective for two reasons. First, it alerts us to the important processes of standardization and social revolution that were engendered by the transformations of economic growth. Second, it challenges us to cast a critical eye on the realities of middle-class Japan during the 1960s. What was and was *not* changing? Did standardization under conditions of economic growth benefit everyone, as the notion of "entirely middle class" suggested, or were there forms of inequity, disparity, and discrimination built into this system? Investigating patterns of work, consumption, agriculture, as well as family, education, gender, the environment, and minorities, can help us approach these questions.

Not all observers at the time were mesmerized by the economic miracle. In the late 1950s, the political scientist Matsushita Keiichi began warning about Japan's degeneration into a mass society. Drawing on theories from the United States, Matsushita argued that Japan's new society of mass consumption and mass production, managed by state technocrats and corporate elites, was sapping the political energy of the people—particularly the working class—who seemed to be willingly trading democracy for shallow self-gratification with their washing machines, refrigerators, televisions, and two-bedroom apartments. But, throughout the 1960s, a growing cadre of antiwar, antipollution, antidevelopment, and student activists also began to mount a frontal attack on the excesses of conservative rule and economic growth. In 1970, the left-leaning *Asahi shinbun* encapsulated these concerns in a provocatively titled series, "Kutabare GNP" (To hell with GNP), while in November of the same year, the fanatical novelist Mishima Yukio and his paramilitary group, the Shield Society, attempted to provoke a coup d'état among SDF forces at the Ichigaya barracks in Tokyo.[24] Although his tactics and objectives differed dramatically from the left, Mishima shared with his leftist contemporaries a common distaste and dissatisfaction for the rampant materialism and seeming lack of political vitality among the Japanese.

On the other side, many vocally celebrated Japan's stunning achievements. During his term as US ambassador from 1961 to 1966, Edwin O. Reischauer repeatedly told Japanese audiences that their country was a success story of modernization in East Asia and hence a model for other developing nations to replicate. Although the country was sidetracked by a period of militarism, Reischauer depicted the overall direction of Japanese modern history as positive. The novelist Shiba Ryōtarō reflected this positivity in his sweeping historical novels of the time. Writing primarily for the new cadre of white-collar salarymen, Shiba's best-selling five-volume work *Ryōma ga yuku* (There goes Ryōma) (1963–1966) on the Meiji Restoration figure Sakamoto Ryōma idealized the hero's rational patriotism based on alliance building and learning from the West. Readers could quite easily project the economic and social transformation about to unfold in Meiji Japan onto the economic miracle happening before their eyes in the present.

Buoyed by the country's rising economy, the successful Tokyo Olympics, and approbation from foreign observers like *The Economist* and Reischauer, throughout the decade scholars such as Aida Yūji and Nakane Chie began to propagate a discourse on the unique and positive characteristics of the Japanese—so-called *Nihonjinron*—which contrasted dramatically with early postwar perspectives that had depicted the Japanese mentality as backward.[25] Such works would only proliferate in the coming years as the Japanese economy continued to outstrip its Western counterparts. Many of these trends were driven by a renewed national sentiment, very often inconspicuous but on occasion unabashed. In 1962, for example, the writer and ultranationalist from the prewar, Hayashi Fusao, caused a stir with a series of articles titled "Dai Tōa Sensō Kōtei Ron" (An affirmation of the Greater East Asian War) in the monthly magazine *Chūō Kōron*. Here Hayashi speciously argued that throughout its modern international history Japan had genuinely striven for the liberation of Asia from the West and had not—as history books would have it—been an aggressor against its region. Less controversial, but nonetheless a similar display of rising national sentiment, was the Meiji Centennial celebration of 1968, which, like Shiba's novel on Sakamoto Ryōma, juxtaposed the successful modernization of the Meiji era against the economic miracle of the present.

But how was this bright new life being experienced on the ground, in workplaces, in villages, and in the apartments of the teeming urban masses? Beginning with the standardized wage bargaining process—*shuntō* or the spring offensive—in the mid-1950s, and reinforced by the monumental defeat of radical labor in the Mitsui Miike dispute in 1960, labor-management relations entered an era of relatively cooperative interactions. Labor disputes were certainly not unusual during the 1960s, rising from 2,222 disputes involving 6.95 million workers in 1960 to 5,283 disputes involving 14.48 million workers in 1969.[26] But workers—both blue- and white-collar—and especially those in private sector unions were also busy forging a kind of social contract with their employers in these years.[27] Enterprise-based unions in large corporations were able to negotiate a number of core benefits for their members, including "lifetime" employment and seniority wages (both with prewar roots), as well as a range of company welfare benefits for employees and their families, like company hospitals, housing, holiday resorts and trips, and social groups for employees' spouses. Although some public sector unions remained combative and resistant to cooperation with management throughout the 1960s, leaders of cooperative private sector unions encouraged their members to adopt a moderate approach to remuneration and other benefits for the long-term well-being of their companies and, hence, their jobs. This approach made sense to many workers in an atmosphere of economic growth. Quasigovernmental organizations, such as the Japan Productivity Center, assisted in this process by sponsoring groups of employees and managers to travel to the United States to study business operations. Moreover, to placate combative public sector unions, in 1964, Prime Minister Ikeda negotiated a compact with the Sōhyō leader, Ōta Kaoru, in which it was agreed that public sector wages would mirror those in the private sector.[28]

Overall, workers benefited from this social contract, although debate remains whether they may have secured a larger slice of the growing economic pie by adopting a more confrontational approach. In 1960, wages rose by 7.8 percent, and they were rising at over 15 percent per annum by the end of the decade.[29] Significantly, income disparity also began to narrow between managers and employees, urban and rural populations, workers in different occupations, and blue- and white-collar workers. Work in family-based businesses continued its decline from the 1950s, as more and more people—men especially—entered paid employment. Thanks to expanding educational opportunities and a maturing economy, the number of white-collar workers began to increase, although most workers were still in lower-paying blue-collar jobs. The urban salaryman phenomenon had been around since the 1920s, but it was during the 1960s that it became a realizable ambition for many more young Japanese men.

Of course, the social contract was not without its shortcomings. So-called lifetime employment was not a principle set in stone, with companies pressuring employees to retire or accept lower-paying postings during downturns. Moreover, despite decreasing disparity over time, conditions for workers in large companies (both blue- and white-collar) were considerably more secure than for those in small- and medium-sized enterprises. Full-time employees—primarily men—in the large corporations could feel safe in their positions and look forward to continued welfare benefits and increasing wages throughout their careers. For this reason, they developed a sense of loyalty to their companies and were willing to accept periodic transfers separating them from their families, as well as long working hours and commuting times. For the 25 to 30 percent of workers in small- and medium-sized enterprises, existence was less certain. As noted earlier, their jobs were extremely vulnerable during economic downturns, and they did not enjoy the same benefits as their counterparts in large companies. Furthermore, while the percentage of women working outside the home increased, the gendered nature of employment practices and income tax incentives meant that they remained a peripheralized section of the workforce.

As figure 4.8 reveals, urbanization and the shift to work as an employee continued to have sweeping ramifications for rural life and agriculture in the 1960s. In 1950, some 41 percent were working in primary industries, but this figure had fallen to 32 percent by 1960 and around 19 percent by 1970 (fig. 4.9). The decrease in young agricultural workers (15–24 years of age) was particularly notable, falling from around 4.67 million in 1950 to 735,000 in 1970.[30] The number of part-time farmers also continued to increase, so much so that the term *san-chan nōgyō* entered the list of popular phrases in 1963. *San-chan* referred to the grandfathers (*jī-chan*), grandmothers (*bā-chan*), and housewives (*kā-chan*) who tended farms and looked after children while husbands worked in wage labor positions in nearby regional cities or even large metropolises. By 1965, the number of farming households whose main source of income came from outside agriculture outstripped those whose main source remained farming.[31] This shift was made possible by rapid mechanization, such as the introduction of mechanical plows, rice threshers, harvesters, and sprayers, but there were other reasons. In response to changing diet, rice production gradually decreased after peaking in 1968, with many paddy fields simply left fallow.[32] The government assisted farmers—a natural constituency of the LDP—in the transition by implementing policies to ensure that rural incomes and standards of living were not left behind compared with those of urbanites. For example, the 1961 Basic Law on Agriculture passed by the Ikeda administration aimed at raising rural productivity, income, and standards of living in the countryside. A mechanism was established under which the government purchased all rice and paid farmers a price higher than that paid by consumers. By covering the price discrepancy, the government artificially enhanced rural incomes. In 1960, average rural household incomes were only around 90 percent those of urban households, but they were close to 120 percent by 1970 and reached a high of near 140 percent in 1975.[33] Conversely, despite government subsidization, consumers were paying up to double the international price of rice.[34]

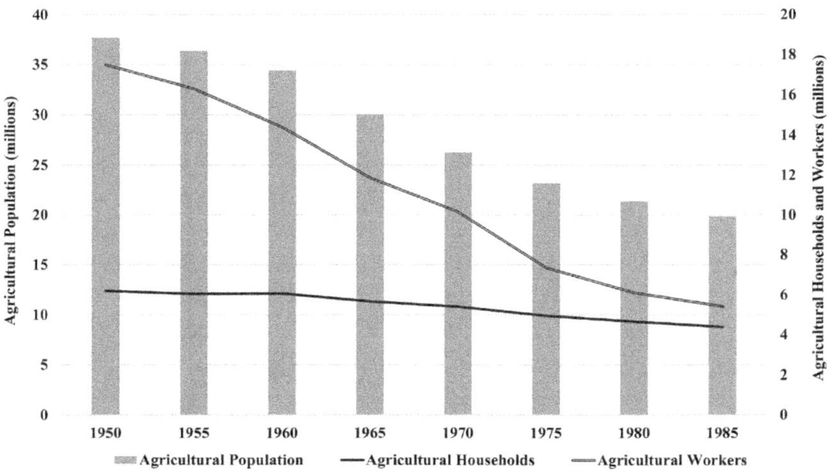

Sources: Sasaki, *Sengoshi Daijiten*, 735; Sōmushō Tōkei Kyoku, "III Henka suru Sangyō."

Figure 4.8. Agricultural Population, Households, and Workers, 1950–1985

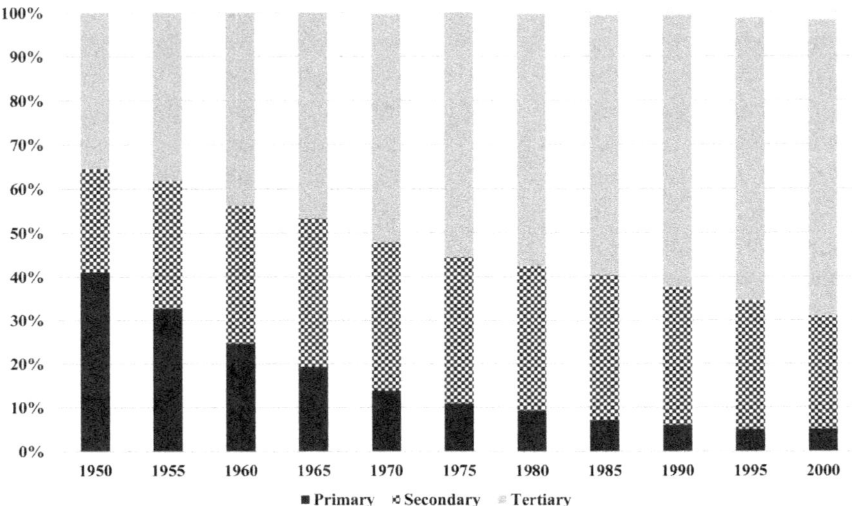

Source: Sōmushō Tōkei Kyoku, "III Henka suru Sangyō."

Figure 4.9. Sectoral Balance of Employment, 1950–2000

Consumers do not appear to have been overly distressed by expensive rice during the so-called Shōwa Genroku—a term that likened society of the 1960s to the cultural efflorescence of late seventeenth century Japan when the cash economy expanded and urban life flourished. The government was quick to identify this trend, observing the "consumption revolution" in new products, like household electrical appliances, in its economic whitepaper of 1959.[35] But the revolution went deeper, involving a fundamental transformation in the balance of household expenditure, rising discretionary consumption, and changes in diet and clothing. As figure 4.10 shows, by 1965, the three "sacred treasures"—electric refrigerators, washing machines, and black-and-white televisions—had almost reached market saturation thanks to falling unit prices and rising incomes. Throughout the 1960s, a new range of consumer durables captured the hearts of consumers. Now people wanted the "3Cs": ***karā terebi*** (color television), ***kūra*** (air conditioner), and ***kā*** (car). Possession of these 3Cs was about more than convenience—owning a color television and a car was proof of having attained the ideal of middle-class affluence.[36]

Uptake of color televisions was relatively fast; air conditioners remained a luxury item and automobiles simply out of reach for most Japanese. Nonetheless, popular interest in automobiles, in particular, increased dramatically. People thronged to auto shows and annually around six hundred thousand sat for their

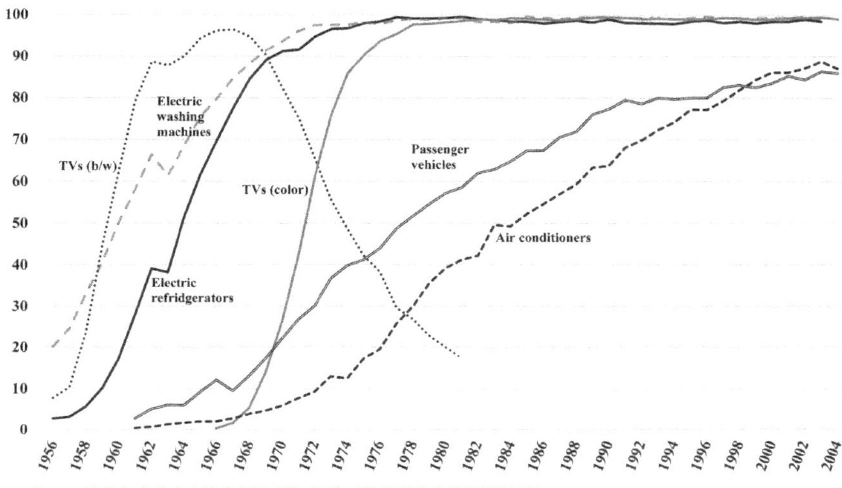

Source: Naikakufu Keizai Shakai Sōgō Kenkyūjo, "Keiki Tōkei, Shōhi Dōkō."

Figure 4.10. Market Penetration of Major Consumer Durables, 1956–2004

driver's license test in Tokyo alone.[37] Automakers responded by manufacturing more reasonably priced smaller cars. In 1960, there were only 513,700 registered passenger vehicles in Japan, by 1965 this figure was 2.28 million, in 1970 it had quadrupled to 8.97 million, and in 1975 it doubled again, reaching 17.46 million registered vehicles. In other words, one in two households owned a car.[38]

Consumption patterns continued trends from the late 1950s. Consumption of rice plateaued, while relative expenditure on meat, dairy products, fruits, and processed foods, like instant noodles, increased dramatically. A December 1960 survey revealed that some 78 percent of households had consumed instant foods at least once.[39] Although daily caloric intake per person per day remained relatively unchanged from 2,104 kilocalories in 1950 to 2,210 in 1970, consumption of animal-based protein essentially doubled from 17.55 grams per day in 1950 to 34.2 grams in 1970.[40]

With respect to clothing, throughout the 1960s consumption continued to shift from homemade items to manufactured clothing that contained more synthetic fibers and was increasingly influenced by fashion trends. In 1957, Japanese purchased around 6.7 kilograms of clothing per capita annually, rising to 9.5 kilograms in 1965 and 12.7 by 1970.[41] At the same time, housewives continued to spend an average of around two-and-a-half hours per day on sewing and clothes making. Using the latest fashion magazines, sewing using electric machines proliferated as did classes for knitting and clothes making.

With restrictions on overseas travel lifted in 1964, wealthier Japanese began to travel overseas. In 1965, Japan Airlines ran its first overseas package tour to Hawai'i costing 36,400 yen—equivalent to the annual salary of a new university graduate. Just over 221,000 Japanese travelled overseas in 1964, but the introduction of affordable package tours, such as JAL PACK in 1965, encouraged more and more people to travel. In 1970, 936,205 people travelled abroad, rising to 2.46 million in 1975 thanks to the introduction of the Boeing 747 jumbo jet in 1970.[42]

Two important aspects of consumption during this era of high-speed economic growth warrant emphasis. First, although exports of manufactured goods showed a remarkable growth, rising elevenfold from 1.46 trillion yen in 1960 to 16.54 trillion yen by 1975, in the years 1955 to 1974, the domestic market—inclusive of consumer demand—absorbed around 90 percent of production.[43] As figure 4.11 shows, it was not until the 1970s and especially the 1980s that the balance of trade was regularly in the black. Thus, at least in the early stages, Japan's economic miracle was homemade, thanks in great part to voracious consumption by ordinary citizens.

But second, while Japanese were busy purchasing the latest electrical goods, they were also judiciously saving. Increasing wages and high costs for housing meant that, throughout the 1960s, Japanese households were saving around 15 percent of their annual income (climbing to an astounding high of 23.2 percent in 1974)—among the

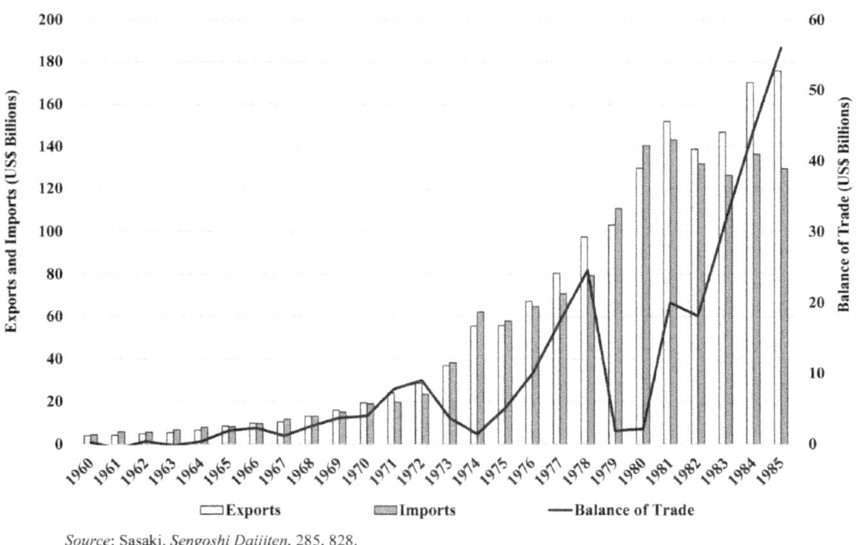

Source: Sasaki, *Sengoshi Daijiten*, 285, 828.

Figure 4.11. Exports, Imports, and Balance of Trade, 1960–1985

highest savings rates in the world. The government, in collaboration with civic groups, did its best to encourage such behavior through various campaigns beginning in the 1950s. As noted in chapter 3, many Japanese housewives deposited their money in postal savings accounts, which, in turn, provided the government with a massive pool of funds for lending and infrastructural investment.

The inexorable shift from extended families to nuclear families continued throughout the 1960s, with the latter coming to account for over 63 percent of all households. Increased urbanization and the associated housing supply crunch meant that most families could not afford more than two children, especially with only the father working full time and the mother at home, perhaps taking on a part-time job. With the exception of 1966—considered an inauspicious year for child-birth—the total fertility rate from 1960 to 1975 was 2.08, steadily decreasing thereafter. With fewer mouths to feed, households now spent more money on education; the 1960s can rightly be seen as an era of education in postwar Japan. Throughout the decade more and more children—both boys and girls—entered high school. In 1950, 42.5 percent of students entered high school, a figure which increased to 57.7 percent in 1960, 70.7 percent in 1965, 82.1 percent in 1970, and 91.9 percent by 1975.[44] Graduation from high school slowly replaced graduation from middle school as the minimum level of education needed for the job market (although only middle school was compulsory and free).

University rates of entry also increased, though more steadily, from 10.3 percent in 1960 to 17 percent in 1965, 23.6 percent in 1970, and 38.4 percent in 1975. Importantly, a gendered pattern emerged in tertiary education, with many young women choosing two-year junior colleges over four-year universities—the assumption being that women would eventually leave the workforce to become full-time housewives and mothers. From around the early 1960s, the number of women entering junior colleges outnumbered those entering universities, a trend that would only reverse in 1995 (fig. 4.12).

Indeed, the gender divide manifested itself in almost every corner of high-growth Japan. Women were expected to take charge of the domestic realm as "professional housewives" (*sengyō shufu*) and "education mothers" (*kyōiku mama*), while their husbands went out into society as corporate warriors. In the home, women generally ruled supreme, controlling household finances, consumption, and the lives of children. Knowing this, companies often directed their advertising campaigns at women as did the state in its various campaigns for saving and hygiene. Despite the shift to nuclear families, women were also often expected to provide care and support for their own and their husband's elderly parents. Those women who did work encountered highly gendered workplaces. In the 1950s and 1960s, the state and industry encouraged young unmarried women to work full time in the

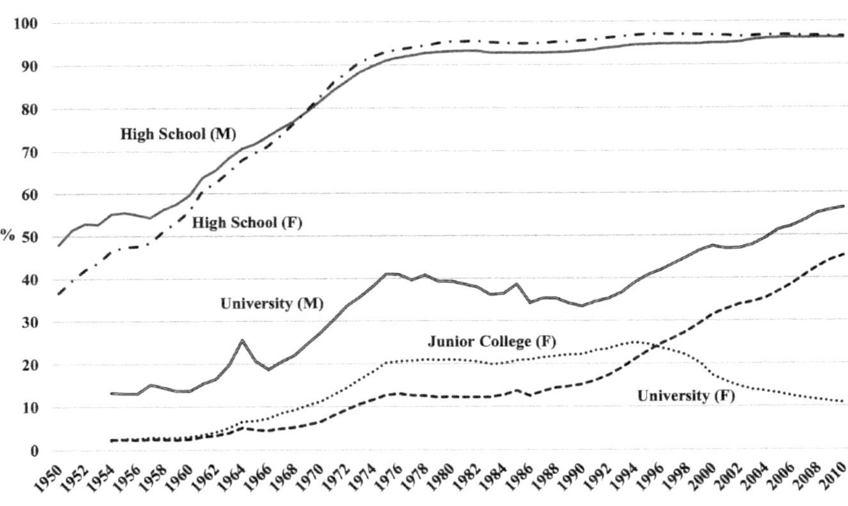

Source: Naikakufu, Danjo Kyōdō Sankaku Kyoku, "Dai-1-setsu."

Figure 4.12. High School, Junior College, and University Entry Rates, 1950–2010

growing manufacturing and service sectors, replacing the textile industry as the hub for female employment of the early postwar years. While men occupied the great majority of upwardly mobile positions, women were mostly relegated to clerical positions. On marriage—usually in their early to midtwenties—women were expected to permanently leave their jobs to concentrate on homemaking and childrearing. As a result, over time a so-called M curve (see chap. 5, fig. 5.6) emerged in women's workplace participation rates: a spike in participation for women in their early twenties, dropping sharply for women in their late twenties and early thirties as they focused on childrearing, rising again for women in their late thirties and forties, and gradually declining thereafter.

Not all women silently accepted this gendered system. In 1964, Suzuki Setsuko sued her employer, Sumitomo Cement, arguing that the company's mandatory requirement for women to retire on marriage violated Article 14 of the Constitution of Japan (banning sexual discrimination) and Article 90 of the Civil Code. Two years later, the Tokyo District Court ruled in Suzuki's favor, but the victory proved a pyrrhic one for workplace gender equality in the long run. Thereafter, companies actively avoided hiring female university graduates and others unlikely to leave on marriage, preferring instead junior college graduates who were more likely to quit. The government also supported this workplace gendering with a taxation system that assumed men to be the breadwinners and women full-time homemakers.

Specifically, primary household income earners could claim a spouse deduction so long as the other spouse (usually the wife) did not earn more than the equivalent of a low-paying part-time job.

Along with women, other groups faced discrimination in Japan's supposedly "entirely middle-class society." Ethnic Korean minorities continued to experience prejudice in marriage and employment, and not until the normalization of relations between Japan and South Korea in 1965 would they become eligible for social security and health benefits. Occasionally their frustrations burst to the surface, as in 1968, when the resident Korean Gwon Hui-ro took guests at a mountain inn hostage after shooting two gangsters dead in a loan dispute. In a media interview prior to his arrest, Gwon spoke of relentless discrimination by police and ordinary Japanese from his childhood, resulting in his criminal recidivism. Unlike Gwon, however, most ethnic Koreans suffered discrimination in silence.

Burakumin communities mentioned in chapter 1, who were ethnically Japanese but had been traditionally discriminated against for working in occupations considered polluting in Buddhist belief, began to push for better treatment in the 1960s. Like ethnic Koreans, they encountered discrimination in marriage and employment. Companies often checked family registers or, when this practice was later prohibited, referred to unofficial lists of Buraku neighborhoods before taking on new employees. The Buraku Liberation League (BLL), formed in the early postwar as a successor of the prewar Levelers Society, adopted a militant approach at first. But the government responded in 1961 by establishing the Dōwa Measures Deliberative Council ("Dōwa" being the government term for the Burakumin), which included cooperative leaders from the Burakumin movement. With the passing of the Dōwa Special Measures Law in 1969, the BLL largely abandoned struggles for equal rights, settling instead for various government-supported forms of compensation, such as import restrictions on leather items and funding for schools, community centers, and housing in Buraku communities. Standards of living undoubtedly improved for the Burakumin but discrimination remained.

Politics in the Age of the Economy

Party Politics

Although media pundits at the time celebrated the glittering new "age of the economy" with its income doubling and astonishing rates of growth, the 1960s were by no means a period of political stagnation nor was the decade short on spirited protest and dispute. On the contrary, rivalries within political parties and changing demographics began to reshape the party landscape, while the excesses of economic growth and obligations under the US-Japan security alliance provoked many ordinary citizens to mobilize in protest or seek justice in the courts. It was Ikeda's successor Satō Eisaku—yet another of Yoshida's bureaucratic progenies and the natural brother of Kishi Nobusuke—who had to deal with these challenges in the late 1960s and early 1970s.

Satō had strong leadership ambitions, only narrowly losing to Ikeda in a vote for the LDP presidency in mid-1964. His chance came earlier than expected when Ikeda suddenly announced his resignation after the closing ceremony of the Olympics due to a cancer diagnosis. Ikeda had certainly been strong on economic policy but his management of the LDP was weak, opening the way for factional power to proliferate within the party. While Satō lacked Ikeda's grand vision, he was a skillful people manager and a flexible realist, making him the ideal leader to smooth factional rivalries led by young guns in the party like Tanaka Kakuei and Fukuda Takeo. Thanks to these qualities, Satō was able to hold on to the prime ministership for almost eight years from late 1964 to mid-1972.

If the Satō administration can be attributed with any distinguishable policy agenda, then it was probably the idea of "social development" (*shakai kaihatsu*), which aimed at rectifying some of the negative aspects of Ikeda's Income Doubling Policy, like housing shortages, poor social infrastructure, regional underdevelopment, meagre social security, and industrial pollution. At the same time, there was no policy about-face during the Satō years, with economic growth still ruling supreme. Under Satō's watch the Izanagi boom (1965–1970) lasting fifty-seven months was the longest and arguably most impressive spurt of economic growth during the miracle years.

The economic good times certainly undergirded the electoral dominance of the LDP, but this was also buttressed by the entrenched malapportionment of electoral districts in favor of rural areas (the LDP's core constituency), the LDP's ability to coax conservative independents to join the party under its "big tent" approach, and the gradual atomization of the opposition. In fact, throughout the 1960s, the LDP's percentage of the total vote continued to decrease, falling below 50 percent in the 1967 lower house election for the first time. Although not as dramatic thanks to malapportionment, the party's number of seats in the lower house also decreased from 294 to 283 in the 1963 election, to 277 seats in 1967, only to bounce back to 288 seats in 1969. This trend was particularly evident in urban districts, where the LDP attracted less than 30 percent of voters.[45] Nonetheless, in all lower house elections from the mid-1950s to 1972, the LDP continued to secure comfortable majorities.

After the 1967 election when the combined vote for the progressive parties hit 49.9 percent, observers began to suggest a new age of "conservative-progressive parity," with some even predicting that the ongoing demographic shift from the country to city and from agricultural to wage labor would inevitably lead to victory by the progressives in the near future—perhaps even by the end of the 1960s.[46] Ultimately such predictions proved woefully wrong for at least three reasons: first, because the LDP managed to modify its policies to effectively capture some of the urban vote; second, because of electoral district malapportionment; and third, due to the atomization of the opposition parties, which effectively split the progressive vote.

Among the political party newcomers was the Kōmeitō or Clean Government Party (CGP), established in November 1964 as the political wing of the lay Buddhist association Sōka Gakkai, a prewar new religion revived after 1945. Early on, Sōka Gakkai drew its membership from the urban lower strata of nonunionized workers, small business owners, and housewives. By the late 1950s, its ranks had swelled to around one million members. In 1955, the religion established the Sōka Gakkai Cultural Division, which helped fifty-one independent candidates win seats in local elections. Buoyed by this success, three Sōka Gakkai candidates ran successfully in the July 1956 House of Councillors election. Following the CGP's establishment in 1964, the party won twenty-five seats in the 1967 House of Representatives election, followed by forty-seven seats in the 1969 election—making it the third largest party with around 11 percent of the popular vote. Responding to media criticisms about the constitutionality of Sōka Gakkai—a religious organization—backing elected representatives, the CGP officially severed ties with the religion in 1970, although Sōka Gakkai members still formed the backbone of the party's electoral base.

In terms of political platform, the CGP—as the name suggests—focused on eradicating political corruption, enhancing welfare, building "Buddhist-style" democracy and world peace, protecting the constitution, and supporting capitalism. Because of the resonances in their policy agendas, early on the CGP frequently supported JSP candidates in elections. But the party began to compete with the JSP for the same urban votes over time. Moreover, as the party's constituency became wealthier, the CGP's policy platform shifted closer to the LDP's and further away from its initial left-of-center position.

While the CGP grew impressively, the JSP continued its gradual decline, undermined by party splits and internecine ideological disputes. The story of the JSP in the era of high-speed growth is essentially one of the party's electoral prospects being undermined by both new parties like the CGP and the rigid ideological stance of the party's hardline left. After Nishio Suehiro and others bolted the party to form the center-left DSP in 1960, the JSP fell under the financial and ideological sway of the Sōhyō labor organization, which demanded a dogmatic strategy of class struggle. This stance made it impossible for the party to broaden its electoral appeal. Peaking at 166 seats in the lower house elections of 1958, throughout the 1960s the party's electoral performance deteriorated, dropping into the 140s in 1960, 1963, and 1967, a crushing 90 seats in 1969, and recovering to only 118 seats in 1972. The JSP's fortunes in the House of Councillors were not much better, falling from a high of 85 seats in 1959 to 66 seats in 1971.

This downward trend seems somewhat counterintuitive given the falling support for the LDP in urban areas, even considering the emergence of competitors like the CGP. However, the problem was more fundamental, connecting to the core objectives and strategies of the party. Nowhere was this more evident than in the failure of the so-called structural reform movement led by Eda Saburō and the other remaining members of the party's minority right wing in the early 1960s. In a nutshell, Eda's structural reform proposal—first aired at the party conference in October 1960—called on the JSP to abandon its policy line of socialist revolution for a more moderate strategy of incremental reformism through parliamentary politics. At a party meeting in Tochigi Prefecture in 1962, Eda outlined his "Eda Vision" based on "clarifying an image of socialism in modern society different from the Soviet Union and China." The four foundations of this vision would be a high standard of living as in America, comprehensive social security as in the Soviet Union, the parliamentary democracy of the United Kingdom, and the Japanese peace constitution. Herein, Eda was attempting to develop a realistic policy line for the party against the backdrop of a rapidly developing Japan. Around the same time, the West German Social Democratic Party changed its policy line in this direction, opening the way for the Willy Brandt government at the end of the 1960s.[47] But no such transformation would happen in the JSP of the time. The hardline left of the party refused to budge, rejecting Eda's proposal as a "revisionist" denial of the party's fundamental principles. Resoundingly defeated, in December 1962 Eda resigned as secretary general of the party. Thereafter the JSP never became a genuine alternative government in the minds of voters.

The JSP's centrist former brethren in the DSP also failed to make any meaningful electoral progress throughout the 1960s, despite their policy line similar to Eda's structural reform. From an initial forty seats in the lower house and seventeen in the upper on its establishment in January 1960, throughout the decade the party never captured more than thirty seats in the lower house and stagnated at around ten seats in the upper house. In hindsight, the DSP's main role seems to have been more to siphon votes away from the flailing JSP than to offer a viable center-left option to voters. The party never managed to capitalize on support from the moderate Dōmei (Japanese Confederation of Labor).

Finally, the JCP's period of extremism in the early 1950s meant that the party would have to devote considerable energy to rebuilding its public image over the coming years. In 1960, the communists held only three seats in each of the houses, but this had improved to fourteen seats in the lower house and seven in the upper house by the end of the decade. The JCP's newly cultivated image as a genuinely independent watchdog of the government and its formal split from the Chinese Communist Party in 1966 resulted in a modest increase in support among urban intellectuals and some professionals. In the following decade, the party's electoral fortunes would continue to improve as the detrimental effects of economic growth became apparent and the LDP was rocked by scandal.

Resisting Excessive Development and Pollution

While conservatives could feel relatively comfortable about electoral politics in the 1960s, the LDP's greatest challenges stemmed from its own economic and security policies. Among these, excessive and lopsided development and harmful environmental pollution were the most serious. The EPA's economic white paper of 1967 frankly recognized this situation, noting that although Japan ranked second among the top six industrialized nations in steel production, it ranked lowest in terms of sewerage infrastructure and housing standards. Among the fifteen welfare indices compared in the white paper, Japan ranked a dismal fifth or sixth in eleven categories.[48] The causes of this situation were complex but stemmed in great part from massive unplanned urbanization, together with a government spending strategy focused on industrial infrastructure at the expense of the social facilities required to raise living standards.

Beginning in the mid-1950s, up to one million people migrated to cities from the countryside annually (fig. 4.13). Greater Tokyo (inclusive of Kanagawa, Saitama, and Chiba prefectures), the Osaka region, and Nagoya absorbed the bulk of these migrants. In 1962, Tokyo became the world's first city of ten million people, and from 1960 to 1975 the Greater Tokyo population swelled from around thirty-five million to over fifty million. Continuing trends from the prewar era, rates of urbanization expanded from around 30 percent at war's end to nearly 50 percent by the mid-1970s.

Urban infrastructure like roads, sidewalks, and schools struggled to keep up with this mass migration, as too did the supply of housing. Although the government's public housing project provided millions of new dwellings, it could not keep up with demand. Surveys throughout the 1960s revealed that between 40 to 50 percent of people were either dissatisfied with their current housing or experiencing housing distress due to high rental costs, inadequate building construction, and poor facilities, like plumbing for toilets and kitchens. Rising land prices also put pressure on renters and made the dream of home ownership out of reach for many. Between 1963 and 1967, land prices rose 891 percent nationally and an astounding 1,210 percent in the six largest cities.[49] For those forced to live on the outskirts of Greater Tokyo or Osaka, daily commutes were long and arduous. Rush hour commuter trains were crammed to 300 percent capacity thanks to JNR employees

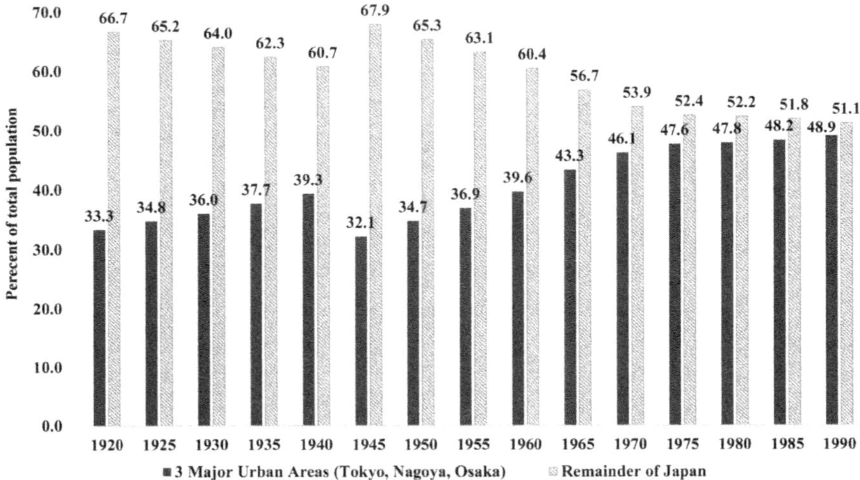

Source: Rōdō Seisaku Kenkyū-Kenshū Kikō, "Hayawakari Gurafu de miru Chōki Rōdō Tōkei."

Figure 4.13. Urbanization in Japan, 1920–1990

specially tasked with shoving people into carriages like canned sardines. Scientists at the time calculated that riding one hour on an overcrowded train was the equivalent of four hours work or eight chicken eggs worth of caloric energy—and many people commuted for much longer.[50]

Municipal governments also struggled to stay on top of the human deluge, which was accompanied by an equivalent torrent of waste. In the early 1960s, per capita daily waste was just below five hundred grams, but this had doubled by the mid-1970s, especially in big cities like Tokyo, where residents were producing over two kilograms of trash per day, prompting the governor to declare a "war on waste" in 1971. New kinds of waste, like plastics and cans, also made disposal more complicated and costly. In 1967, the per capita waste disposal cost was less than 1,500 yen, but this had increased almost sevenfold to 9,915 yen by 1976.[51]

The blight of environmental pollution closely followed the advent of mass production and mass consumption. Throughout the 1960s, Japanese citizens across the archipelago endured multiple forms of pollution, including contamination of rivers and bays, air pollution, noise and vibration from aircraft and Shinkansen, odors from industrial effluent, and shocking cases of food contamination. In the big cities, especially industrial areas like Kawasaki, automobiles and factories emitted dangerous levels of nitrogen dioxide and carbon monoxide. Conditions became so bad that the Tokyo Metropolitan Government erected electronic pollution signboards with real-time emissions readings in crowded downtown areas in the late 1960s. In July 1970, students at a girls' high school in Tokyo's Suginami ward were rushed to the hospital after collapsing in the school grounds due to photochemical smog inhalation. Thereafter, Tokyo and other local governments began issuing regular chemical smog warnings. Outside of the cities, residents faced destructive industrial pollution, as at Tashinoura Bay south of Tokyo, where industrial sludge dumped from local paper mills emitted foul smelling odors, contaminated the water, and devastated fishing stocks in nearby Suruga Bay.

Residents did not sit by idly as their living environments were destroyed and their health impacted. Throughout the 1960s and early 1970s, at Tashinoura and thousands of other locations nationwide, movements opposing development and pollution mobilized. At their height in 1973, hundreds and thousands of local residents were active in around three thousand movements. National networks, like the Independent Forum on Pollution led by the University of Tokyo chemist Ui Jun, helped to connect local activists and spread knowledge about movement strategy and the science of pollution. Groups of social and natural scientists, like the Research Committee on Pollution, also provided expert advice to local communities dealing with the ravages of pollution and excess development.

One of the earliest movements to resist industrial development was in the cities of Mishima, Shimizu, and Numazu in Shizuoka Prefecture. Here local teachers, storeowners, fishermen, and farmers mobilized to stop construction of a petrochemical plant. Using novel citizen science techniques, locals proved that air currents in the area would result in dangerous levels of air pollution for residents if the plant was constructed. Under extreme pressure from their electorates, mayors of the three cities eventually yielded, scrapping their approval for the petrochemical plant that promised to inject millions of yen into the local economy.

The triumph of the Shizuoka movement inspired residents across the nation, although not all would share the same success. In 1966, for example, residents in Yokohama mobilized to stop construction of a new freight line in their neighborhood as part of a Yokohama Municipal Government plan to alleviate pressure on commuter lines. Activists challenged city officials' appeals to the so-called public interest, pitting this against their local rights. They questioned the logic of a "public interest" that would destroy their living environment simply to transport workers to their offices faster. In the end, however, the freight line was constructed. In a similar way, in 1966, farmers and local storeowners in the Sanrizuka-Shibayama area of Chiba Prefecture mobilized against the planned construction of the New Tokyo International Airport (now Narita International Airport). The decision to build the airport was made in 1960 and the site chosen in 1965. Farmers and other residents were advised that they were required to sell their land to the government to make way for the airport. For many locals, however, their holdings were about much more than income. Many residents were returnees from Japan's wartime colonies. They had been forced to abandon everything and start from scratch after returning in 1945. Feeling themselves to have been victims of Japan's failed experiment in colonialism, they were loath now to relinquish their land to the government.

In 1966, Tomura Issaku, a local store owner, artist, and devout Christian, assumed leadership of the opposition movement, comprising around three thousand farmers and residents. Over the coming years, the movement was also periodically supported by students, the JSP and JCP, anti–Vietnam War protesters, and activists from other movements. To avoid forced eviction, residents and their supporters constructed elaborate barricades and tunnels and even engaged in violent exchanges with riot police on occasion. These tactics greatly delayed construction of the airport, and the refusal of some farmers to sell meant that runways could not be constructed as long as originally planned. Nonetheless, construction began in 1969, only to be completed in 1978, many years behind schedule.

While many local residents struggled to stop construction projects like airports, petrochemical combines, and railroads, thousands of others confronted the horrific

Figure 4.14. Tomura Issaku, chairman of the Sanrizuka-Shibayama United League Opposing the New Tokyo International Airport, is surrounded and beaten by police officers outside the Narita Municipal Office during the struggle against airport construction (February 26, 1968). Courtesy of The Asahi Shimbun Company.

consequences of industrial pollution. Nowhere was this problem more disturbingly revealed than in the so-called Big Four pollution cases that first appeared in the 1950s and continued until their conclusions in the courts in the early 1970s. More than any other phenomenon of the period, these instances of industrial pollution and its devastating effects on human health stimulated many ordinary citizens to begin questioning the logic of unbridled economic growth.

The appearance in the early 1950s of methylmercury poisoning among residents of the picturesque Minamata Bay area in southern Kyūshū was the first warning sign. Locals initially noticed unusual behavior among cats that began exhibiting strange dance-like convulsions followed by sudden death. Soon after, residents began displaying various neurological impairments, including headaches, ear ringing and hearing loss, severe fatigue, loss of sensation and tremors in the limbs, loss of mobility, narrowing of fields of vision, and language impairments. Some became bedridden after losing control of their bodily functions. Newborns also displayed severe neurological symptoms, requiring full-time nursing care from birth. In 1956, researchers at the Kumamoto University Medical Faculty identified the cause as methylmercury contamination in the seafood residents had consumed from the bay. The source of this contamination was traced to effluent from a local factory manufacturing acetaldehyde, used for plastics like polyvinyl chloride. In 1958, research from the Ministry of Health and Welfare also identified the factory as the cause, but the owner, the Chisso Corporation, and its allies in business, politics, and academia refuted the claims.

Seeking some form of recompense, residents organized a mutual assistance group in 1959, which negotiated an informal settlement with the company: Chisso would offer "sympathy" payments but not admit responsibility and recipients would agree not to pursue legal remedies in return. Not all in the Minamata community supported this approach, with some three hundred fishermen even storming the factory precincts in 1959. Only in 1968 did the government finally recognize the irrefutable science identifying the Chisso factory as the contamination source. When victims were pushed to their limits economically, socially, mentally, and physiologically, they turned to lawyers who commenced legal proceedings for compensation in 1969.

Minamata disease, as it would come to be known, was widely reported in the domestic and international media. In 1969, the author Ishimure Michiko touched Japanese readers' hearts with her book *Kukai jōdo: Waga Minamata byō* (*Paradise in the Sea of Sorrow: Our Minamata Disease*), while the American photojournalist Eugene Smith caused a sensation in 1975 with the publication of his photographic account, *Minamata: The Story of the Poisoning of a City, and of the People Who Choose to Carry the Burden of Courage.*[52]

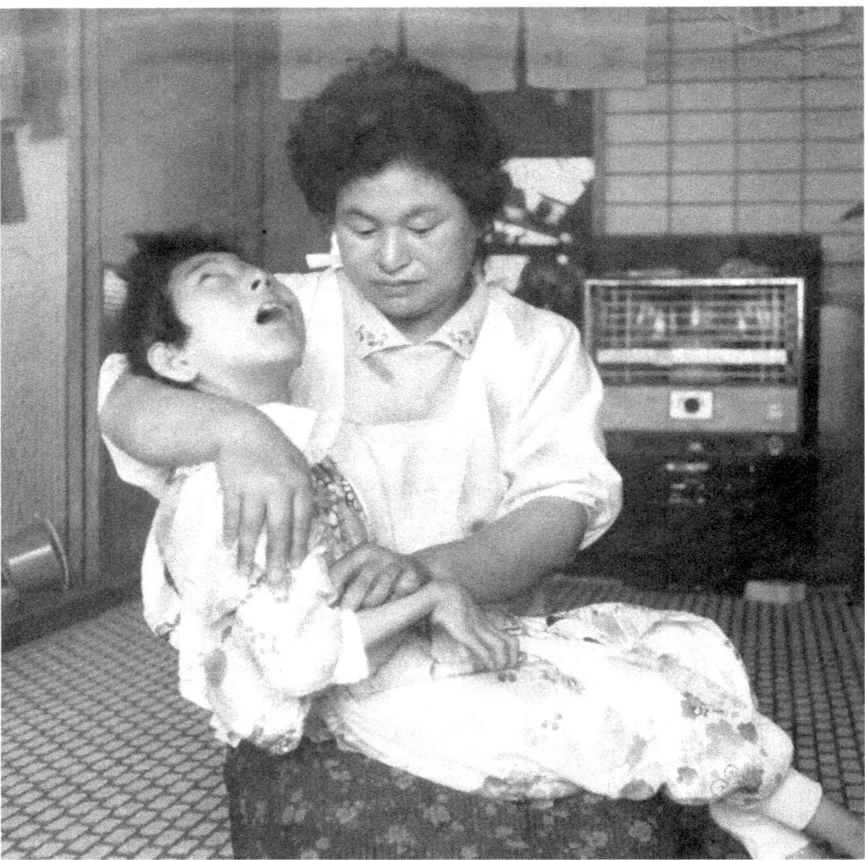

Figure 4.15. Uemura Tomoko, a fetal-type Minamata disease patient, is cradled by her mother, Yoshiko, on her thirteenth birthday (June 10, 1970). Courtesy of The Asahi Shimbun Company.

As the tragedy at Minamata was unfolding, three other high-profile pollution cases captured public attention. In 1965, residents along the Agano River in Niigata Prefecture began to exhibit similar symptoms to those in Minamata. On investigation, it was revealed that they too had been poisoned with methylmercury due to effluent released by the Shōwa Denkō factory. Unlike their counterparts in Minamata, residents in Nagano wasted no time in seeking legal compensation, with thirteen plaintiffs filing suit against the company in mid-1967. In the same year, residents living around a massive petrochemical complex in Yokkaichi City in Mie Prefecture filed suit against companies for causing debilitating—and sometimes lethal—bronchial asthma due to smokestack emissions from the complex. If this was not enough, in 1968, some five hundred victims of cadmium poisoning living along the Jinzū River in Toyama Prefecture filed suit against the Kamioka plant of the Mitsui Mining and Smelting Company. In this case, poisoning occurred when residents used contaminated water from the river to irrigate their rice fields. Colloquially known as *itai itai-byō*—literally "it hurts, it hurts disease"—cadmium poisoning made bones brittle to the point that even coughing could result in excruciatingly painful fractures.

From 1971 through 1973, Japanese courts delivered landmark decisions in favor of the plaintiffs in all of the Big Four pollution cases. For the victims, their families, and the devastated communities and natural environments, of course, these victories only provided a partial—if gratifying—remedy. Many had their lives and livelihoods cut short and others were burdened with caring for severely disabled family members and offspring.

The Big Four cases together with other localized industrial pollution outbreaks in Kawasaki, Amagasaki (Osaka), and many other locales around the nation also reverberated in politics. Fed up with the growth-at-all-costs policies of the central government and determined to protect their local living environments, throughout the 1960s, citizens elected progressive mayors and governors one after the other. The unified local elections of 1963 saw progressive mayors elected in Osaka, Kitakyūshū, and Yokohama. In April 1967, the leftist academic economist Minobe Ryōkichi was elected governor of Tokyo with endorsement from both the JCP and JSP. Thereafter, progressive administrations were elected in Osaka in 1971; Okinawa, Saitama, and Okayama in 1972; Kagawa and Shiga in 1974; and Kanagawa and Shimane in 1975. At its height, there were ten progressive governors and 126 mayors nationwide—hardly a majority, but enough to worry LDP heavyweights.[53] These administrations passed landmark pollution abatement ordinances and instituted a range of progressive social policies such as the Tokyo Minobe Administration's free health services and public transportation for the elderly. In Yokohama City, the mayor Asukata Ichio established public forums called "ten thousand citizen assemblies" to promote direct citizen participation in politics.

Concerned about a possible national electoral backlash—especially in the cities—the LDP responded with a swath of new laws and policies. In 1968, the party's Urban Policy Investigative Committee, led by the up-and-coming Tanaka Kakuei, released a set of principles on urban policy, calling for extravagant public spending on redevelopment in metropolises and regional centers. The previous year, the government passed the Basic Law on Pollution Control together with laws relating to cities and the siting of factories. In 1970, at a historic meeting of the Diet later called the "Pollution Diet," some fourteen environmental laws were either strengthened or newly passed, giving Japan some of the strongest environmental regulations in the world. The following year, the Environmental Agency was established—one of the first in the world—and, in 1973, the government created a bureaucratically administered mechanism for pollution dispute mediation and a compensation scheme for victims. Such developments only transpired after much human misery and environmental destruction, but Japan was finally turning the corner on its pollution and overdevelopment nightmare by the end of the decade. Albeit reluctantly and slowly, the Satō administration was admitting that there were identifiable and necessary limits to economic growth.

Antiwar and Student Activism in the 1960s

Along with industrial pollution, Satō also faced a rising wave of protest against Japan's involvement in the Vietnam War. As discussed in chapter 5, Satō's long-term strategy was the return of Okinawa. To this end, he was open to providing extra logistical and other support for the Americans as their military involvement in Indochina intensified following the commencement of aerial bombing on North Vietnam in early 1965. Although indirect, Japanese involvement in the Vietnam War was far reaching. US nuclear-powered submarines and aircraft carriers utilized Japanese ports like Yokosuka and Sasebo. Okinawa—still under US military administration—provided logistical support and served as a staging ground for troop deployments and B52 bombing raids on the north. Like the Korean War, the US military procured a variety of materials from the Japanese such as ammunition, clothing, textiles, tanks, and food supplies. Japanese companies were commissioned to construct and expand US bases, roads, runways, communications facilities, and barracks, as well as to provide repairs and maintenance on aircraft, ships, and military vehicles. Closer to the battlefield, US forces utilized Japanese-built landing ships. Hundreds of Japanese worked on US military bases and in transportation services in Vietnam and the Pacific. Businesses around US bases provided recreation services to military personnel on leave. At the same time, Japanese businesses capitalized on the conflict abroad, expanding their trade with countries in Southeast Asia. Anticipating a rise in exports to the United States with the escalating conflict, Japanese steelmakers invested heavily in new blast furnaces, rotary kilns, and strip mills, while other corporate giants like Toshiba and Mitsubishi directed resources into petrochemicals and shipbuilding. Without the Vietnam War, these industries may not have been able to develop at such a pace.[54]

Opposition to the Vietnam War arose almost immediately, led by the JSP, JCP, Sōhyō, students, and a pioneering civic organization known as Beheiren or the Citizens League for Peace in Vietnam. Formed in April 1965, Beheiren grew out of the energies and activists of the Anpo Treaty protests in 1960. Its main spokesperson was the charismatic novelist, Oda Makoto, who was joined by other eminent intellectuals and artists like Kaiko Takeshi, Tsurumi Yoshiyuki, and Muto Ichiyo. The movement had significant transnational connections to antiwar intellectuals like Jean-Paul Sartre and Simone de Beauvoir in France and to members of the Student Nonviolent Coordinating Committee, civil rights activists like Stokely Carmichael, singers and actors such as Joan Baez and Jane Fonda, and intellectuals like Howard Zinn in the United States.

Participants in Beheiren distinguished their movement from the hierarchical established organs of the left, preferring instead a loose organization based on individual freedom, deliberative decision-making, and individual responsibility. The movement also differed from the strongly Marxist class-based focus of earlier leftist activism. For this reason, Beheiren marked the emergence of the so-called new social movements in Japan, which broke sharply with earlier styles of top-down activism and opened the way for a new politics of identity. In this sense, the many Beheiren movements of the late 1960s resonated with the thousands of loosely organized antidevelopment and antipollution residents' movements and the new breed of independent student movements discussed later in this chapter.

Among its activities, Beheiren held international antiwar conferences, assisted conscientious US military deserters, staged protests outside US military facilities, and targeted Japanese corporations for profiteering from the war. Beheiren also made significant ideational breakthroughs. Thanks to the ideas of Oda and others, antiwar pacifism transformed from its earlier focus on the Japanese people's victimization by the state and the United States to a more mature recognition of Japanese citizens' position as both victims and aggressors in the Vietnam War. Activists were challenged to look at the complicity of their daily lives in the conflict—how was Japanese affluence connected to the misery in Vietnam? This awakening had important long-term consequences, especially in terms of activists' attention to Japan's history of aggression in Asia, which had been little explored until that point.

Alongside Beheiren, students also returned to the political limelight in the late 1960s, following the defeat of Anpo and a period of internecine sectarian disputes. In 1967, armed students took to the streets around Tokyo's Haneda Airport to—unsuccessfully—prevent Prime Minister Satō from traveling to Southeast Asia to meet with the US-supported South Vietnamese government. The ensuing melee with riot police resulted in the death of a student militant from Kyoto University, Yamazaki Hiroaki. The Haneda struggle was but a precursor to the student protests that would erupt on campuses across the nation in 1968 and 1969, drawing Japan into the wider global student movements of the time.

Closely connected to the anti–Vietnam War movement, on October 21, 1968—International Antiwar Day—student protests exploded nationwide, most graphically at Tokyo's Shinjuku train station, where students raided the platforms and attempted to stop a train loaded with jet fuel to be utilized by the US military at its base in Tachikawa in western Tokyo. The protest grew out of an incident in 1967 when a train transporting jet fuel had ignited at the station. The student occupation of Shinjuku station was accompanied by acts of destruction and violence, including the burning of vehicles. On the same day, large numbers of students armed with wooden sticks invaded the Defense Agency premises in Tokyo's Roppongi area.

University campuses also witnessed radical student upheavals, beginning with a dispute at the elite University of Tokyo. The initial spark came from medical school students who were dissatisfied with an unremunerated internship system, which they characterized as exploitative. In January 1968, members of the medical students' association entered an indefinite strike. In response, university officials used an altercation between students and medical administrators as a pretext to punish seventeen students of whom six were summarily expelled from the university. With this, on June 15, 1968, medical students occupied the Yasuda Auditorium at the

Figure 4.16. Students from the University of Tokyo Zenkyōtō group aiming to blockade the university (left) clash violently with students opposed to the blockade (right) outside the main library on November 12, 1968, resulting in around forty injuries. Such scenes quickly turned public opinion against militant campus activism. Courtesy of The Asahi Shimbun Company.

center of the campus, prompting university authorities to send in twelve hundred riot police to forcibly eject them. In response, around six thousand students from across the university organized an emergency protest, thereafter reoccupying and barricading Yasuda Auditorium. The standoff between the students and university authorities would continue until January 1969 when riot police finally prevailed.

Throughout 1968 and 1969 protests spread like wildfire to other campuses nationwide, with students expressing their dissatisfaction over increases in fees, university corruption, unreasonable punishments, and problems in student dormitories. They demanded managerial transparency and a greater voice for students in university governance. Students connected campus problems to Japan's wider "neo-imperialism" within the American world order and they demanded the immediate reorganization or dismantling of Japan's universities. Into 1969, many campuses were forced to close due to student occupations of classrooms and other university facilities. Daily television news programs broadcast chaotic scenes of armed students violently clashing with riot police.

A characteristic feature of these student mobilizations of the late 1960s was the rise of so-called All-Campus Joint Struggle Councils or Zenkyōtō, comprising students who had no affiliation with existing sects and were organized based on direct democracy, similar to Beheiren. To this extent, the Zenkyōtō students were part of the important transition in Japanese social activism. At the same time, escalating violence distinguished the student movement of the late 1960s from Beheiren and most of the antipollution and antidevelopment movements. Indeed, it was this violence that gradually turned public opinion against the students.

By the early 1970s, some elements of the movement had even transformed into terrorist groups. In 1972, members of the Japanese Red Army became involved in a violent clash with police at the Asama Mountain Retreat in Karuizawa after taking the manager's wife hostage. The police assault on the facility was broadcast on live television to massive ratings. Infighting within these terrorist groups resulted in lynchings and murders that only further exacerbated public antipathy and played into the hands of the Satō government, which was keen to stamp out student extremism.

International Matters

The US-Japan security alliance continued to deeply shape Japan's interactions with the outside world throughout the age of the economy in the 1960s and early 1970s, particularly the country's relations in East Asia. In 1961, Ikeda Hayato made official visits to Pakistan, India, Burma, and Thailand to settle wartime reparations issues, as well as to expand aid and pave the way for new business connections. Although still modest, Japan's ODA increased from around US$1.42 billion in the mid-1960s to US$3.59 billion by 1969. Importantly, the focus of ODA shifted noticeably from South Asia to East and Southeast Asia. Japan also extended international loans to Taiwan, Thailand, Malaysia, and Indonesia for infrastructure projects like railways, dams, and ports. Where possible, the Japanese government utilized institutions such as the Asian Development Bank for its aid to Asia to avoid any impression of a second "invasion."

Relations with the PRC remained quite delicate in the 1960s, occasionally showing signs of improvement only to quickly degenerate. With no official relations, the two countries technically remained in a state of war. In the late 1940s and early 1950s, Yoshida Shigeru had encouraged the development of discrete trade with the PRC while officially upholding the US policy of containing the communist nation. However, this approach collapsed under Prime Minister Kishi, who abruptly shifted emphasis to recognition of the Republic of China (Taiwan) in the late 1950s.

In keeping with his more general policy of rebuilding ties with Asia, on coming to power, Ikeda Hayato attempted to recalibrate the relationship with the PRC by separating economics from politics. In the early 1960s, unofficial discussions between the PRC and Japanese government officials became more frequent, resulting in the Liào-Takasaki Trade Agreement—also known as the LT Agreement—in 1962. Named after its lead negotiators—Liào Chéngzhì on the PRC side and Takasaki Tatsunosuke on the Japan side—this agreement formalized both parties' willingness to separate politics and economics. As a result, a form of quasi-officially managed trade developed in which Japanese companies that met certain PRC conditions—such as not having business ties with Taiwan or the United States—were allowed to engage in commercial activities. Trade increased accordingly, such that Japan was the PRC's major trading partner by 1965. Chinese officials were particularly keen to develop trade due to the failure of the Great Leap Forward and the souring of ties with the Soviet Union. Following in Yoshida's footsteps, Ikeda viewed mainland China as a natural trading partner for Japan and he believed that the Asian giant should be reincorporated into the international system—something he emphasized in a meeting with President Kennedy.[55] Nonetheless, relations remained fragile and prone to political interference.

With the PRC's detonation of an atomic bomb in 1964, the escalation of the Vietnam War from 1965, and the Cultural Revolution from 1966, relations between the two countries cooled somewhat in the late 1960s. The LT Agreement was replaced by the Memorial Trade Pact in 1968, which, although endorsing commercial activities, was far more limited than the previous agreement, requiring renegotiation annually. Relations would remain in this precarious state until the momentous transformations of the early 1970s.

Relations with South Korea made progress in the 1960s after over a decade of stop-start dialogues on normalization. As noted earlier, discussions between the two nations began in 1951 but were constantly hindered by the reckless remarks of Japanese officials, the implementation of the Rhee Line in 1952 and subsequent seizure of Japanese fishing vessels, Japan's refusal to characterize all resident Koreans as South Koreans, and disagreements over reparations and historical interpretations. Conditions shifted significantly following the military coup by Park Chung-hee in South Korea in 1961 and America's increasing military entanglements in Indochina. A former Imperial Japanese Army officer, Park was arguably pro-Japanese to begin with, but he also desired normalization for the economic benefits it could bring. The Americans also sought Japanese-South Korean détente to facilitate coordination among their military bases in both countries in anticipation of escalated hostilities in Vietnam.

In early 1965, Satō sent his foreign minister, Shiina Etsusaburō, to South Korea to resuscitate the stalled dialogues. At this meeting, the Japanese promised substantial financial aid and recognition for Koreans in Japan, while both sides acknowledged fishing entitlements in the Sea of Japan. The Treaty on Basic Relations Between Japan and the Republic of Korea was signed in February 1965 together with four agreements on fishing rights, the position of Koreans resident in Japan, bilateral economic cooperation, and cultural assets and exchanges. It did not, however, resolve all the complex issues complicating relations between the countries. First, although Article II of the treaty nullified all earlier treaties and agreements signed between the Empire of Japan and the Empire of Korea, both sides adopted contrasting interpretations. For the South Koreans, the terminology "already null and void" was interpreted to mean that the annexation treaty of 1910 and all earlier treaties had been invalid from the outset. The Japanese, however, interpreted this article to mean that only with the signing of the 1965 treaty were earlier treaties abrogated. This latter interpretation made it possible for some conservative Japanese politicians to assert that the earlier treaties were not coercive and that Japanese colonization was beneficial to Korea.[56] Second, although the Rhee Line was effectively removed, the issue of sovereignty over the disputed Takeshima (in Japanese) or Dokdo (in Korean) islets in the Sea of Japan remained unresolved, with both sides skirting the issue and simply shelving it for the future. Third, by recognizing the South Korean government as the solitary legal government on the Korean peninsula, pathways to normalization with North Korea were effectively closed. Fourth, controversies around compensation remained. Under the treaty, both sides agreed to abandon their rights to reparations claims arising from the period of colonization. In return, Japan agreed to pay a US$300 million grant in economic aid, US$200 million in low-interest loans, and US$300 million in private credit for economic development. Nonetheless, interpretations differed on either side as to whether these payments were "compensation" or "economic aid." Some on the Korean side argued that the treaty did not settle the individual claims of Korean citizens for personal damages suffered during the colonial era.

These divergences, along with the Cold War politics underlying the treaty, prompted activists in both countries to come out in protest. However, the emphasis of their protests differed in subtle yet important ways. Japanese protesters lambasted the Park regime and the role of the United States, while South Korean protesters focused on the unresolved colonial legacies and Japan's "reinvasion" of Korea. As discussed later in this book, these differences in perspective and interpretation would continue to trouble Japan-South Korean relations in the coming decades.

CHAPTER FIVE

Japan, the Economic Superpower, 1970s–1980s

The Return of Okinawa and the 1970 Security Treaty Renewal

Along with the historic phase of economic growth under his watch, Satō Eisaku is also credited with successfully negotiating the return of Okinawa to Japan in 1972. For many Japanese people, US control over the islands represented an ongoing vestige of the country's occupation and humiliation after the war and, hence, was something to be settled as soon as possible. Soon after assuming office in 1964, Satō directly addressed this sentiment, declaring that the postwar era (meaning the US-led Occupation) would not be genuinely finished until the return of Okinawa. Satō made the same point to President Lyndon B. Johnson during their first meeting in 1965, at which time Johnson gave an in-principle agreement to reversion in two to three years. In August 1965, Satō reiterated his desire for reversion when he became the first postwar Japanese prime minister to visit the islands. In a speech during his trip, Satō promised that returning Okinawa to the "motherland" would be a policy priority for him.

Movements on the ground in Okinawa bolstered Satō's drive for reversion. As early as 1960, the Okinawa Prefecture Homeland Reversion Council was established with a platform of immediate, unconditional, and complete return of the islands to Japan. The reversion movement gained steam in the late 1960s as it intersected with growing anti–Vietnam War sentiment stemming from US military use of bases in Okinawa for attacks on North Vietnam. In the first election for leader of the Ryūkyū government held in November 1968 (leaders were previously appointed by the American administrators), Yara Chōbyō—former chair of the Okinawa Board of Education and leader of the Reversion Council—was elected with strong endorsement from the leftist parties. Although his authority was still subject to American oversight and veto, Yara's election gave reversionist Okinawans a powerful public voice.

Just months after Yara assumed office, a US B52 bomber crashed and exploded close to a US nuclear weapons storage facility, prompting Yara and fellow Okinawan activists to demand that all such facilities be removed after reversion. In response, Satō was forced to promise that, in the reversion negotiations with the Americans, the

Japanese government would require that any remaining US military bases on Okinawa be nuclear weapons free—in line with the situation on mainland Japan. This commitment followed Satō's pronouncement in the House of Representatives Budgetary Committee in 1967 of the Japanese government's "three nonnuclear principles": not possessing, not producing, and not permitting the introduction of nuclear weapons into the country. As discussed below, these principles would subsequently be watered down by a secret agreement between Satō and President Richard Nixon.

Indeed, the reversion negotiations benefited greatly from Nixon's arrival at the White House in January 1969. The new president was looking for an honorable exit from the Vietnam War, as well as greater defense burden sharing by America's Asian allies—his so-called Nixon Doctrine. The negotiations were led by Secretary of State Henry Kissinger and Satō-appointed negotiator, Wakazumi Kei, a well-connected academic from Kyoto Sangyō University. To maintain secrecy, the two referred to one another as "Dr. Jones" and "Mr. Yoshida" in all communications. Following an official meeting at the White House in November 1969, Nixon and Satō released a joint communiqué in which the United States agreed to return Okinawa to Japan in 1972 and both sides reiterated their commitment to the Anpo Treaty—including the continuity of US bases on Okinawa. Concerning Japan's nonnuclear principles, the Americans promised that nuclear weapons would not be stored on US military bases on the islands after reversion. Only many years later was it revealed that, in return for removing nuclear weapons from Okinawan military bases, Nixon demanded that Satō sign a secret agreement—which he did—consenting to the reintroduction of nuclear weapons in the event of a security crisis.

Unaware of this agreement, the Japanese public was generally favorable toward Satō's seeming "nuclear free" reversion settlement, although opposition to the ongoing presence of US military bases persisted among many Okinawans, some of whom even desired outright independence for the islands. Okinawan anger was further inflamed in 1970 after US authorities failed to equitably resolve the death of an Okinawan woman in a hit-and-run accident involving a military vehicle. Some five thousand Okinawans subsequently clashed with military police as they sacked US facilities in the infamous Coza Riot. Such instances of American military crimes and local resentment would persist after reversion.

The bilateral agreement for reversion was signed in 1971, followed by Okinawa's official return as a prefecture of Japan with Diet representation on May 15, 1972. His job completed, Satō quietly stepped down from the prime ministership in early July. Of course, despite its "reversion" and the sense of sovereignty regained, US military bases continued to dominate the Okinawan landscape, representing 75 percent of all US bases in Japan in a prefecture with only 0.6 percent of the country's land area. Finally, in one of the more farcical codas of postwar Japanese political history, the

Norwegian Nobel Committee awarded Satō Eisaku its Nobel Peace Prize in 1974 for his three nonnuclear principles undergirding the return of Okinawa.

Satō's successful reversion negotiations set the stage for the largely uncontested automatic extension of the Anpo Treaty in 1970. Groups like Zenkyōtō, Beheiren, the Antiwar Youth Committee of Workers, and various New Left sects did clash with the authorities in Tokyo, sometimes in violent exchanges involving Molotov cocktails and riot squads armed with tear gas. But the established leftist parties could offer only feeble opposition. Above all, the protests received almost no popular support from a general public more and more hostile to student violence after the campus upheavals of 1968 and 1969. Indeed, with the automatic extension of the treaty and the imminent return of Okinawa, many student and civic activists began to reconsider their strategies and agendas, opening the way for a new generation of civic activism to develop in the coming decades

Politics in the 1970s: The Rise and Fall (and Afterlife) of Tanaka Kakuei

The Nixon Shocks

While Richard Nixon had actively used clandestine diplomacy and secret agreements with the Japanese government in the Okinawa negotiations, on other issues he kept quiet, dumbfounding the Japanese with sudden paradigm-shifting policy announcements. The two most significant of these so-called Nixon Shocks came one after the other in 1971. In mid-July, the Nixon administration announced that Secretary of State Kissinger had made a secret visit to the PRC, where he arranged with Premier Zhou Enlai for President Nixon to make an official visit the following year, at which time relations would be normalized. This announcement came as a major shock to the Japanese, who were only informed by the Americans immediately prior to the official press release. Satō and his conservative associates were rightly infuriated at being blindsided, particularly because they had faithfully continued to resist pressure from pro-China conservatives in the LDP who were pushing for normalization with the PRC in Japan's economic interests. The subsequent meeting between Nixon, Zhou, and Mao Zedong in February 1972 resulted in the United States recognizing the PRC as the legitimate government of China—inclusive of Taiwan. By doing so, the Americans hoped to exploit the growing rift between the PRC and the Soviets while also halting Chinese support for the North Vietnamese, thus paving the way for a speedy conclusion to the war in Indochina. Despite their displeasure with Nixon's tactics, ultimately this "shock" opened the way to the resumption of diplomatic ties between Japan and the PRC soon after.

The second Nixon Shock came exactly one month later in mid-August, this time in the form of an economic bombshell. Against the backdrop of rising outlays for the Vietnam War and dollar outflows exceeding gold reserves, Nixon announced a new economic policy under which the United States would abandon the Bretton Woods Agreement of 1944, ending the convertibility of the US dollar to gold. To protect the US dollar against the expected currency fluctuations, a 10 percent tariff would also be imposed on all imports and quotas implemented for textiles. US trade officials also began negotiations with foreign countries on exchange rates to devalue the US dollar and raise the competitiveness of American products globally. Nixon's announcement came as yet another body blow for the Japanese, who had benefited greatly from an artificially low exchange rate of 360 yen to the dollar since the Dodge Line of the late 1940s.

Under the new economic regime, Japanese exports would become considerably more expensive. As stock markets worldwide slumped in response to Nixon's announcement, the Japanese government reacted by purchasing over US$4 billion to prop up the yen and maintain the existing exchange rate. After a brief interlude of floating exchange rates, the finance ministers of the ten major industrialized nations met at the Smithsonian Institution in Washington, DC in December 1971. Here they agreed to revalue both the Japanese yen and the West German deutschmark against the US dollar and institute a system of exchange rate ranges pegged to the dollar. The yen was set at 308 to the dollar, representing an almost 17 percent appreciation.

But this Smithsonian Agreement also proved short lived. In February 1973, Japan joined other industrialized nations by floating its currency on the international exchange market. With this move, the yen strengthened even further, rising to 261 yen to the dollar on the day after floating and continuing to appreciate thereafter. The revaluation of the yen worried Japanese business executives and politicians, who feared for the international competitiveness of Japanese exports.[1] Conversely, a stronger yen meant cheaper prices for the imported raw materials needed by industry. It also encouraged Japanese industry to move across borders, especially into East Asia.

Perhaps the most significant legacy of Nixon's "Dollar Shock" was the advent of inflation in Japan. The Japanese government had already begun lowering the official discount rate before the shock in response to an economic downturn in 1970. This monetary easing continued into 1971 and 1972 as officials tried to slow the rising value of the yen, but their efforts proved fruitless as the currency continued to rise. What did remain, however, was an inflation time bomb, which would soon be ignited by a flamboyant new prime minister and an energy crisis of historic proportions in 1973.

Tanaka, the Modern-Day Regent

Satō Eisaku could bathe in the glory of Okinawa's reversion and his place as Japan's longest serving prime minister at that time (seven years and eight months), while happily leaving the fallout from the Nixon Shocks for his successor to deal with. Several contenders including Ōhira Masayoshi, Miki Takeo, Fukuda Takeo, and Tanaka Kakuei stepped forward to contest the LDP leadership after Satō, but the race was ultimately between Fukuda and Tanaka. Given the unsettled economic circumstances, Fukuda—a former bureaucrat from the MOF and cut from the same cloth as Ikeda and Satō—was seen as the most likely successor. In the first round of voting for the LDP presidency in July 1972, Tanaka (156) and Fukuda (150) were neck and neck, with Ōhira and Miki capturing only a small number of votes. But voting swung dramatically in the direction of Tanaka in the runoff, when he comfortably defeated Fukuda 282 to 190 votes with support from the other factions.

Tanaka's public popularity no doubt played a role in his triumph. Then Japan's youngest prime minister at fifty-four years of age, Tanaka was a politician lacking an academic or bureaucratic pedigree. He was first elected to the Diet in 1947, thereafter holding various ministerial posts under Yoshida, Kishi, Ikeda, and Satō. Tanaka had a strong public image as a self-made man of the people thanks to his exploits as president of a construction company in his native Niigata Prefecture. With his thick regional accent and rugged style, the charismatic Tanaka cut a remarkably different figure from his rather colorless predecessors. The media quickly dubbed him the "people's prime minister," "Kaku-san," "the computerized bulldozer" (for his supposed economic prowess), and the "modern-day regent," which likened Tanaka to the sixteenth-century samurai Toyotomi Hideyoshi who had risen from lowly birth to become the emperor's regent. Thanks to this image, at the start of his administration in 1972, Tanaka's cabinet enjoyed historic approval ratings in the sixtieth percentile, surpassing previous highs enjoyed by Yoshida Shigeru after the Treaty of Peace with Japan in 1952.

Although Tanaka's prime ministership would be short lived, his influence over politics—particularly in the selection of LDP leaders—would continue until the late 1980s. His faction grew to become the largest and most powerful in the LDP thanks primarily to Tanaka's ability to provide financial support for his followers. Although money and related scandals had certainly been a part of conservative (and even progressive) politics in Japan since the early postwar years, with the rise of Tanaka, both the scale and the corrupting influence of money reached new heights.

Tanaka's first major achievement—and arguably the easiest to realize—was dealing with Nixon's China shock. He was assisted here by both business and political

Figure 5.1. Tanaka Kakuei leading three cheers (*banzai*) after his election to the LDP presidency on July 5, 1972. Courtesy of The Asahi Shimbun Company.

initiatives to build better ties with the PRC. In September 1971, soon after Nixon's China announcement, a multipartisan group of politicians called the Diet Members Alliance to Promote Sino-Japanese Normalization (formed in 1970) had travelled to the PRC, where they signed a declaration proclaiming the Japan–Republic of China (Taiwan) Treaty invalid. Throughout the year, numerous prefectures and municipalities also passed resolutions calling for the normalization of diplomatic ties, while business delegations from Tokyo and Osaka prefectures visited the PRC. Both the Japanese and Chinese were eager to restore ties: the former attracted by the business possibilities of such a massive market, the latter reeling from the economic reverberations of the Cultural Revolution. As noted earlier, trade between the two countries had continued throughout the 1960s, if intermittently interrupted by politics.

Before making any formal overtures, in August 1972, Tanaka travelled to Hawai'i to meet with Nixon, who gave his stamp of approval for Sino-Japanese normalization. The following month, Tanaka and his chief cabinet secretary, Nikaidō Susumu, visited the PRC, where they negotiated the details of normalization with Zhou and Mao. With great fanfare in September 1972, Tanaka and Foreign Minister Ōhira Masayoshi signed the joint communiqué with Zhou and Mao. Similar to the American normalization agreement, the Japanese recognized the PRC as the "sole legal government of China"[2]—including Taiwan; the treaty between Japan and the Republic of China (Taiwan) was thereby annulled; the state of "abnormal relations" (i.e., state of war) between the two nations ended; and an agreement was made to sign a Treaty of Peace and Friendship in the near future (ultimately in 1978). Importantly, the preamble to the communiqué also included a Japanese recognition of past transgressions saying, "The Japanese side is keenly conscious of the responsibility for the serious damage that Japan caused in the past to the Chinese people through war, and deeply reproaches itself."[3] Although no longer formally recognized, Taiwan was not completely abandoned in this process. In December 1972, the Japanese Embassy in Taipei was replaced by the Interchange Association (later the Japan-Taiwan Exchange Association), which provided diplomatic and consular services thereafter. Moreover, the Japan-Taiwan Exchange Nongovernmental Agreement was signed in 1973.

In relation to Nixon's Dollar Shock of 1971, Tanaka arguably did not so much manage as exacerbate its inflationary pressures through his flagrantly expansionary economic policies. Around a month before ascending to the prime ministership in mid-1972, Tanaka published his best seller *Nihon rettō kaizō ron* (*Building a New Japan: A Plan for Remodeling the Japanese Archipelago*), written with the assistance of bureaucrats and selling over a million copies. The book detailed Tanaka's ambitious plan to revitalize regional areas through the decentralization of industry, the establishment of new regional cities of around 250,000 people, the construction of a national high-speed rail and road network, policies to deal with environmental pollution and overdevelopment, and a comprehensive restructuring of social welfare. In essence, Tanaka's grand plan was very much a continuation of the policies for economic growth instituted under Ikeda Hayato, but it came at a highly inopportune moment with Nixon's Dollar Shock of 1971 followed by the First Oil Shock of 1973.

Among the arguably positive outcomes of Tanaka's plan were improvements in social welfare—short lived though some of them were. Here Tanaka built on Satō Eisaku's notion of "social development" for addressing the excesses of high-speed growth, while simultaneously trying to steal back the welfare agenda captured by progressive local administrations elected in the late 1960s. In 1972, for example, medical care was made free of charge for persons over seventy years of age, and family payments for national health insurance were reduced in the following year. Pension payments for retirees were also increased and indexed to inflation. Together, these reforms led to 1973 being dubbed "Year One of the Welfare Era." Although not strictly welfare, the government also instituted a new compensation system for industrial pollution victims, and supported small business with government loans and a new law restricting the growth of large retail chains. Not all were supportive of such moves, especially fiscal conservatives who watched in horror as government spending increased 25 percent annually from 1972 to 1975 in welfare, public works, new Shinkansen lines, and road infrastructure like tunnels and bridges.[4] As government finances deteriorated throughout the decade, calls for a "reconsideration of welfare" gradually intensified, resulting in a scaling back of some supports in the 1980s.

The increased government spending under Tanaka and his successors—much of it for political pork-barreling—further exacerbated the country's inflation problem. Throughout the high-growth years from 1960 to 1972, consumer prices had remained in the 4 to 6 percent range, but they rose by over 11 percent in 1973 alone—a figure that more than doubled the following year. Anticipating a development boom from Tanaka's plan, corporations and individual investors—flush with cash thanks to the government's monetary easing after the Nixon Dollar Shock—began to engage in real estate speculation, while trading companies hoarded commodities such as timber to reap larger profits from construction demand. In response, the government was forced to pass a law in July 1973 prohibiting hoarding or intentionally restricting the supply of fourteen everyday necessities. Residential land prices, especially in the big cities, were already rising at a rate of 20 percent throughout the 1960s, but they rose an astounding 42.5 percent in the speculative climate of 1973, pushing many buyers out of the market.[5]

Tanaka incurred the wrath of voters for these excesses. Brimming with confidence after his triumph in China, he called a general election in November 1972 in the expectation of a massive victory. Although the LDP claimed a comfortable majority with 271 seats, it lost seventeen. Meanwhile, the JSP and JCP made impressive gains in urban constituencies like Tokyo and Osaka, where voters were struggling with skyrocketing costs of living and land prices. Tanaka's electoral pain continued under the shadow of the First Oil Shock. In the July 1974 upper house election, the LDP lost five seats despite the prime minister pouring a reported twenty billion yen of his own money into the campaign and flying around the country in a helicopter.[6] Fed up with Tanaka's tactics and perhaps sensing political blood, Minister of Finance Fukuda Takeo and Deputy Prime Minister Miki Takeo tendered their resignations from the cabinet following the election. After initially high ratings, Tanaka's approval percentage had fallen into the midtwenties and his non-approval into the sixties by late 1973.

But it was not the strained economic conditions that precipitated Tanaka's downfall. Rather, it was the exposure of the rampant corruption and money politics fueling his prime ministership. In October 1974, a maverick reporter, Tachibana Takashi, published a scathing exposé detailing Tanaka's political fundraising through shady real estate dealings, his use of vote buying to secure the LDP leadership, and his illegal tax evasion. Tanaka attempted damage control through a cabinet reshuffle, but the mounting party and public pressure was relentless. His two-year prime ministership finally collapsed with his resignation on November 26, 1974. A US Senate committee hearing into the lobbying practices of American multinationals in 1976 further exposed the entrenched corruption under Tanaka. The hearing revealed that the Lockheed Corporation had paid bribes to various Japanese politicians, bureaucrats, and executives via the trading company Marubeni and with assistance from the infamous Yakuza crime boss Kodama Yoshio. Tanaka had received five hundred million yen to ensure that All Nippon Airlines (ANA) purchased Lockheed's Tristar jets instead of those of its competitor, McDonnell Douglas. In the subsequent fallout, Tanaka was arrested and brought to trial on charges of having received bribes and for violations of foreign exchange laws. In 1983, the court delivered a guilty verdict, sentencing the former prime minister to a four-year prison sentence and a heavy fine. Tanaka was freed on bail pending appeal, but the case was dropped in 1993, following his death due to long-standing complications from a stroke in 1986. Nonetheless, through all the upheaval, Tanaka stayed on as an independent Diet member until 1990. Thanks to his financial clout and powerful faction, Tanaka would shape the fate of the next five prime ministers.

Politics in Tanaka's Shadow

Politics "after" Tanaka have been described by one historian as a tale of "musical prime ministers," with no less than four LDP leaders from December 1974 to

November 1982—an average of around two years per prime minister.[7] Following Tanaka's resignation, Ōhira Masayoshi and Fukuda Takeo emerged as likely contenders. However, to avoid a messy internecine struggle for power and a possible party split, LDP vice president Shiina Etsusaburō intervened to broker a compromise among the major factions. Miki Takeo, leader of a small, progressive-leaning faction, was chosen as a caretaker replacement for Tanaka thanks to his clean image and distance from the big factions. He was charged with cleaning up and modernizing the party in the wake of the scandals, with support from Fukuda as deputy prime minister and Ōhira in the finance portfolio. Miki set himself a bold—and ultimately unattainable—reform agenda centered on regulating political donations, instituting a primary vote in LDP presidential elections inclusive of grassroots party members, and revising both the electoral and antimonopoly laws. Coming from a minority faction, however, meant that Miki was unable to realize much substantive change. The decision by his cabinet in 1976 to limit defense spending to 1 percent of GDP was among the few relatively enduring legacies of his administration.

In the wake of the Lockheed incident, Miki's prime ministership came under increasing pressure from Tanaka faction members due to his staunch refusal to protect their leader from prosecution. After leaving jail on one-hundred-million-yen bail, Tanaka began to conspire for Miki's downfall, supported now by Ōhira and Tanaka-rival Fukuda. The December 1976 House of Representatives election provided the opportunity to strike, as the LDP failed to secure a majority on its own for the first time in the party's history. The poor electoral performance was exacerbated by the departure in June of Kōno Yōhei and four others in protest of the Lockheed scandal. Their New Liberal Club (NLC) party grew to eighteen members after the election thanks to support from irritated conservative voters. The LDP subsequently managed to gain a majority by coaxing independent conservatives to join the party, but the blow to Miki proved fatal. In December 1976, he resigned, taking responsibility for the electoral carnage.

With Miki gone, the way was now open for Tanaka's great rival, Fukuda Takeo, to swoop on the prime ministership. Like Miki, Fukuda came to the position with a reform agenda and was quickly dubbed the "cleaning minister" (*sōji daijin*)—a play on the Japanese term for "prime minister" (*sōri daijin*). But his aloof bureaucratic style never drew popular support and, within the LDP, his hold on power was constantly dogged by resistance from Ōhira and Tanaka. Nonetheless, Fukuda pushed forward with party reform. In 1977, his party reform committee decided on a new process for LDP presidential elections. The first stage would involve a primary vote among party members and friends at the grassroots, followed by a second stage of voting by LDP Diet members. The aim here was to try and eliminate the influence of the factions in presidential elections. Unfortunately for Fukuda, however, the reform backfired spectacularly. As the LDP presidential elections approached in November 1978, Ōhira—assisted by the Tanaka political machine—managed to encourage 1.5 million supporters to join the party as members or friends. In the presidential primary election on November 26, Ōhira convincingly defeated an outmaneuvered Fukuda. The "shadow shogun" Tanaka had struck again, with Fukuda meekly resigning after the first-round primary vote.

Ōhira's prime ministership was hardly more productive than those preceding it in recent years. Acting on economically sound but politically dangerous advice from the MOF, Ōhira decided to push for the implementation of a consumption tax in 1980 to help reduce government debt. He took the policy to the polls in the October 1979 lower house election, which the LDP hoped would break the emerging parity between conservative and progressive representation in the Diet. But the backlash over the proposed consumption tax among small business owners and others plagued the campaign, so much so that Ōhira was forced to promise that no new tax would be implemented in 1980. The LDP still performed poorly, gaining only 248 seats—one less than the 1976 election outcome that had forced Miki's resignation. Once again, Ōhira was only able to secure a majority for the LDP by bringing independent conservatives into the party. Pressure for Ōhira's resignation from the Fukuda, Miki, and Nakasone factions intensified thereafter, with the Tanaka faction as Ōhira's only lifeline.

In May 1980, Fukuda and Miki brought matters to a head by absenting themselves from a routine no-confidence vote on the Ōhira cabinet, instituted by the opposition. So virulent was the internal wrangling that LDP members were willing to side with the opposition to bring down the party leader—which eventuated when the Diet passed the motion. With this extraordinary "happening," as the press dubbed it, Ōhira had no choice but to dissolve the Diet and call an election.

The June 1980 ballot was the first combined upper and lower house election in the postwar era. Adding to the drama, in late May, an embattled Ōhira was hospitalized after suffering a heart attack, and he died two weeks later. Thanks in great part to an outpouring of sympathy for Ōhira, the LDP won over 55 percent of seats in the House of Councillors, while in the House of Representatives, twenty-six more of its candidates were elected than in 1979, giving it a comfortable majority of 284 seats. After another round of factional bargaining following the election, Suzuki Zenkō—yet another uninspiring figure from the Ōhira faction—stepped into the prime ministership as a peacemaker. But his lack of vision and leadership meant he would only be warming the leadership seat for his successor, Nakasone Yasuhiro.

How are we to understand the unsettled politics of the 1970s and the persistence of LDP rule? To begin with, throughout the decade, the LDP's grip on power appeared to be tenuous, with its percentage of the popular vote decreasing (only to rise again in 1980). Nonetheless, the party managed to secure majorities in the lower house by absorbing independent conservatives. This tended to compensate for losses to breakaway conservative parties, like the reform-minded NLC. Factions also supported their members by providing the money needed to build grassroots constituencies. LDP politicians' involvement in the party's Policy Affairs Research Council (PARC) helped them to develop expertise and influence in specific policy areas, like construction, agriculture, and defense. Not only did such expertise give LDP politicians greater leverage over bureaucrats in policymaking but it also afforded them a distinct advantage over opposition parties that were locked out of resource allocation decisions.

Another reason for the LDP's survival during the 1970s had to do with the ongoing division among the opposition parties. Although parties like the CGP and the DSP made electoral gains in elections from 1972 to 1980, support for the JSP dwindled, while the JCP experienced, at best, fluctuating support in lower house elections. As table 5.1 also shows, the opposition parties made essentially no gains in House of Councillors elections throughout the decade. The JSP's seats steadily declined, similar to the party's fate in the House of Representatives. Interestingly, the combined number of seats held by the opposition parties in both houses in these years was not dramatically different from the LDP, raising the interesting counterfactual question about what a unified opposition may have been able to accomplish in these years.

Table 5.1 Diet Seats of Major Parties after National Elections, 1970–1980

	LDP	NLC	CGP	DSP	JSP	JCP	Combined Opposition[a]
			House of Representatives				
1972	271	—	29	19	118	38	204
1976	249	—	55	29	123	17	224
1979	248	4	57	35	107	39	238
1980	284	—	33	32	107	29	201
			House of Councillors[b]				
1971	131	—	22	13	66	10	118
1974	126	—	24	10	62	20	126
1977	124	3	25	11	56	16	125
1980	135	3	26	11	47	12	101

Source: Jichishō Senkyobu, *Shūgiin giin sōsenkyo*, pp. 20, 62.

[a] Combined Opposition includes Diet members not belonging to the major parties.

[b] Figures for the House of Councillors include seats not up for election.

The Economy in the 1970s and Early 1980s: Shocks and Transitions

The First Oil Shock, 1973

Japan's high-speed economic growth had begun to slow in the wake of the Nixon Dollar Shock, and Tanaka Kakuei's redevelopment vision only served to spur inflation. The economy faced yet another crisis in December 1973, when the ten member nations of the Organization of Arab Petroleum Exporting Countries (OAPEC) announced an oil embargo on countries that had supported Israel in the Fourth Arab-Israeli War. Along with the United States, Canada, and the United Kingdom, Japan was subjected to progressive restrictions on its oil supplies. This came as a huge blow, given that crude oil represented over 70 percent of Japan's primary energy needs by the early 1970s, of which close to 80 percent came from the Middle East. Aggravating the pain, OAPEC gradually decreased crude oil production, while members of the Organization of the Petroleum Exporting Countries (OPEC) agreed to raise their prices. The result was an almost 300 percent increase in the price of oil from $3 per barrel before the crisis to around $12 per barrel when the embargo was lifted in early 1974.

The impacts in Japan were immediate and painful. In late 1973, wholesale prices spiked by 22 percent, while consumer prices rose by over 13 percent. The rampant inflation—or "skyrocketing prices" as it was called in the media—continued into 1974, when the wholesale price index rose to almost 35 percent and the consumer price index to around 25 percent. All kinds of products were impacted, from daily necessities to consumer durables and automobiles. Opportunistic price gouging and hoarding of commodities like toilet paper, detergent, soap, and sugar by suppliers and retailers further exacerbated the crisis; prices for consumer electronics and passenger vehicles, which should have risen by around 3 percent, actually increased by over 15 and 23 percent, respectively.[8]

Panicked by rumors of shortages, consumers rushed to stock up on toilet paper and soap. Newspapers carried images of security guards struggling to control frenzied shoppers, and reports emerged of school children stealing toilet paper from school lavatories. Wages also rose in response to the sudden spike in the cost of living, putting further pressure on business costs and price inflation and precipitating a classic instance of a price-wage spiral. For the first time since 1955, the Japanese economy was in a state of stagflation in 1974: in other words, negative economic growth combined with high inflation. Due to the rising cost of oil, Japan's balance of payments experienced a trade deficit in 1973, although this would be short lived and only repeated briefly again after the Second Oil Shock of the late 1970s.

Figure 5.2. Shoppers line up at a Tokyo supermarket to purchase sugar, detergent, and toilet paper—all believed to be in short supply—following the First Oil Shock in November 1973. Courtesy of The Asahi Shimbun Company.

The First Oil Shock dealt a lethal blow to Tanaka's grand redevelopment plan. After the sudden death of Minister of Finance Aichi Kiichi in late November 1973, Tanaka was forced to appoint his rival, the fiscal conservative Fukuda Takeo, to the position. Fukuda's appointment complemented the cabinet's "Outline of Emergency Measures for Petroleum" released around ten days earlier. This outline called for an overall reduction in government spending; a 10 percent reduction in consumption of oil and electricity; a request to retailers like restaurants, cinemas, bars, and nightclubs to switch off neon signs and reduce opening hours; the temporary halting of late-night television broadcasts; self-restraint in the use of highways; voluntary temporary closures of gasoline stands; and a reduction in the number of pages in daily newspapers. In December, the Diet passed two emergency laws: the Petroleum Supply and Demand Adjustment Law, aimed at reducing oil consumption and stabilizing its distribution and price; and the National Livelihood Stabilization Emergency Measures Law, which gave the state powers to initiate rationing measures when needed. Fukuda also used the FY1974 budget to dampen aggregate demand by significantly tightening public spending—killing some of Tanaka's pet projects like new Shinkansen lines, highway projects, and a bridge linking Honshū and Kyūshū Islands. He was supported by business organizations, like the Keidanren, which endorsed measures to bring inflation under control.

The government's countermeasures were largely successful—almost too successful—as the economy slipped into negative growth and a short period of stagflation in 1974. The initial aim had been to cut crude oil consumption by 10 percent but, in a massive show of national self-restraint, the country realized a massive 25 percent reduction. On the diplomatic front, in November 1973, the government modified its pro-Israeli policy in a desperate bid to restore secure and affordable supplies of crude oil. Japan now demanded Israel's immediate withdrawal from the Occupied Territories and its recognition of the rights of the Palestinians. In December, Tanaka sent Deputy Prime Minister Miki Takeo to the Middle East as a special envoy, where he visited oil-producing countries to reinforce Japan's close friendship and beg for the lifting of the export restrictions on Japan. The trip proved successful with oil supplies beginning to recover thereafter.

The government's final task after the First Oil Shock was to address the threat of recession in the wake of the economic belt-tightening and negative growth in 1974. The FY1975 budget addressed this issue with a restoration of some public works projects and other forms of stimulus, followed by the issuing of government bonds in a supplementary budget later in the year. The Bank of Japan pitched in by lowering the official discount rate. In turn, the economy responded positively, with economic growth in 1975 registering 3.2 percent.

Economic Transitions in an Era of Stable Growth

Following the First Oil Shock, "energy conservation" (*shōene*) became a popular buzzword in all corners of society. Businesses responded by adopting "lean management" approaches through office automation and computerization, increased use of robotics, worker productivity–raising initiatives, and energy-efficient investments. By 1982, Japan had around fourteen thousand industrial robots, which represented an amazing 63 percent of robots worldwide.[9] But lean management also had a harder edge, involving gradual reductions in the number of regular full-time employees and greater use of easily "disposable" temporary workers and contract labor—many of whom were women. This latter trend would become more and more prominent in the 1980s and 1990s. Those who did enjoy the benefits of secure employment (mostly male workers) were subject to frequent job rotations and transfers, often taking them away from their families. The guarantee of employment also entailed a commitment to working long hours of overtime—much of this being unpaid "service" overtime—resulting in increasing cases of so-called death from overwork (*karōshi*). According to 1987 statistics from the Ministry of Labor (MOL), at 2,150 hours annually, Japanese employees were working 226 hours more than those in the United States and 495 more than those in West Germany—the equivalent of around 9.4 and 21.5 days more per year respectively.[10] The weakened labor movement did little to resist such trends, especially in terms of providing support for nonregular workers who did not fit under its traditional remit. Despite growing numbers of deaths from overwork and support from activist lawyers for bereaved families, the MOL only recognized a handful of cases each year, while many companies preferred to settle quietly out of court, helping to keep the phenomenon out of the media and public attention.

After having successfully navigated the First Oil Shock, Japan faced yet another energy upheaval late in the decade. On December 17, 1978, OPEC suddenly announced that crude oil prices would be raised by 15.5 percent in stages throughout 1979. A week later, oil production in Iran stopped due to the country's Islamic Revolution. Together, the two events precipitated the Second Oil Shock worldwide. Having learned from the 1973 crisis, Japanese economic officials were quick to respond, tightening monetary policy via three official discount rate rises in late 1979 and early 1980. As a result, inflation did not exceed 10 percent after the shock. The economy was able to sustain steady growth of around 3 to 4 percent into the 1980s, while maintaining an unemployment rate of around 2 percent compared to an average of 7.3 percent for member countries of the Organisation for Economic Co-operation and Development (OECD).[11] This stood the Japanese economy in stark contrast to other developed economies, like the United States, where protracted stagflation took root. So resiliently did the Japanese economy respond that the Bank of Japan felt comfortable enough to actually lower the official discount rate two times in 1980.[12]

While Japan came out of the second crisis relatively unscathed, the Oil Shocks of the 1970s served as catalytic forces in the transformation of Japanese industry. As figure 5.3 reveals, the relative contribution of sectors to GDP continued to gradually shift from the primary to the secondary and, ultimately, the tertiary industries such as financial services, retail, transport and communications, and real estate. Manufacturing not only shrank but also transformed in terms of outputs. In Japanese, this process has been characterized as a transition from the production of "heavy, solid, long, and large" (*jūkōchōdai*) to "light, lean, short, and compact" (*keihakutanshō*). The heavy and petrochemical industries like shipbuilding, steelmaking, paper, fertilizers, and aluminum, which were already on the precipice of decline, were hit particularly hard by the shocks. Under the administrative guidance of economic bureaucrats, production facilities in certain petrochemical industries were reduced by almost 30 percent. The steel industry experienced major reductions, with furnaces closing at some of the giants like Yahata and Kamaishi. Workers in steel and shipbuilding were redeployed into other operations, sent to subcontractors, or even pressured into early retirement. Blue-collar workers in declining industries often found themselves

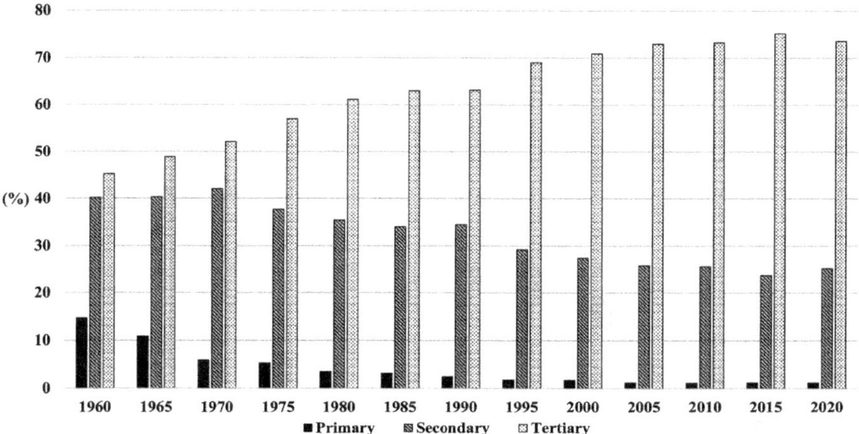

Sources: Inoue, "Heisei 24nen Keizai Sensasu"; and Yoshikawa and Miyakawa, "Sangyō Kōzō no Henka."'

Figure 5.3. Trends in the Composition of Industry as a Percentage of Nominal GDP, 1960–2020

absorbed into the service divisions of their corporations as sales representatives or even restaurant managers and waiters.[13] To assist in the transition, the government passed laws in 1978 and 1983 to better define the prerequisites for recognition as a declining sector and the nature of official support.

While the industrial giants of the high-growth era declined, new industries—many of which owed their emergence and early growth to the heavy and petrochemical industries—thrived in the wake of the Oil Shocks. Among these were automobiles and consumer electronics, along with hi-tech industries like semiconductors, advanced electrical machinery and robots, and computers (fig. 5.4). In 1980, passenger vehicle exports increased by 30 percent from 3.1 to 3.95 million units, continuing to grow thereafter to a peak of 4.57 million units in 1987—despite the implementation of voluntary export restrictions to the United States (discussed later in this chapter).[14] Electronics showed a similar growth, with companies like Sony, Toshiba, Fujitsu, and NEC becoming household names worldwide and capturing large shares of global markets for semiconductors, new consumer appliances, and office equipment such as facsimile machines.

The tertiary sector of the economy centered on services also developed rapidly in the wake of the Oil Shocks, rising from 52.1 percent of GDP in 1970 to 63.1 percent in 1990 and over 70 percent by the turn of the century.[15] Companies in this sector included banking, investment, insurance, securities trading, media and communications, advertising, and education services (so-called cram schools to prepare

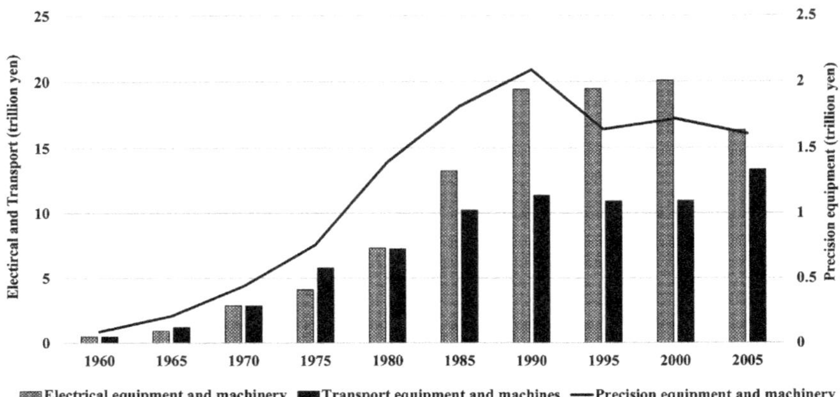

Yoshikawa Hiroshi and Miyakawa Shūko, "Sangyō Kōzō no Henka to Sengo Nihon no Keizai Seichō," *RIETI Discussion Paper Series*, 09-J-024, accessed January 16, 2023, https://www.rieti.go.jp/jp/publications/summary/09090001.html.

Figure 5.4. Manufacturing Performance in Electrical, Transport, and Precision Equipment Industries, 1960–2005

students for demanding university entrance exams). Property and real estate companies—often run by shady operators—also rose to prominence in the 1970s and, more so, the 1980s. Their speculative dealings would precipitate a ruinous asset price bubble in the late 1980s.

Thanks to these industrial transitions, the Japanese economy was able to withstand the Oil Shocks with greater resilience than many other industrialized nations globally. The development of new industries also meant that Japanese exports would continue to grow—sixfold in the years from 1970 to 1990—expanding the profile of Japanese companies and their brands worldwide.[16] Indeed, it is during the late 1970s and throughout the 1980s that Japan came to be seen as a global economic superpower. Yet there were negatives associated with this new status. In the early 1970s, it resulted in violent backlashes from citizens in Southeast Asian countries fearful of an economic invasion. In the 1980s, it became the basis for cantankerous trade frictions with the United States.

The Oil Shocks also precipitated a shift in Japan's energy profile. As figure 5.5 shows, prior to the First Oil Shock, Japan's reliance on crude oil for primary energy was greater than 70 percent but, by 1990, this had decreased to around 55 percent.[17] Diminishing imports of oil required a restructuring of the country's energy portfolio. The government turned to new sources of energy, such as imported liquid natural gas (LNG), hydroelectric power, and nuclear power, which became more prominent after the shocks.

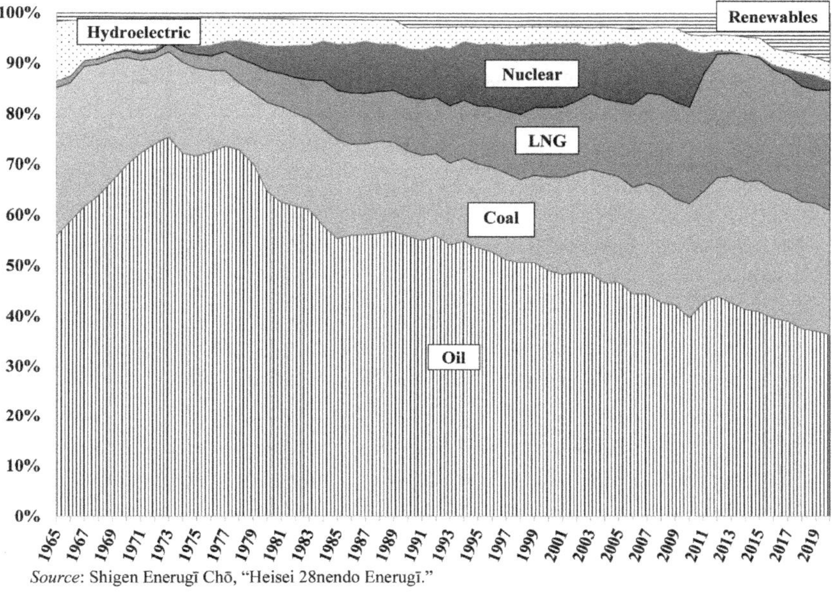

Source: Shigen Enerugī Chō, "Heisei 28nendo Enerugī."

Figure 5.5. Changes in Domestic Supply of Primary Energy in Japan, 1965–2020

Development of the peaceful use of nuclear energy for electricity production had a much longer history in Japan, beginning soon after President Eisenhower's famous "Atoms for Peace" speech at the UN General Assembly in 1953. In response, the following year, the young conservative politician Nakasone Yasuhiro and others arranged for a special budget to support research and development of nuclear power in the country. In 1955, the US-Japan Nuclear Power Agreement was signed, giving Japan access to enriched uranium. The Diet also passed the Basic Law on Nuclear Power along with two other nuclear-related laws to enable research and development on nuclear power for peaceful applications. Thereafter, the government established the Nuclear Power Committee under the chairmanship of Shōriki Matsutarō, a former policing bureaucrat in the Ministry of Home Affairs and now owner of the conservative-leaning *Yomiuri shinbun*. Shōriki had spent time in Sugamo Prison as a suspected war criminal at the end of the Asia-Pacific War, where he became a close comrade of fellow detainee, Kishi Nobusuke. After his release, Shōriki developed covert connections with the CIA, which the Americans utilized to influence policymaking in areas such as nuclear power.

With the legal and political infrastructure in place, the Japan Nuclear Research Laboratory was established at Tōkaimura in Ibaraki Prefecture in 1956. When its experimental reactor reached criticality in that year, the media proclaimed the dawn of Japan's nuclear age. A decade later, the Tōkaimura facility became the site of Japan's first commercial nuclear power plant, using modified technology from the British General Electric Company. During the 1960s, power companies began construction of light water reactors, which came online in the 1970s. Thus, even before the Oil Shocks, the Japanese government was well along the path of nuclear power development.

At the Osaka World Exposition in 1970, power companies cooperating in nuclear power development exhibited an actual-size replica of a nuclear reactor core, while energy for the exposition was supplied by the Tsuruga Nuclear Power Station in Fukui Prefecture, which commenced operations on the opening day of the event. In the decades during and after the Oil Shocks, nuclear power plant construction proceeded apace. In the 1970s, nineteen new reactors began operations in Fukui, Shimane, Saga, Fukushima, Shizuoka, and Ehime prefectures. A further sixteen reactors came online in the 1980s and the same number again in the 1990s, raising the profile of nuclear power generation in Japan's energy portfolio.

Opposition to nuclear power emerged almost as soon as power plant construction started in the 1960s. Local residents initiated various lawsuits and campaigns to stop plant siting in their communities, while scientists and other civic activists mobilized against nuclear power as inherently dangerous. Such activism was supported by intermittent nuclear accidents in Japan and abroad, like the leakage of radiation from Japan's first—and only—nuclear powered vessel, *Mutsu,* in 1974, the Three Mile Island accident in America in 1979, and the Chernobyl disaster of 1986 in Ukraine. Fearing widespread resistance to nuclear power development, Tanaka Kakuei and MITI officials arranged for the passing of the so-called Three Power Source Development Laws in 1974, which provided huge subsidies and incentives for communities hosting nuclear power plants.

Ironically, from an environmental perspective, the overall energy transition away from crude oil after the Oil Shocks did not lead to a reduction in Japan's greenhouse gas emissions, which continued to grow, increasing from around 899 million tons in 1973 to 1.16 billion tons in 1990 and reaching a peak of 1.32 billion tons in 2013.[18] Although electricity generation from nuclear power increased, Japan also satiated its energy needs through increasing consumption of liquid natural gas and continued reliance on imported coal. More nuclear power plants also meant greater risk of accidents in a seismically active country—as would eventuate some four decades later at the Fukushima Daiichi Nuclear Power Plant.

Society and Social Energies in the 1970s and 1980s

Demographic Transformations

Many of the social and demographic trends traced in previous chapters continued throughout the 1970s and 1980s, often becoming more prominent and even worrying for Japan's leaders. Thanks in part to excellent health care, life expectancy for Japanese people continued to rise during these decades. At war's end, the average Japanese man lived to 50.1 years of age and the average woman to 54 years. By 1970 these numbers had risen to 69.3 and 74.7, respectively, reaching 73.4 and 78.8 in 1980 and 71.9 and 81.9 by 1990—making Japanese life expectancy among the highest in the world.[19] In turn, the percentage of the elderly population (those over 65 years of age) continued its steady rise from 4.9 percent in 1950 to 7.1 percent in 1970, 9.1 percent in 1980, and 12 percent by 1990. Officials and media pundits began to speak of Japan's "aging society problem" (*kōreika shakai mondai*), which was further compounded by the country's ever-decreasing fertility rate. After a brief second "baby boom" from 1971 to 1974, Japan's fertility rate began its precipitous decline, going from 2.14 in 1973 to 1.57 by 1989. This "1.57 Shock" forced the government to recognize declining birth as a serious problem in need of policy responses supportive of families and work-life balance. But, as explained in the following chapter, countermeasures were insufficient and did not stop the decline.

While some conservative politicians condescendingly attributed the falling birth rate to "selfish" young women delaying marriage and childbirth, the core of the problem lay in the incentives and impediments of the postwar socioeconomic system. From 1970 to 1990, the proportion (and absolute amount) of monthly expenses devoted to children's education almost doubled from 2.7 percent (2,212 yen) in 1970 to 5.1 percent (16,827 yen) by 1990, putting more pressure on family budgets. The average age of marriage also slowly crept upwards from 26.9 years for men and 24.2 years for women in 1970 to 28.4 for men and 25.9 for women by 1990. In turn, this change was reflected in women giving birth to their first child at a later age. Societal pressures on women to care for aging parents served to further exacerbate the trend to have fewer children and at a later age. Rising costs of urban life only compounded such incentives.

The economic transitions following the Oil Shocks accelerated the already-shifting employment balance in the economy. In 1970, primary industries accounted for 19.3 percent of employment, secondary industries 34 percent, and tertiary industries 46.6 percent. But, by 1990, primary industries only represented 7.1 percent, secondary industries remained stable at 33.3 percent, and tertiary industries had grown noticeably to 59 percent—trends which would continue into the 1990s. The number working in agriculture declined from just over ten million in 1970 to 5.65 million by 1990, with a conspicuous shift from rice production to higher value products such as livestock (especially beef) and varieties of fruit and vegetables. Generous governmental support for farmers meant that agricultural incomes tracked on average at least 30 percent higher than those of employed workers throughout the 1970s and 1980s. The other side of rural depopulation was persistent urbanization in the 1970s and 1980s or, perhaps more accurately, "Tokyozation." Throughout these decades, the number of people moving to the Greater Tokyo region increased yearly, while the two other big cities of Osaka and Nagoya actually experienced out-migration. Japan's economic prowess also encouraged an influx of foreigners eager to share in the spoils of Japanese riches. In 1970, there were just over 708,000 registered foreigners in Japan, but the number was over one million by 1990 (see chap. 7).

Gender and Youth

NHK surveys from around the early 1970s onward reveal a slow but growing desire among women to continue working after marriage. But the combination of tax incentives and social expectations, together with economic developments after the First Oil Shock, meant that many women would still leave full-time employment for an extended period after marriage, only to return into part-time work many years later—the so-called M-curve pattern for women's work in Japan as shown in figure 5.6. The high-growth system was constructed based on this fundamental gender division with men as the breadwinners and women as homemakers, child bearers, and child rearers—or "good wives, wise mothers" as the traditional term described them. This gender division was institutionalized in workplaces, where women were slotted into clerical support roles as "tea makers" for men doing the "substantive" work. The division resulted in significant wage disparities, with women earning on average only 50 percent that of men annually. In the period from 1970 to 1990, women were only paid 60 percent the wages of men with similar education levels.[20]

The opportunity to change this situation came with International Women's Year in 1975 and the Convention on the Elimination of All Forms of Discrimination against Women, adopted by the UN General Assembly in 1979. Japan's ratification of this convention in 1980, together with pressure from women's advocates, pressured the government to address institutionalized forms of discrimination in areas such as family law and employment. The amendment to the Nationality Law in 1984 to give citizenship rights to the children of Japanese women married to foreign nationals was a first step, followed in 1985 by the passing of the Equal Employment Opportunity Law (EEOL).

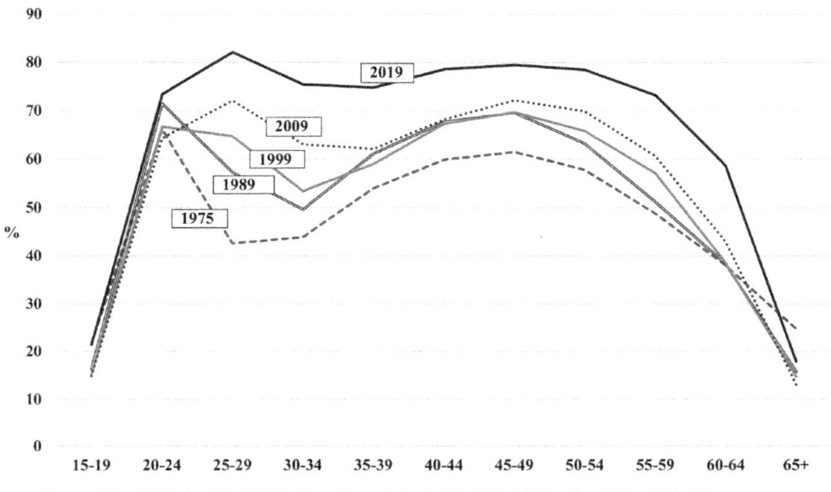

Sources: Kōsei Rōdōshō, "Zuhyō 1-3-8 Josei"; and Kokudo Kōtsūshō, "(3) Josei no Shūgyō Jōkyō."

Figure 5.6. Changes in Female Labor Force Participation Rates by Age, 1975–2019

As we saw in the previous chapters, women wanting to continue their careers had gone to court as early as the 1960s in pursuit of their rights. This activism continued into the 1970s, intersecting with Japan's international commitments to gender equality made late in the decade. The EEOL was one concrete outcome of these processes, as lawmakers and business leaders realized that they could no longer evade putting in place a legal-institutional framework for gender equality.

The EEOL stipulated gender equality in hiring (such as eliminating job ads for "men only") and in career development. But the law lacked teeth and even produced some contrary outcomes in its original iteration. Notably, on the request of business organizations, the EEOL contained no penalties for noncompliance nor any enforcement functions, merely requiring employers to "strive" for gender equality in the workplace. Many organizations simply renamed their gender-specific career tracks as "comprehensive" (primarily men) and "general" (primarily women) streams, the latter being less secure and primarily clerical. Employers also successfully lobbied for amendments to the Labor Standards Law, eliminating overtime restrictions and menstrual leave for women. As a result, while the EEOL may have provided equality of *opportunity* for women, it did not connect to equality in *outcomes*.[21] The law was subsequently revised in 1997 to include provisions for preventing sexual harassment and, in 2006, to ban discriminatory treatment due to career interruptions such as pregnancy and childbirth. But gender equality remained a work in progress in the 1980s and beyond.

The EEOL was not the only notable piece of legislation in 1985, with the Law for Worker Dispatch Operations (LWDO) coming into effect in the same year. The LWDO was initially devised to facilitate labor mobility for an emerging sphere of highly skilled workers who provided part-time or contract services. For this reason, the occupations covered under the law were initially quite limited. But these occupational limitations were gradually eased and eventually eliminated over the coming decades. In hindsight, the LWDO was reflective of a wider trend toward nonregular employment in the Japanese labor market, beginning from around the end of the 1970s and picking up pace in the 1980s.

Initially, some saw new, positive possibilities in styles of work different from those developed under the high-speed growth regime. Youth who rejected the excessively regimented career paths and lifeways of their workaholic fathers and stay-at-home mothers in favor of nonregular, temporary employment were called *shinjinrui* or a "new breed of human." In 1985, singer-songwriter Nagakubo Tetsu helped coin the term *furītā* or "freeter" (a combination of the English "free" and German *Arbeiter* [meaning "employee"]) to describe these freewheeling youth who passionately pursued their aspirations. The part-time job magazine *Furomuē* further defined freeters in 1987 as "a new liberated species" of "radical workers" who "reject traveling along the path already laid, holding on tightly to their dreams as they navigate through society."[22] This early lionization of nonregular employment would erode quickly in the 1990s as precarity replaced freedom for a whole generation of youth. In the exuberant affluence of 1980s Japan, however, such futures were almost unimaginable.

Social Energies

Following the university campus protests of the late 1960s and early 1970s, observers began to speak of a decline in civic activism in Japan, with some even declaring the onset of a social movement "ice age." While violent street protests like the ones witnessed in 1968 certainly did subside, the depiction of a waning in civic activism in the country in the 1970s and 1980s is misleading. On the contrary, these decades witnessed the rise of a plethora of new movements involved in issues concerning the environment, safe food, community building, welfare, feminism, nuclear power, and relations with Asia.

Though weakened by setbacks in earlier decades, the labor movement soldiered on through its springtime wage offensives, which sometimes involved millions of workers. In the 1970s, public sector employees continued to struggle for the right to strike, but defeat on this issue in 1975 heralded the waning of their influence. By

1989, the JSP-aligned Sōhyō had run out of steam and was disbanded. Most of its members joined with the DSP-affiliated Dōmei to form the moderate Japan Trade Union Federation or Rengō, comprising some eight million members. Around 1.4 million JCP-affiliated workers, who did not wish to join Rengō, formed the National Confederation of Trade Unions or Zenrōren, while a smaller number—around five hundred thousand—formed the National Trade Union Council or Zenrōkyō. The rise of Nakasone Yasuhiro to the prime ministership in 1982 precipitated the final decline of Sōhyō and militant labor activism in Japan.

With student and labor activism on the wane, the energy for social change shifted now to a new realm of grassroots civic movements. Many of the founders of these movements had cut their activist teeth in student and labor activism, so their new initiatives in the 1970s and 1980s often grew out of frustration and disappointment with these earlier experiences. Rejecting established repertoires of violent protest and opposition—which they believed had failed—these activists promoted strategies of "proposal" and "creativity" over dissent. Rather than simply criticizing and attempting to destroy political, economic, and social institutions, why not try and rebuild them from the bottom up in the form of new alternative lifestyles? Concern for the environment and human health was often at the center of the new movements' agendas.

A pioneering example of such "proposal-style" activism was the Association to Preserve the Earth, established in 1974 by the former student activists Fujita Kazuyoshi and Fukumoto Toshio following their release from jail. Their movement aimed at creating an alternative to the mainstream system of mass production and mass consumption through the distribution of organic vegetables from farmers to urban consumers. At the core of their movement was the idea that food is not only for sustenance but also for self-reflection and self-transformation regarding consumption and the environment. The Lifestyle Club Cooperative, established in the late 1960s, shared similar values and aspirations to Fujita and Fukumoto's movement. The co-op's founders, Iwane Kunio, a photographer, and Yokota Katsumi, a self-proclaimed "Marx boy," began by supplying low-cost milk to co-op members, later expanding operations to the delivery of groceries to teams of housewife members making collective purchases. Into the 1980s, the Lifestyle Club became involved in initiatives for natural soap, food safety, and environmental protection. It also started the so-called Proxy Movement in which female candidates were supported to run in municipal elections on progressive, housewife-focused platforms such as opposition to synthetic detergents. Terada Etsuko was the first proxy to be successfully elected to the Kawasaki City Assembly in 1983.

Other comparable movements of the time included the eco-focused Kansai Recycling Movement and the Nara Tampopo Association, which operated a sheltered workshop for the disabled. By the mid-1980s, these new proposal-style movements had become a significant force in Japanese civil society. In 1986, prominent members of the new movements organized a networking cruise to the islands of Okinawa on the fittingly-named *New Utopia,* involving over five hundred leaders from around 170 movements. Thereafter, these groups published a networking list of over thirteen hundred groups that helped to further grow the sector. Importantly, these networking movements provided a strong foundation for the burgeoning of Japanese civil society in the 1990s.

At the same time, however, the new groups' commitment to constructive activism and avoidance of overt confrontation also resonated curiously with the neoliberal shift in conservative policymaking during this era based on small government and individual and societal self-responsibility. The fact that these movements were aimed at and primarily operated and supported by Japanese housewives, who lacked access to the centers of political and economic power ("bicycle citizens" as one political scientist has described them), also helped shape this intriguing conservative-progressive convergence.[23]

Of course, civic activism throughout the 1970s and 1980s was not only about proposal, cooperation, and self-help. Some activists continued to staunchly advocate for and struggle over contentious issues. The early 1970s witnessed the emergence of Japanese feminism and women's liberation, most symbolically with the release of the activist Tanaka Mitsu's provocative essay "Liberation from the Toilet" (Benjo kara no kaihō), arguably the earliest manifesto of the movement. Thereafter, in books such as the 1972 *Inochi no onnatachi e* (To women with spirit), Tanaka criticized sexual discrimination and asked probing questions about femininity. Together with fellow activists, Tanaka formed the Group of Fighting Women in 1970. Based at the Liberation Shinjuku Center in Tokyo, the group served as a hub for the spread of feminist ideas and networking through its publications and events.

Resonating with second-wave feminism worldwide, Japanese women's liberation activists criticized the patriarchal, male-dominated organization of the economy, society, and politics. They mounted a frontal attack on the concept of motherhood so central to earlier women's movements like the 1950s Japanese Congress of Mothers (chap. 3).[24] Women also led local movements, such as the Association for the Protection of Nature and Children formed in the 1980s. Here, housewives in Zushi City to the south of Tokyo mobilized to stop construction of a US military housing project in the Ikego forest. The women activists adopted a range of creative strategies to save the forest, including lawsuits and a recall election for the local mayor.[25]

Transnational grassroots movements between Japanese and fellow Asian activists involved in women's, environmental, and democratization issues were another notable development in Japanese civic activism during the 1970s and 1980s. Earlier movements such as the anti–Vietnam War movement had certainly been alert to Asian issues, but it was not until these decades that sustained transnational interconnections began to develop. While shining a spotlight on the excesses of Japanese economic involvement in Asia, these movements were also important in awakening activists to the unresolved legacies of Japan's earlier war in Asia. In turn, such awakenings opened the way for a recalibration of the victim mentality that had dominated many forms of activism throughout the postwar era.

The earliest of these movements involved the newspaper journalist Matsui Yayori, feminists, and Christian activists who established the Women's Group Opposing Kisaeng Tourism in 1973. Japan's growing affluence and expansion into Asia had been accompanied by increased overseas tourism, some of which involved organized sex tours to South Korea and elsewhere in Asia. Working transnationally with Christians and university students in South Korea, Matsui and colleagues managed to bring this sex tourism to the attention of the public and political elites, such that both governments were eventually forced to ban the practice. For the Japanese participants, the movement also became an opportunity to examine issues from the past, like military sexual violence and prostitution carried out by the Japanese army during the Asia-Pacific War—the so-called comfort women issue (see chap. 6).

At around the same time, environmental activists became aware of Japanese corporations relocating their pollutive industrial processes to Asia in the wake of stricter environmental legislation in Japan from 1970 onwards. Activists first became aware of this "pollution export" problem while attending the UN Conference on the Human Environment in Stockholm in 1972. The following year, Japanese activists joined with Thai counterparts to protest contamination of the Chao Phraya River in Bangkok by a subsidiary of the Japanese Asahi Glass Company (part of the Mitsubishi Group). In an era of landline telephones and telegrams, activists in both countries managed to organize simultaneous demonstrations against the company in Bangkok and its Tokyo headquarters. Similar transnational antipollution export movements developed with activists in South Korea to stop Japanese companies relocating pollutive mercurochrome plants to the Ulsan Industrial District. Later in the 1970s, Japanese activists joined with Filipino counterparts to stop the industrial giant Kawasaki Steel from relocating a pollutive sintering plant to Mindanao. Not all of these mobilizations were successful, but the negative media and public attention made companies carefully consider overseas relocation of their most pollutive industrial processes.

Japanese activists also joined with Christians, academics, and lawyers in South Korea in the late 1970s in support of the movement for democratization under the authoritarian regime of Park Chung-hee. Once again, involvement in this transnational solidarity movement offered Japanese activists an opportunity to reconsider the enduring legacies of Japan's colonization of that country.[26] Into the 1980s, Japanese nongovernmental organizations like the Japan International Volunteer Center, Shapla Neer, and Alter Trade Japan initiated various initiatives in Asia, such as training in agricultural methods; water sanitation and hygiene; and fair trade in bananas, coffee, sugar, and other commodities. Against the backdrop of Japan's environmentally destructive "throwaway" consumerism, these initiatives sent out a message to the Japanese people to reconsider the costs of their comfortable lifestyles for the environment and for people in developing nations. Japanese activists also became more and more involved in global environmental initiatives in the 1980s, such as movements to address stratospheric ozone damage, rainforest destruction, biodiversity depletion, and climate change.[27]

Another important element of civic activism during the 1970s and 1980s was growing opposition to nuclear power. Local movements opposing the construction of nuclear power plants began as early as the 1960s, intensifying throughout the 1970s and 1980s due to the rush of new plant constructions. In response, the government passed laws to generously reward communities that accepted nuclear power plants. Established antiatomic weapons movements were divided over the question of nuclear power in Japan. Gensuikin, affiliated with Sōhyō and the JSP, joined with local groups to oppose nuclear power plant siting and construction, while the JCP-affiliated anti–A-bomb movement, Gensuikyō, supported the peaceful use of nuclear energy.

Opposition to nuclear power intensified after the nuclear power plant accident at Chernobyl in Ukraine in April 1986. Initially, people were more concerned about the risk of contaminated food from northern Europe entering Japan than they were about nuclear power. But polls by the *Asahi shinbun* in the months after the disaster revealed that only 34 percent of respondents supported nuclear power, with 41 percent opposed—the first time opposition had exceeded support in a survey on the issue.[28] Interestingly, however, only 9 percent of respondents wanted existing power plants to be shut down, while a massive 60 percent supported the status quo—suggesting that many Japanese believed that such an accident was not likely to occur at a Japanese nuclear power plant. To address concerns over food safety, the Ministry of Health and Welfare issued standards for radiation levels in foods and bolstered testing procedures on imports in November 1986.

Antinuclear activists led a flurry of rallies and protests against nuclear power in the wake of Chernobyl. Organizations like the Citizens Nuclear Information Center, established by the nuclear scientist Takagi Jinzaburō and others in 1975, highlighted the material risks of nuclear power in Japan. This new wave of antinuclear protest shared many of the same characteristics as the movements discussed above, led by women and youth and not aligned to any particular political party. In 1988, for example, the bread-baker activist Ohara Yoshiko organized the Group for Daily Life Without Nuclear Power Plants, which staged a rally outside the headquarters of the Shikoku Power Company to oppose planned testing at the Ikata Nuclear Power Plant in Ehime Prefecture. Youth were also involved in antinuclear activism in the 1980s. In 1984, university students organized the "Atomic Café Festival," a concert held at Tokyo's Hibiya Open-Air Concert Arena. Student musicians even came close to having their satirical antinuclear adaption of Elvis Presley's *Love Me Tender* recorded under the EMI label, only to be thwarted at the last minute when Toshiba, EMI's parent company and a major player in the nuclear industry, stopped the release.[29] Nonetheless, these students made full use of newsletters, leaflets, amateur FM radio broadcasts, and cassette recordings to relay their antinuclear message. The interconnection of this antinuclear sentiment with environmentalism, feminism, food safety, and artistic creation gave the post-Chernobyl movements a genuinely 1980s ambiance, quite different from the combative and often violent student movements of the 1960s and early 1970s. Social activism had certainly changed, but it was by no means in an "ice age."

The Culture of Affluence

Cuisines: Fast and Fancy

An increasingly standardized urban culture of mass consumption continued to flourish through the inflationary years of the early 1970s and into the ebullient bubble era of the late 1980s. It was fueled by the medium of television commercials and a vibrant sphere of weekly and monthly magazines, brimming with advertisements for the latest products, foods, and fashions. As Japanese incomes rose, the proportion of family income spent on food decreased, declining from 34.1 percent in 1970 to 29 percent in 1980 and 25.4 percent in 1990.[30] Conversely, discretionary spending on eating out increased in both absolute terms and as a percentage of food expenditure, rising from 9 percent (2,413 yen) in 1970 to 15.6 percent (12,349 yen) by 1990. Accompanying this shift, the early 1970s witnessed the arrival of American fast-food chains like Kentucky Fried Chicken, which opened an outlet at the Osaka World Expo in 1970 followed by its first store in Nagoya later that year. McDonald's Japan arrived in 1971, opening its first store in the glitzy Ginza region, while Mister Donuts began operations in Minō City, Osaka. With its sidewalk counter service, McDonald's opening was timed perfectly to coincide with the beginning of Ginza's weekend "pedestrian paradise," when the shopping strip was closed to automobiles (fig. 5.7). Customers formed long queues to order the fabled burgers and shakes. McDonald's was not the first fast-food hamburger chain in the country, an honor claimed by the Japanese-owned Dom Dom Hamburgers.

The 1970s also witnessed the appearance of so-called family restaurants, like Skylark in Tokyo's Kunitachi (1970), Royal Host in Northern Kyūshū (1971), and the American-owned Denny's in Yokohama (1974). Instant foods continued their meteoric rise, notably with the release of Styrofoam cup noodles in 1971. Previously, instant noodles were supplied in plastic packaging and required a bowl or cup for preparation. Styrofoam packaging made things more convenient, albeit at four times the cost (100 yen). This new product quickly became a mainstay meal for emergency workers like police and firefighters, and even SDF personnel, not to mention ordinary instant noodle enthusiasts. The 1970s culture of convenience was further bolstered with the opening of the first 7-Eleven convenience store in Tokyo's Kōtō Ward in 1974. True to its name, the store initially operated from seven in the morning until eleven in the evening.

Cuisines previously out of reach for middle-class Japanese gradually became more accessible during the 1970s and 1980s. Throughout the postwar era, French cuisine had been limited to exclusive restaurants in upmarket hotels, but small

Figure 5.7. The first McDonald's restaurant in Tokyo's Ginza area (March 26, 1971). Courtesy of The Asahi Shimbun Company.

French restaurants run by chefs who had apprenticed in the kitchens of Paris, Provence, and elsewhere began to pop up in suburban areas throughout the 1970s. Of course, dining at such establishments still remained an aspiration for many.[31] University students were among the first to frequent these new restaurants, mostly on the advice of popular magazines like *Popeye* and *Hotto doggu puresu,* which became "training manuals" for young men eager to win the hearts of their dining partners. In the 1980s, a French restaurant craze swept the country, as young men booked tables up to three months in advance for a romantic, high-class Christmas dinner with their companions. At the height of the boom, many restaurants had three or more sittings on Christmas Day.[32]

Demonstrating the growing popularization of cuisines previously reserved for the sophisticated classes, food critics began writing for the masses, who now had the financial elbow room to indulge in European culinary delights. A typical example is Kariya Tetsu's manga comic series *Oishinbo* (The gourmet) contained in the publication *Biggu komikku supirittsu* from 1983. Here Kariya attempted to help ordinary people understand "true flavor" in an age when "gluttony" and "food fashion" were fast becoming dominant.

The French cuisine craze was followed in the 1980s by an ethnic food boom, as Southeast Asian and South Asian foods began to spread in what some called a "poststructuralist" reaction to the glorification of Western food (and all things Western) throughout modern Japanese history.[33] The growing popularity of so-called B-rank gourmet (*B-kyū gurume*), consisting of the everyday foods of the working class like omelet rice (*omuraisu*), beef bowl (*gyūdon*), chicken and egg bowl (*oyakodon*), ramen, and curry rice, was yet another expression of this postmodern shift in mentality in the 1980s. Indeed, such trends resonated seamlessly with the emergent cultural nationalism of 1980s Japan (see chap. 6).

New Gadgets, Spaces, and Places

If the late 1950s and 1960s belonged to the three "sacred electrical treasures," then the 1970s and 1980s undoubtedly marked the beginning of an age of "gadgetopia." In 1975, the Epoch Company released its "TV Tennis" game, heralding the birth of the video-game era. Costing a hefty 19,500 yen, the company sold around five thousand units in the first year. The black-and-white game consisted quite simply of two paddles that were maneuvered up and down to hit a ball back and forth across the screen. Karaoke began to grow in popularity after its invention in the 1970s, especially following the opening of the first automatic karaoke "box" in Okayama Prefecture. These boxes made karaoke easily accessible to enthusiasts beyond the traditional restaurants, bars, and banquet halls. Music culture was further revolutionized with the release of Sony's Walkman in 1979—a portable cassette player

Figure 5.8. Cover of the first stand-alone edition of Kariya Tetsu's popular manga *Oishinbo* (1984). Shōgakkan.

with wired headphones that enabled people to listen to music anywhere. The Walkman was Sony's second hit product after the release of its transistor radios in the mid-1950s.

Office automation was greatly enhanced in 1978 when the Toshiba Corporation released its first word processor while, in 1985, the earliest mobile phones, utilizing technology from car phones that had appeared in 1979, went on sale. Nippon Telegraph and Telephone Corporation (NTT)'s so-called shoulder phone consisted of a handset attached to a hefty 3-kilogram (6.6 pound) box with a shoulder strap. Mobile phones began to spread widely only from the 1990s when a second generation of handheld models, much smaller and with better reception, were released.

Reflecting the new throwaway culture, Fujifilm released its disposable camera "Sharundesu" in 1986. The culture of plastic also intensified with plastic (PET) bottles first used for soy sauce in 1977 and then for beverages, following an amendment to the Food Hygiene Law in 1982.

The 1980s were also the decade of theme parks, resorts, and galleries. In April 1983, Tokyo Disneyland opened its turnstiles at Urayasu City, just outside Tokyo. Over ten million visitors flocked to Disneyland in its first year, stimulating a theme park construction boom across the country. With the passing of the Resort Law in 1987, a similar boom occurred in resort construction. The law provided various incentives, like special tax breaks, low interest loans, and easing of regulations, to encourage private developers in both urban and rural areas. These incentives exacerbated the real estate price bubble of the late 1980s. In the decade from 1987, around six million hectares or 16 percent of Japan's total land area was swallowed up by resort developments such as golf courses, ski fields, and marinas—many of which ended up as decaying ruins in the wake of the bubble economy.[34]

Ordinary Japanese did not benefit from such developments either, as most people could not afford expensive golf club memberships or yachts. On the contrary, government statistics revealed that around 40 percent of people were still living in substandard housing in the early 1980s—an increase from 35 percent a decade earlier despite growing affluence.[35] Japanese political elites were left red faced in 1987, when a prominent British researcher labelled Japanese dwellings "rabbit hutches." Moreover, the intensive development of resorts, marinas, and theme parks continued to deplete Japan's natural environment. Throughout the 1970s, natural coastline decreased to 60 percent, falling to 50 percent by 1989. Conversely, social infrastructure like parks, paved roads, and sewerage lagged behind other industrialized nations—a condition that one critic labelled the "Japanese disease" in 1989.[36]

Along with theme parks and resorts, the 1980s witnessed the burgeoning of a new urban culture centered around galleries, theatres, and department stores. The Saison Group, led by the entrepreneur and writer Tsutsumi Seiji, was at the

Figure 5.9. In downtown Osaka, a young woman listens to a music cassette tape through headphones on the newly-released Sony Walkman attached to her belt. According to the *Asahi shinbun*, at the time (1979), the Walkman, roller skates, and digital wristwatches were considered the "three sacred treasures" of youth fashion. Courtesy of The Asahi Shimbun Company.

forefront of this cultural efflorescence. Tsutsumi had a fascinating background, having joined the JCP during his days as a student radical only to be expelled from the party. Thereafter, he published many novels and poetry collections under the penname Tsuji Takashi—all the while building his corporate empire. Although Tsutsumi would become an icon of Japan's consumerist culture of the 1980s, amusingly, he clung firmly to his identity as a "leftist."[37] The Saison Group's rise began with the opening of Parco department stores in Tokyo's Ikebukuro in 1969 and Shibuya in 1973, followed by many art galleries and theatres. Tsutsumi's great innovation was to fashion a new urban culture based around department stores and exploit the distribution revolution discussed in chapter 3. "Anchor" department stores at railway hubs, like Ikebukuro and Shibuya, became consumer magnets with their foreign brands, specialist stores, theatres, and art galleries. Single young women—many in dead-end clerical jobs, still living at home, and with high disposable incomes—became the engines of this glittering consumer culture of fashion, art, and cuisine.

Affordable overseas travel also became possible for millions of Japanese during the 1980s. By the late 1970s, around three million Japanese were already travelling abroad annually, but this number had more than tripled to ten million by 1990, 40 percent of whom were women. Overseas travel spiked noticeably in the late 1980s thanks to the strengthening of the yen following the Plaza Accord of 1985. The number of overseas travellers doubled from five to ten million in these years. Busloads of Japanese tourists, led by flag-bearing guides, became common sights in major cities around the world, while Japanese bookstores devoted generous shelf space to the best-selling travel guides, *Chikyū no arukikata* (How to travel the world), aimed at a new generation of solitary travellers. The (belated) opening of the New Tokyo International Airport in 1978 greatly facilitated this upsurge in overseas travel.

Ideologies of Affluence

Japan's stunning economic growth of the 1960s, its subsequent resilience after the Nixon Shocks and Oil Shocks, and the new cultures of consumption in the 1970s and 1980s provided fertile ground for the emergence of various forms of cultural nationalism at this time. As mentioned in chapter 4, this cultural nationalism found expression in the so-called *Nihonjinron* or "theories on the Japanese people," which developed into a flourishing—and profitable—sphere of books, articles, and commentaries. Such works pointed to the supposed homogeneity of the Japanese, their unique cohesiveness, and their penchant for collective decision-making—expressed most clearly in business and employment practices like lifetime employment, seniority wages, company welfare, enterprise unionism, quality control, and technological

Figure 5.10. Patrons socialize at the stylish rooftop beer garden of the Parco Ikebukuro store in 1980. Courtesy of The Asahi Shimbun Company.

innovation. These theories connected the success and resilience of Japan's economy to the "unique"—almost genetic—features of a monolithically imagined nation.

Although by no means a work of *Nihonjinron,* the Harvard sociologist Ezra Vogel's 1979 work, *Japan as Number One: Lessons for America,* published simultaneously in English and Japanese, was particularly important in arousing national pride. Selling over seven hundred thousand copies in Japan—making it the highest selling work of nonfiction by a foreign author in Japan at that time—Vogel's book praised Japan's bureaucracy, the diligence of Japanese employees who apparently enjoyed going to work, and the top-class and egalitarian education system. Vogel hoped that these lessons from Japan's success might be adopted and adapted into an ailing America of the late-1970s, although his work ultimately appears to have been more important in reinforcing the sense of cultural superiority taking root in Japan. The Nippon Steel Corporation's 1978 *Nippon: Sono sugata to kokoro* (published in English in 1982 as *Japan: The Land and Its People*) contained many of the same themes as Vogel's work, with specific emphasis on employee loyalty and group mentality as the secrets to Japan's success. Such works were preceded by classics of *Nihonjinron* like the psychiatrist Doi Takeo's 1971 *Amae no kōzō* (*The Anatomy of Dependence*), first published as a series of articles in the 1950s. Doi's work explained the Japanese psyche on the basis of unique dynamics between inner feelings (*hone*) and external behavior (*tatemae*), and inside (*uchi*) and outside (*soto*). The social anthropologist Nakane Chie's 1967 work, *Tate shakai no ningen kankei: Tan'itsu shakai no riron* (*Japanese Society*), identified Japanese uniqueness in the construction of human relations based on place (or social position) as opposed to attribute (for example, profession). While works such as the latter were often emphasizing potential limitations in Japanese mentalities and modes of reaction, in Japan of the 1980s, critical analysis often gave way to the seductive combination of uniqueness, nationalism, and economic success.

From the late 1970s spanning into the 1980s, *Nihonjinron* evolved further as cultural nationalism gradually fused with celebratory consumerism. Authors like the economist Murakami Yasusuke and the commentator Yamazaki Masakazu began to reconceptualize Japanese uniqueness through a neoconservative postmodern lens focused on the "new urban masses" and their affluent lifeways. Works such as Murakami's 1979 *Bunmei toshite no ie shakai* (*Ie Society as a Pattern of Civilization*) and Yamazaki's *Yawarakai kojinshugi no tanjō* (The birth of gentle individualism) lauded Japan's ability to incorporate systems from the West, such as capitalism and consumerism, while maintaining its unique trait of group cohesiveness over rampant individualism. In this way, Japan had arguably been able to avoid many Western "diseases," like unemployment and social alienation.

These perspectives were reflected in official discourse, such as in Prime Minister Ōhira's "brain trust" advisory committee, the Ōhira Masayoshi Policy Research

Group. In 1980, the group released a report arguing that, since Japan had attained "modernity (industrialization, Westernization)" and was now an "advanced industrial society," there no longer existed any "model" to "catch up" with. "From now on," the report said, the Japanese must trace their own unique path.[38]

Tanaka Yasuo's 1981 novel *Nantonaku kurisutaru* (*Somehow, Crystal*), about the exploits of Mari, a returnee from overseas now working as a model, and Jun'ichi, a band leader, succinctly captured the subtle fusion of cultural exuberance and the unbridled pursuit of self-interest among affluent urban youth in postmodern 1980s Japan. Tanaka's fresh, conversational style of writing shared by others of his generation like Yoshimoto Banana and Murakami Haruki challenged established literary conventions. The breezy culture portrayed in these works provoked the ire of Old Left intellectuals who scoffed at the "slavery to comfort" colonizing the mentalities of affluent youth.[39] Such criticisms, however, were barely audible at this moment of cultural and economic euphoria.

Nakasone and the "Final Settlement" of Postwar Politics

Nakasone Yasuhiro's ascension to the prime ministership in 1982 was in many ways the perfect political manifestation of the economic, social, and cultural trends unfolding throughout the 1970s and 1980s in Japan. The sixty-four-year-old Nakasone was a political veteran, first elected to the Diet in 1947, with impeccable credentials as a law graduate of the elite Tokyo Imperial University followed by service as an officer in the Imperial Japanese Navy. In the 1950s, Nakasone served as director of the Science and Technology Agency under Kishi Nobusuke and, in the late 1960s and early 1970s, as minister of transport and thereafter director of the Defense Agency in the Satō administration. After mobilizing his small faction in support of Tanaka Kakuei's run for the LDP presidency in 1972, Nakasone was rewarded with cabinet portfolios for science and technology and then trade and industry, followed by a stint as director of the administrative management agency under the short-lived Suzuki Zenkō administration (1980–1982).

Nakasone's support for the "shadow shogun" Tanaka proved critical in his own run for the LDP leadership in 1982. Although Tanaka had been forced to resign from the party due to the Lockheed scandal, his faction members helped push Nakasone well ahead of his rivals in the LDP presidential election. Tanaka's payoff was the inclusion of seven faction members in the first Nakasone cabinet, prompting the media to snipe about "Tanakasone" rule. But Nakasone would not be Tanaka's handmaiden and, in fact, the Tanaka legacy was oftentimes a burden for him. In the December 1983 House of Representatives election, for example, for the third time since its establishment, the LDP failed to gain an outright majority until absorbing independent conservatives into the party to reach 50.7 percent. One cause of the poor performance was the Tokyo District Court's handing down of a guilty verdict against Tanaka just months earlier for his receipt of bribes.

Indeed, Nakasone came to the prime ministership with his own grand plans for achieving a "comprehensive settlement of postwar politics." In his major policy speech before the Diet in January 1983, Nakasone argued that the postwar history of Japan was at a "turning point" and, thus, the time had come to "reconsider existing systems and mechanisms without any taboos."[40] Here Nakasone was mounting a critique on the fundamental elements of the 1955 System, including, first, Japanese dependence on the United States and the associated norm of nonmilitarization and, second, a large government based on Keynesian-style policies to stimulate demand alongside a limited welfare state.

Instead, Nakasone wanted a more assertive Japan internationally, through an equal partnership with the United States and a gradual military buildup. Central in this vision was Nakasone's desire to revise the pacifist elements of the constitution, such as Article 9. In terms of fiscal policy, Nakasone wanted to rein in the excessive government spending of his predecessors—including supporters like Tanaka—instead relying on the energies of the private sector. With this combination of neoconservatism and neoliberalism, Nakasone was effectively trying to replace the long-held policy platforms of both the democratic and liberal streams of the LDP with a neonationalist agenda all his own.

Nakasone also injected a new energy, prominence, and influence into the prime ministership not witnessed since Tanaka. His charismatic personality and strong public speaking skills made Nakasone a darling of the media, especially television, which he used to his great advantage. The close personal relationship between Nakasone and President Ronald Reagan—"Yasu" and "Ron" as they called each other—only further cemented the prime minister's image as a strong and respected leader internationally. In turn, this image resonated with the cultural nationalism intensifying among Japanese in the 1980s although, as noted later in this chapter, only to a certain extent. Institutionally, Nakasone worked to strengthen the power of the prime minister vis-à-vis the bureaucracy and the LDP's party factions by establishing a range of deliberative and advisory committees reporting directly to him on important policy matters. Drawing on experts from elite universities and major corporations, Nakasone established personal advisory panels for information technology, economic policy, education, and the controversial Yasukuni Shrine. He then utilized the reports of these panels to shape public opinion and generate support, thereby attempting to circumvent the established policymaking process in which legislation was drafted by the bureaucracies, then passed through the LDP's PARC, the cabinet, and finally the Diet.

Figure 5.11. Prime Minister Nakasone Yasuhiro and his wife, Tsutako, entertain President Ronald Reagan and his wife, Nancy (left), with a tea ceremony at the Hinode Mountain Retreat on the western outskirts of Tokyo during the president's visit to Japan in November 1983. Courtesy of The Asahi Shimbun Company.

Administrative reform aimed at small government was a centerpiece of Nakasone's drive to fundamentally restructure postwar politics, and it distinguished him from almost all postwar prime ministers—the so-called conservative mainstream—with the exception perhaps of Yoshida Shigeru and Fukuda Takeo. The key slogan for Nakasone was "fiscal reform without tax increases" (*zōzei naki zaisei saiken*). Nakasone emphasized the fundamental dilemma of public finance in Japan since at least the 1960s in which government revenues were gradually decreasing, while expenses for social welfare, economic pump-priming (inclusive of pork-barrel spending), and support for sunset industries were ballooning (fig. 5.12). Instead, borrowing from the neoliberal policies of Margaret Thatcher and Ronald Reagan, Nakasone argued that the state should only do that which the private sector "absolutely" could not do.[41] Fiscally speaking, Nakasone's perspective had sound factual grounds. Throughout the 1970s, government expenditures for economic stimulus packages and social welfare had increased. With falling tax revenues, these costs were funded increasingly by issuing government bonds, leading to compounding government debt. Even before Nakasone, governments had tried to balance the budget, but government debt continued to rise.[42]

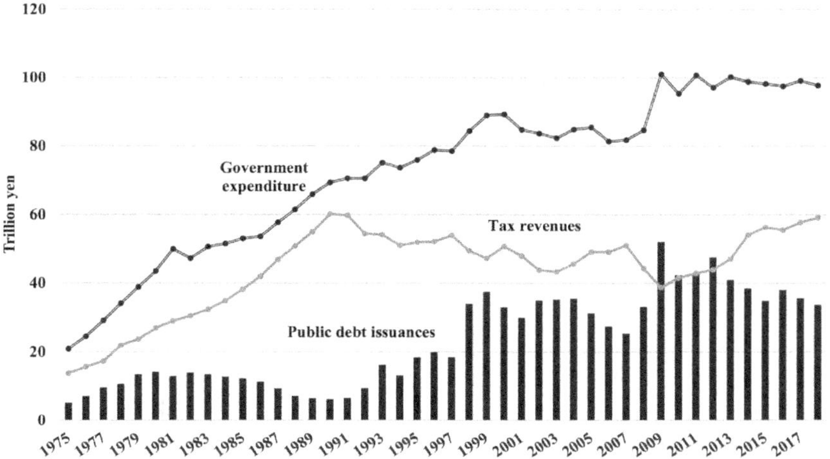

Source: Zaimushō, "Zaisei ni kansuru Shiryō: Ippan Kaikei Zeishū, Saishutsu Sōgaku oyobi Kōsai Hakkōgaku no Suii," online, December 13, 2022, https://www.mof.go.jp/tax_policy/summary/condition/a02.htm.

Figure 5.12. Japan General Account Expenditures, Revenues, and Public Debt Issuances, 1975–2018

The Second Provisional Commission on Administrative Reform, Rinchō in Japanese, was established in 1981 under Nakasone's predecessor Suzuki Zenkō and responsible to Nakasone, first as director of the Administrative Management Agency and then as prime minister. Rinchō was charged with formulating a comprehensive fiscal reform package. In its various reports, the commission—chaired by former Japan Business Federation (Keidanren) president Dokō Toshio—recommended the simplification of central and local government functions; the reduction of public expenditures in areas like national health insurance, national pensions, and social welfare; the privatization of public corporations; and private sector revitalization.

Nakasone moved immediately on privatization, with Japan Tobacco and Salt Corporation and NTT privatized in 1985 and JNR broken up into six private railway corporations the following year. The privatization of JNR had much to do with overstaffing, underutilized lines, excessive debt, and inefficiencies in the massive organization, but it was also a blatant strategy by Nakasone to break the back of the militant Kokurō railway workers union. In turn, the demise of Kokurō weakened Sōhyō—which disbanded in 1989—effectively depriving the JSP of one of its largest support bases. Nakasone's union-busting policy met with little resistance from a public annoyed by Kokurō's disputes over "the right to strike," which caused interruptions during commuter rush hours.

Along with privatization of state entities, social welfare was cut back under Nakasone in the 1980s. Free medical care for the elderly was replaced by a copayment system. The government began to advocate for a "welfare society" as opposed to a "welfare state," in which families (primarily women), volunteers, and nongovernmental organizations would take responsibility for care of the elderly, disabled, and needy in society. To strengthen and liberalize financial and other markets and enhance private sector competitiveness, controls over foreign exchange and other regulations were loosened, resulting in an increase in inward FDI in the 1980s (although not to a level acceptable to the Americans). After a landslide victory in the 1986 double election, Nakasone also attempted to renege on the promise of no new taxes by offering income tax cuts in return for the implementation of a 5 percent sales tax to bolster government revenues. But opposition from within the LDP and from consumers, small businesses, and workers forced him to abandon the plan, just as his predecessors had.

The other critical aspect of Nakasone's "settlement" of postwar politics revolved around the country's military and national defense posture. His desire for remilitarization resonated with America's military buildup in the face of mounting tensions with the USSR in the early 1980s. In a meeting with Ronald Reagan in Washington, DC, in mid-January 1983, Nakasone told the president that Japan and the United States belonged to a "community of fate" binding together the democratic nations of the Pacific. In an interview with the *Washington Post,* Nakasone depicted the Japanese archipelago as an "unsinkable aircraft carrier" that would serve as a shield for the United States in the event of Soviet attack. Here the new prime minister went a step too far for most Japanese—as perhaps reflected in the 1983 electoral drubbing—and thereafter Nakasone noticeably toned down his language on security matters. Pacifist public opinion also forced constitutional revision of Nakasone's policy agenda. Nonetheless, Nakasone began slowly chipping away at some of the postwar norms surrounding national security, including ending the ban on arms exports in 1984 and officially scrapping the 1 percent ceiling on defense spending in FY1987 when this item increased to 1.004 percent.[43]

Underwriting Nakasone's national security agenda was a staunch nationalism aimed at revitalizing Japanese patriotism and national pride. Such revitalization, he believed, would enhance Japan's "internationalization" as a productive and proactive nation, exporting its outstanding culture to the world. Nakasone insisted that education must instill the correct values of patriotism in young Japanese and, to this end, in 1985, the MOE made raising the national flag and singing the national anthem compulsory at school ceremonies.

Controversially, on August 15, 1985 (the fortieth anniversary of war's end), Nakasone led his cabinet members in an official visit to Tokyo's Yasukuni Shrine, which enshrines the spirits of Japan's war dead, including fourteen convicted Class A war criminals who were quietly enshrined in 1978. Nakasone had made previous visits as prime minister, but not on such a politically charged anniversary. Moreover, nor was he the first prime minister to visit the shrine, with Miki Takeo having visited in a private capacity on the anniversary of war defeat in 1975 to placate the right wing of the party. Thereafter subsequent prime ministers and cabinet members continued this private ritual. But Nakasone's official 1985 visit, coming after the enshrinement of the war criminals, provoked vehement protestations from East Asian countries, with the PRC angrily criticizing his actions as "hurtful to the hearts of Asians." Questions about the constitutionality of the visit also provoked lively debate, since officials had used government vehicles to travel to the shrine, arguably violating Article 20 on the separation of state and religion. Nakasone shrewdly sidestepped the issue by claiming that the visit was not religious because he had not performed the usual two bows, two claps, and third bow.

As Nakasone's 1986 landslide electoral victory of three hundred seats revealed, many Japanese were willing to accept this level of nationalist display from the prime minister, despite remaining unmoved on the issue of constitutional revision. Thanks to this electoral performance, LDP members agreed to change party rules, allowing Nakasone to extend his prime ministership for a second term until November 1987, making him the third longest serving prime minister in postwar Japan at that time after Yoshida and Satō. Nakasone would remain an influential LDP player until his retirement from the Diet in 2003 at age eighty-five. Moreover, his reforms in public finance and national security and his nationalist stance would strike deep roots in conservative politics and policies thereafter.

Japan: The Regional and Global Power

The Power of the Yen

Internationalization (*kokusaika*) was one of Nakasone's favorite mantras, although for him it was mostly a one-way process of exporting Japan's economic and cultural products to the world. In reality, Japan's international entanglements in the 1970s and 1980s were far more complex and complicated. The strengthening yen after the shift to floating exchange rates in the early 1970s encouraged many companies to expand operations overseas to address rising labor and material costs. The Nixon Dollar Shock of 1971 stimulated the first phase of intensive FDI into Asia, North America, and Europe. In 1970, Japanese FDI outlays were just over US$900 million, reaching $3.28 billion by 1975, $4.69 billion by 1980, $12.2 billion by 1985, and peaking at $67.5 billion in 1989 at the height of the economic bubble. As figure 5.13 shows, outward FDI increased fivefold during the 1970s, a further 2.5 times from 1980 to 1985, and then another 5.5 times in the four years to 1989. In the space of around two decades FDI had thus increased an astounding 75-fold.[44] The regional focus of FDI evolved over time, too, increasing in most countries and regions with a notable concentration in the United States, which attracted 48 percent of Japanese outward FDI in 1989 compared with 12 percent for Asia and 13 percent for Europe. Among some of the more high-profile Japanese investments of the time were the acquisition of Firestone Tire and Rubber by the Bridgestone Corporation in 1988, the purchase of the Rockefeller Center in New York by Mitsubishi Estate, Sony Corporation's takeover of Columbia Pictures in 1989, and the purchase of the Pebble Beach Golf Course by Cosmo World in 1990.

Despite the strong yen, Japanese exports continued to surge. From 1970 to 1980 exports increased four times, followed by a further 1.2-fold increase during the 1980s when the yen was at its strongest.[45] The United States and Asia accounted for more than 60 percent of these exports (over 30 percent, respectively), with the relative weight of exports to Asia increasing throughout the decade.[46] Japan's growing influence in international trade and investment led to its inclusion in the G5 industrialized nations in 1973 (later expanded to the Group of Six and then Group of Seven). The country also fortified its international contributions, with ODA more than tripling from US$3.53 billion in 1970 to $7.7 billion in 1980 and $11.47 billion by 1990.[47]

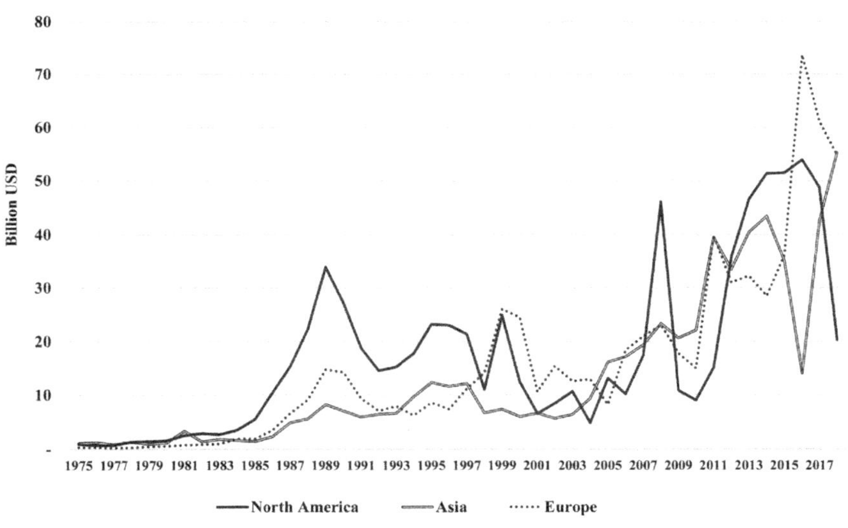

Source: Japan External Trade Organization, "Chokusetsu Tōshi Tōkei."

Figure 5.13. Japanese Outward Foreign Direct Investment, 1975–2018

But not all was smooth sailing for the new economic superpower. As Japan overtook the United States as the major investor and ODA provider in East Asia in the early 1970s, Japanese politicians and businesses faced increasing hostility from citizens in the region who were worried about the spread of Japanese industries and the proliferation of Japanese products—what one Filipino critic labelled Japan's "second invasion."[48] Tanaka Kakuei felt this anger firsthand during a visit to Southeast Asian nations in 1974. After a largely smooth trip to the Philippines, thanks to the heavy hand of dictator Ferdinand Marcos, Tanaka met with violent riots in Indonesia. Protesters destroyed the premises of Japanese companies, overturned and set alight Japanese branded vehicles, and pelted the Japanese embassy with stones. President Suharto had no choice but to shuttle Tanaka to the airport by military helicopter, where he made a speedy exit to Thailand. Although not violent, Tanaka's reception in Bangkok was hardly more welcoming, with crowds of protesters forming a human chain around the Japanese embassy and even government officials criticizing the arrogance of Japanese companies and tourists.

Japanese elites were genuinely shocked by this reception from Asians, since they believed that their country's investments and aid were contributing to the development of the region. Few recognized how many Asians still carried bitter memories of Japanese militarism in the region and how these memories connected to images of a new Japanese economic invasion based on exploitation and environmental destruction. It was left to Prime Minister Fukuda Yasuo to mend bridges in Southeast Asia. In a speech delivered in Manila during a trip to the region in 1977, Fukuda announced his so-called Fukuda Doctrine in which he promised that Japan would forever renounce militarism and nuclear weapons, contribute to peace in the region, and proactively build "heart-to-heart" relations with the people of the Asia.

Fukuda's overture was received positively at the time, but a controversy in 1982 once again fostered distrust and resentment toward Japan throughout East Asia. The matter began when Japanese media outlets reported that the MOE—under pressure from conservative politicians—had required authors of school history textbooks to change certain terminology and descriptions of historical events relating to the Asia-Pacific War. Descriptions of Japan's "invasion" of China in 1937 were amended to "incursion" or "advance," while the horrific Nanjing Massacre of 1937 was attributed to obstinate resistance by Chinese forces rather than a blatant atrocity by the Japanese military. South Korea also expressed its annoyance at depictions of the March First independence movement of 1919 as a "riot" and use of the term "draft" to characterize the forced labor imposed on Koreans during the war. The PRC led the backlash from Asia, lodging an immediate protest with the Japanese government and calling Japan's actions a betrayal of the spirit of the treaty of friendship signed under Fukuda in 1978. The Chinese were joined by a chorus of protestations from North Korea and South Korea, Taiwan, Hong Kong, Singapore, and a host of other Southeast Asian nations. Criticism also spread in Japan with thousands of citizens sending letters of protest to newspapers.

Although the MOE initially denied interference, the backlash both domestic and international forced Prime Minister Suzuki Zenkō and his Chief Cabinet Secretary Miyazawa Kiichi into damage control. Miyazawa promptly met with Asian officials, promising Japanese government action to rectify the issue. In a public statement released in August 1982, Miyazawa confirmed that the government would revise the relevant sections of the textbooks, and that the certification criteria would thereafter consider the "development of friendship and goodwill" with "neighboring Asian countries." Specifically, the textbook certification conditions were now to include a "neighboring countries stipulation," requiring consideration of diplomatic relations with other countries. With this, the diplomatic brouhaha subsided, but the incident did little to inspire Asian countries' trust in Japanese leaders. Moreover, it provided welcome fuel for nationalists in other countries, who could depict Japan as unrepentant and an ongoing threat in the region. This would not be the last textbook controversy, with another flaring up in 1986. It was evidence of how the Japanese continued to struggle with the unresolved legacies of colonization and militarism over forty years after war's end.

Trade Frictions

Relations with the United States in the 1980s were hardly any smoother than they were with Asian countries, despite the celebrated friendship of "Yasu and Ron." The story of the 1970s and 1980s was one of Japan's meteoric rise as a manufacturing and exporting superpower in automobiles, consumer electronics, and integrated circuits. One problematic outcome of this exporting miracle was a growing trade imbalance with the United States, European countries, and nations throughout Asia. In 1979, the trade imbalance with the United States stood at 1.3 trillion yen but, a mere six years later in 1985, it had ballooned more than sevenfold to 9.3 trillion yen (fig. 5.14).

In the early 1980s, Japanese exports accounted for 70 percent of the US trade imbalance, stoking the ire of US political and business leaders alike.[49] Japanese exports of passenger automobiles attracted particular attention in America, growing from around 712,000 units in 1975 to 2.2 million in 1985, as consumers switched to smaller, more energy-efficient vehicles in the wake of the Oil Shocks. As US automakers' sales declined and workers were laid off, calls for a boycott of Japanese vehicles intensified from around the late 1970s. Strident voices began to accuse Japan of being an unfair trader that imported very little and whose exports were destroying the livelihoods of hardworking Americans in the Midwest. In the

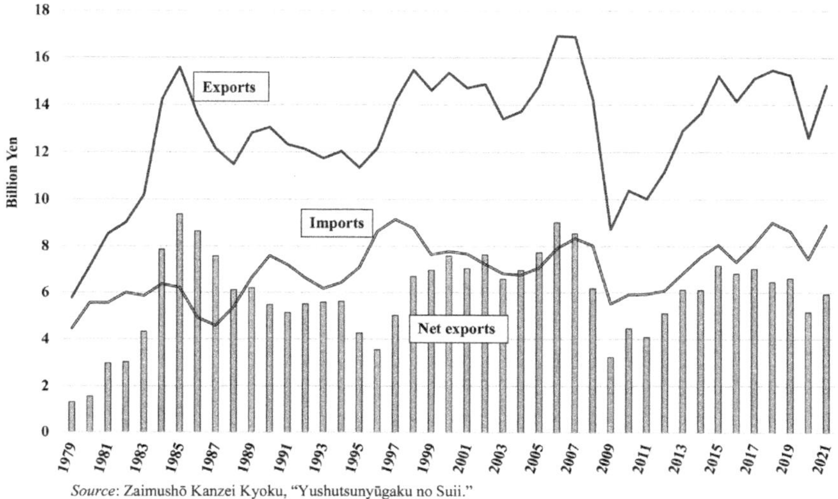

Figure 5.14. Japanese Imports from, Exports to, and Net Exports to the United States, 1979–2021

mid-1980s, Lee Iacocca, chief executive of the Chrysler Corporation, toured America calling for an all-out "trade war" with Japan, while author Daniel Burstein published the menacingly-titled *Yen!: Japan's New Financial Empire and Its Threat to America* in 1988.[50]

Cooler heads ultimately prevailed but, beginning in the late 1970s and continuing throughout the 1980s, American trade negotiators began pressuring the Japanese to restrain exports of certain products—voluntarily or, if necessary, by the imposition of numerical targets. The first such agreement came in 1978, when the two countries agreed on a floor import price for Japanese steel to protect the US domestic industry. Nonetheless, thereafter Japanese steel imports continued to grow, resulting in a 1984 agreement by Japan to voluntarily restrain its exports—a so-called VER (voluntary export restraint). Japanese televisions and machine tools also faced import restrictions: the former subject to an "orderly market agreement" restricting exports, the latter transitioning from price controls in the late 1970s to a VER in 1986.

Negotiations over automobiles—among the more contentious of products, given the political and economic implications on both sides—resulted in a series of VERs limiting Japanese exports to the United States to 1.68 million units from 1981 to 1983, 1.85 million units in FY1984, and 2.3 million units in FY1985.[51] Ironically, the VERs encouraged Japanese automakers to increase profit margins by upgrading exported models and manufacturing more expensive midsized automobiles. Moreover, to circumvent the VERs, makers such as Honda, Nissan, and Toyota set up local production facilities in the United States, further contributing to the globalization of the Japanese automobile industry.

The final stage in the US-Japan trade frictions was the so-called Structural Impediments Initiative (SII) of the late 1980s, which focused on the supposedly obstructive aspects of the Japanese market, like cheap capital, exclusionary keiretsu relationships among firms, a prohibitively complicated distribution system, and other more dubious claims about the Japanese saving too much and working too long. Whereas the earlier focus was on unfair Japanese export practices, now American political and business leaders turned their attention to the supposed barriers to American companies gaining fair access to the Japanese market. Even before the SII negotiations began in 1989, American negotiators had the Japanese decrease (and then abandon) import quotas on US beef and citrus fruits. In 1986, a secret agreement was reached between the two governments in which the Japanese side committed to assisting US semiconductor manufacturers attain a 20 percent market share in Japan.

In the final report of the bilateral SII committee submitted to President George H. W. Bush and Prime Minister Toshiki Kaifu in 1990, the Japanese side committed to encouraging Japanese firms to purchase more supplies from abroad and implementing market deregulation. As seen in the neoliberal policies of Nakasone Yasuhiro, the push for deregulation and opening up the economy was already a policy priority for Japanese conservatives, hence such *gaiatsu* or pressure from the outside actually helped their cause. But, as observers note, the SII was only successful in domestic industries already supportive of opening up, such as retail and distribution. Other sectors like agriculture and construction continued to remain closed and comparatively inefficient.

Throughout this period of internecine US-Japan trade strife, officials and political elites attempted to assuage tensions with frothy gestures, like Nakasone's 1985 call on all Japanese to purchase US$100 of imports to cut the trade deficit by US$12 billion, and the government's designation of October as "Import Promotion Month" with its slogan "spread friendship worldwide by promoting imports."[52]

Not all Japanese meekly accepted America's demands. In 1989, the nationalist politician and novelist Ishihara Shintarō and Sony Corporation president Akio Morita coauthored the provocative *"No" to ieru Nihon* (*The Japan That Can Say "NO": Why Japan Will Be First Among Equals*) in which they called on Japanese leaders to more forcefully defend the country's interests against the "racist" Western world.[53] Resonating with the cultural nationalism discussed earlier, the book emphasized the "superiority" of Japanese workers, education, and technology compared with the West—strengths that needed to be marshalled to assert Japan's rights internationally. Coming in 1989, Ishihara and Morita's book was perfectly timed for the dizzying heights of an economic bubble just about to burst.

The Bubble Economy

In 1985, the heads of central banks from the G5—the United States, the United Kingdom, West Germany, Japan, and France—met at the Plaza Hotel in New York City, where they collectively agreed to intervene in currency markets to address the strong dollar by raising the value of the deutschmark and, especially, the yen. The Americans hoped that such a move would serve as another lever to reduce the massive trade imbalance with Japan. In theory, a stronger yen would make imports cheaper, incentivizing Japanese consumers and businesses to purchase more from abroad. Following their meeting, G5 members aggressively sold US dollars and purchased yen, resulting in a massive appreciation in the yen, which rose from 220 yen to the dollar just prior to the accord to 160 yen to the dollar by July 1986, followed by a historic high (for the time) of 121.25 yen to the dollar on December 28, 1987 (fig. 5.15). Fearing the onset of a "strong-yen recession," the Japanese government responded by aggressively lowering the official discount rate on five occasions beginning in January 1986, taking it from 5 percent to 2.5 percent by 1987—its lowest

Source: Macrotrends, "Dollar Yen Exchange Rate (USD JPY)."

Figure 5.15. Japanese Yen to US Dollar Exchange Rate, 1971–1999

rate ever. At the same time, responding to American demands to stimulate domestic demand, the Nakasone administration lowered corporate tax rates and began pumping finances into public works in 1987.

As a result of these measures, the Japanese economy entered a state of excess liquidity, as corporations and local governments found themselves with an overabundance of capital reserves—much of which was unrealized. Instead of investing this capital in research and development as might have happened during the years of high-speed growth, under the spell of affluence, attention turned to speculative investment in real estate, stocks, and even expensive works of art by van Gogh and others. Known as *zaiteku* or "financial engineering," a dangerous cycle emerged in which corporations used gains from speculative investments to report massive earnings on financial reports. As long as corporations could show unrealized capital gains, they could increase their fundraising capacity and legitimize further investments, leading in turn to more speculative activity, which pushed markets ever upwards. The *zaiteku* boom mesmerized investors of all hues, including large corporations, government agencies, local governments, consumer cooperatives, and ordinary investors.

The result was rampant asset inflation manifest in spiraling land and share prices in the late 1980s. Both residential and industrial properties, especially in the Tokyo, Osaka, and Nagoya regions, experienced massive price increases, exacerbated by land speculators or *jiageya* from Yakuza groups who would intimidate landowners until they agreed to sell. In 1984, residential land cost just over two hundred thousand yen per square meter, but prior to the economic meltdown in 1991, it had risen fourfold to eight hundred thousand yen. Similarly, industrial land stood at around one million yen per square meter in 1984, rising to over eight million yen in 1991.[54] The passing of the Resort Law in 1987 only further fueled the upsurge. So valuable did real estate become that the land under the Imperial Palace in Tokyo was supposedly worth as much as the state of California, and Tokyo worth more than the entire United States.[55]

Giants of the Japanese banking industry like Sumitomo joined the speculative hysteria, approving loans for—in hindsight—greatly overvalued properties and securities investments. Many of these loans would remain as bad debts on the books of banks throughout the 1990s. Stock prices also surged in the late 1980s. The Nikkei 225 index rose from 12,666.95 yen on September 20, 1985 (just prior to the Plaza Accord) to a high of 39,915.87 on December 29, 1989. In the space of four years, stock prices more than tripled. The global stock market crash of October 19, 1987—so-called Black Monday—shaved 14.9 percent off the value of the Nikkei 225, but the index had recovered within six months and kept increasing thereafter.

With greed as the motivating force, the bubble years witnessed numerous instances of corruption and bribery. Prestigious securities companies were found to have compensated important clients—including public organizations and large corporations—for losses made on shoddy investments. In 1989, the Nomura Securities company was ordered to cease operations for a month for violations under the Securities Trading Law, relating to its dealings in railway shares. In the fallout, the company's president and vice president were forced to resign after revelations of investments in companies with Yakuza connections. As detailed in chapter 6, the demise of Prime Minister Takeshita Noboru also resulted from shady dealings in stocks.

Not all companies shared in the delights of the bubble, however. Many small factories producing machine tools and other components for large industry found their contracts either greatly reduced or suspended as the high yen encouraged corporations to relocate operations overseas or to source materials from abroad.

Government officials finally admitted that the economy was dangerously overheated and, in 1989 and 1990, raised the official discount rate three times. Moreover, to reign in real estate speculation, the MOF issued the Regulation on Aggregate Real Estate Financing in April 1990, which directed banks to keep the growth of real estate lending below that for loans overall. The hope was that such measures would cool down both stock market and real estate speculation—which did indeed ensue.

But few anticipated the wider economic carnage that would follow. Having successfully navigated the shocks of the early 1970s and the massive appreciation of the yen, the view from the late 1980s looked decidedly positive. Japan was "number one" and life was "somehow crystal" for many ordinary citizens. Few would have believed that the "sun also sets" as Bill Emmott, Tokyo bureau chief at *The Economist* magazine, declared in his 1989 book of that title. Yet, as we have seen, the economic, social, and political systems and practices forged throughout the 1970s and 1980s also brought with them a dark underbelly of corruption, worsening public finances, a ticking demographic timebomb, a growing stratum of nonregular workers, and unresolved questions about Japan's place in the region and the world. These issues would dominate Japanese attention in the wake of the bubble era.

CHAPTER SIX

The 1990s: Era of Unraveling

Death of an Emperor

On September 19, 1988, the Japanese nation was plunged into an atmosphere of solemn melancholy when the media reported that Emperor Hirohito had been hospitalized in a serious condition due to complications from chronic pancreatitis. Only later would people learn that the emperor had in fact been diagnosed with late-stage pancreatic cancer. For the next 111 days, the media consistently reported on the emperor's deteriorating condition, offering detailed descriptions of the monarch's temperature and pulse, his "vomiting of blood," and his frequent "bloody bowel discharges."

The emperor's declining health brought the unfettered exuberance of the economic bubble to a sudden standstill—at least in public—replaced now by a mood of gloom and spontaneous displays of self-restraint. Playing cheerful music and dancing in public suddenly became inappropriate, festivals were cancelled, drum beating at baseball games was abandoned, upbeat television commercials were edited, comedy programs were rescheduled, weddings and other celebrations were either cancelled or greatly toned down, and celebratory foods like red bean rice taken off the shelves of stores—replaced now with signs reading "sales temporarily suspended." Citizens flocked to sign get-well registers established by the Imperial Household Agency at twelve locations across the archipelago. By November 1988, these registers contained some sixty million messages.

The inevitable came on January 7, 1989, when the eighty-seven-year-old emperor finally succumbed to his illness at 6:33 in the morning. Following Hirohito's death, government agencies, banks, stores, and other organizations flew flags at half-mast. The funeral of the following month was attended by dignitaries from 164 countries and 28 international organizations.

Emperor Hirohito left a complicated legacy, spanning the agonizing history of militarism and wartime destruction and the postwar story of reconstruction and economic success. Within Japan and in the countries of survivors from Japan's last war, critical retrospectives of the Shōwa Emperor appeared, with some denouncing the late sovereign as a war criminal. Emblematic of the controversy surrounding Hirohito, the mayor of Nagasaki, Motoshima Hitoshi, was shot by a right-wing

Figure 6.1. Funeral procession for Emperor Hirohito (the Shōwa Emperor) at Shinjuku Gyoen, February 24, 1989. Courtesy of The Asahi Shimbun Company.

group in 1990 for raising the issue of the emperor's war responsibility—something largely swept under the carpet by the US occupiers forty-three years earlier.

Controversy aside, Hirohito's passing contributed to a larger sense of ending in 1989, reinforced by the deaths of the great manga artist Tezuka Osamu (of *Astro Boy* fame) in February, the founder of Matsushita Electric Industrial Company (later Panasonic Corporation) Matsushita Kōnosuke in April, and the popular singer Misora Hibari in June. Soon after the Imperial Household Agency announced the emperor's death from cancer, Chief Cabinet Secretary Obuchi Keizō proclaimed the new era name, Heisei, meaning "attaining peace." Hirohito was succeeded by his eldest son, the fifty-five-year old Akihito who, along with his "commoner" wife Michiko, would occupy the throne for the next thirty years until his abdication in early 2019.

After the Economic Miracle

The Bubble Bursts

Globally, the years from around 1989 to 1991 also witnessed historic endings with the collapse of the Cold War framework in Europe, as the Soviet Union, its satellite states, and its allies abandoned state socialism one by one. Following Soviet president Mikhail Gorbachev's policies of glasnost (freedom of information) and perestroika (domestic reform), Gorbachev and American president George H. W. Bush held a historic meeting on the island of Malta in 1989, where they declared the Cold War over. Thereafter, Poland, Hungary, and Romania conducted free elections and moved to open multiparty systems. In November 1989, Germans in the east and west collectively knocked down the Berlin Wall, followed by elections in a united Germany in 1990. The following year witnessed the dissolution of the Warsaw Treaty, bringing an end to the East European socialist bloc. After a failed attempt by conservatives to maintain the USSR, in 1991, Ukraine, Estonia, Latvia and most other areas declared their independence from the union. In December, Boris Yeltsin became president of the Russian Federation and, together with surrounding states including Ukraine and Belarus, formed the Commonwealth of Independent States. For many Japanese, these events in far-off Europe seemed a world away, but the tectonic shifts they precipitated would have profound implications for Japanese foreign relations in the coming decades.

Closer to home, the years 1989 to 1991 corresponded with nothing short of a meltdown in the stock and real estate markets or, as it would come to be known, the "bursting" of the economic bubble. As we saw in the previous chapter, the origins of this economic bubble lay in the sharp appreciation of the yen following the Plaza Accord of 1985. Within the space of a year, the yen appreciated from 235 yen to the dollar to around the 150-yen mark. Fearing the negative effects of a strong yen on the export-driven Japanese economy, beginning in 1986, the Bank of Japan responded to calls from business to decrease the official discount rate. As noted, in 1986 alone, the Bank of Japan announced four rate cuts, taking the official discount rate from 5 percent to 3 percent. A further fifty basis point cut in February 1987 took the discount rate to 2.5 percent—the lowest in its history and just half of what it had been a year earlier. With cheap money flowing freely and corporations flush with cash, capital flowed into speculative investment in real estate and securities, creating an economic bubble. By early 1988, land values in Tokyo and its surrounds were up over 60 percent compared with just a few years earlier, while the Nikkei 225 index exceeded 30 thousand yen for the first time. So long as prices of land and stocks were rising, financial institutions felt comfortable about lending even more, despite loans being secured by unrealized assets.

Not everyone was blinded by the skyrocketing markets. As early as 1986, Tamura Yoshirō, Land Bureau Chief at the then National Land Agency (NLA), recommended to the Ministry of Finance and the government that the land tax system be reformed and bank lending for real estate more tightly regulated to stem the flow of speculation. But Tamura's suggestion was disregarded. Similarly, in late 1986, Bank of Japan chairman, Mieno Yasushi, wanted to halt further discount rate decreases, but he too was rebuffed as MOF bureaucrats and political elites like

Prime Minister Miyazawa focused their concerns on the risk of a "strong-yen-led recession." As the former president of Fuji Bank (later Mizuho Bank) Hashida Taizō later recalled, "interest rates should have been raised" once the stock market began to recover after Black Monday (October 1987), but a policy of monetary easing was adopted, resulting in huge investments in real estate, golf club memberships, and works of art.[1]

By 1989, it was no longer possible for regulators and many others to ignore the dangerously overheated economy. The term "bubble" appeared 28 times in the pages of Japan's leading economic newspaper, the *Nihon Keizai shinbun* in 1989, climbing to 252 appearances in 1990, a year of stock market carnage in the country.[2] The Bank of Japan's monetary tightening policies—beginning in May 1989 with an enormous seventy-five basis point increase in the official discount rate—precipitated the collapse. Smashing the "myth of eternally low interest rates," thereafter, the Bank of Japan raised the discount rate in quick succession, taking it from 2.5 percent to 6 percent in the space of fifteen months. Compounding the shock, the government introduced its long-delayed sales tax of 3 percent in April 1989. With this, Japanese governmental economic policy shifted from one of attempting to suppress the appreciation of the yen to controlling the overheated economy. In hindsight, however, this adjustment probably came too late.

Around the same time, the government adopted several measures to bring real estate prices under control. To oversee real estate dealings, a special land price monitoring system was established within the NLA. In April 1990—four years after Tamura's initial advice—the MOF imposed a regulation on the total volume of real estate lending. Herein, banks were required to keep lending for real estate below the growth rate for loans overall, with the aim of dampening the real estate bubble. The regulation immediately restricted bank lending in a range of sectors, including construction, real estate, and nonbank institutions like leasing and consumer finance companies. With this action, the MOF "sent a clear signal" that it was determined to prevent any further price increases in the real estate market.[3] The MOF reinforced this position by instituting a reform of the land tax system. Working in lockstep, the Ministry of Construction implemented new regulations on land use.

The effect of these policies was immediate and dramatic. After reaching an all-time high of 38,915 yen in late December 1989, the Nikkei 225 began to fall precipitously (fig. 6.3). By October 1990, the index had slumped to below twenty thousand yen, representing a 49 percent drop from its previous high and prompting the Japanese-language edition of *Newsweek* to run a story on the "Shocking Tokyo Crash." Thereafter, the Nikkei recovered to reach around twenty-six thousand yen, but another steep decline from late October 1991 plunged the index below fifteen thousand yen on August 9, 1992—the first time in close to six-and-a-half years.

Figure 6.2. Panic on the Tokyo Stock Exchange as prices crash in late February 1990. Courtesy of The Asahi Shimbun Company.

Figure 6.3. Nikkei 225 Stock Market Index, 1980–2022

This drop represented a massive 62 percent decrease from the index's peak in 1989. Apart from a few occasions, thereafter the Nikkei 225 struggled to exceed twenty thousand yen until well into the new millennium. Moreover, proving that the crash was a specifically Japanese phenomenon, stock markets around the world were left relatively unscathed.

The collapse of real estate prices came around one year after the stock market crash (fig. 6.4). Following the peak in land values in 1991, prices for both residential and commercial real estate in all of Japan's major metropolises and most regional towns declined, although Tokyo and its surrounds as well as the Osaka area were hit particularly hard. Compared with 1990, in the six major cities of Tokyo, Yokohama, Nagoya, Kyoto, Osaka, and Kobe, by 1995 commercial property values had dropped by close to 42 percent, residential land by 57 percent, and industrial land by 67 percent, with an overall average decrease of 54.7 percent.[4] Prices continued to plummet until 2001, followed thereafter by a gradual improvement led by the greater Tokyo region. Both lenders and borrowers were battered by the descent. Banks and other lending institutions were left with trillions of yen in loans secured by collateral whose value was devastated by the land price crash. Individuals, corporate investors, and property developers alike found themselves trapped with either worthless or greatly devalued real estate along with massive loans now incurring larger servicing costs due to increased interest rates.

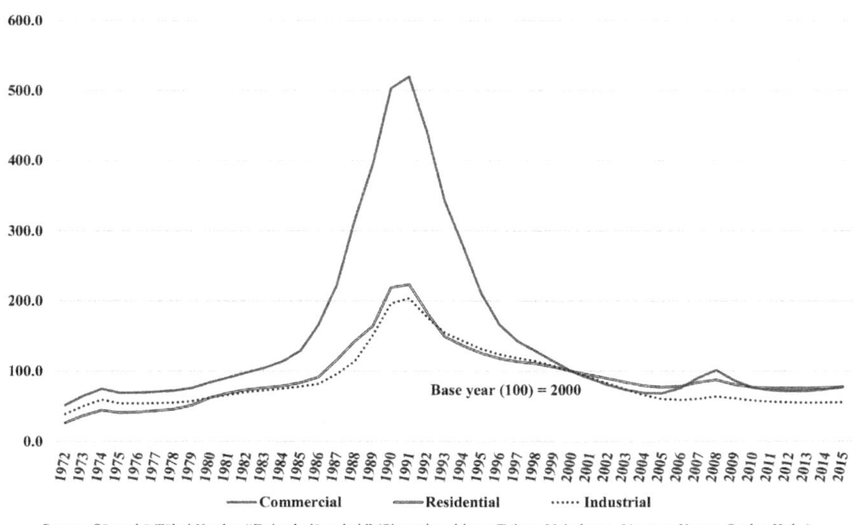

Source: Sōmushō Tōkei Kyoku, "Dai-rokujūgo-kai." (Six major cities = Tokyo, Yokohama, Nagoya, Kyoto, Osaka, Kobe)

Figure 6.4. Urban Land Price Index (Six Major Cities), 1972–2015

The bankruptcy of numerous real estate developers and market speculators surprised no one. But the subsequent collapse of financial institutions—some previously seen as unshakable—in the wake of the stock and real estate market crashes raised concerns about the very foundations of Japan's economic system. Due to the Bank of Japan's monetary easing policy during the 1980s, the amount of bank loans more than doubled, with most of this financing going to real estate companies or individuals and enterprises involved in real estate investment. At the beginning of the 1990s, some 25 percent of bank investments were tied up in the real estate or construction industries and, if we include indirect investment, around 55 percent of bank loans were in one way or another dependent on land, leaving these institutions highly exposed to market adjustments.[5]

The year 1995 witnessed the collapse of several financial institutions that had been decimated by the crash: the Cosmo Credit Association in July, followed by the Kizu Shinkumi Bank of Osaka and the Hyōgo Bank of Kobe in August. The most high-profile bankruptcy of 1995 was the Jūtaku Senmon Kin'yu Kaisha (abbreviated as "Jūsen"), comprising seven financial institutions that specialized in the provision of home loans. Jūsen traced its roots to the 1970s, when several major and regional banks came together to offer residential loans, which had been largely neglected by major banks that chose to focus on corporate financing. Into the 1980s, however, corporations found themselves awash in cash and, hence, in less need of bank financing. In response, major banks more aggressively targeted the home loan market, prompting members of Jūsen to provide more and more financing for speculative real estate investments. The impact of this shift on Jūsen was catastrophic. In the late 1980s, 96 percent of Jūsen assets consisted of residential loans, but this had dropped to just 21 percent by the end of the 1990s. As early as autumn 1992, the MOF was aware of Jūsen's massive, accumulated debts following the real estate market collapse. But the deep-seated belief—or perhaps hope—that property prices would increase prevented bureaucrats from taking proactive action. Moreover, many officials felt that liquidating Jūsen would only further dent market confidence, contributing to the already dire economic conditions. The fact that chief executive officers (CEOs) of six of the seven Jūsen companies were former MOF bureaucrats also did not predispose officials in the ministry to directly intervene.

By the mid-1990s, however, the Jūsen collapse could no longer be avoided. At a rambunctious session of the Diet in June 1995, members passed a law authorizing the use of public monies to dispose of Jūsen's mountain of bad loans. This injection of around seven hundred billion yen of taxpayer money to bail out Jūsen proved highly controversial, but it was just the first in a series of government bailouts thereafter.

Indeed, the years from 1997 to 2000 proved to be a disastrous period in the financial history of postwar Japan, as the excesses of the bubble era came back to haunt leading banks and securities companies. In 1997, it was revealed that several high-profile banks and brokerages had been making illicit payments to so-called *sōkaiya*—corporate blackmailers from organized crime groups who threatened to disrupt annual general meetings if executives refused to pay up. Nomura Securities was the first institution to admit paying off *sōkaiya* in March, followed by the Daiichi Kangyō Bank—which had even been investing in a *sōkaiya* company—in May, Yamaichi Securities in July, and Daiwa Securities in September. CEOs and other executives were forced to resign in all cases.

Accompanying the scandals came a procession of bankruptcies in the financial services industry. November 1997 marked the bleak beginning, as Sanyō Securities, Hokkaido Takushoku Bank, and Yamaichi Securities all filed for voluntary liquidation. Hokkaido Takushoku Bank was strapped with 2.3 trillion yen in bad, unsecured loans and had no choice but to declare bankruptcy after being unable to raise funds. In 1998, the Long-Term Credit Bank of Japan, founded by the Yoshida Shigeru administration in 1952 to fund industrial growth, declared bankruptcy and was temporarily nationalized with 3.5 trillion yen in bad debts. Similarly, the Nippon Credit Bank, established in 1957 with assets from the former Chōsen Bank of colonial times, was nationalized with bad loans amounting to 270 billion yen. Given their proximity to the government and association with Japan's economic miracle, the collapse of these institutions greatly dented Japan's economic prowess and confidence. The year 2000 witnessed collapses in the insurance industry, with both the Kyoei Life Insurance and Chiyoda Life Insurance companies declaring bankruptcy with debts exceeding four trillion yen. These high-profile collapses were accompanied by further bankruptcies among regional banks and other life and general insurance companies during these years. The psychological blow to business and consumer confidence was enormous as companies hesitated to invest and consumption slumped. Japan's former corporate warriors could only watch helplessly as many bankrupt financial institutions were gobbled up by US investors specializing in the acquisition of failed businesses.

The collapse of the Yamaichi Securities Company in 1997 was emblematic of the kind of problems Japanese financial institutions created for themselves during the bubble years. Founded in 1897, Yamaichi was one of Japan's "big four" brokerages, attracting young talent from elite universities and exerting great influence in both political and economic circles. Yamaichi's customer profile read like a who's who of corporate Japan, with multinational juggernauts like the automaker Toyota among its clients. In order to retain these clients, Yamaichi—and other brokerages—had engaged in a practice called *nigiri* (literally "grasping" or "holding on to"), under which a rate of return was informally guaranteed to clients regardless of the market performance of their investments. Brokerages utilized *nigiri* after the

Figure 6.5. CEO Nozawa Shōhei weeps before a crowded media conference following Yamaichi Securities' bankruptcy in November 1997. Courtesy of The Asahi Shimbun Company.

stock market crash of Black Monday in 1987, compensating corporate customers like Hitachi, Matsushita, and Toyota for market losses. In essence, these brokerages were operating like banks, and the investments of clients treated almost like secured deposits with guaranteed rates of return. To keep these losses secret, around reporting time, Yamaichi engaged in another practice called *tobashi* (literally "transferring"), which involved temporarily shifting liabilities to a related company. During the bubble years when markets were constantly on the rise, Yamaichi executives could be confident that such losses would eventually be covered by future gains. But when the market collapsed—as it did in 1990—Yamaichi was left saddled with massive liabilities and unable to keep its informal commitments to large clients. Standing before a packed media conference on November 24, 1997, Yamaichi CEO Nozawa Shōhei accepted full responsibility for this failure and, in a memorable display of sobbing emotion, begged people not to blame company employees because it was all the fault of management.

The bankruptcies and scandals of the late 1990s put an end to the speculation of the bubble era. Burdened with bad loans and risk averse to even seemingly safe loans, bank lending in construction, real estate, and to nonbank financial institutions plummeted. In turn, corporate investments in plant and equipment stagnated, with ripple effects for personal consumption and employment as well. The fundamentals of the Japanese economy had certainly been dealt a heavy blow throughout the 1990s, but just as important was the loss of confidence and expectations for a "bright future" that had inspired the Japanese people for the better part of three decades.

Government Responses

Both corporate Japan and ordinary citizens looked to the government for solutions, which initially involved a mix of monetary and fiscal responses. In a reversal of the interest rate hikes of the late 1980s, beginning in July 1991, the Bank of Japan successively lowered the official discount rate nine times from 6 percent to 0.5 percent. Another series of decreases in 2001 took the discount rate to a historic low of 0.1 percent. But, as noted above, banks remained hesitant to lend for fear of exacerbating their already massive inventory of nonperforming loans.

In an effort to more directly pump prime the economy, governments in the years from 1992 to 1997 under prime ministers Miyazawa Kiichi, Hosokawa Morihiro, and Murayama Tomiichi implemented economic stimulus packages, mainly public works projects such as highways. The Miyazawa administration's "Comprehensive Economic Measures" package of August 1992 involved a huge 10.7 trillion yen in government spending. Despite the change in government in 1993, the new non-LDP prime minister, Hosokawa, followed up with a further "Emergency Economic Measures" package. Hosokawa also initiated a policy of deregulation to free up economic activity. Initially some ninety-four areas were deregulated. Under the Murayama government from 1995, this deregulation was extended into real estate, financial services, the securities industry, and insurance.

Although government spending put great strain on public finances, it contributed to a muted economic recovery of sorts. From negative growth in 1993 (-0.5 percent), real GDP recovered to 1.5 percent in 1994, 3.2 percent in 1995, and 2.9 percent in 1996. The strong-yen woes also appeared to be receding. After hitting a historic high of 82.85 yen to the dollar in May 1995, by the end of 1996, the yen had weakened to 116.3 yen. In response, plant and equipment investment in the manufacturing industry rose in the years from 1994 to 1997. Other statistics were not so positive, however. Unemployment increased from 2.3 percent at the beginning of the decade to 4.7 percent by the end (thereafter peaking at 5.4 percent in 2002).

After the resignation of JSP prime minister Murayama (see later in this chapter), the LDP once again assumed power under the leadership of Hashimoto Ryūtarō in January 1996. Hashimoto's rise to power coincided with another economic downturn thanks in part to the implementation of an increase in the consumption tax from 3 to 5 percent (approved in 1994). Hashimoto was initially concerned primarily with the sorry condition of public finances and embarked on an expansive agenda of administrative reform and fiscal stringency to cut back on government wastage and inefficiencies. Declaring 1997 "year one of the era of structurally reforming public finances," Hashimoto committed to reducing government bond issuances to zero and shrinking the deficits of local and national governments to 3 percent of GDP by the year 2003. On top of this, Hashimoto oversaw an increase in patient copayments for health care and the abandoning of certain tax breaks.

In principle, the reforms under Hashimoto, based on reigning in government spending while bolstering revenues with a consumption tax increase, made sense.

But the timing of the tax increase and reform program proved toxic for a still-bruised economy. In the mid-1990s, most of the major banks were just starting to rein in their bad loans by posting losses. However, the consumption tax increase in 1997 only served to precipitate another nosedive in land prices, in turn causing more loan defaults. Hashimoto had no choice but to jettison his fiscal stringency line for more phases of stimulus spending and government bailouts. The Law Concerning Emergency Measures for the Stabilization of the Functions of the Financial System of February 1998 allowed the government to inject around 1.8 trillion yen into twenty-one major financial institutions, although most realized that this amount only scratched the surface of the problem. The so-called Financial Revitalization Law of October 12, 1998, was subsequently passed to enable the liquidation of the Long-Term Credit Bank of Japan and the Nippon Credit Bank. Under this law, the Financial Reconstruction Commission was able to temporarily nationalize financial institutions deemed to be insolvent, and their nonperforming loans were disposed of by the newly established Resolution and Collection Corporation. Finally, the passing of the Financial Function Early Strengthening Law on October 16, 1998, paved the way for the injection of a further 7.5 trillion yen into fifteen major and regional banks in March 1999—four times the capital injection of late 1998.

During the period 1998 to 2004, government capital injections to save and strengthen ailing financial institutions amounted to 12.4 trillion yen.[6] In the wake of these interventions, Japanese banks entered a period of mergers and consolidations. All in all, ten banks merged to create the three mega banks we see today. In 2001, Sakura Bank merged with Sumitomo Bank to become the Mitsui Sumitomo Bank; in 2002, Daiichi Kangyō Bank merged with Fuji Bank and the Industrial Bank of Japan to create the Mizuho Bank; and, in 2005, the Tokyo Mitsubishi Bank merged with UFJ Holdings to form Mitsubishi Tokyo UFJ.

Along with the bank bail outs, Hashimoto—despite being a self-proclaimed "fiscal reformer"—announced a massive stimulus package of sixteen trillion yen to address poor (and sometimes negative) GDP growth (fig. 6.6). As part of his economic revitalization policies, Hashimoto launched his financial "Big Bang" in November 1996, which involved extensive deregulation of the financial services industry and system. The three core aims of the policy were "free," "fair," and "global"—all aimed at making Tokyo into a financial center the equivalent of London or New York.[7] The extent to which this vision was realized is debatable. Hashimoto himself later admitted that economic policies under his watch may have been mistimed, thus contributing to the worsening of economic conditions. The onset of the Asian Financial Crisis of 1997, beginning with the collapse of the Thai Baht, also did not assist in economic recovery.

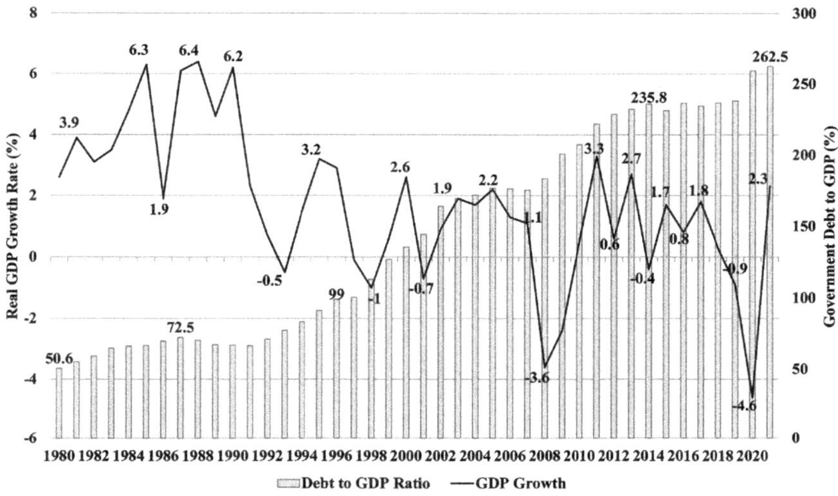

Figure 6.6. Annual Growth of Real GDP and Government Debt as Percentage of GDP, 1980–2021

The "Lost Decade"?

Apart from the financial services industry, many other industries, including construction, automotive, steel, and electronics, suffered from bankruptcies and severe downturns during the 1990s. Laden with debt, the Nissan Motor Corporation—ranked second only to Toyota in sales volume—was forced to enter an alliance with the French automaker Renault in 1998. Adding to the humiliation, Renault appointed Carlos Ghosn—the so-called cost killer—as chief operating officer in 1999 (president in 2000, CEO in 2001), after which he engaged in a merciless restructuring of the company through cost cutting, factory closures, layoffs, and severing ties with long-time suppliers. Three years into Ghosn's reign, Nissan had made an astounding turnaround to become one of the most profitable global automotive manufacturers, although at great cost to many laid-off employees and bankrupted suppliers.

Not all Japanese manufacturers were as lucky. Electronics manufacturing, for instance, reached its apex in 2000, declining sharply thereafter in the face of competition from South Korea, China, and elsewhere. Observers blamed the decline on a failure on the part of Japanese electronics makers to adapt to the changes wrought by globalization and new technologies linked to the internet. Companies like Matsushita (Panasonic) and Sony remained wedded to traditional products, like televisions, and continued to produce products in separate divisions rather than moving in the direction of product integration. Matsushita, for example, developed its whole business strategy around the production of televisions linked to video cassette recorders and video cameras using analog technologies. Concerned only about domestic market share, the company arguably lost sight of external changes. Little capital was injected into research and development of digital technologies and networking—a decision that would put the company at a great disadvantage with the rise of the internet and competition from South Korea and China. Nakamura Kunio, president of Panasonic from 2000 onward, later recalled his shock on the release of Microsoft's Windows 95 operating system in 1995.[8] Faced with extinction in a newly networked world, the company thereafter shifted emphasis away from televisions into renewable technologies, such as rechargeable lithium batteries.

While Panasonic managed to survive thanks to its size and ability to belatedly adapt, others did not. In 2009, Sanyo Electric became insolvent and was made into a subsidiary of Panasonic, while the Sharp Corporation was acquired by the Taiwanese Foxconn Group and Toshiba Home Appliances by the Midea Group of China in 2016. Japanese semiconductor companies, once the pride of Japanese manufacturing alongside automobiles, were gradually overtaken by competitors from the United States, Korea, and Taiwan. In 1990, six Japanese companies were in the top ten semiconductor manufacturers in the world with NEC, Toshiba, and Hitachi occupying the first three places, respectively. But Japan only had one company in the top ten by 2012: Toshiba at number five.

Not surprising, then, that by the end of the 1990s observers were beginning to speak of Japan's "lost decade." Of course, as the discussion above reveals, it is an exaggeration to simply classify the whole decade as "lost." The economy actually grew from 1994 to 1996—albeit at a lower rate than the US and West European economies. Moreover, economic mismanagement also arguably exacerbated the country's conundrums. The Japanese government failed to constrain the bubble before it got out of hand and, afterwards, did not effectively and swiftly deal with the problem of nonperforming loans, resulting in a major financial crisis. Ill-timed policies like the consumption tax hike of 1997 hit the economy just when it seemed to be moving in a positive direction. More than a lost decade then, the 1990s may be better viewed as a decade of lost opportunities and even lost hope in what, then, was still the world's second largest economy.

Political Disorder

Disorder and disruption in the political world only added to the sense of turmoil and unraveling in the early Heisei era. The turnover of prime ministers was staggering. In the thirty years of Heisei there were seventeen prime ministers (with Abe Shinzō serving twice), whereas in the previous forty-four years there had only been sixteen prime ministers. The quality of many of these leaders arguably played a role in their quick demise, but so too did intensifying partisan conflict within both the LDP and its rivals, amplified by substantial reforms in the electoral system. Throughout the Heisei era, close to fifty political parties with Diet representation were either newly established or created through amalgamations and ruptures. Voters appear to have become increasingly disenchanted with politics. Until the 1990s, voter turnout for general elections had hovered around 70 percent but, thereafter, it barely exceeded 60 percent except for 2009 when the DPJ was swept to power. The drop in voting among youth became particularly conspicuous, especially among those in their thirties and even more so for those in their twenties, of whom less than 40 percent were voting in the 1990s and beyond.

Scandal in the LDP

Part of this voter apathy had to do with fatigue over repeated instances of political scandal and corruption, but it also grew in reaction to the byzantine undulations within Japanese politics of the 1990s, especially in the years from 1989 to 1997. In fact, the first cracks in the 1955 System appeared at the start of the economic bubble in February 1985, when then minister of finance Takeshita Noboru established the Sōseikai, ostensibly a "study group" within the Tanaka faction but in reality a rudimentary new faction—in other words, a faction within a faction. Some eighty-five members of the 130-strong Tanaka faction, the Mokuyōkai, initially expressed an interest in joining Takeshita, but only forty ultimately agreed thanks to Tanaka's desperate efforts to convince them otherwise. Nonetheless, Takeshita's Sōseikai included some of Tanaka's leading protégés, like Ozawa Ichirō, Kanemaru Shin, Hata Tsutomu, and Obuchi Keizō.

Takeshita's move grew out of the frustration he and others with leadership aspirations had toward Tanaka's strategy of only supporting those from other factions for prime minister, while using his factional numbers to control them. When Tanaka suffered a sudden stroke that would leave him severely incapacitated and barely able to speak in late February 1985 (soon after the establishment of the Sōseikai), Takeshita's window of opportunity began to open. Thereafter, the Tanaka faction survived only as a fragile alliance of Takeshita adherents and Tanaka loyalists until mid-1987. At that point, Takeshita finally made his move, defecting to establish the new Keiseikai faction with 113 Tanaka-faction rebels. This internal division within the powerful Tanaka faction, which had exerted so much influence over the LDP and Japanese politics since the early 1970s, opened the way for some stunning political realignments in the 1990s.

As he had promised, the highly popular Nakasone Yasuhiro ended his term as LDP president and prime minister in late 1987, opening the way for one of three frontrunners to take the helm: Takeshita, LDP general council chairman Abe Shintarō, and Minister of Finance Miyazawa Kiichi. When dispute arose over whether there should be a party election for the next LDP president or a backroom decision though factional negotiation, Nakasone intervened, brokering a deal in which Takeshita would assume the presidency and prime ministership, while appointing Miyazawa deputy prime minister and Abe LDP secretary general—in essence, creating a leadership group among the three rivals.

Takeshita's time as prime minister from November 1987 to June 1989, however, was tainted with scandal. In terms of policy, his one notable achievement was the passing of an unpopular 3 percent consumption tax in late 1988, which both of his predecessors Ōhira and Nakasone had been unable to accomplish. But the Takeshita administration is remembered mostly because of the so-called Recruit Cosmos scandal, which bubbled to the surface during this time.

The scandal originated with a report in the *Asahi shinbun* in June 1988, which identified a Kawasaki city official who had apparently obtained unlisted shares in the Recruit Cosmos Corporation (involved in publishing, telecommunications, property, and development), later selling these for a huge profit when the company went public. Weeks later, the newspaper followed up with a damning exposé on how leading politicians in the LDP and opposition parties, together with high-ranking bureaucrats, had also pocketed huge profits after selling unlisted Recruit Cosmos shares. In its July 6, 1988 edition, the *Asahi* reported that LDP heavyweights like Nakasone, Abe, and Miyazawa were among the politicians to have struck stock market gold with their shares. As more details gradually emerged from the shadows, it was revealed that the president of Recruit Cosmos, Ezoe Hiromasa, had been flagrantly distributing unlisted shares to elites in government, business, the bureaucracy, and mass media to gain favors and win influence. Ezoe himself was arrested in 1989 for paying bribes to executives of NTT.

The political fallout from the scandal was immediate and made worse by the popular discontent over the new consumption tax. Miyazawa was the first to fall, resigning in December 1988. In April of the following year, Takeshita released the findings of an internal investigation into the matter before the Lower House Budget Committee, revealing that his secretary had received (and repaid) a personal loan from Recruit amounting to fifty million yen and had accepted a 151-million-yen donation for Takeshita's political war chest. Appalled by the revelations, young LDP politicians led by Takemura Masayoshi formed the "Utopia Political Research Group," which began to advocate for political reform and whose members voluntarily made their political finances public. With his political approval nosediving into the single digits (as low as 4.4 percent in some polls), Takeshita was left with no choice but to resign the prime ministership in disgrace in early June 1989.

Resistance to Reform and Rebellion in the LDP

After the scandal, Takeshita's main rivals—Miyazawa and Abe—were both ruled out as successors since they had also profited from the unlisted Recruit Cosmos shares. In search of an "untainted" caretaker, the party settled on the seemingly innocuous Uno Sōsuke, minister of foreign affairs under Takeshita and member of the Nakasone faction. Uno was, in fact, the first non-leader of a faction to serve as prime minister since the LDP's inception, but his prime ministership would last just sixty-nine days thanks to a ludicrous personal scandal and a damaging electoral failure. The scandal, which surfaced in the weekly magazine *Sunday Mainichi* just prior to the July 1989 House of Councillors election, involved Uno's insensitive treatment of a former geisha who had supposedly been his mistress some years earlier. Under the cloud of yet another scandal and facing backlash to the consumption tax, voters punished the LDP in the upper house election. The party managed to win only 36 of the 126 seats up for election, leaving it with just 109 out of 252 seats in the upper house—18 short of a majority. Conversely, the JSP—now under the leadership of the charismatic female leader, Doi Takako—won 46 seats, taking its total in the upper house to 68 seats.

Doi proposed a new agenda for the JSP focused on gender, regional communities, and generational issues. The policy line was quite at odds with the class-based ideological platform previously enforced by the party's hardline left and closer to Eda Saburō's earlier advocacy of structural reform. For the most optimistic, Doi seemed to represent a turning point from which the JSP might remold itself into a party with broad appeal capable of winning power. This perspective was further emboldened by the relative success of women candidates in the election. In what the media condescendingly dubbed the "Madonna boom," some twenty-two women were elected—admittedly still only a small number, but a great improvement on the previous record of ten. Yet the optimism born of Doi's success was rather fleeting, and the JSP would continue its slow decline after a brief high point in government in the mid-1990s. Uno's demise, however, was far more immediate, as he was forced to resign the prime ministership in embarrassment after the election debacle and geisha fiasco.

Uno's successor, the youthful fifty-eight-year-old Kaifu Toshiki, represented the LDP's second attempt at presenting the Japanese public with a plausibly clean, reform-minded leader and, for the most part, he fit the bill. For prime ministerial hopefuls like Miyazawa and Abe, Kaifu was an acceptable and unthreatening interim leadership solution, coming as he did from a minor faction.

Thanks to Kaifu's smooth and soft-spoken persona, the LDP performed better in the 1990 general election than the carnage anticipated by many, capturing 275 seats compared to 300 before. The JSP also continued its brief renaissance, winning 136 seats versus its previous 85. Sensing growing support for reform among elements inside the LDP and the general public, Kaifu pursued policies aimed at making political contributions more transparent and reforming the lower house electoral system—seen by many to be a root cause of Tanaka-style money politics and corruption.

But Kaifu's reformist agenda met with vehement opposition from both the old guard in the LDP and opposition lawmakers, who all feared that any electoral reform would disproportionately disadvantage them. Despite approval ratings among the highest of any postwar prime minister, the LDP's new powerbroker, Kanemaru Shin, and allies deliberately set out to sabotage the upstart Kaifu and throttle his drive for reform. In October 1991, Kanemaru and allies withdrew support for the prime minister in his bid for reelection to the party presidency. Lacking the party votes needed to survive, the popular Kaifu was forced to resign, his reform agenda wholly unrealized.

In November 1991, the party installed the seventy-two-year-old Miyazawa Kiichi as prime minister. Fluent in English and with extensive experience abroad, Miyazawa was a party veteran, having entered the Diet in 1953 after a career in the MOF and thereafter serving in various high-level ministerial and party posts across numerous cabinets. Miyazawa's "LDP business-as-usual" image was reinforced when he appointed three individuals implicated in the Recruit Cosmos scandal to his cabinet. His most notable policy achievement was the passing of historic legislation approving deployment of SDF units for overseas peacekeeping missions (discussed later in this chapter), but this was overshadowed by yet another scandal that would finally split the LDP.

Like the Recruit Cosmos scandal, the so-called Sagawa Express scandal involved the receipt of illicit monetary payments, gifts, and services from the Sagawa Express company by LDP heavyweights like Kanemaru. As the scandal unfolded from late 1992, it was revealed that Sagawa Express had mobilized gangsters to threaten opponents of Takeshita. Even worse, LDP vice president Kanemaru Shin was found to have received five hundred million yen in undisclosed funds from the company prior to the 1990 general election, for which he was fined two hundred thousand yen for violations of the Law to Regulate Political Finances. The public was left flabbergasted when a police investigation of Kanemaru's residence in 1993 uncovered illegally-obtained gold bars worth one billion yen, resulting in Kanemaru's indictment on tax evasion.

With Kanemaru's arrest, a power struggle ensued in the Keiseikai faction, which Kanemaru had led after Takeshita's elevation to the prime ministership. Just as had unfolded in the division of the Tanaka faction, two sides emerged: one including Ozawa, Hata, and others in favor of political reform and the other supporting Takeshita and his preferred factional leader Obuchi Keizō. In the ensuing struggle, Obuchi prevailed, prompting Ozawa and colleagues to initially create yet another intrafactional faction—the "Reform Forum 21" or "Hata" group—and then, in November 1992, depart Takeshita's faction altogether.

Now free to pursue their own agenda, Ozawa, Hata, and colleagues began to push for fundamental reform of the electoral system and political financing. They found a receptive public audience thanks to the seemingly endless procession of LDP scandals and corruption, coupled with revelations of corporate connections to organized crime groups, brokerages engaging in *nigiri* compensation of client losses, and national bureaucrats found to have been wined and dined by the very financial institutions they were responsible for regulating. All in all, the system—now seemingly in freefall in the stock and real estate markets—appeared to be rotten to the core.

The Ozawa and Hata group continued to apply pressure to Miyazawa to move on electoral reform. He eventually acquiesced and introduced reform bills to the Diet. But when Miyazawa was unable to secure support for the bills from within the LDP, he proposed delaying their passage in the current sitting. With this, the proponents of reform had had enough. On June 16, 1993, the JSP proposed a vote of no confidence in the Miyazawa government—a motion usually doomed to failure—but on this occasion the Hata group swooped, allowing the motion to pass. With this act of "treachery" from within the LDP, Miyazawa had no choice but to call a general election, in turn sparking a period of unparalleled disruption in Japanese politics.

Regime Change and Political Reform

Alongside its traditional opponents—the JSP and JCP—the LDP faced several new rivals in the July 1993 election. In late June, Hata, Ozawa, and forty-two colleagues promptly departed the LDP after supporting the no-confidence vote, forming the Japan Renewal Party (JRP). This desertion left the LDP with less than a majority in the lower house and had party officials scrambling to identify a swath of new candidates to compete against the JRP rebels in their districts. The LDP was dealt a further blow around the same time when Takemura Masayoshi, Hatoyama Yukio, and eight others who had established the Utopia Political Research Group following the 1989 Recruit Cosmos scandal deserted the LDP to form the New Party Sakigake (NPS). Alongside these former LDP-based parties was the Japan New Party (JNP), established without fanfare in May 1992 by the former governor of Kumamoto Prefecture, Hosokawa Morihiro, with the aim of substantive political reform.

Despite hailing from a family of elite samurai leaders and being the grandson of Prince Konoe Fumimaro (chaps. 1 and 2), Hosokawa projected an image of reform-minded openness starkly different from the jaded political insiders of Tokyo. In the JNP he brought together a new generation of reformist politicians intent on ousting the LDP, including Edano Yukio, Noda Yoshihiko, Maehara Seiji, and Koike Yuriko—all of whom would feature prominently in local and national politics in the coming decades. Koike Yuriko proved particularly valuable for the JNP, leveraging her public profile as a television newscaster to promote the party.

In the ensuing election on July 18, 1993, the non-LDP parties captured a combined majority of 288 out of 511 seats. The JRP, NPS, and JNP all increased their representation, together winning 103 seats. The JSP suffered significant losses, with many of its seats being devoured by the new center-left parties like the JNP. Conversely, the LDP won 223 seats—meaning that most of its losses could arguably be accounted for by the defections rather than any massive voter swing away from the party. Nonetheless, for the first time since its establishment in 1955, the LDP did not have a majority in the House of Representatives (it was thirty-three seats short). After an agonizing month of negotiations brokered by Ozawa, an alliance of eight opposition parties stretching from right to left (but excluding the JCP) formed a fragile collation under the leadership of Hosokawa. The majority of the twenty-one cabinet posts were held by representatives from the JRP (6), JSP (6), and CGP (4), including three women and two private sector appointees. The JNP was represented by only Hosokawa in the cabinet, with Koike Yuriko—who had played such an important role in the rise of the party—only appointed parliamentary vice minister for management and coordination.

The new coalition government brought together parties from across the political spectrum and, hence, was destined to be an unwieldy entity from the outset. Essentially only two things held the coalition together: a desire to oust the LDP and a commitment to reform, although the details of the latter proved challenging to agree on. In this sense, the affable Hosokawa was extremely important as the glue holding together the ideologically divergent extremities of the coalition. Faced with the worst economic conditions since war's end and high public expectations for the emergence of a strong center-left political force, Hosokawa promised sweeping reforms in the electoral system, public administration, and taxation, along with comprehensive political decentralization. He was supported in this endeavor by deputy prime minister Hata Tsutomu, who had developed a reputation in the LDP as "Mr. Political Reform" based on his quest to eliminate the money politics dominating elections.

Although not in the Hosokawa cabinet, the JRP's Ozawa Ichirō also exerted great influence over Hosokawa's policy agenda. In his 1993 book *Nihon kaizō keikaku* (*Blueprint for a New Japan*), Ozawa laid out a starkly neoconservative and neoliberal political vision built upon decentralization, deregulation, and national and individual self-reliance. He leveled a scathing critique at the LDP for advancing protectionist policies and entrenching pork barrel politics. As Ozawa explained, many younger politicians like himself had felt trapped in the LDP machine, wherein political survival depended on securing exorbitant funding from powerful factional bosses who demanded absolute allegiance. Diplomatically, Ozawa called on Japan to become a "normal country" by removing the supposed manacles imposed by its pacifist constitution. Ozawa's political vision and his penchant for control did not sit comfortably with leftist members of the coalition like the JSP.

Such differences aside, however, the Hosokawa administration's first priority was reform of the lower house electoral system and, in principle, all members of the coalition were supportive. The midsized multimember district system in operation since 1947 was seen as a major cause of the problems in Japanese politics. Under this system, several LDP politicians often belonged to the same electoral district, meaning that, come election time, they needed to compete based on clientelism, pork barreling, and political favors instead of policy. This kind of political clientelism demanded large sums of money which, in turn, incentivized LDP politicians to join the powerful party factions (like Tanaka's) capable of providing them with resources. In this way, money arguably came to dominate politics under the 1955 System, opening the way for institutionalized corruption, weak leadership, and suboptimal policy outcomes. Advocates of electoral reform like Hata and Ozawa wanted to scrap this multimember system in favor of a single-member district (SMD) model. The latter system, they argued, offered numerous benefits. Since LDP candidates would only be pitted against opposition parties, theoretically the old clientelist system would recede, and along with it the power of LDP factions. Elections would be fought out through policy debate and not "pork." With factional influence eliminated, the power of the prime minister and the central executive of the party would be enhanced. Moreover, an SMD system would also encourage consolidation among opposition parties (since competing against one another would simply split the non-LDP vote). It was envisaged that, ultimately, a Westminster-style two-party system would emerge in which power would regularly shift between two major centrist parties. Advocates argued that electoral reform in this direction would produce nothing short of a fundamental revolution in Japanese politics, expunging the undesirable aspects of the 1955 System.

Of course, the electoral reform that eventuated inevitably reflected the complexities of Hosokawa's fragile coalition and, in this sense, was a compromise. After much political wrangling, the Diet passed a law establishing the new House of Representatives electoral system in March 1994. At the same session it amended the law regulating political finances to limit annual corporate political donations and to make public reporting of donations over fifty thousand yen compulsory. Another new law was also passed establishing a government-funded subsidy system for political parties. Of the three pieces of legislation, the electoral reform proved by far the most contentious, drawing support and resistance from within the coalition and in the LDP. After some members of the JSP in the upper house voted against the bill in late 1993, Hosokawa had to rely on reformers within the LDP like Kōno Yōhei to secure passage.

The new system initially consisted of five hundred seats of which three hundred were SMDs alongside two hundred seats based on proportional representation (PR) across eleven district blocks nationwide. The latter system emerged out of a compromise: smaller parties felt that, without the resources of the LDP, they would be uncompetitive in an entirely single-member district system. The PR system, they believed, offered at least a fighting chance of survival. This outcome was not entirely the system Hosokawa, Ozawa, and others wanted, but if politics is the art of the possible, then it must be seen as a significant accomplishment by what was a very fragile coalition government.

The Return of the LDP and Demise of the JSP

Hosokawa's celebrations were to be short lived, however, because in the following month he was forced to resign and his coalition rapidly collapsed. Ironically enough, Hosokawa's enemies managed to dig up some financial dealings he had had with none other than the Sagawa Express company in 1982. At a press conference, Hosokawa explained that he borrowed around one hundred million yen from the company to purchase an apartment in Tokyo and to repair the gate and wall of his house in Kumamoto. An investigation by the JCP's official mouthpiece *Akahata,* however, revealed that Hosokawa had purchased the apartment months before borrowing the money and that the repairs to his gate were made over a year after receiving the loan. Under this cloud of suspicion, the prime minister whose entire agenda was based on eliminating corruption and money politics could not survive. On April 4, 1994—a mere 242 days after assuming the prime ministership—a crestfallen Hosokawa announced his resignation.

With the departure of Hosokawa, cooperation among members of the anti-LDP coalition proved difficult. In late April, Hata Tsutomu of the JNP emerged as Hosokawa's successor, but his elevation to the prime ministership provoked the JSP to desert the coalition, claiming that former LDP "right-wing" elements under Ozawa's influence were attempting to usurp control.[9] Without the JSP, Hata could only form a minority government, which soon came under pressure, acutely so in June when the LDP and JSP threatened to cooperate on a vote of no confidence.

Figure 6.7. People on the street in Tokyo's Shinjuku area watch a live broadcast of Prime Minister Morihiro Hosokawa's press conference announcing his resignation in 1994. Courtesy of The Asahi Shimbun Company.

Hata initially planned to dissolve the Diet and call a general election but, following a marathon dialogue with Ozawa, he agreed to resign on June 30 after just sixty-four days in office.

Developments after the resignation of the Hata cabinet are among the more bizarre in postwar Japanese political history. In December 1994, Ozawa advanced his quest to create a second large political party capable of competing with the LDP with the establishment of the New Frontier Party (NFP). The NFP brought together eight parties, including members of the defunct Hosokawa collation (JRP, JNP, some from the CGP, DSP), Kaifu Toshiki and several other reform-minded defectors from the LDP, and excluding the JSP and NPS. At its founding, the NFP, led by Kaifu with Hata as his deputy and Ozawa as secretary general, held 176 seats in the lower house and 38 in the upper, making it second only to the LDP with 239 seats.

More extraordinarily, however, the JSP, which had just deserted the coalition over claims of right-wing machinations, now announced that it would be entering into a coalition government with the LDP and NPS—the first time the JSP had been in power for forty-seven years. Dumbfounded Japanese citizens learned that Murayama Tomiichi from the left wing of the JSP would be appointed prime minister in a cabinet stacked with sixteen LDP ministers and only six from the JSP and two from the NPS. Joining this unlikely coalition meant that the JSP had to abandon many of its core policies (for example, the unconstitutionality of the SDF), a move which undoubtedly undermined the party's already-declining legitimacy among its traditional supporters.

As we have seen, throughout the years, some like Eda Saburō and Doi Takako had attempted to move the party in a social-democratic direction to give it more mainstream appeal, but abruptly joining with the LDP now reeked of precisely the kind of political opportunism that the JSP had so stridently condemned throughout its history. To be sure, by the middle of the 1990s, JSP leaders clearly recognized the party's downward spiral, as support from the union movement dwindled and the new electoral system portended inevitable decline. Murayama and others believed that joining with the LDP might provide the party with one final opportunity to bring about change. But apart from Murayama's important statement on the fiftieth anniversary of the end of the Asia-Pacific War in 1995, the JSP achieved little in its eighteen-month marriage of convenience with the LDP. After departing the coalition in January 1996, the party officially changed its name to the Social Democratic Party (SDP), but cosmetic modification could not halt the party's inexorable decay.

After a period of great instability in Japanese politics—all against the backdrop of mounting economic troubles and social upheaval—Prime Minister Murayama abruptly resigned in January 1996, opening the way for the LDP to regain the prime ministership. Murayama had come under intensive political and media scrutiny due to the government's poor response to the earthquake in Kobe City in January 1995 and the Tokyo sarin gas subway attacks a month later (see later in this chapter). He was succeeded by Hashimoto Ryūtarō, a member of Takeshita's Keiseikai (now renamed the Heisei Seiji Kenkyūkai). As noted earlier, Hashimoto came to the position promising administrative reform and economic revitalization. To preserve a lower house majority, he had no choice but to maintain the coalition with the SDP (formerly the JSP) and NPS.

Hashimoto led the coalition to the first general election held under the new electoral system in October 1996. Ozawa's NFP managed to claim 156 seats, a somewhat disappointing result given that the party went into the election with 160 seats and high hopes of success as the second major party under the new system. In fact, dissatisfaction with Ozawa's leadership thereafter prompted some members to desert the NFP in mid-1995. In 1997, it collapsed altogether, splitting into a plethora of small parties.

The DPJ—essentially the second experiment after the NFP in creating a credible rival of the LDP—was established in the month before the election by Hatoyama Yukio, Kan Naoto, and Diet members from the JNP, CGP, SDP, and NPS. The DPJ maintained its fifty-two seats from prior to the election, making it relatively small but serving as the foundation for the party's subsequent expansion (both Hatoyama and Kan would later serve as prime minister).

The LDP under Hashimoto managed to increase its seats from 223 to 239 in the 1996 election—short of the necessary 251 for a majority, but an improvement. When the SDP and NPS declined cabinet posts, offering only to cooperate from outside the government, Hashimoto was forced to form a minority government, but his fortunes changed in September 1997 when members from Ozawa's NFP returned to the LDP, restoring its lower house majority. By around 1998, the wheels of politics had turned full circle, beginning with the LDP's loss of power in 1993 and ending with its return as the sole party of government in 1997.

Against the backdrop of bankruptcies in the banking and financial services sectors, Hashimoto pushed forward with an agenda of administrative reform. One of the most important legacies of his administration was to institute a comprehensive reorganization and consolidation of the national bureaucracies, partly as a cost-cutting measure but also in response to bureaucratic scandals and policy failures following the bubble and the Asian Financial Crisis of 1997. Under the Basic Law on Reforming Central Ministries, passed in June 1998, the existing twenty-two ministries were consolidated into twelve (effective 2001). The Prime Minister's Office was transformed into the Cabinet Office (CAO) and, together with the Cabinet Secretariat (CS), became responsible for policy planning and coordination and administrative matters. In a (largely futile) attempt to control government spending, the Hashimoto government also passed the Fiscal Structure Reform Act in late 1997 aimed at reducing national and local government deficits below 3 percent of GDP by 2003, reducing deficit bond issuances to zero, and reducing public works and social security spending. Just over a year later, however, Hashimoto's successor froze the act to allow more government spending for economic recovery.

As with other prime ministers of the 1990s, Hashimoto's term was short lived. In the upper house election of July 1998, the LDP managed to win only 44 out of the 126 seats up for election, with gains going to the DPJ and a resurgent JCP. After two-and-a-half years in office, Hashimoto was forced to resign as punishment for the poor performance, replaced by Obuchi Keizō, yet another progeny of Takeshita. Japanese politics would not settle until the arrival of Koizumi Jun'ichirō in 2001.

Japan in the Post–Cold War World

Alliance Pressures

With its rise as a global economic superpower in the 1980s, forces both inside and outside of Japan began to push for a more active role for the country in international affairs. The first significant test for Japan came after President Saddam Hussein ordered Iraqi forces to invade Kuwait on August 2, 1990, on the pretext that Kuwait had been increasing oil production in violation of OPEC agreements, causing great damage to the Iraqi economy. Soon after, the UN Security Council flatly rejected the grounds for Iraq's invasion and demanded an immediate withdrawal. Together with its allies, the United States organized a multinational response force under the aegis of the UN. The force was deployed to Saudi Arabia and the Persian Gulf in August 1990, where it instituted a maritime embargo on Iraq.

Soon after the Iraqi invasion, President George H. W. Bush contacted then-Prime Minister Kaifu to request that Japan send an SDF minesweeper to the Gulf as part of the multinational force. Although some in the LDP like Ozawa Ichirō argued that Japan could dispatch SDF forces under Japan's current legal-constitutional framework, Kaifu adopted a cautious approach based on the accepted principle that the SDF could only provide national self-defense. Kaifu first attempted to build a domestic consensus for the deployment by passing a new International Peace Cooperation Law through the Diet in October, but it met with stiff opposition. The JSP and JCP pushed Kaifu to clarify whether the law meant his government was revising the accepted cabinet interpretation that the overseas deployment of SDF forces was prohibited. They also sought a clear explanation of conditions required to warrant overseas deployment and the extent of SDF involvement. Kaifu and other officials explained that official definitions remained unchanged, but their clarifications were inconsistent and conflicting. In the face of growing public skepticism, Kaifu was forced to abandon the bill in late November 1990.

With the commencement of the Gulf War—so-called Operation Desert Storm—in January 1991, the Kaifu government reverted to alternative methods of support, such as the transportation of food, water, and medical supplies, and the deployment of medical teams. Most significantly, Japan contributed a total of US$13 billion to the multinational response: an initial three tranches totaling US$4 billion after the invasion in 1990 and a further US$9 billion following the commencement of Operation Desert Storm. In April 1991, when hostilities had ended, Kaifu gained Diet approval to dispatch SDF minesweepers to assist in the Gulf—the first official overseas deployment of the SDF under the postwar constitution (although this had occurred secretly during the Korean War). Despite Japan's hefty monetary contribution, few in America or other countries of the multinational coalition appreciated its size and, on the contrary, Japan was criticized in the foreign media for its "checkbook diplomacy" and its supplying of "money" over the "blood" of its soldiers. Even the official expression of thanks by the American government to its allies in US newspapers after the war failed to mention Japan.[10]

For some observers, one outcome of this rather chilly treatment of Japan was the country's own version of "Gulf War Syndrome." This came in the form of a right-wing backlash against the country's "unilateral pacifism" and was accompanied by a push for constitutional revision, more robust legislation for military emergencies, and the authorization of collective self-defense.[11] In 1992, the LDP government succeeded in passing the peacekeeping operations legislation through the Diet, allowing SDF forces to participate in UN Peacekeeping operations in noncombat situations where the warring parties had agreed to a ceasefire. The first deployment under the law came soon after, with the dispatch of ground, maritime, and air SDF units to Cambodia, where they oversaw a ceasefire and supported the reconstruction of villages, roads, and bridges. The SDF subsequently participated in UN Peacekeeping operations in areas such as Mozambique (1993–1995), the Democratic Republic of the Congo (1994), the Golan Heights (1996–2013), and, into the new millennium, in East Timor, Nepal, Sudan, and Haiti. SDF units also provided protection for refugees in Rwanda (1999), Afghanistan (2001), and Iraq (2003), as well as post-disaster support following the Honduras hurricane (1998), the northwestern Turkey earthquake (1999), the Gujarat earthquake in India (2001), the Bam

Figure 6.8. Japanese SDF members scanning for land mines in Takéo Province, Cambodia, in October 1992 before the arrival of the full UN Peacekeeping operations force. Courtesy of The Asahi Shimbun Company.

earthquake in Pakistan (2003), and in Thailand and Indonesia following the Indian Ocean earthquake and tsunami (2004–2005)—to list but a few of its many overseas deployments. As discussed in the following chapter, laws were either passed or amended to allow the deployment of SDF forces to provide rear support in the Afghanistan War (2001) and Iraq War (2003).

These developments harmonized with the Americans' desire to have Japan play a more proactive role in the security alliance. In 1997, the two allies agreed to an update of the US-Japan Defense Guidelines of 1978, which outlined the nature of military cooperation in the event of an attack on Japan but offered no guidance on collective action in situations or regions surrounding Japan. The new guidelines "expanded defense cooperation" to include "crisis situations in 'areas surrounding Japan'" for the first time, potentially giving the SDF a role in contending with regional conflicts, although only through logistical support in noncombat areas.[12] The guidelines also authorized SDF cooperation with US forces in peacekeeping operations, humanitarian and disaster relief scenarios, and inspecting ships to enforce UN-mandated economic sanctions.[13] These agreements were subsequently codified in the Surrounding Areas Emergency Law of 1999 and, together with the International Peace Cooperation Law, represented a significant alteration to Japan's relatively low defense and security posture under the postwar Yoshida Doctrine. Subsequent LDP administrations would continue to chip away at this doctrine, gradually expanding the scope of SDF activities while staying within the limits imposed by Japan's peace constitution.

The US-Japan alliance was made even more complicated by the incessant crimes of military personnel at bases across Japan, particularly in Okinawa Prefecture. Okinawa hosts over 70 percent of the US military bases in Japan, despite representing only 0.6 percent of Japan's total land area. Throughout the 1970s, 1980s, and 1990s, Okinawa housed close to thirty thousand troops. Okinawans endured ceaseless American military offenses, such as traffic violations, robberies, and sex crimes. Tensions escalated to extreme levels in early September 1995, when three servicemen from Camp Hansen near Kin Bay abducted a twelve-year-old schoolgirl on her way home from shopping and brutally raped her at a nearby beach. The Okinawa police subsequently issued arrest warrants for the three, but under the Japan-US Status of Forces Agreement, the US military was not required to hand over personnel who had not been charged with crimes. In response, Governor Ōta Masahide and the Okinawa Prefectural Assembly called for an immediate revision of this agreement and passed a motion of remonstration. In late October, some eighty-five thousand incensed locals attended the Okinawa Residents Collective Protest Rally at which they demanded a fundamental recalibration of Okinawa's position and status in postwar and post–Cold War Japan.

Figure 6.9. In October 1995, over 85,000 Okinawans gather in Ginowan City to protest the brutal rape of a local schoolgirl by US miliary servicemen. Courtesy of The Asahi Shimbun Company.

Facing strong domestic pressure, Prime Minister Hashimoto began negotiations with US president Clinton in 1996 for the return of Futenma base, located in the densely populated city of Ginowan (and for this reason one of the most dangerously sited among Okinawa's military bases). With the shadow of the rape threatening to undermine Japanese public acceptance of military bases, in a symbolic gesture, the Americans agreed to return the Futenma base and ten other military facilities, but only on condition of an alternative site being provided within the prefecture for the construction of a thirteen-hundred-meter heliport facility. As locals realized, this quid pro quo for eliminating Futenma ironically threatened to increase rather than decrease the US military presence and its associated dangers. On learning of the agreement, communities across Okinawa mobilized to oppose construction of this new facility in their backyards. Eventually the pristine Henoko Bay was chosen as the site for an offshore base, but opposition erupted over the inevitable destruction of the coral reef and its ecosystem, including endangered dugongs. Despite protests, lawsuits, and political action, construction on the project eventually began, but it has been repeatedly delayed due to persistent controversy and remains uncompleted at the time of writing.

Japan and Asia in the 1990s

Japan's relations with its regional neighbors continued to deeply shape economics, politics, national identity, and historical consciousness throughout the 1990s. As discussed in chapter 5, economically, the years following the 1985 Plaza Accord and the resulting appreciation of the yen witnessed an explosion of Japanese FDI into the region. This trend began to slow with the economic downturn in Japan of the early 1990s, except toward China, where Japanese FDI remained strong until around 1995. Seeing this growing interdependence between Japan and its regional neighbors, politicians, officials, and media pundits began to advocate for a new Asian regionalism in which Japan could—together with the rising Asian "tigers" of South Korea, Hong Kong, Taiwan, and Singapore—construct a vibrant East Asian community. Throughout the decade, publications on Asia proliferated in Japan as too did interest in the ethnic cultures and cuisines of the region. In 1994, the historian Hiraishi Naoaki wrote of the "Asia boom in Japanese publishing," pointing to the flurry of new works on Asian history, culture, and society.[14] Prominent business leaders, like Fuji-Xerox chairman Kobayashi Yōtarō, called for the "re-Asianization" of Japan, while the former diplomat Ogura Kazuo advocated a "new Asianism" to challenge the hegemony of the West.[15] In a more strident tone, the right-wing author and politician Ishihara Shintarō in his 1994 book *No to ieru Ajia: Tai Ōbei e no hōsaku* (*The Voice of Asia: Two Leaders Discuss the Coming Century*) coauthored with the Malaysian prime minister, Mahathir Mohamad, called on the Japanese to recognize anew Japan's Asian origins.[16] The time had come for Japan and its Asian neighbors to resolutely push back against Western domination, according to Ishihara. Others, like the *Asahi shinbun* journalist Funabashi Yōichi, proposed a more inclusive "Asia-Pacific fusion," with Japan acting as a bridge between East and West.[17]

This regionalist discourse was put to the test during the 1997 Asian Financial Crisis (AFC), when the currencies of Thailand, South Korea, Hong Kong, and elsewhere collapsed one after the other. Despite its financial-sector crisis at home, the Japanese government quickly proposed the creation of an "Asian Monetary Fund" to help regional economies survive the AFC, but this initiative was promptly stymied by the United States, which feared the creation of a "yen bloc" in East Asia. Nonetheless, Japan's response evidenced its commitment to the region, which would only further deepen thereafter.

As economic ties increased, so too did the number of Japanese traveling elsewhere in Asia for work and leisure during the late 1980s and into the 1990s. Moreover, the number of foreign workers from other Asian countries arriving in Japan also increased noticeably, such that some would even begin describing the country as a de facto "immigrant nation" (see chap. 7).

But while trade, investment, and travel between Japan and countries in the region flourished, the country's relations with its neighbors continued to be troubled by unresolved historical issues that intermittently bubbled to the surface throughout the 1990s. In 1991, for example, a South Korean woman, Kim Hak-sun, revealed publicly that she had been the victim of Japanese military sexual violence and coercion as a so-called comfort woman. Thereafter she commenced proceedings for compensation in the Tokyo District Court. Kim's revelation came after a provocative 1990 Japanese television documentary in which a former soldier of the Imperial Japanese Army confessed to having forcibly recruited women. Such claims gained further credibility in 1992, when the historian Yoshimi Yoshiaki uncovered documents in the Japanese Defense Agency evidencing the involvement of the Japanese military in the administration of military brothels.

Civic groups in Japan, South Korea, and elsewhere subsequently mobilized in movements to pursue Japanese government responsibility and seek compensation and apologies for the victims. In 2000, the Violence Against Women in War-Network Japan, together with sixty-four victims and one thousand participants from thirty countries, organized the Women's International War Crimes Tribunal for the Trial of Japan's Military Sexual Slavery. Although lacking enforceability, the tribunal held in Tokyo found Emperor Hirohito and nine other Japanese leaders criminally liable for rape and sexual slavery in the 1930s and 1940s as crimes against humanity and called on the Japanese government to accept responsibility, apologize, and pay compensation to the victims.[18]

Alongside the "comfort women" issue, during the 1990s and beyond, the Japanese government and corporations faced legal action from individuals subjected to forced labor during the Asia-Pacific War. Activist academics such as Ōnuma Yasuaki, Ustumi Aiko, and Tanaka Hiroshi initiated "postwar responsibility" initiatives to bring public attention to Japan's former victims of sexual violence, forced labor, and forced conscription, as well as Koreans deserted by Japanese forces as they retreated from Sakhalin Island at war's end. Indeed, by the fiftieth anniversary of the end of the Asia-Pacific War in 1995, an intense and often vehement debate swirled around the unresolved history of Japanese colonial empire and militarism.

The comfort women issue proved particularly volatile in Japanese-South Korean bilateral relations. Facing international and domestic pressure after Kim Hak-sun's court action in 1991 and Yoshimi's revelations in January 1992, Prime Minister Miyazawa admitted in the Diet that Japanese military involvement in the system could not be ruled out. During a visit to South Korea in the same month, Miyazawa offered a formal apology to the president and promised to undertake investigations. Following the release of a special government report, Chief Cabinet Secretary Kōno Yōhei released a statement in 1993—the so-called Kōno Statement—admitting to

Japanese military involvement in wartime prostitution to which he expressed his "sincerest apologies" and "remorse."[19] In 1995, the government, together with Ōnuma Yasuaki and other intellectuals and activists, supported the creation of the Asian Women's Fund to provide compensation to the former comfort women. But the initiative was undermined by controversy over its nongovernmental status, which critics argued evaded the issue of Japanese state responsibility. Payments from the fund were accompanied by an official apology letter from Prime Minister Murayama. In 2015, Prime Minister Abe Shinzō and Korean president Park Geun-hye again attempted to resolve the issue by setting up another compensation fund, but this agreement similarly collapsed in 2019 under President Moon Jae-in.

The emergence of these historical issues, the approaching fiftieth anniversary of the end of the Asia-Pacific War, and the brief calamity within the LDP in the early 1990s offered progressive-minded leaders, like Hosokawa Morihiro and Murayama Tomiichi, a window of opportunity to express unequivocal apologies to Japan's war victims. At his first press conference on assuming the prime ministership, Hosokawa referred to the war as a "war of aggression" and a "mistaken war"—the first Japanese prime minister to use such categorical language. He followed this up with an apology to Asian countries in his first major policy speech in the Diet in August 1993, along with an apology to South Korean president Kim Young-sam later that year. Hosokawa's actions met with fierce domestic resistance from groups such as the Japan War-Bereaved Families Association and right-wing LDP politicians, who branded the apologies as "masochistic" and "poisoned by the Tokyo Tribunal view of history."[20] In response, Hosokawa slightly modified his language, shifting from Japan's "war of aggression" to "acts of aggression." It should also be noted that some LDP prime ministers had earlier expressed forms of remorse, such as Kaifu Toshiki who apologized for Japanese transgressions during the colonial years while visiting Seoul in 1991 and Prime Minister Takeshita who apologized to North Korea for wartime acts in 1989.

The most significant—and also toned down—of war apologies appeared at the time of the fiftieth anniversary of war's end in 1995. The JSP prime minister Murayama wanted to make an unconditional statement of apology to Asian countries on this important anniversary, but the coalition he had entered with the LDP and NPS—coupled with resistance from conservatives in the opposition like Ozawa Ichirō—thwarted his aims. Opponents objected to any Diet resolution directly describing Japan as having engaged in "aggressive acts," "invasion," and "colonial rule." Others even pushed for the exclusion of the term "apology" from the resolution. After much contention and debate, the final statement—the Diet Resolution on the 50th Anniversary of War—fell on the side of ambiguity. Japanese colonial rule and acts of aggression were contextualized within the "many instances" of similar acts by other countries worldwide throughout history, and the Diet offered "sincere condolences" to "victims of war . . . all over the world," rather than specifically to the victims of Japan's war. In other words, according to this statement, Japan's earlier actions were like those of many other countries, so it was no exception. In a veiled appeal to Asian countries to stop regurgitating the past, the resolution called on countries to "transcend differences over historical views," and it vowed to "learn humbly" from history to "build a peaceful international society."[21]

Japan's Asian neighbors were understandably dissatisfied with the statement. The South Korean media reported how terms such as "apology" and "war renunciation" were removed from the final draft of the resolution. Chinese media retorted that their people did not want "insincere apologies," and the Singapore press lamented that Japan had missed its final opportunity for apology.[22] Murayama and his JSP colleagues were similarly disappointed with the Diet Resolution so, on August 15, 1995, the anniversary of Japan's surrender, Murayama released his personal corrective in the so-called Murayama Statement. Delivering the statement in a televised broadcast, Murayama said that the war was a mistake and that it proceeded on the basis of aggression and colonial rule. He offered his sincerest "remorse" and "apology," particularly to the peoples of Asia and Allied POWs for the suffering inflicted on them by the Japanese military. Thereafter, Murayama's statement would become the gold standard for all official utterances on the war by Japanese prime ministers.

Commentaries by Murayama, Hosokawa, and others on the war almost inevitably provoked a right-wing backlash and historical revisionism within Japan. In 1995, the University of Tokyo scholar of education, Fujioka Nobukatsu, together with conservative commentators, political scientists, writers, and manga artists, established the Liberal View of History Study Group to combat what they considered "masochistic" and "arbitrary" presentations of history by leftist historians and politicians like Murayama. Instead, they called for "correct" interpretations of history to impart a sense of patriotism and national pride in young Japanese. Building on this right-wing revisionism, the scholar of German literature Nishio Kanji and others established the Japanese Society for History Textbook Reform in 1997, which subsequently published a middle-school history text focused on instilling pupils with national pride. Although the textbook passed official government screening, it was only adopted by a few schools. Nonetheless, the rising revisionist tide resulted in references to issues such as the comfort women gradually disappearing from, or being toned down in, many mainstream textbooks in the coming years.[23]

Vindictive anti-Asian sentiment and historical denialism also found a home in online communities of hate, with groups sporadically mobilizing to oppose historical exhibitions, documentary films, or art shows dealing with controversial historical issues. In reality, such groups hardly represented the mainstream in Japan, but their strident voices reverberated across the seas, undermining Japan's relations with its neighbors. Of course, progressive-minded individuals did not stand by idly. For example, historians from Japan, China, and South Korea came together in collaborative research projects to produce history textbooks that tried to reflect the perspectives of all countries.[24] Such initiatives were not without their controversies and hurdles, but they revealed the potential of transnational collaborations and solidarities to combat chauvinism.

Society and Culture in Flux

The Great Hanshin-Awaji Earthquake

A number of shocking events added to the sense of unraveling in 1990s Japan, with two incidents in 1995 bringing the nation to a standstill. At 5:46 on the morning of January 17, 1995, residents in Kobe City and nearby Awaji Island were jolted by the largest earthquake ever recorded in the region. The 7.3 magnitude Great Hanshin-Awaji Earthquake was, in fact, the largest quake to strike Japan since the destructive Great Kantō Earthquake that flattened the Tokyo region in 1923. In total, the disaster claimed 6,434 lives; injured 43,792; and forced over 300,000 to evacuate their dwellings. The shortage of emergency shelters meant that many people were left homeless in the immediate aftermath of the quake. News helicopters broadcast confronting scenes of a fire-ravaged Kobe City, dotted with damaged buildings and infrastructure. Segments of the elevated Sanyō Shinkansen rail bridge had collapsed, as too had numerous subway tunnels and sections of the city hall and Kobe West Citizens' Hospital. The Hanshin raised expressway—supposedly "earthquake-proof"—spectacularly buckled in numerous places and, along with the devastated buildings and strewn rubble, made areas of Kobe look like a war zone. The concentration of old wooden structures in downtown Kobe and the occurrence of the earthquake at breakfast time caused massive fires that razed the area and claimed many lives. Lifelines to the city, like railways, roads, electricity, tap water, and telephones, were interrupted or cut off completely. Two artificial islands—Port Island and Rokko Island—both built on reclaimed land in the bay off Kobe, suffered from extensive liquefication and land subsidence, resulting in critical damage to buildings. Around 241,000 residential dwellings around Kobe were damaged in the quake, of which some 174,000 were totally destroyed or burned to the ground. Experts estimated the cost of the damage at around ten trillion yen.

Exacerbating the disaster, the coalition government under Prime Minister Murayama was shamefully slow to react, exposing its woeful crisis management

Figure 6.10. A bus hangs perilously on a collapsed portion of the Hanshin Expressway in Nishinomiya, Kobe, following the Great Hanshin-Awaji Earthquake (January 17, 1995). Courtesy of The Asahi Shimbun Company.

Figure 6.11. Nagata Ward in downtown Kobe still in flames nine hours after the Great Hanshin-Awaji Earthquake (January 17, 1995). Courtesy of The Asahi Shimbun Company.

skills to fierce media and public criticism. Only later would it emerge that Murayama and his cabinet had relied almost entirely on the media for information about the unfolding disaster in Kobe. Bureaucratic red tape meant that SDF forces and emergency services from outside of the prefecture could not be quickly deployed. Offers of assistance from abroad were similarly delayed due to incomprehensible procedures such as foreign search and rescue dogs needing to undergo quarantine before entering the country.

This poor response to the Kobe quake greatly undermined support for Murayama, whose administration would end in January 1996. One of the positive outcomes, however, was the establishment of the Cabinet Crisis Management Center at the prime minister's official residence in Tokyo in 1996 and the appointment of a deputy chief cabinet secretary for crisis management from 1998 onward.

Another positive legacy stemming from the tragedy in Kobe was the flowering of volunteering and civil society in Japan. While officials floundered in their response, hundreds and thousands of youth flooded into the Kobe area—many on foot—to provide assistance. In the month after the quake around twenty thousand volunteers were active daily, assisting at emergency shelters, distributing supplies, preparing and serving meals, and searching through the rubble. Around 50 percent of the volunteers were in their twenties and close to 70 percent had no prior volunteering experience. Over 60 percent traveled from outside of Hyōgo Prefecture. So impressive was the volunteer response of around 1.37 million people, that 1995 became known as "Year One of the Volunteer Era" and January 17 was eventually designated as National Disaster Volunteering Day. Volunteers would continue to figure prominently in subsequent disasters, with ninety-five thousand helping after the Niigata Chūetsu Earthquake of 2004 and 1.45 million assisting following the Great East Japan Earthquake in 2011 (chap. 7).

The volunteer response also convinced political leaders across the political spectrum of the urgent need to reform the regulatory infrastructure supporting nonprofit activities in Japan. Until this time, gaining incorporated legal status as a nonprofit organization was subject to strict bureaucratic oversight, meaning that many groups remained informal and, hence, were unable to engage in simple procedures like renting premises, opening bank accounts, and signing contracts. Recognizing the potential social worth of these groups, civic activists and politicians began a movement for regulatory reform after Kobe.

In fact, civil society advocates had been pushing for reform of the sector since the 1980s. As discussed in chapter 5, networking among civic groups during the 1980s brought together a core of activists committed to strengthening and professionalizing the sector along the lines of the United States and Western Europe. The Kobe earthquake crystalized these energies into a powerful movement that resulted in the passing of the historic Law for the Promotion of Specified Nonprofit Activities, or simply, the NPO (nonprofit organization) Law in 1998. With this new law, NPOs could now easily incorporate and enjoy all the benefits of legal status. As of 2024, there were over fifty thousand NPOs involved in areas including disaster relief, health services, welfare provision, environmental protection and conservation, local community building, lifelong education, and international cooperation. Among these, 50 percent had annual earnings over ten million yen, still comparatively small but an impressive growth in the almost twenty-five years since the law's passing.

From a broader historical perspective, it is also clear that the move to promote NPO activities among lawmakers was about more than the Kobe earthquake. Since the days of Nakasone Yasuhiro, Japanese leaders had been concerned about ballooning government expenditures, especially for welfare and health services in a rapidly aging society. In this context, NPOs fit the emerging neoliberal vision of smaller government built around the retrenchment of public services to the private sector. Nonetheless, the Kobe quake was a crucial stimulus for the growth of civil society in 1990s Japan.

Terror on Tokyo's Subways

A little over two months after the Kobe disaster, the Japanese were jolted by another shocking incident. On March 20, members of the Aum Shinrikyō cult boarded the Marunouchi, Hibiya, and Chiyoda subway lines in central Tokyo at around 8:00 a.m., after which they proceeded to release sarin, a highly toxic nerve agent used in chemical warfare. In the ensuing carnage, thirteen subway employees and commuters lost their lives and over six thousand people were injured, some completely paralyzed and bedridden for life. Two days after the attacks, police raided around twenty-five sites belonging to the Aum cult in Kamikuishiki Village, Yamanashi Prefecture, east of Tokyo, where they uncovered chemicals used in the production of sarin. On May 16, the NPA deployed a massive contingent of police to find and arrest the cult's leader, Asahara Shōko (real name Matsumoto Chizuo), who was discovered hiding in the roof of one of the cult's facilities.

Asahara, a legally blind yoga instructor, founded the sect under the name Aum Shinsen Association (Ōmu Shinsen no Kai) in 1984. Early on, the group only numbered in the tens and focused on Asahara's yoga instruction. But it began to grow rapidly after a female member reported to various magazines that Asahara had superhuman powers, including the ability to levitate. Following a 1986 tour of India and Tibet to study Buddhism, Asahara founded Aum Shinrikyō in 1987. The cult drew on a curious concoction of ideas drawn from Buddhism, Christianity, New Age belief, and science fiction, all tied together by pseudoscientific rituals and a

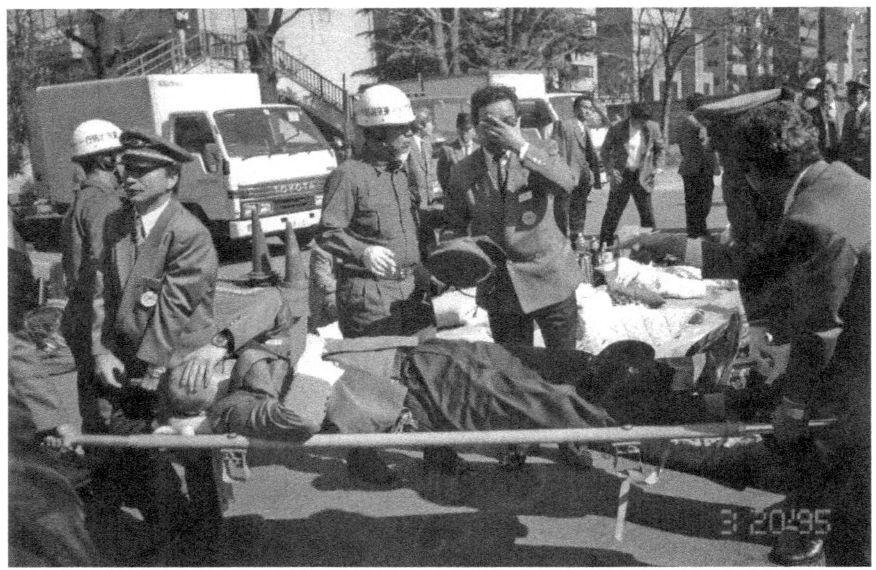

Figure 6.12. Subway employees injured in the sarin gas attack are assisted by emergency responders in Tsukiji, Tokyo, on March 20, 1995. Courtesy of The Asahi Shimbun Company.

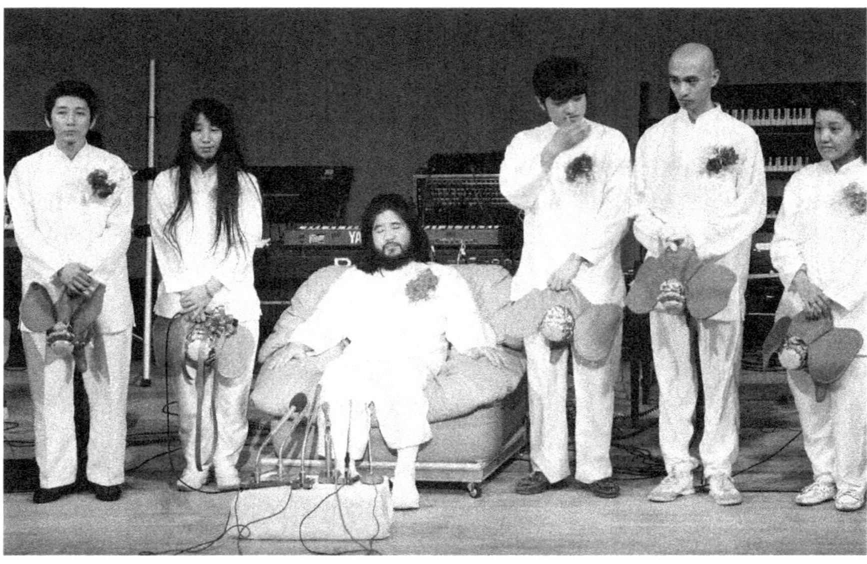

Figure 6.13. Asahara Shōko (a.k.a. Matsumoto Chizuo, seated center), leader of the Aum Shinrikyō cult, surrounded by followers during his abortive run for the House of Representatives in 1990. Courtesy of The Asahi Shimbun Company.

millennialist belief in the coming Armageddon. In 1989, the cult was certified as a religious legal entity by the Tokyo government (later withdrawn in 1995)—ironically, the same year that it began to spiral into murderous violence. In November 1989, on orders from Asahara, six of the cult's young adherents broke into the home of thirty-three-year-old lawyer Sakamoto Tsutsumi, where they strangled him, his wife, and their one-year-old daughter, thereafter injecting them with potassium chloride and burying their bodies in the mountains of Niigata Prefecture. Asahara had become infuriated with Sakamoto for spearheading a movement to expose the nefarious operations of the cult. Only after their arrest in 1995 did members admit to the murders and disclose the whereabouts of the bodies.

In 1990, Aum made an abortive effort to gain political representation, running twenty-five candidates in the general election. The bizarre campaign involved dancing, singing, and rallies led by cult members dressed in all-white unforms and wearing large mask effigies of Asahara. None of the Aum candidates were elected, and it is believed that this failure provoked Asahara and cult leaders to turn to terror. In the meantime, Aum's annual income continued to grow, reaching an estimated one billion yen by 1994 thanks to new members. Using these funds to "arm" itself, members released sarin in Matsumoto City, Nagano Prefecture in June 1994, killing eight people in what is believed to have been a dress rehearsal for the subway attacks of the following year.

One of the worrying aspects of the Aum incident for many Japanese was Asahara's success at attracting highly educated youth into the cult. It seems that many young people were drawn to Aum out of a desire to break away from the excesses of contemporary Japan, which they felt was approaching its final days. In a sense, Aum Shinrikyō became an extreme manifestation of Japan's bubble economy years, when people exchanged reality for the pursuit of the "fictitious."[25] Similarly, within Aum, members pursued a bizarre program for advancement. Only through the completion of predetermined offerings (including cash) and ascetic rituals could members increase their power and rank in the cult. On reaching so-called enlightenment or liberation, members were rewarded by becoming "warriors" in the "plan for salvation." According to some, this process of collecting various treasures and completing tasks to advance within the cult mimicked the escapism of adventure video games.[26] It offered youth an illusory ecosystem inside which they could vent their anxieties. To be sure, the superficial materialism and ultimate fragility of the economic bubble, the ceaseless corruption of political and business leaders, and the pressures of a society in which youth were forced into rigid career paths and predetermined lifeways left many with a sense of futility and spiritual emptiness. It is also a fact that only a handful of youth who felt this way chose to join Asahara's murderous cult.

As with the Kobe quake of the previous month, the government was criticized for its serious failings in defending public security. It was revealed that the police had, in fact, been monitoring the cult before the incident, yet they had failed to foil its lethal deeds by taking proactive action. Such criticisms may have been somewhat unwarranted given the challenges authorities faced in balancing civil liberties and public safety. But the incident made many Japanese feel even more anxious about the future of their society in the new Heisei era.

As the economy and politics seemed to be unraveling, so too did social order and public morals. The Heisei era had actually begun somewhat ominously with the arrest of the twenty-seven-year-old serial killer Miyazaki Tsutomu, a partially disabled recluse who strangled and decapitated four young girls aged four to seven years, recording his grizzly acts on videotape. After burying the victims' torsos in a remote forest, Miyazaki cooked and consumed their craniums. Two years after the Aum subway attacks, a fourteen-year old boy was arrested after murdering an eleven-year old acquaintance and placing the victim's severed head at the entrance to his school with a note signed "Sakakibara Seito." These horrific crimes, combined with revelations of schoolgirls engaging in prostitution for pocket money, cast a dark shadow over Japan's future in the unsettled decade of the 1990s.

Culture After the Bubble

Subtle changes in popular fashion preferences in the 1990s were also indicative of a shift from the bubble to post-bubble mentality in Japan. Fashion in the 1980s had been dominated by the upmarket "DC" brands—short for Designers and Characters—produced by foreign designers like Armani and homegrown talent such as Issey Miyake and Yohji Yamamoto. Government surveys reveal the peak of annual household spending on clothing to be 302,000 yen in 1991, when apparel sales at exclusive department stores reached 6.1 trillion yen and overall sales exceeded 15 trillion yen—around 50 percent more than in 2019.[27] But as purse strings began to tighten in the 1990s, the DC brands quickly gave way to so-called fast fashion, symbolized by international brands like Gap and H&M, offering mass-produced, low-priced clothing. Domestic competitors also emerged like the ubiquitous UNIQLO, although it claimed to be different from the fast fashion brands due to its maintenance of regular product lines. The shift to cheap, fast fashion had negative environmental costs owing to the massive increase in wastage, as product lines were continuously removed from shelves and disposed of to make way for new arrivals. In 1990, the amount of clothing being supplied in Japan (around 1.196 billion items) was close to the amount being consumed (around 1.154 billion items). By 2017, however, supply (2.798 billion items) was about double that being consumed (1.343 billion items). Consumers were certainly paying less, but this came at the expense of massive wastage, environmental destruction, and violations of the rights of textile workers in developing countries.

Food culture also entered an era of so-called price destruction (*kakaku hakai*). The earlier craze for expensive French cuisine gave way to what might be called a culture of food convenience. During the Heisei era, consumption of bread overtook that of rice. As more women entered the labor market—by choice, economic necessity, or both—the market for ready-made meals exploded. In turn, as retailers competed to offer the lowest prices in recessionary Japan, food handling and labelling scandals proliferated. Into the early years of the 2000s, the media frequently reported on wholesalers and retailers who had falsely labelled the sources or use-by dates of products.

Despite the bursting of the bubble, the 1990s witnessed the continuing growth of the leisure industries—perhaps an indication of popular desires to escape gloomy realities. The gradual shift to a five-day school week in elementary and middle schools (previously five-and-a-half days) and official promotion of "relaxed learning" (*yutori kyōiku*) meant that youth and children had more free time. Accordingly, leisure activities like karaoke, which had primarily been a pastime for patrons at drinking establishments, now became wildly popular among youth. Buildings with

Figure 6.14. "Price destruction" at outdoor ramen stalls in Fukuoka in 2001. The sign reads "300-yen ramen every Tuesday." Courtesy of The Asahi Shimbun Company.

rows of karaoke boxes spread dramatically during the 1990s, growing from around 50,000 in 1990 to 160,000 by 1996, thereafter levelling off at around 130,000 in the early years of the 2000s.[28] In 1995, Taitō and Kyocera Multimedia Corporations released the first household karaoke transmission service via its "X-55 media box," which was connected to a television and a phone line, allowing for the downloading of karaoke songs, information, and games.[29]

Such phone line services would be quickly supplanted in the 1990s by a more thoroughly transformative phenomenon: the internet. Several companies such as ASCIInet, Nikkei Mix, PC-VAN, and NIFTY Serve had been providing rudimentary data transmission and networking services since 1985, following the passing of the Telecommunications Business Law. The decisive turning point came in 1995 with the release of Microsoft Corporation's Windows 95 personal computer operating system. With this, use of the internet in Japan expanded from a narrow group of academics and computer enthusiasts to the wider population—so much so that 1995 was also christened "Year One of the Internet Era." In 1995, internet diffusion was only around 2 percent of the population, but this had increased fifteen-fold to 30 percent by 2000. In 2003, close to half the population were connected at 48 percent, and this figure had risen to 90 percent by 2020—more or less equivalent to the United States.[30] In the late 1990s, then, Japan began the transition from

Figure 6.15. Revelers at a karaoke box in Tokyo's Shibuya Ward in July 1992. Courtesy of The Asahi Shimbun Company.

a "television society" to a "net society"—although, as we have seen, many of the country's electronics makers were slow to recognize and respond to this shift.[31]

Interestingly, Japan also temporarily led the world in the provision of mobile internet services with the launch of i-MODE by NTT in 1999. Subscribers to i-MODE were the first in the world able to access a limited array of internet services through their clamshell mobile devices. This technology, however, would subsequently be outmoded by smartphones. The Kobe quake also played a role in shaping public perceptions about the potential of the internet as a useful new communication tool. After the earthquake, computer enthusiasts volunteered their services to set up numerous networks to connect volunteers and to help coordinate the disaster response at the grassroots. Internet service providers like NIFTY Serve established an earthquake information service just hours after the event. The internet would serve as a critical communication and coordination tool in coming natural disasters—especially after the Great East Japan Earthquake of March 2011 (chap. 7).

Traditional media, such as newspapers, magazines, and television, were all impacted by the proliferation of the internet and move to digitalization. NHK and free-to-air television stations were joined by new cable television services, resulting in the bourgeoning of new stations. Newspaper circulation reached its peak in 1997 as younger readers began to switch to online news sources, threatening the very structure of newspapers' postwar business model based on subscriptions and local delivery agencies. For other forms of media, like manga and computer or console games, the 1990s represented a new era of growth and globalization. The early 1990s marked the peak in sales of hard copy manga magazines. The magazine *Shūkan shōnen janpu,* for instance, recorded its highest sales of 6.53 million copies for its 1995 March-April edition. Famous titles—some of which would attract a global audience—included *Dragon Ball Z, Slam Dunk, Detective Conan, Sailor Moon, Chibi Maruko-chan, Crayon Shin-chan,* and *Pokémon.* At this time, manga represented around 40 percent of all print publications in Japan.[32] With rising competition from computer games and consoles, however, sales of hard copy manga magazines began to wane from the mid-1990s, but manga continued to thrive domestically and internationally through book series like *One Piece,* which first appeared in 1997. The *One Piece* series sold over 320 million copies worldwide, earning it a place in the *Guinness World Records* as the all-time best-selling comic series by a single author. Such Japanese manga proved extremely popular throughout East Asia, with television drama remakes of works such as *Hana yori Danshi* in South Korea, Taiwan, and China.

In response to the growing manga industry, in 2000, Kyoto Seika University established a Department of Manga, which was later elevated to the Faculty of Manga. Around 85 percent of students in the faculty come from China. In recent

Figure 6.16. The first stand-alone edition of the best-selling *One Piece* manga series published in December 1997. Shūeisha.

years, the digitalization of manga works has also gained in popularity. In 2014, print manga sales stood at around 225 billion yen compared to 88 billion for digital sales. But this situation had reversed with digital sales exceeding 171 billion yen versus 161 billion for print by 2017. The burgeoning of these cultural industries offered some glimmers of hope in the wake of the 1990s and its discouraging chronicle of economic gloom, political upheaval, and social malaise.

CHAPTER SEVEN

Japan in the New Millennium

Populists and Democrats: Politics in the Early Decades of the Twenty-First Century

The new millennium did not bring any quick relief to the sense of unease and insecurity born during the tumultuous 1990s. Indeed, as timepieces and computer systems ticked toward the year 2000, officials watched with bated breath as the so-called Y2K bug threatened to cripple power generation and water supplies, short-circuit essential medical equipment, paralyze communications infrastructure and financial services, and—in a worst-case scenario—unleash calamitous meltdowns in the country's nuclear power plants.

Although the new year ticked over without incident, the following decades continued to present the Japanese with manifold challenges stemming from far-reaching demographic transformations, precarity and decreasing social mobility, an international scene dominated by a war on terror and tectonic shifts in the geopolitics of East Asia, and a looming environmental crisis. For some, the years after 2000 even heralded an "age of anxiety" in which terrorism, natural disaster, foreign hazards, and socioeconomic decay all combined to undermine a system that had once seemed so indestructible.[1] At the same time, Japan was still a wealthy country with a complex economy, high standards of living, low crime rates, excellent health care and education, a diligent and hardworking populace, and long life expectancy. What seemed to be lacking most of all was the sense of confidence about the future that had been so palpable in the glory days of high-speed economic growth.

This atmosphere of anxiety arguably opened the way for several experiments in political populism in Japan in the first two decades of the millennium, as new political entrepreneurs appealed to the public with glossy solutions for national renewal. Following the resignation of Hashimoto Ryūtarō after the LDP's poor showing in the upper house election of mid-1998, Obuchi Keizō stepped into the prime ministership in what was viewed as yet another "seat-warming" administration while the party searched for more sturdy leadership. Surprisingly, Obuchi made an impressive start, convincing LDP-defector Ozawa Ichirō—now leader of the LP—to join in coalition with the LDP in January 1999, followed by the CGP coming onboard in August. But

Obuchi's honeymoon was short lived. In April 2000, Ozawa's party abruptly deserted the coalition after Obuchi refused to disband the LDP and create a new party with Ozawa. The stress of this wrangling took its toll on the prime minister, who suffered a stroke on April 5 and would die from complications around a month later.

In his place, the LDP installed Mori Yoshirō, an LDP stalwart and rugby fanatic but hardly the stuff of strong leadership. Quite predictably, voters were uninspired. In the lower house election of June 2000, the LDP only managed to maintain power thanks to its coalition with the CGP and the Conservative Party (consisting of defectors from Ozawa's LP who wished to remain in the coalition). Mori's fortunes deteriorated further when, in February 2001, the media reported that he had continued to play golf after learning that an American nuclear-powered submarine, the *USS Greeneville,* had collided with a Japanese vessel, killing nine passengers including four high school students. Faced with some of the lowest approval ratings on record—a dismal 7.2 percent at its nadir—the Mori Cabinet resigned the following month, replicating the wearying cycle of short-lived administrations.

It was against the backdrop of this political tedium that a new populist energy emerged in Japanese politics in the form of the energetic and charismatic fifty-nine-year-old Koizumi Jun'ichirō. Unlike Hashimoto, Obuchi, and others from the Tanaka lineage, Koizumi could not draw on strong factional support in his bid for the LDP leadership, instead strengthening his position through populist appeals to the public. In the election for the LDP presidency following Mori's resignation, Koizumi faced off with Hashimoto, who was keen for another chance at leadership, and Asō Tarō, who boasted an impressive political lineage as the grandson of Yoshida Shigeru (chap. 2) and great-great-grandson of the Meiji leader Ōkubo Toshimichi (chap. 1). Despite belonging to the LDP, during the campaign, Koizumi shrewdly portrayed himself as an "enemy" of the LDP establishment, with its vested interests, corruption, and money politics. The strategy proved quite appealing to a politics-weary public; fearing electoral blowback for defending the status quo, in the subsequent party presidential election of April 2001, LDP members voted overwhelmingly in favor of Koizumi for the party presidency and hence the prime ministership. Koizumi won 298 votes compared to Hashimoto's 155 and Asō's disappointing 31.

Koizumi continued to capitalize on this populist energy in building his new administration and advancing its audacious policy platform. The norm of appointing cabinet ministers based on factional numbers was unceremoniously scrapped, with a record five female ministers and three nonpoliticians, including the Keio University economist, Takenaka Heizō, who served as Minister of State for Economic and Fiscal Policy. In an interesting irony given his commitment to destroying LDP sacred cows, Koizumi appointed Tanaka Makiko—the daughter of "Mr. Money Politics" Tanaka Kakuei—to the important post of foreign minister.

Figure 7.1. Koizumi Jun'ichirō after his election to the LDP presidency on April 24, 2001. Courtesy of the Asahi Shimbun Company.

However, her term would be tarnished by internecine conflicts with bureaucrats that played out in a farcical media drama.

With his lion-like mane of hair and penchant for Elvis Presley, the enigmatic Koizumi cut a powerful public image as a decisive leader willing to stake everything on bringing about genuine reform. In television appearances and press conferences, Koizumi became king of the catchphrase, firing out self-assured slogans like "reforming Japan even if it means demolishing the LDP," "no economic recovery without structural reform," and "structural reform with no sacred cows." Two weeks after assuming office in 2001, Koizumi cleverly tapped into popular sympathies when he announced that his administration would not appeal a court ruling against the government on compensation for Hansen's disease (also known as leprosy) sufferers forced to live in isolated sanitoriums. Intentionally amplifying the drama of the moment, Koizumi met publicly with the victims, shaking their hands and offering his sincerest apologies for institutional discrimination in the past.

But despite his initial popularity and approval ratings over 80 percent, at the lower house election of 2003 two years into Koizumi's term, the LDP won 10 fewer seats than the previous election (down from 247 to 237), although it still managed to hold onto power thanks to the CGP coalition. Meanwhile, the DPJ—now led by the dashing former civic activist Kan Naoto—gained 40 seats (up from 137 to 177). The gap between the government and the opposition was narrowing rapidly thanks to the new electoral system. Without the boost from the popular Koizumi, the LDP may very well have lost the election.

Foreign Policy and National Security Under Koizumi

US-Japan Relations

Following the terrorist attacks on the United States by Al-Qaeda adherents in September 2001, like many other American allies, the Koizumi government quickly pledged allegiance to President George W. Bush's "war on terror," promising a more proactive role for Japan in what arguably became a "golden age" in the security alliance.[2] In October 2001, the government passed the Anti-Terrorism Special Measures Law, which authorized the SDF to provide rear support, such as refueling and supplying provisions to American-led forces in the Middle East. This law was subsequently extended until 2007 and then—against fierce opposition—replaced with a new law continuing support until 2010. At the time of its enactment in 2001, opposition parties pushed the government to clearly define "rear support," whose meaning remained contentious and ambiguous—seemingly including everything from the provision of food supplies to refueling and the repatriation of wounded soldiers.

The dispatch of a supply ship and two escort vessels to the Persian Gulf to provide rear support following the enactment of the law represented a milestone in postwar defense policy in Japan: until then, the SDF had only been deployed for UN Peacekeeping operations missions during ceasefires. Moreover, different from the deployment of a minesweeper following the Gulf War in 1991, this deployment to the Gulf was the first case in the postwar era of the SDF providing rear support for the American military in an active combat situation. After the initial dispatch, Japan would subsequently send more escort vessels, supply ships, and minesweepers to the Gulf.

Following the outbreak of the Iraq War in 2003, the Koizumi administration passed the Act on Special Measures concerning Humanitarian Relief, Reconstruction Work, and Security Assistance in Iraq in 2004. This act authorized SDF forces to undertake peacekeeping operations and postwar reconstruction projects in the country. Thereafter, ground SDF forces were dispatched to Samawah in southern Iraq, where they engaged in reconstruction work. Interestingly, SDF forces were not allowed to retaliate even if attacked, once again sparking debate over the ambiguity between "combat" and "noncombat" operations.

More controversial and far-reaching than the relief and reconstruction law, however, was a suite of legislation for national emergency responses passed around the same time, collectively known as the Laws for Emergency Situations. LDP governments had, in fact, been considering such legislation for close to twenty-five years but always hesitated due to strong pacifist public sentiment. But the war on terror and regional threats from North Korea opened a window of opportunity for the Koizumi government to bring this legislation to the Diet. The three pieces of legislation—the Law on Countermeasures for Armed Attack Situations, an amendment to the Self-Defense Forces Law, and an amendment to the Law for Establishment of the National Security Council—were passed through the Diet and promulgated in 2003 thanks to cooperation between the LDP and DPJ and despite strong resistance from other opposition parties and civic groups. The fourth piece of legislation, the National Protection Law, passed the Diet the following year.

Overall, the new legal framework enhanced the state's powers of command and control in emergency situations and allowed for restraints on civil liberties. Critics pointed to several worrying possibilities arising from the laws. For example, under the Surrounding Areas Emergency Law of 1999 (chap. 6), local governments, businesses, and landowners had been able to refuse to support Japanese and US forces during emergencies. But the new framework gave the government sweeping powers to enforce compulsory cooperation in the use of transportation thoroughfares, airports, ports, utilities, medical facilities, and communications infrastructure. SDF forces could now appropriate land in anticipation of an attack instead of waiting until an attack actually began. Some argued that now it would not be illegal, for example, if an American tank ran a red light on a Japanese road. Moreover, in the event of an armed conflict, wounded US soldiers or SDF forces would arguably take priority over injured civilians in medical treatment, and medical staff could be mobilized for this end. Although the laws stipulated that fundamental human rights were to be protected to the "fullest extent," skeptics claimed that they promised the very opposite given the new powers bestowed on the state.

Moreover, other ambiguities and concerns remained, such as whether an attack on SDF forces abroad would be considered an armed attack on Japan proper and whether these laws might further open the way for Japan to be drawn into US military action abroad. There is little doubt that the new laws increased state powers vis-à-vis society, gave the US military greater latitude in operations within the country, and moved Japan closer to a nation capable of fighting a war despite its pacifist constitution. As discussed below, this legal framework would be further strengthened under the second Abe government from 2012.

Relations with the Region

The emergency situations legislation was conceived of with the threat from North Korea in mind, so it was ironic (or perhaps intentional) that leaders of the hermit nation decided to approach Japan around the same time to resurrect stalled negotiations on normalization and to secure economic assistance. The Japanese side had three requirements from the North Koreans for normalization: a de-escalation of tensions, an end to the North's nuclear weapons program, and the safe return of Japanese citizens abducted by North Korea decades earlier.

In yet another instance of carefully constructed political theatre, on September 17, 2002, Koizumi, Deputy Chief Cabinet Secretary Abe Shinzō, and a delegation from Japan travelled to Pyongyang for a historic meeting with the country's supreme leader, Kim Jong-il. During the meeting, Kim formally admitted that, decades earlier, agents from the country had furtively entered Japan by boat and abducted thirteen Japanese nationals, who were forced to provide interpretation services and Japanese language instruction. Kim advised that eight of the thirteen were now deceased. The Japanese government has officially recognized seventeen Japanese citizens as having been abducted by North Korea during the 1970s and 1980s, although the Japanese police suspect that up to eight hundred missing persons may have been abducted. During their meeting, Koizumi and Kim signed the Pyongyang Declaration in which Japan apologized for its colonization of Korea and relinquished all claims to assets left in the country after the collapse of empire. The Japanese also promised to settle accounts of the past by providing economic aid after the normalization of relations. In October 2003, the Japanese nation came to a standstill as five of the abductees made an emotional return home, although the government remained skeptical about the total number abducted and demanded more evidence from the North Koreans, particularly regarding the supposed deaths.

Figure 7.2. Prime Minister Koizumi Jun'ichirō and Supreme Leader Kim Jong-il after signing the Pyongyang Declaration in North Korea on September 17, 2002. Courtesy of The Asahi Shimbun Company.

Figure 7.3. Five Japanese nationals abducted by North Korea return to Tokyo's Haneda Airport on a charter flight after twenty-four years away on October 15, 2002. Courtesy of The Asahi Shimbun Company.

Koizumi made yet another visit to North Korea in May 2004, during which both parties agreed to fulfil their obligations under the Pyongyang Declaration and work toward normalization. However, to date, this has not eventuated. In fact, relations subsequently deteriorated, with the North periodically launching ballistic missiles near to, and sometimes over, the Japanese archipelago. Moreover, the abductee issue reached no resolution under the new regime of Kim Jong-un beginning in 2011. In 2014, both countries signed the so-called Stockholm Agreement, under which the North Koreans promised to undertake a thorough investigation into the whereabouts of all unaccounted-for abductees and missing Japanese persons. The investigation was to include scientific inspections of remains and the graves of deceased Japanese, interviews with spouses of Japanese, and the provision of details about other remaining abductees and missing persons. But anomalies and outright fabrications in the report from the North Korean side only further complicated matters.

While relations with North Korea appeared to be moving in a tentatively positive direction in the Koizumi years, this was not necessarily the case for relations with South Korea and China. On the positive side, the cohosting of the 2002 FIFA World Cup by Japan and South Korea portrayed an image of regional integration and was accompanied by a Korea boom as Japanese watched popular television dramas like *Fuyu no Sonata* (*Winter Sonata*) and eagerly consumed South Korean products and foods. But tensions were never far from the surface. Koizumi continuously stoked the ire of Japan's Asian neighbors with his annual official visits to the Yasukuni Shrine to pay respects to Japan's war dead—including the convicted war criminals. His initial visit in 2001, as expected, provoked a wave of criticism from South Korea, China, and elsewhere in the region. Even the nationalist Nakasone was concerned, warning Koizumi about the negative diplomatic backlash from regional giants like the PRC.[3] Koizumi's most controversial visit was in 2006—his final year in office—when he fulfilled a promise made during the LDP leadership race to visit the shrine on August 15, the anniversary of war's end.

Koizumi's provocative Yasukuni visits from 2001 onwards further enflamed diplomatic relations with Asian neighbors, who were already infuriated by the Japanese MOE's April 2005 announcement that it had approved a new edition of a nationalistic history school textbook written by the right-wing Japanese Society for History Textbook Reform (chap. 6). In response, anti-Japanese sentiment erupted in cities across China, as angry mobs smashed the storefronts of Japanese retailers and convenience stores and chanted angry slogans outside the Japanese embassy in Beijing and consulates elsewhere.

Viewed from outside Japan, Koizumi's Yasukuni visits and the approval of rightist textbooks seemed to suggest that Japan was heading down a rightward path.

At the same time, rising nationalism and domestic issues in China also undoubtedly played a role in the disturbances of 2005. Moreover, as relations with Japan's closest neighbors deteriorated in the Koizumi years, a racist and xenophobic movement focused particularly on South Korea began to gain strength within Japan. It was fueled by hate speech and historical denialism disseminated over the internet and in manga series like Yamano Sharin's *Kenkanryū* (*Anti-Korean Wave*). Such developments revealed how, even sixty years after the collapse of its empire and the defeat of militarism, the prominence of nationalist voices on the past within Japanese society and politics continued to undermine the construction of positive relations with Japan's regional neighbors.

Economic Policy Under Koizumi

In the realm of economic policy, Koizumi vociferously championed the merits of "structural reform," forcefully shifting emphasis from the fiscal spending and monetary easing of his predecessors (with the exception of Nakasone) to an unabashed neoliberal agenda based on downsizing government and deregulating markets. There would be "no growth without structural reform," Koizumi and his economic guru, Takenaka Heizō, asserted. The two argued that government needed to be made smaller by shifting the "public to the private" and the "national to the local" to ease fiscal pressures in areas like health and social security. Koizumi's "Robust Policy 2001" attempted to quantify these aspirations by limiting government bond issues to thirty trillion yen, reforming the social security system, repairing local government finances, cutting government spending, privatizing state entities, and structurally reforming the economy by shifting resources from unproductive to productive sectors.

To advance this policy agenda, Koizumi established several consultative bodies within the CAO. The Council for Regulatory Reform became the mouthpiece for Koizumi's neoliberalism, advocating for comprehensive deregulation and reform in health, welfare, education, childcare, labor, agriculture, and other heavily regulated sectors. Meanwhile, the Council on Economic and Fiscal Policy, chaired by Takenaka, attempted to seize policymaking control from the MOF and put it in the hands of the prime minister and his closest advisers. To this end, the council proposed dividing the policymaking process into three stages: the first, a planning stage during which a deliberative council would set specific economic priorities; the second, an approval stage by the cabinet; and the third, the implementation stage by the MOF. Needless to say, this approach threatened to short-circuit the powerful stranglehold economic bureaucrats had enjoyed over economic policymaking throughout the postwar era.

In terms of policies ultimately implemented, government spending did decrease under Koizumi, while individual copayments for services such as health provision increased. More discretion and responsibility were placed on local governments in fiscal matters, resulting in the consolidation of localities across the country and arguably exacerbating the wealth disparity between metropolitan and regional areas. Deregulation proceeded apace via the establishment of special "deregulation zones," as too did the privatization of government entities, including national universities, the National Oil Corporation, and some national highways.

The privatization of Japan Post (JP) proved to be the most controversial of Koizumi's endeavors, compelling him to fully unleash his populist arsenal. As discussed in chapter 3, JP's postal savings and insurance operations, utilized by millions of Japanese, helped to fund the Fiscal and Investment Loan Program from which the Japanese state made investments in strategically important industries and projects during the years of high-speed economic growth. However, Koizumi and other critics argued that the permanent availability of this massive pool of money had engendered poor investments and encouraged pork-barrel politics. Only by privatizing JP, Koizumi and his economic team asserted, could this institutionalized wastage be eliminated and the logic informing fiscal decision-making restored to a basis of responsibility.

Koizumi's cabinet approved the JP privatization legislation in late 2004, but it hit a significant roadblock the following year when LDP members in the upper house refused to support the legislation because of opposition from within their constituencies. With this defeat, Koizumi threw down the gauntlet, dissolving the Diet and calling an immediate general election—the so-called Postal System Election of 2005. In the ensuing campaign, Koizumi portrayed those within the LDP who had opposed his bills as "reactionary forces." He melodramatically vowed to "stake his life" on the privatization of JP, even if it meant "destroying the LDP." In language reminiscent of President George W. Bush's war on terror, Koizumi depicted voters' choice in zero-sum terms: they could be either "for or against reform" and "for or against Koizumi." In the election, Koizumi refused to endorse LDP incumbents who had opposed the privatization legislation or who would not pledge to support it after the election. To prove his point, in the electoral districts of the recalcitrants, Koizumi endorsed alternative candidates on the LDP ticket, who the media colorfully dubbed "Koizumi assassins" and "Koizumi children."

Koizumi's stratagems proved to be electoral gold. Voters lapped up the prime minister's theatrics, giving the LDP-CGP a landslide victory of 327 seats. An astounding eighty-three of the "Koizumi children" were victorious, including former JNP member Koike Yuriko, now reborn as a Koizumi "child." Somewhat confirming the shallow populism behind Koizumi's victory, however, only ten of his "children" would be reelected in 2009. But, at least in 2005, no one could deny the maverick prime minister's decisive victory over the LDP old guard. The JP legislation passed through the Diet in October and, in 2007, postal services were divided into four companies under the control of Japan Post Holdings.

The LDP that Koizumi wanted to destroy was the party of money politics, backroom deals, corruption, and personalities like Tanaka Kakuei and his scions Takeshita, Hashimoto, and Obuchi. In the early 1990s, Ozawa Ichirō had made a futile attempt to destroy this system by abandoning the LDP and trying to build a viable opposition. Conversely, Koizumi chose to stay within the LDP, turning to populist politics and using the media to paint himself as the true champion of reform.[4] In the long term, however, Koizumi's achievements in bringing about fundamental structural reform of the economy were mixed. Moreover, whether or not ordinary Japanese were better off as a result is questionable, since his neoliberal policies based on deregulation, free markets, small government, and self-responsibility arguably tended to widen the gap between the "the winners" and the "losers."

The LDP Flounders

At the expiration of his term in September 2006, Koizumi stepped down—the first prime minister to do so since Nakasone in 1987. What ensued was another period of extreme instability in leadership, with three prime ministers serving in three years—short even in the context of earlier governments during the Heisei era. Koizumi's immediate successor was Abe Shinzō, the son of former LDP heavyweight Abe Shintarō and the maternal grandson of Kishi Nobusuke. Thanks to his public profile for facilitating the abductee issue under Koizumi, LDP members viewed him as a good option in a new age of public image. Abe also promised to restore stability to the party after the turmoil of the Postal System Election, welcoming back former LDP members forced out of the party for opposing privatization. Of course, while popular within the party, Abe's magnanimity suggested to many that the LDP would be returning to the old-guard, business-as-usual approach under his watch. Abe did, however, maintain several trends evident under Koizumi, such as attempting to increase the power of the prime minister over cabinet ministers, although this move arguably resulted in a lack of coordination in policymaking.

In speeches and publications like his 2006 book, *Utsukushii Kuni e* (*Towards a Beautiful Country*), Abe also advanced a strongly nationalist agenda, notably calling for an end to the "postwar regime" (e.g., postwar pacifism and the peace constitution). He similarly focused his energies on hawkish issues like national security, the abductees problem, educational reform aimed at instilling national pride, and revision of the war-renouncing clauses of the constitution. In preparation for constitutional revision, the Abe government passed legislation in May 2007 enabling a national referendum on constitutional revisions if supported by the necessary two-thirds majority in the Diet.

Outside of formal politics, Abe developed an intricate web of personal and organizational ties. Along with many of his LDP colleagues, Abe belonged to the ultranationalist organization Nippon Kaigi, which propagated many of the same right-wing policies he was pursuing in the Diet. At the same time, however, Abe attempted to balance his nationalist zeal with diplomatic realism, choosing not to visit the Yasukuni Shrine and restarting high-level diplomacy with South Korea and the PRC, which had stalled under the Koizumi administration. The month after assuming office in 2006, Abe made official visits to both countries.

Economically, Abe's first term failed to accomplish much, despite proclamations about bringing government expenses under control. On the contrary, his administration was plagued by scandals involving the abuse of political finances by cabinet ministers, questions over Abe's use of political money, and a massive brouhaha concerning the Social Insurance Agency's mismanagement of pensions. The latter incident unfolded in 2006–2007, when it was revealed that some fifty million pension accounts had not been correctly integrated into a new system, meaning that payment records were either unrecorded or incorrect and, in some cases, that pension payments were lower than actual entitlements. Voters, who were largely indifferent about Abe's nationalist agenda, punished him for the pension fiasco in the upper house election of 2007, handing the DPJ an impressive victory and stripping the LDP-CGP coalition of its majority. Facing extreme pressure from within the LDP and suffering from an acute bout of ulcerative colitis, Abe resigned in September on account of his deteriorating health but also to accept responsibility for the pension debacle.

Abe was followed by two even more unremarkable successors, Fukuda Yasuo and Asō Tarō. Fukuda faced monumental difficulties from the outset of his administration, with the DPJ controlling the House of Councillors in what the Japanese call a "twisted Diet" (i.e., opposing parties controlling each chamber). Try as he might, Fukuda was unable to negotiate a coalition agreement with the DPJ, and with the legislative process hamstrung by the twisted Diet, he was forced to resign in September 2008, just one year after assuming office. The beginning of Asō's administration under the slogan "making Japan a brighter, stronger country" lamentably coincided with the onset of the Global Financial Crisis (GFC), which was anything but "bright." Asō responded with numerous immediate countermeasures such as a one-time cash payment to citizens, tax breaks for home loans and eco-friendly automobiles, and discounts on highway tolls. But he was openly criticized by LDP politicians, who remained faithful to the neoliberal Koizumi-line of small government and fiscal responsibility. Asō's approval ratings sank from an uninspiring 42 percent at the outset of his administration to a dismal low of 14 percent after just a few months. With a lower house election due by October 2009, in late July, Asō dissolved the Diet and called a general election for August 30.

The Rise and Fall of the Democratic Party of Japan

The ensuing election delivered the DPJ a fairytale and the LDP a corresponding nightmare. The DPJ, with 115 seats prior to the election, captured 308 out the total 408 seats—a remarkable 193-seat increase. The party made impressive gains in both the single member and proportional representation districts. Conversely, the LDP captured only 119 seats (down from 296), and its coalition partner CGP 21 seats (down from 31). The new electoral system proved critical in the DPJ's victory, particularly in the SMDs in which the party won 73 percent of seats with around 47 percent of the vote, while the LDP only secured a paltry 21 percent of seats with 39 percent of the vote.

For proponents of the new electoral system this outcome heralded the arrival of a genuinely two-party system with periodic regime change. It also confirmed that landslide victories were possible in SMD, winner-takes-all electoral systems (albeit

Figure 7.4. DPJ leader Hatoyama Yukio following the party's stunning lower house election victory. The rose markers for seats won reveal the extent of the DPJ's triumph over the LDP (August 31, 2009). Courtesy of The Asahi Shimbun Company.

modified by the PR districts). The election outcome was historic on several levels. It was the first time that non-LDP forces had held a majority in both houses since 1955 and, moreover, that an opposition party had managed to win a majority in its own right in the lower house. Furthermore, it was only the third time in the postwar era that a regime change happened due to an election: the first being from the Yoshida to Katayama government in 1947 and the second from the Kaifu to Hosokawa government in 1993—although in both cases these outcomes were not so much a result of shifting voter preferences as they were divisions within political parties. The victory was certainly an endorsement of the DPJ's potential but, at the same time, it was also arguably just as much a voter repudiation of poor leadership by the LDP after Koizumi.

The new prime minister, Hatoyama Yukio, together with his brother and fellow politician Kunio, was born into a family of conservative politicians stretching back into the late nineteenth century. Notably, his father Ichirō served as prime minister in the mid-1950s, helping to oversee the formation of the LDP (chap. 2). Initially a member of the LDP, Hatoyama joined the reformist Utopia Political Research Group (chap. 6), established in response to the 1989 Recruit Cosmos scandal. In 1993, Hatoyama and Kunio deserted the LDP to help form the NPS, later joining the DPJ in its first iteration from 1996. Hatoyama was joined in the DPJ by Kan Naoto, a leftist civic activist who cut his teeth in the student movement of the late 1960s and later in progressive grassroots politics, supporting figures such as Ichikawa Fusae. Kan entered politics in 1976 as a member of former JSP secretary general Eda Saburō's breakaway progressive party, the Socialist Democratic Federation (SDFR). With the dissolution of the SDFR in 1994, Kan joined the NPS, serving as minister of welfare in the short-lived JSP-LDP-NPS coalition of the mid-1990s. During this time, he gained public respect for uncovering and resolving a scandal in which hemophiliacs were given HIV-infected imported blood plasma. Japanese officials initially recommended a stop to these imports but quickly reversed this decision under pressure from pharmaceutical marketers.

The third character in the victorious DPJ triumvirate was Ozawa Ichirō—the great "shadow shogun" of politics in the Heisei era. Ozawa joined the DPJ in 2003 following a whirlwind of defections and maneuverings throughout the 1990s, when he was trying to forge a viable LDP alternative among the atomized opposition forces. Ozawa served as leader of the DPJ from 2006 but was forced to resign in early 2009 over yet another political donation scandal involving one of his secretaries. For Hatoyama, Kan, Ozawa, and others in the DPJ, the electoral victory in August 2009 represented the realization of an aspiration they had been working toward for around two decades, but their joy would be short lived.

Although holding a healthy majority in the lower house, the DPJ leadership chose to form a coalition with the SDP and the People's New Party (PNP), consisting of a group of LDP ultraconservatives, like Kamei Shizuka, who had deserted the LDP in opposition to Koizumi's economic policies in 2005. This coalition was necessary for support in the upper house where the DPJ lacked an outright majority. The Hatoyama Cabinet started with relatively high approval ratings of around 65 percent—equivalent to Kaifu, Murayama, and Abe, but over ten points less than Hosokawa and Koizumi.

Hatoyama appointed Kan as deputy prime minister and minister in charge of the NSO, which would be responsible for budgetary reform (and, later, political strife for the new government). Fukushima Mizuho of the fading SDP came on board as minister for consumers and declining fertility, while Kamei Shizuka of the PNP assumed the finance and postal reform portfolios. As these cabinet appointments reveal, the DPJ-SDP-PNP coalition was one of ideological extremes. The same can also be said about the DPJ itself, which combined conservative former LDP hawks like Ozawa with leftist-defectors from the defunct JSP.

The Hatoyama government set out its policy agenda in a glossy "manifesto"—the first of its kind in the postwar era. In the sphere of governance, the DPJ committed to replacing the bureaucratic-dominated system in Japan with genuine "leadership by politicians." This would involve decoupling the nefarious relations between the ministries and the politicians, as well as the interest groups that benefited from them. To help fashion a politician-led system based on rational long-term planning for the good of the people, Hatoyama created two new institutions within the CAO and CS. First, the NSO was to be the command center for policymaking—similar in function to the Council on Economic and Fiscal Policy under Koizumi. But, as observers note, "the NSO's role was ambiguous and the institution was never fully developed or utilized. Its purview was limited to economic policies, but it was never fully staffed."[5] Second, the Government Revitalization Unit was created as a mechanism for transparent oversight of all government spending in an attempt to improve accountability. Alongside these new institutions, to enhance political leadership in policymaking, the DPJ government introduced new processes of budget screening and created committees of ministers, vice ministers, and senior bureaucrats to collectively make policy decisions.

In the sphere of welfare, the DPJ shifted emphasis from neoliberal cost-cutting, pork-barrel public spending, and single-minded policies for economic growth to a focus on citizen welfare—a shift from "concrete" to "people," as some described it.[6] It planned to realize this shift through initiatives like child allowances for families, free high school education, and the removal of highway tolls. In foreign relations, Hatoyama advocated for closer relations with East Asia, particularly the PRC and

South Korea, with ideas such as "fraternity" (*yūai*) and the construction of an East Asian Community. At the same time, Hatoyama aimed for a recalibration of the US-Japan security alliance, most notably in his promise to Okinawans that the controversial US military base at Futenma would be relocated outside of their prefecture and even outside of Japan.

Hypothetically, at least, the DPJ's policy agenda appeared to be aimed at eliminating some of the least desirable aspects of the 1955 System, while also offering a genuinely social democratic alternative to both Koizumi-style neoliberalism and single-minded economic growthism. But governing proved far trickier than winning the hearts of voters with impressive policy manifestos. The DPJ's welfare policies were necessarily dependent on increased government spending—a condition that successive Japanese governments had actually been trying to bring under control for the better part of thirty years. This condition was further complicated by the immediate pressures on government revenues in the wake of the GFC, leaving the party in the difficult situation of maintaining fiscal responsibility while keeping its election promises.

Ultimately, the Hatoyama government had no choice but to make a large issuance of government bonds to fund its welfare initiatives. Moreover, many of its policy proposals would not survive or would go unrealized altogether. Child allowances and toll-free highways both ended in 2011, and guaranteed incomes for farming families never materialized. Free high school education, moreover, was only partially realized in 2010 through a system of government subsidies for students based on an assessment of family income.

The DPJ also faced problems of governance. Internally, the party was ideologically diverse—even fragmented—with far-left and far-right wings that tended to undermine unity. Despite their time in the LDP or LDP coalitions, the DPJ leadership of Hatoyama, Kan, and Ozawa also lacked the preparation for high-level leadership, resulting in naïve decisions that undermined the party's public credibility. The DPJ's aim to put power in the hands of politicians made sense and resonated with earlier initiatives made under the Hashimoto administration to streamline the bureaucracies and Koizumi's moves to enhance the powers of the prime minister. But, in their rush to push this agenda, DPJ leaders managed to alienate and antagonize the bureaucrats on whom they were dependent for the provision of expert advice and policy implementation. Without bureaucratic support, the novice government was destined to flounder.

A lack of strategic thinking further undermined the new regime. Hatoyama's desire to engage with the country's regional neighbors had merit, but not if it threatened to destabilize the relationship with the United States. His popular election promise to relocate the Futenma base outside of Okinawa quickly became a matter of dispute with coalition allies, the SDP and PNP. Moreover, the Americans—wary of Hatoyama's Asia "pivot"—were opposed to relocation anywhere other than the agreed site of Henoko. Under extreme pressure from all directions, in May 2010, Hatoyama announced a reversal of his promise: the relocation from Futenma to Henoko would proceed as planned.

With this, the SDP unceremoniously quit the coalition, while Hatoyama's public support plummeted for having reneged on a campaign promise and seemingly given in to the demands of the United States. Thereafter, developments were all downhill for the new prime minister. In December 2009, Hatoyama was dealt a further blow when the media revealed anomalies in his (and Ozawa's) use of political funding and office expenses. Faced with questions about his leadership and integrity, Hatoyama announced his resignation in June 2010—a worrying stumble for the new regime.

Developments continued to move in a negative direction for the DPJ thereafter—some of their own making, others due to simple bad luck. Kan Naoto was selected as Hatoyama's successor in June, but the following month he suffered a brutal blow in the upper house election when the DPJ and its coalition partners lost their majority, despite the DPJ being the largest party in that house. The resulting "twisted Diet" made passing legislation without LDP support next to impossible. The Kan administration sustained another blow with the Great East Japan Earthquake—the so-called Triple Disaster—of March 2011, when massive tsunamis ravaged the east coast of northern Honshū, resulting in catastrophic meltdowns at the Fukushima Daiichi nuclear power plant (discussed later in this chapter). The government's poor crisis management came under extreme scrutiny—even from Ozawa and his allies within the DPJ—and, facing a vote of no confidence, Kan agreed to step down in September 2011.

Next in line for the prime ministership was Noda Yoshihiko, a center-right politician who entered the Diet on the JNP ticket (Hosokawa) in 1993, following a time in prefectural politics. The Noda administration was marked by an overall reversal of many of the DPJ's core policy promises. Committed to fiscal responsibility rather than expanding social welfare, Noda settled on a staged increase in the consumption tax from 5 to 10 percent with LDP support—a move that incensed Ozawa and forty-nine followers who promptly deserted the DPJ.

Noda was also forced to backtrack on Hatoyama's policy line of "fraternity" with Asia due to the reigniting of regional tensions, most conspicuously in relation to the disputed Senkaku/Diaoyu Islands. Tensions had, in fact, begun to escalate in December 2008, when two Chinese vessels entered Japanese waters surrounding the uninhabited islands. In September 2010, conditions deteriorated further when a JCG patrol boat collided with a Chinese fishing vessel it was attempting to move outside of Japan's contiguous zone. Crew members of the Chinese vessel were subsequently arrested, resulting in various reprisals from the PRC, including the suspension of ministerial-level meetings, a ban on Chinese rare earth exports to Japan and, most provocatively, a PRC declaration that the Senkaku/Diaoyu Islands were Chinese sovereign territory. Thereafter, incursions by official PRC vessels and Chinese fishing boats continued to escalate around the Senkakus and in other East Asian territories that the PRC wished to stake a claim on.

Bilateral relations hit an all-time low in August 2012, following the arrest and deportation of a Chinese national for swimming to the islands. In response, the far-right nationalist governor of Tokyo, Ishihara Shintarō, announced that the municipality had plans to purchase the islands from their current owner. Hoping to prevent such a move, in September, Prime Minister Noda announced that the islands would be nationalized, sparking anti-Japanese protests and attacks on Japanese supermarkets and factories in cities across China, similar to those in 2005.

In sum, by December 2012, the policy platform of the DPJ centered on leadership by politicians, expanded welfare and social-democratic initiatives, and a focus on Asian community was in tatters. So too was the party, following Ozawa and others' unceremonious exits and the left and right factions at loggerheads. Japan's second post-1955 experiment in non-LDP rule was on the verge of collapse.

The Triple Disaster of March 11, 2011

While politics in the first decade of the new millennium caused mild consternation, irritation, and occasional excitement among the Japanese, it was a natural disaster in 2011 that shook society to its foundations. On March 11 at 2:46 p.m., a catastrophic magnitude 9.0 earthquake struck about 130 kilometers off the coast of the Oshika Peninsula in Miyagi Prefecture to the north of Tokyo. The earthquake generated a massive tsunami that destroyed coastal communities in the Tōhoku region incorporating Iwate, Miyagi, Fukushima, and Ibaraki Prefectures. In Tokyo, bewildered office workers watched in horror as buildings and other structures swayed like palm trees. Commuters were forced to walk by torchlight out of subway tunnels. With the communications and transport infrastructure in most of east Japan inoperative or overloaded, people rushed to secure hotel rooms or hail taxies, while others walked or cycled marathon distances to their homes in surrounding prefectures. Television news around Japan and the world broadcast live aerial shots of the tsunami as it swallowed up the landscape of Tōhoku, leaving carnage in its wake. Social media such as Twitter (now X) became a critical source of information exchange, with many images and videos of the destruction appearing online in real time.

The so-called Great East Japan Earthquake was the strongest recorded in Japanese history and the fourth largest earthquake in the world since 1900, according to the United States Geological Survey. Different from the Kobe quake where tremors, fire, and subsidence caused most damage, in Tōhoku, the tsunami was the main villain. Exceeding thirty meters in some areas due to coastal topography, the tsunami easily cleared the fifteen-meter seawalls constructed along the Tōhoku coastline to protect residents from such an event. Despite the region's documented history of tsunamis, the stone monuments erected to indicate the height of earlier tsunamis, and the reassuring presence of supposedly tsunami-proof seawalls, thousands were swept away to their deaths. Others lost their lives by underestimating the height of the tsunami, which swallowed up low-rise buildings like city halls.

According to statistics from the NPA, as of March 2022, the number of deaths resulting from the disaster stood at 15,900, while 2,523 people were still classified as missing.[7] Close to four hundred thousand structures were either totally or partially destroyed.[8] At its peak three days after the disaster, around 470,000 people were taking refuge in emergency shelters or staying with relatives and acquaintances. One year after the disaster, 159,168 people were still unable to return to their radiation-contaminated homes and businesses, 62,267 of whom were forced to relocate outside Fukushima Prefecture. As of February 2022, 33,365 people were still living in a forced state of evacuation from their homes—many of whom had been displaced due to radioactive fallout from the other villain of the Triple Disaster: the nuclear reactor meltdowns at the Fukushima Daiichi nuclear power plant.[9]

The tsunami struck the Fukushima plant—run by the Tokyo Electric Power Company (TEPCO)—around fifty minutes after the quake, severing power from the electricity grid and crippling the emergency backup generators needed to cool the reactors. Reactors 1, 2, and 3, which were operational at the time, could not be cooled, resulting in meltdowns around three days after the disaster. In a desperate bid to cool the reactors, plant officials injected water, which, in turn, triggered powerful hydrogen explosions that destroyed the buildings housing the reactors, especially Reactor 2. Radioactive material from the explosions was released into the atmosphere, spreading out over a wide radius, making many areas uninhabitable and raising concerns about the effects on human health, crops, soil, water, flora, and fauna.

The International Atomic Energy Agency (IAEA) initially categorized the Fukushima accident as level 5 (accident with wider consequences) on its International Nuclear and Radiological Event Scale, but this was later upgraded to the highest level 7 (major accident) after the meltdowns came to light. So serious was the crisis that Emperor Akihito made an unprecedented, televised address on March 16 in which he expressed his sadness for the victims and thanked the SDF, police, firefighters, JCG, and other institutions involved in the response.

Figure 7.5. A tsunami crashes over a levee near the mouth of the Hei River in Miyako City, Iwate Prefecture, at 3:21 p.m. on March 11, 2011. The Mainichi Newspapers.

Figure 7.6. Aerial image showing extensive destruction of the reactors and facilities at the Fukushima Daiichi nuclear power plant taken on March 20, 2011. Courtesy of The Air Photo Service.

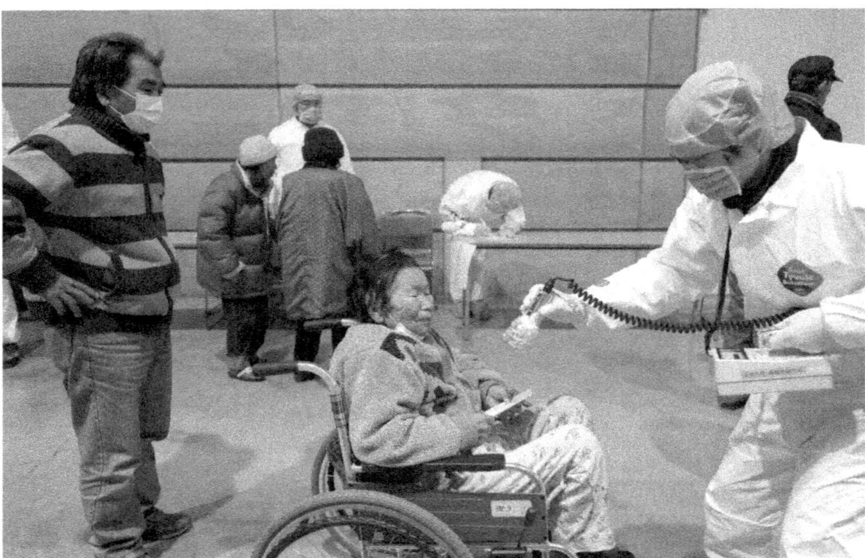

Figure 7.7. Residents of Tomioka Town and Kawauchi Village in Fukushima Prefecture undergo radiation checks before being reevacuated to Sugito Town, Saitama Prefecture, at 1:57 p.m. on March 17, 2011. Courtesy of The Asahi Shimbun Company.

The DPJ government under Prime Minister Kan Naoto was faced with a mammoth task, responding to both the aftermath of the earthquake and tsunami and the deteriorating situation at the nuclear power plant. In relation to the latter, the government declared an immediate nuclear emergency. Due to concerns over radiation contamination, local residents were initially evacuated outside a three-kilometer radius from the plant, but this was subsequently extended to twenty and then thirty kilometers as conditions worsened. Areas suspected of contamination of twenty millisieverts or above were classified as "planned evacuation zones," forcing over one hundred thousand people to abandon their homes and businesses immediately.

But not all went smoothly in the disaster response. Communication between the government, TEPCO, and the Fukushima plant was patchy, eventually causing the prime minister's temper to fray as he sought concise and timely updates on conditions at the crippled plant. Citizens also became concerned about the veracity of government reporting on conditions, some even choosing to flee southwards away from possible radioactive fallout. Sensing this public concern, in May, Kan ordered the temporary shutdown of reactors at the Hamamatsu nuclear power plant in Shizuoka Prefecture south of Tokyo due to safety concerns. Thereafter, most of

Japan's nuclear plants would go offline for an extended duration as support for nuclear power plummeted and the DPJ declared a policy of abandoning nuclear power altogether. Nonetheless, many Japanese were deeply dissatisfied with the government's handling of the Triple Disaster and they began to question the crisis management capabilities of the Kan administration. In turn, such dissatisfaction would serve as a critical factor in the downfall of the DPJ in 2012.

While the government suffered a significant dent in support due to its emergency response, the SDF, which was deployed to provide disaster relief and reconstruction assistance, greatly enhanced its public image and trust. Citizens watched live scenes of SDF helicopters flying dangerously close to the Fukushima plant to douse water on its melting reactors. The SDF was assisted in this task by US forces involved in so-called Operation Tomodachi, (*tomodachi* means "friendship"), begun almost immediately after the disaster. Apart from helping at Fukushima, the Americans assisted with cleanup work at the flooded Sendai Airport, reconstruction of schools and other critical infrastructure, and support for disaster victims.

Building on the learning experience of volunteering after the Kobe earthquake of 1995, this time the civic response was carefully managed through close cooperation between government institutions and volunteer organizations. The isolation of many of the affected areas in the Tōhoku region meant that volunteers could not make their own way to help. Instead, bus companies organized "volunteer tours" and government Social Welfare Councils set up volunteer registries and managed volunteer deployment. The government encouraged universities to provide students with "volunteer credits," while large companies began to offer employees "volunteer leave." On the positive side, the highly professionalized volunteer response evidenced the maturation of Japanese civil society since the mid-1990s but, for some critics, it also confirmed that a once spontaneous sphere of civic activity had fallen victim to regimentation, management, and neoliberal governance.

Volunteering was by no means the only civic response following the disaster. As facts about the Fukushima plant began to emerge, leading intellectuals, civic leaders, and literati like the novelist Ōe Kenzaburō organized antinuclear rallies, one of which in September 2011 attracted more than sixty thousand participants. For some observers, this contentious activism heralded the birth of a new "cycle of protest" in Japan, but such predictions proved incorrect as the demonstrations declined over time.

In the wake of the Triple Disaster—especially the Fukushima meltdowns—people began to ask whether appropriate preparations had been put in place to deal with such a catastrophe, and whether—as some claimed—the disaster was simply "unforeseeable." To be sure, there was an undeniable history of accidents—sometimes fatal—at nuclear power plants in Japan. In December 1995, for example, the public learned that the experimental fast-breeder reactor known as Monju, run by the Power Reactor and Nuclear Fuel Development Corporation in Fukui Prefecture, had experienced a fire caused by the leakage of radioactive sodium. Matters were made worse when it was revealed that plant officials had delayed informing authorities and whitewashed their report. In 1997, over twenty people were exposed to radiation after solidified radioactive waste caught fire at a nuclear fuel fabrication facility in Tōkaimura in Ibaraki Prefecture. This incident was followed in 1999 by a so-called criticality accident caused by improper handling of liquid uranium at a fuel reprocessing facility run by the Japan Nuclear Fuel Conversion Company, also in Tōkaimura. The accident resulted in 666 people being exposed to radiation, two of whom would die. In 2002, executives at TEPCO were forced to resign after revelations that reports on accidents at nuclear facilities had been covered up or altered and repair and maintenance records systematically falsified. Finally, after the Niigata Chūetsu Earthquake in October 2004, a fire broke out in Reactor 3 at the Kashiwazaki-Kariwa nuclear power plant in Niigata.

Thus, by 2011, nuclear-related accidents—including those caused by earthquakes—were hardly unforeseeable. Indeed, reports following the Fukushima disaster confirmed that TEPCO officials had failed to heed warnings from experts about the dangers earthquakes and tsunami posed to the company's nuclear reactors. TEPCO's own simulations in the years leading up to the disaster confirmed that the seawalls protecting the Fukushima plant were too low, but such warnings were ignored due to the one-billion-yen price tag to upgrade.

In hindsight, this amount proved minuscule given that the Japanese people will need to pay 35–80 trillion yen to clean up the mess in the coming forty years.[10] Just prior to the Triple Disaster in 2011, the government's Nuclear Safety Commission granted an extension to the aging Fukushima plant's operating license, but only on condition that the emergency electricity generators be replaced and relocated due to the risk of inundation by tsunamis.[11] But no action was taken. After initially exonerating itself of all responsibility for what was an "unforeseeable" event, three damning investigations in 2012 forced TEPCO to admit that "human error" and "institutionalized complacency" played into the disaster, as too did the company's failure to act on its own findings.[12]

The DPJ's decision to abandon nuclear power after Fukushima had broad public appeal at the time but, as critics warned, there were still no concrete answers as to how Japan would secure reliable energy substitutes in a world moving toward decarbonization. With all of its reactors offline after Fukushima, Japan immediately reverted to importing fossil fuel substitutes like LNG, coal, and crude oil. This caused the country's balance of payments to fall into the red for the first time in thirty-one years and, more worryingly, its energy self-sufficiency to drop to 6 percent—the lowest among the advanced economies.[13]

By 2022, with a depreciating yen and rising energy prices, antinuclear sentiment began to wane in the country as ordinary Japanese faced rising living costs for the first time in decades. In a March 2022 poll, a small majority backed restarting the reactors for the first time since the Fukushima disaster, while another poll in July reported 48.4 percent in support of restarts and 27.9 percent opposed.[14] Against this backdrop of changing public opinion, in mid-2022 Prime Minister Kishida Fumio announced that seventeen of the thirty-three idled nuclear reactors were to be reactivated within a year and that the government would begin developing and constructing the next generation of nuclear power plants.[15] Cleanup at the crippled Fukushima plant continued (and will do so for at least another thirty years), with the Japanese Nuclear Regulation Authority approving the release of treated radioactive wastewater from the plant into the ocean in 2023—much to the consternation of Japan's neighbors in the Asia-Pacific region, but with the cautious approval of the IAEA.[16]

Economy, Disparity, and Precarity

Brief Economic Recovery and Global Financial Crisis

Into the new millennium the Bank of Japan, economic bureaucrats, and LDP leaders continued their efforts to revive the Japanese economy with some early signs of improvement. Beginning in 1999 and stretching though the following decades, the bank pursued a zero-interest policy coupled with monetary quantitative easing aimed at stimulating corporate borrowing and investment. Thanks to a relatively weaker yen, growing exports, and a US economy riding high on the information technology bubble, the economy briefly recovered from around 2003 to 2007. Average real GDP growth in those years was a modest 1.64 percent but a marked improvement compared to the 0.48 percent for the previous five years (including negative growth in 1998 and 2001). Unemployment, which peaked at 5.4 percent in 2002, dropped to 4.1 percent and, after another brief spike, would stabilize at around 2.6 percent by 2022. Per capita income also steadily increased in the years from 2002 to 2012, rising from around US$33,000 to US$49,000. Thus, though some would later speak in the plural of "lost decades" after the original lost decade of the 1990s, Japan's economic performance was hardly so moribund.

But just as the economy was showing signs of moderate improvement, it was hit by the shock of the GFC, known in Japan as the "Lehman Shock" after the American financial services firm, Lehman Brothers, which sparked the calamity on its collapse in 2008. The Japanese economy was hit particularly hard by the shock due to exporters' reliance on credit from companies such as Lehman Brothers.

Following the shock, the Nikkei 225 slumped to its lowest level in twenty-six years and Japanese exports dwindled. GDP growth for 2008 and 2009 was –.6 and –2.4 percent, respectively (although this would bounce back to 3.3 percent in 2010). Against the backdrop of a sluggish domestic economy and external shocks, Japan's famed high household savings rate also began to decline from over 10 percent of household annual income in 1997 to less than 2 percent by 2012. In 2013 and 2014 household savings were actually negative.

Moreover, demographic factors (see later in this chapter) also began to encumber economic performance. As figure 7.8 shows, the number of working-age Japanese decreased from 85.9 million in 1990 to 73.4 million in 2020, meaning that the aggregate number of working hours was gradually decreasing in Japan after 1990. As a result, productivity increases have been the only way for the Japanese economy to grow but, as the number of workers continues to decline (a projected fifty million by 2050), other solutions will be required.[17]

"Cool Japan" to the Rescue?

While the economy struggled on, the international influence and popularity of Japan's cultural and creative industries expanded notably during the Heisei era, accompanied by a burgeoning of inbound tourism in recent decades. None of these industries promised (or even desired) to revive the high-growth economic "miracle"

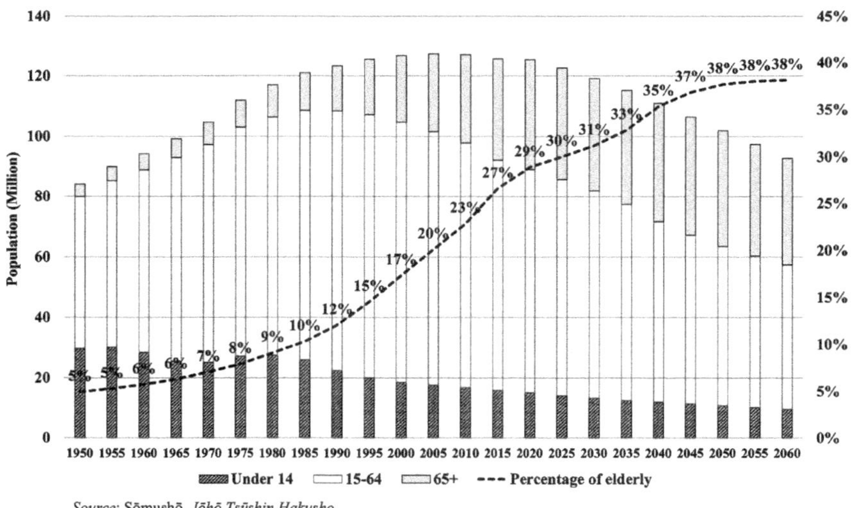

Figure 7.8. Population Composition by Age Group and Percentage of Elderly (≥65yrs) in Postwar Japan, 1950–2060

of old, but they hinted at creative potentialities still largely untapped in contemporary Japan. Foreign observers also began to notice the new phenomena. In a 2009 article for the magazine *Foreign Policy,* journalist Douglas McGray pointed to Japan's expanding "Gross National Cool," thanks to the global popularity of the country's culture industries and products.[18] As McGray explained, "Instead of collapsing beneath its political and economic misfortunes, Japan's global cultural influence has only grown. In fact, from pop music to consumer electronics, architecture to fashion, and food to art, Japan has far greater cultural influence now than it did in the 1980s, when it was an economic superpower."[19]

Japanese consumer electronics and automobile brands had become household names worldwide by the 1980s, but now they were joined by an array of new cultural products and icons, including Sony's PlayStation, Nintendo video games like Pokémon and Super Mario Bros., J-pop artists such as Amuro Namie and SMAP (both wildly popular throughout Asia), the Sanrio Corporation icon Hello Kitty, the animated movies of Miyazaki Hayao and Studio Ghibli like *Spirited Away* (2001), the novels of Murakami Haruki, and bestselling manga series such as *One Piece.* Japan had certainly witnessed the potential of cultural exports before with the popularity of the NHK series *Oshin* in the 1980s, but the effect then was minuscule by comparison.

In the early years of the new millennium, Japanese officials began to acknowledge the economic potential of Japan's culture industries. As early as 2000, an education whitepaper noted the growing international popularity of manga. Under the Koizumi administration (2001–2006), the prime minister and his officials began promoting cultural exports and nation branding through industries like film, animation, and fashion. A range of specialist committees and projects such as the J-Brand Initiative and funding for the annual World Cosplay Summit were subsequently implemented.[20] In a 2006 speech, the foreign minister Asō Tarō declared that "pop culture" must be a critical component of Japan's cultural diplomacy into the future and, in the same year, he inaugurated the Japan International Manga Award for the best manga by a foreign artist.[21] Thereafter, the Ministry of Foreign Affairs (MOFA) appointed the animation character Doraemon as "Anime Ambassador," while three young women became MOFA's official "Pop Culture Transmitters" (also known as "Ambassadors of Cute"). More concrete initiatives ensued with the establishment of the Cool Japan Promotion Office by the Ministry of Economy, Trade and Industry in 2010 and the CS's Council for the Promotion of Cool Japan in 2013. In the same year, the public-private sector initiative "Cool Japan Fund" began supporting a range of commercial projects to promote Japanese products and services worldwide, including media content, food, fashion, daily products, services, advanced technology, leisure goods, local products, and tourism.[22]

Just how important such government initiatives were in advancing Japan's culture and service industries is debatable. Moreover, their tendency to present an image of "Japan" and "Japanese culture" as somehow unique and homogeneous was often at odds with the actual diversity of the country and the transnational aspects of its cultural products. Nonetheless, there is no doubt that Japan's "Gross National Cool" kept expanding across the Heisei years, nowhere more evident than in the rising popularity of Japan as a tourist destination. Starkly different from the 1980s when "tourism" and "Japan" signified throngs of Japanese tourists travelling to destinations across the globe, in recent decades Japan has emerged as a tourism magnet, thanks in great part to the international influence of its culture industries. By way of comparison, in 2003 around 5.2 million tourists visited the country. But by 2014, this number had grown to 13.4 million, and by the eve of the COVID-19 pandemic in 2019, an astounding 31.8 million were visiting the country annually. Visitors from East and Southeast Asia accounted for 82.7 percent of inbound tourism.[23] Initiatives started by the Koizumi administration in 2003 such as the global "Visit Japan Campaign" began to reap success from around 2010, as the numbers of foreign travellers increased dramatically. In response, the Japan Tourism Agency was established in 2008, with an initial budget of 6.3 billion yen, which would increase to 71.1 billion yen by 2019.[24] The government's Basic Plan for the Promotion of a Tourism Nation of 2017 aimed at forty million annual visitors in 2020, and were it not for the pandemic, that target may have been reached.[25]

At the same time, the other side of Japan's tourism miracle has been growing concerns about so-called over-tourism, especially its deleterious impacts on the environment and carbon footprint. Moreover, the benefits of growing cultural exports and inbound tourism have not been evenly spread, concentrating in the big cities and prominent tourist destinations. Indeed, while "Cool Japan" may have produced a feel-good effect, in terms of socioeconomic challenges and concrete solutions, it is largely a peripheral phenomenon.

Growing Disparity

How did changed economic conditions impact the lives of ordinary Japanese throughout the Heisei era? For some observers, economic stagnation brought with it growing income inequality and poverty in Japan. In 1998, the economist Tachibana Toshiaki sparked a lively debate with his provocative book *Nihon no Keizai Kakusa: Shotoku to Shisan kara Kangaeru* (Economic inequality in Japan: An income and assets perspective).[26] Using the Gini coefficient, which measures wealth and income inequality in nations, Tachibana argued that inequality had increased dramatically in Japan after the bursting of the economic bubble. In the years from 1981 to 2017, Japan's Gini coefficient did indeed rise moderately from 0.314 to 0.372.[27] According to Tachibana, this change reflected the onset of a society of "winners" and "losers" in Japan, replacing the former condition of relative equality among a broad middle class. Contemporaneous observations about the "collapse of education," the "disintegration of the middle class," and the increase in nonregular employment tended to support Tachibana's thesis. At the same time, however, in government surveys, over 90 percent of respondents continued to report their status as "middle class," just as they had in the 1970s. Some, like then Minister of Internal Affairs Takenaka Heizō, went even further, causing a minor controversy in 2006 when he claimed that poverty was not a problem in need of solving in Japan.[28]

To be sure, people were becoming less confident that the future would be better than the past, with only 10 percent answering this question affirmatively in the first decade of the 2000s compared to 30 percent during the years of high-speed growth. The poorest segment of society was also arguably expanding and becoming poorer. The number of households in receipt of social welfare increased from around six hundred thousand in the mid-1990s to over one million in 2004. So too did the number of households with no savings, rising from 5 percent in the late 1980s to 22.8 percent by 2005.[29] Another indicator of growing economic hardship in Japan is the poverty rate, which measures the percentage of households whose income is less than half the median household income of the total population. According to OECD statistics, Japan's poverty rate was 15.7 percent in 2018, the second worst among the G7 nations (after the United States) and ninth out of forty-one OECD countries.[30] This rate represented around a 2 percent increase since the early 1990s. Needless to say, the poverty rate for certain groups such as single parents and elderly women living alone is much higher than the average. Of course, from a historical perspective, this is nothing new since the same situation existed during the years of high-speed economic growth.

One worrying trend, however, has been the increase in child poverty in the country, rising from 10.9 percent in 1985 to 13.5 percent by 2018.[31] The recent appearance of nonprofit groups providing after-school meals to children may also indicate increasing forms of hidden poverty in the country; in other words, families who are not technically categorized as being in poverty because of their income but are nevertheless struggling to get by—the so-called working poor. Also, while poverty has increased in certain groups such as children and youth, another feature of the period after the bubble is that poverty became more visible, whether in makeshift dwellings erected by homeless people in major cities or in advocacy by civic groups in the media and elsewhere.

Precarious Work

Measurements of poverty based on the simple definition of people living below the median annual income also neglect the reality of growing precarity that more and more Japanese faced in the wake of the bubble, as nonregular forms of employment proliferated. With the bursting of the bubble, some of the pillars of the Japanese system like lifetime employment and seniority wages for regular male workers in large corporations began to crumble, and along with them, the transformation of the labor market overall. Companies unable to sustain systems based on seniority or lifetime employment began to encourage early retirement and introduce performance-based remuneration. "Restructuring" (*risutora*) became a buzzword of the early Heisei years as companies used a variety of methods to shed mid- and late-career employees through early retirement, redeployment, merit-based appraisal, and age-based salary reductions. Many youths entering the labor market in the mid- to late 1990s were unable to find permanent work in what became known as the "employment ice age." The ratio of advertised positions to university-graduate job seekers peaked at 2.86 jobs per graduate in 1997, collapsing to 0.99 in 1999, recovering slowly to 2.14 by the time of the GFC, deteriorating again, and finally reaching around 1.7 by the beginning of the 2020s.[32] Many in this "lost generation" of the late 1990s were never able to find regular employment, instead forced to eke out a living from one nonregular job to the next.

As regular, full-time employment declined, nonregular forms such as part-time, contract, and so-called dispatch labor, in which workers are sent from employment agencies to companies, began to increase. For those employees who did secure a regular position, pressures to sacrifice everything for the company intensified. In the 2010s, the media began to report on "black corporations" that forced full-time employees to work excessive hours, sometimes without appropriate remuneration. Labor market statistics evidence the considerable growth in nonregular employment in Japan during the Heisei era. As figure 7.9 shows, around 20 percent of workers were in nonregular forms of employment in 1990, but this figure had reached 37.8 percent by 2019. The absolute number of nonregular employees increased from 8.7 million in 1990 to 35.21 million in 2019.

Nonregular workers had certainly been a significant part of the labor market previously, but what differed now was the rate of increase and the sheer number of both men and women engaged in such employment. The increase was particularly noticeable among advanced career (55–64 years old), the elderly (65 years and over), and female workers. In 2019, around 55 percent of women in their forties were in nonregular employment compared to 8.1 percent for men. This figure climbed to around 60 percent for women in their fifties compared to 10 percent for men.

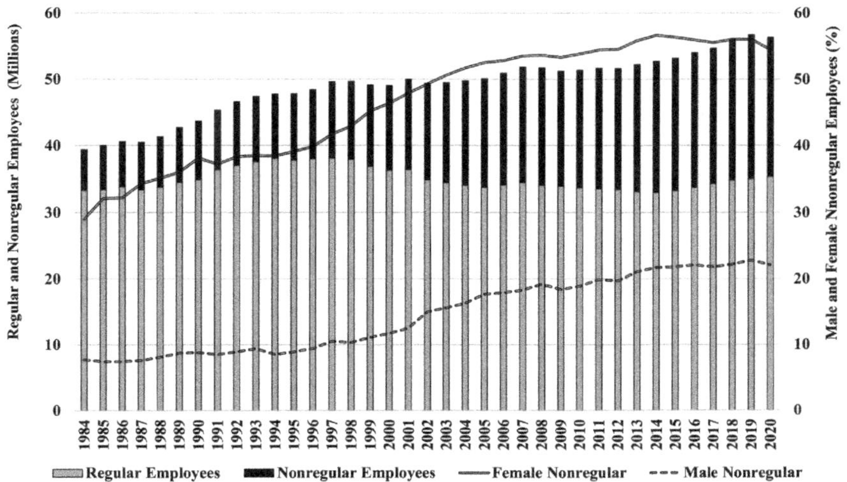

Source: Rōdō Seisaku Kenkyū-Kenshū Kikō, "Hayawakari Gurafu de miru Chōki Rōdō Tōkei, II."

Figure 7.9. Numbers of Regular and Nonregular Employees and Proportion of Nonregular Employees by Gender, 1984–2020

While economic conditions were important in the rise of nonregular employment during the Heisei era, it is also important to recognize the role played by the government through regulation. As we have seen, the Nakasone government passed legislation in 1985 making possible certain forms of dispatch labor previously prohibited under labor law. Initially, this new law was aimed at improving Japan's international competitiveness by allowing specialized workers to offer their technical skills to more than one enterprise. But throughout the 1990s, the number of occupations covered under the law was gradually extended such that by 1999, it included all forms of employment.

By the first decade of the 2000s, the plight of precarious workers trapped in the cycle of nonregular work had become a topic of social concern. The term "freeter"—symbolic of the confident "new species" of liberated workers in the 1980s (chap. 5)—now became associated with a "lost generation" of miserable nonregular workers. Along with freeters, observers also began to express concerns about NEET, referring to youth who were "Not in Education, Employment or Training," "parasite singles" who survived thanks to their parents' financial support, and *hikikomori* or persons suffering from acute social withdrawal. Concerned government agencies began to collect statistics on people in these groups, who loomed as a future "burden" for the welfare system. After an NHK television special on the "working poor" in 2006 brought widespread attention to the problem of precarity in Japan, a youth named Akagi Tomohiro captured the desperation of many freeters in a provocative essay in which he expressed his desire that Japan become involved in a war so that his lost generation might find something—anything—"significant" to do.[33] Others like Amamiya Karin called on society to have more sympathy toward freeters in her book *Ikisaero! Nanminka suru wakamonotachi* (Let them live! Youth made into refugees) (2007), while the economic analyst Morinaga Takurō attempted to provide useful advice in his book *Nenshū 300manen jidai o ikinuku keizaigaku* (The economics of surviving in an age of the three-million-yen yearly income) (2003).

The effects of precarity were often only subtly perceptible—for instance, in relation to marriage. In 1990, only 5 percent of men did not marry but this figure had risen to 23 percent by 2015. Some of this increase had to do with changing lifestyles but it also resulted from precarity. Undoubtedly the most visible expression of precarity in Japan was the New Year's "Dispatch Workers' Village" set up by nonprofits over the new year period of 2008–2009. With the onset of the GFC in 2008, many nonregular workers found themselves out of employment and, in turn, unable to pay for housing and food. In response, a coalition of nonprofit groups and others set up tents in downtown Hibiya Park to provide food and other necessities to the ill-fated workers. This space was carefully chosen, with the Ministry of Health, Labour and Welfare (MHLW)—a key player in the deregulation of the Japanese labor market—located just across the road. With media reporting on the dire situation of freezing homeless people during the most important celebration of the Japanese calendar year, ministry officials felt obliged to temporarily open up their heated offices for use by the "village" patrons. The then-DPJ government undertook to address the inequities experienced by nonregular workers but, over the coming decade (2009–2019), their numbers would increase by close to four million.

Women and Work

Throughout the Heisei era working conditions and expectations among and for women began to change, albeit glacially. The unwritten rule of retirement at marriage and childbirth began to fade, although significant inequalities remained, such as the comparatively low number of women in managerial positions. The demand for greater gender diversity in Japan's rigidly circumscribed workplaces also began to appear more in political and public discussions, as women seized educational opportunities and drew on the experiences of women in other countries. Indicative of the change, the number of women attending four-year universities outstripped those at two-year junior colleges in 1996. On a symbolic level, the magazine *Shufu no tomo* (Housewife's friend)—an icon of Japan's gendered society—published its final edition in 2008 after ninety-one years in operation. Even conservative stalwarts felt increasingly obliged to pay at least lip service to the new discourse. At the beginning of his second term as prime minister in 2013, Abe Shinzō expressed his desire to "attain a society in which women can shine."

Along with such political speak there were some significant regulatory developments in relation to women and work during the Heisei era. The EEOL of 1985 was amended in 1997 and 2005—the former to strengthen provisions for the elimination of discrimination in recruitment advertising, hiring processes, placements, and promotion, and the latter for the eradication of sexual harassment in workplaces. In 1999, the Diet approved the Basic Law for a Gender-Equal Society, which set out the key concepts for forming a gender-equal society and the kinds of measures government, business, and citizens might take to this end. The 2003 Law on Measures to Support the Development of the Next Generation required companies of over three hundred employees to "make efforts" to support childrearing through parental leave and other support. Finally, the Law for the Promotion of Female Participation and Career Advancement of 2015 (strengthened in 2022) required companies to produce action plans for the promotion of women's advancement in their workplaces. Once these plans are certified by the government, companies can use the certification seal on their stationery and advertisements, and they may also be eligible for low-interest government loans and merit points in public procurement bids.

In the new millennium, some Japanese companies also began to proactively develop workplace diversity and inclusion. For example, Teijin Limited, involved in chemicals, pharmaceuticals, and information technology, established an Office for Women's Advancement, while the Nissan Motor Corporation set up its Diversity Development Office. Many other companies and local governments followed suit. Nonetheless, the task of creating workplaces in which women can confidently develop their talents remains a work in progress.[34]

The year 1997 was particularly important for women and work during the Heisei era. In this year wages hit their peak, thereafter declining overall. As a result, the model of male breadwinner and full-time housewife portrayed in magazines like *Shufu no tomo* began to collapse. That year also marked the turning point when the number of households with both spouses working began to outnumber single-income households. This transition was in part due to more women wanting to work, but it was also a product of economic realities. In deflationary Japan when wages were stagnant and many men were in nonregular employment, female partners had no choice but to work to support family budgets. Hence, this shift to dual-income households was partially "negative" in the sense of it being due to necessity rather than choice.[35] Moreover, as before, most of the women entering the labor market were employed in nonregular positions that were generally lower paid, lacking benefits, and precarious. According to government statistics, the number of women employed in nonagricultural labor was 17.38 million in 1989, but this number had climbed to 25.64 million in 2017—a 48 percent increase. At the same time, as figure 7.10 reveals, while the number of working women has been increasing, so too has the number of women in nonregular employment. In 1990, of the 17.65 million working women, 6.46 million or 38 percent were in nonregular employment. In 2005, this number had climbed to 52.5 percent of the 22.43 million working women, and by 2020 it was 54.4 percent of 27.03 million.

The number of women continuing to work after the birth of their first child only began to increase noticeably in the second decade of the new millennium. Throughout most of the Heisei era, around 40 percent of women retired at the birth of their first child. This trend began to reverse from the 2010s, with 53.8 percent of new mothers continuing to work in 2019 (fig. 7.11). Among women in regular employment, the rate was closer to 70 percent.[36] As also evidenced in figure 7.11, the implementation of parental leave schemes in companies meant that many more women (and some men) began to utilize such leave before returning to their positions full time.

Such statistics and practices suggest some positive trends for female workplace participation in Japan, but challenges remain. According to the OECD, the number of highly educated women going into the full-time workforce is relatively low compared with other advanced economies like Sweden, Germany, France, and the

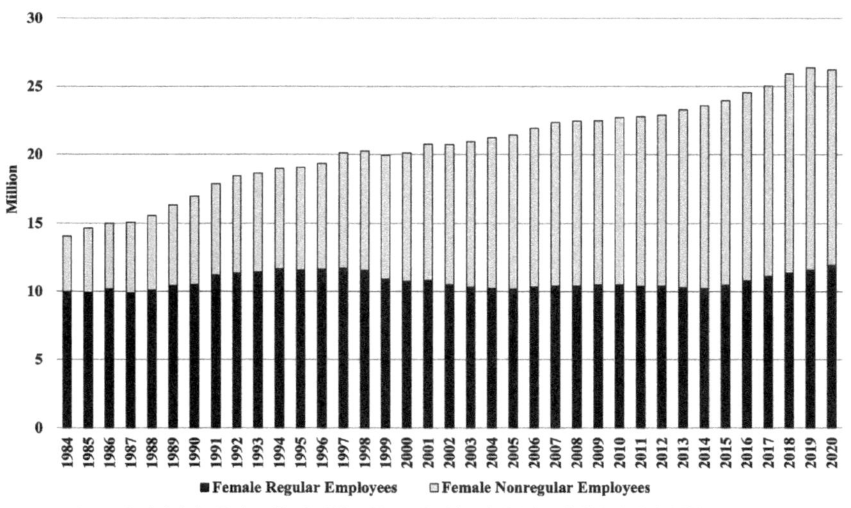

Source: Rōdō Seisaku Kenkyū-Kenshū Kikō, "Hayawakari Gurafu de Miru Chōki Rōdō Tōkei, II."

Figure 7.10. Number of Female Employees Differentiated by Employment Status, 1984–2020

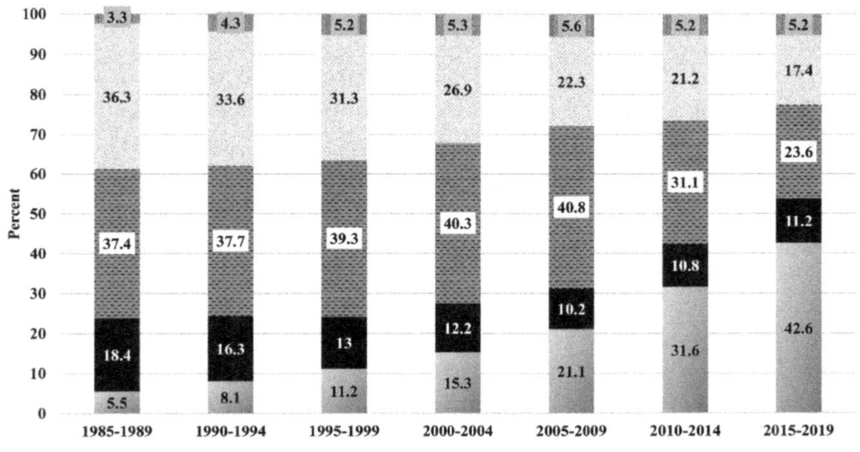

Source: Kokuritsu Shakai Hoshō-Jinkō Mondai Kenkyūjo, "Dai-16-kai," 67.

Figure 7.11. Employment Trajectory of Women after Birth of First Child, 1985–2019

United Kingdom. Also, while the number of women managers has increased (exceeding 10 percent in 2004), Japan still lags behind North America, Europe, and Southeast Asia. Indeed, in 2014, 42 percent of female managers at large firms were single while 15 percent were married with no children—suggesting that "talented women have been forced to choose between career and family, a factor that contributes to Japan's dropping fertility rate."[37]

Demographics, Diversity, and the Environment

Aging and Declining Fertility

Along with Japan's economic woes, demographics became an issue of major concern for the country's leaders throughout the Heisei era. The key demographic challenges facing the country have been the rapid increase in the elderly population, the declining birth rate, and the resultant transformation in the population profile. In the early 1990s, Japanese marveled at the centenarian twin sisters, Kin-san and Gin-san, who appeared in a popular television commercial. The pair were emblematic of increasing lifespan in Japan, which only continued to lengthen over the Heisei years. In 1990, Japanese men lived an average of 75.92 years and women 81.9, but by 2020, this had risen to 80.93 and 87.65, respectively. In turn, as figure 7.8 shows, the proportion of elderly people (over 65 years) in the population rose from 12 percent in 1990 to 29 percent in 2020. This figure is projected to rise to 38.8 percent by 2050.

Japan's increasing longevity evidenced the success of the country's health system and lifestyle and was a praiseworthy achievement in itself. But the growing number of elderly persons has been made problematic by a demographic trend at the other end of the life cycle: namely, the declining birth rate. As figure 7.12 shows, the total number of births and the fertility rate have been gradually declining since the second baby boom of the early 1970s—1973 being the last year that Japanese fertility rates exceeded the replacement rate of 2.07. The Heisei era began with the so-called 1.57 Shock of 1989, when the fertility rate dropped below its previous low in 1966, considered an inauspicious year for childbirth. The rate 1.57 was important because of the risks it posed for the future sustainability of the state and the economy. No country whose fertility rate has dropped below 1.50 has yet been able to push its rate above this again. Worse still, as figure 7.12 reveals, Japan's fertility rate continued to plummet, reaching a historic low of 1.26 in 2005 (only to recover somewhat to 1.36 by the end of the Heisei era).

The government did not embark on any substantive efforts to deal with declining birthrates until the late 1990s. The Basic Plan for the Reduction of the Declining Birthrate of December 1999 called for an expansion of daycare services and support

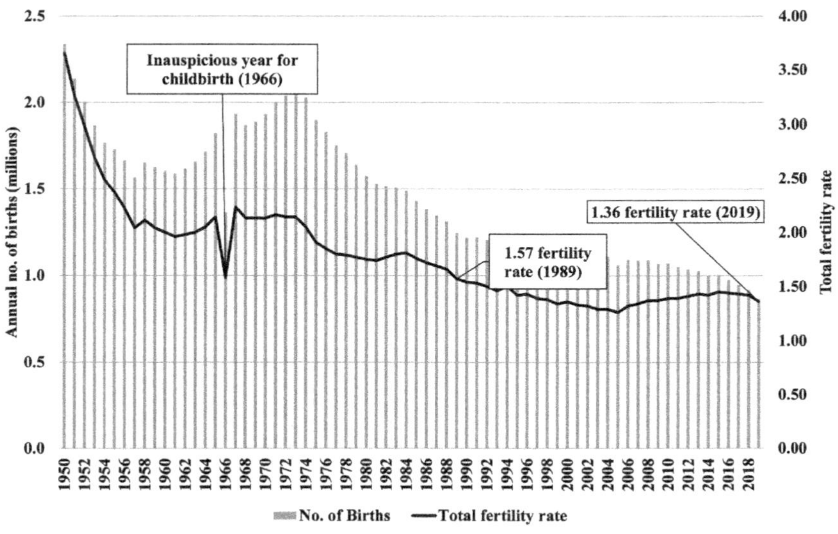

Source: Kōsei Rōdōshō, *Reiwa 2nen-ban*.

Figure 7.12. Annual Number of Births and Total Fertility Rate in Japan, 1950–2019

for childrearing through parental leave. This plan was followed in 2003 by the Law on Measures to Support the Development of the Next Generation mentioned earlier. Such initiatives arguably contributed to the slight improvement in the fertility rate by the end of Heisei, but it remains stubbornly below 1.5 and a great distance from the replacement rate of 2.07.

The causes of declining fertility are manifold, but later marriage, changing values, and growing precarity in employment have clearly been important factors. Uncertainty about the future has contributed to a reluctance among some young people to marry and have children. In 1990, the percentage of unmarried women under 30 years of age was 13.9 percent, but this figure had climbed to 34.6 percent by 2015. The percentage of people in the 50–54 age range who have never married also increased from around 5 percent for both men and women in 1990 to 16.5 percent for women and 26.6 percent for men in 2020.[38] For some in this group remaining single has been a life choice, but there are also many who refrain due to concerns about financial security. Other factors like the shortage of adequate daycare also affected the fertility rate and women's workplace participation. In 2016, a young mother caused a sensation with a blog entry reading "I couldn't get a daycare space for my child. Japan, go to hell!!" Left with no options, the woman had no choice but to leave her job. Opposition political parties subsequently brought the issue to the floor of the Diet, while a grassroots signature campaign presented 27,600 signatures to the MHLW, demanding remedial measures in support of working parents. In response, the government announced funding for more daycare centers, but there remained a shortage of trained daycare workers.

The combined effect of aging (figure 7.8) and declining fertility (figure 7.12) throughout the Heisei era has fundamentally transformed Japan's population profile. While the population over 65 years of age will remain relatively stable in the coming decades, the population under 65 is predicted to continue decreasing, resulting in numerous challenges for labor supply, economic productivity, public finances, and revenue streams for the health and pension systems. Social security expenditures, for example, continued to increase throughout the Heisei era, while the number of people making contributions to the system gradually declined. At the same time, the increasing elderly population exerted greater pressures on both the pension and health care systems—now supported by a declining working-age population. The problem of caring for this growing elderly population troubled policymakers and ordinary Japanese alike. With the decline in multigeneration households and the growth of double-income households, the "hidden asset" of the family (essentially women) providing eldercare began to collapse.[39] In 1989, 40.7 percent of households were still multigenerational, but this declined to 11 percent by 2017.

In turn, the number of elderly people living alone rose precipitously from 1.18 million in 1985 (80 percent women) to 5.93 million in 2017 (67 percent women).[40] The government responded in 1997 with the Long-Term Care Insurance Law, which facilitated the provision of in-home care services for the elderly to be funded by premiums paid by subscribers to the national health insurance system. On its launch in 2000, the system served some 2.18 million users. By 2015, this number had more than tripled to six million. Faced with a shortage of eldercare workers, the government began to explore solutions such as foreign workers and robots, but the reality remains that, for many, the only solution is to leave employment to look after infirm parents or parents-in-law. In 2017, close to one hundred thousand people were forced to make his choice—many of whom were women. Beginning in 1999, Japanese companies were required to provide up to ninety-three days of eldercare leave for regular employees, but this measure did little to help those needing to provide continuous care for elderly relatives.

Diversity: Foreign Workers and Minorities

Japan's demographic transformations and the looming challenges for business, government, and society have, in recent years, stimulated some discussion and limited reforms on the status of foreigners in Japan and the availability of pathways to long-term residency and citizenship. While millions of Japanese travelled overseas in the years of the bubble economy thanks to their newfound wealth, the country's economic superpower status also stimulated a reverse phenomenon of foreigners coming to Japan in search of employment. Throughout the Heisei era, the number of registered foreign residents increased from less than one million in 1989 to around 2.9 million by 2020. Of these, some 833,000 were Chinese nationals followed by Koreans, Vietnamese, Filipinos, and Brazilians of Japanese descent (fig. 7.13). The latter group was granted special status to work in Japan in 1990 to cover a labor shortage in the construction and other industries eschewed by young Japanese—the "three K" jobs: *kiken* (dangerous), *kitanai* (dirty), and *kitsui* (demanding). It was believed that the Nikkei (Japanese lineage) South Americans with their Japanese heritage would more easily assimilate into Japan, although finding a permanent place in Japan proved elusive for many of them.[41]

The Japanese government adopted a curious approach to these newcomer foreigners, treating them as temporary workers and interns—rather than as immigrants—due to popular concerns about the potential social disruption from permanent immigration. Emblematic of this approach was the system of foreign "technical trainees" established in 1993. This system essentially became a "back door" for temporary unskilled laborers to work in Japan without the usual rights of employees.[42] Only in 2018 did the government create a new visa category of

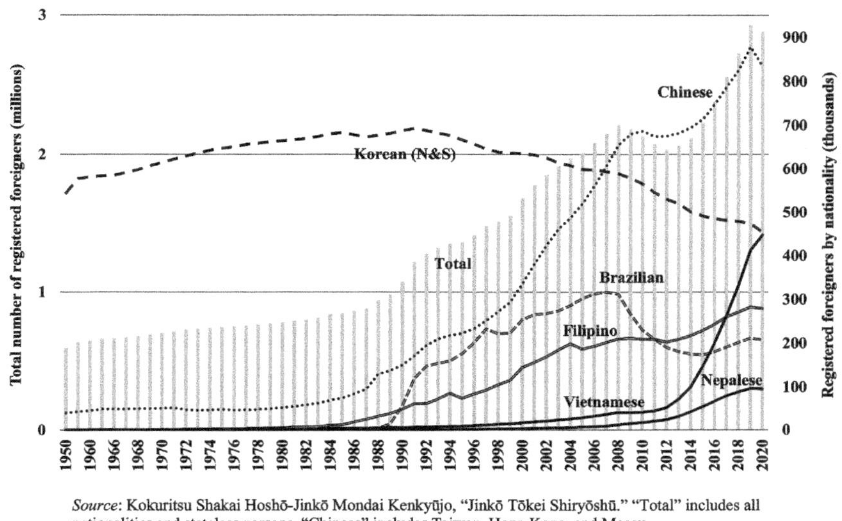

Figure 7.13. Trends in Total Number of Registered Foreigners and Major Foreigner Nationalities, 1950–2020

"specified skilled worker," which accepted manual workers in fourteen industries and offered them a pathway to permanent residency. This was the first time foreign manual labor had been attributed official status in the postwar era.[43] The reality Japan faces is that these workers are needed to perform essential services in agriculture, fisheries, manufacturing, retail, and a range of other sectors.

Alongside foreign workers, Japanese minority groups continued to occupy an ambiguous status throughout the post-bubble years, empowered on the one hand by the diffusion of new international norms, Japan's deeper involvement in international organizations, and transnational movements, but restrained on the other by enduring institutional and social barriers. In the Heisei era, the Japanese state responded to international pressure, transnational activism, and expectations surrounding its hosting of events like the 2020 Tokyo Olympics by passing nebulous laws for minorities that were "designed to diffuse international and domestic pressure" while "reinforcing . . . ideological norms of homogeneity and heteronormativity."[44] As before, laws relating to minorities often lacked enforceable penalties and tended to focus more on the "promotion of public awareness and understanding" than on securing rights or substantively addressing inequalities.[45]

The Ainu Cultural Promotion Law of 1997 and its successor, the Ainu Policy Promotion Law of 2019, clearly evidenced this logic. Even though the 2019 Law recognized the Ainu as an indigenous ethnic group, it did not grant them indigenous rights in terms of the UN Declaration on the Rights of Indigenous Peoples, which Japan had ratified in 2007.[46] This marginalization of minorities was further demonstrated in state legislation against hate speech, which became a particular problem for Japan's ethnic Korean minorities in the 2010s. With the Tokyo Olympics looming in 2020 and court decisions against groups such as the far-right Zaitaokukai (Association of Citizens Against the Special Privileges of the Zainichi Koreans), the government passed the impressively named Law to Promote Efforts to Eliminate Unfair Discriminatory Speech and Behavior against Persons Originating from Outside Japan (or simply, the Hate Speech Law) in 2016. Despite being a law to protect minority groups with roots in Japan from the prewar years, the implication of the law's title was that longtime resident Koreans are, in the end, foreigners. Moreover, directed as it is to "outsiders," the law provides no protection for other minorities like Ainu, Burakumin, or sexual minorities. Although Japan has supported UN resolutions opposing violence and discrimination against LGBT communities, as of this writing, the legal framework is still comparatively weak. In mid-2023, the Japanese Diet passed legislation to promote understanding of LGBT persons and protect them from "unfair discrimination." But this law only passed after the initial draft was watered down due to opposition from conservative lawmakers. Critics argue that the resulting law tacitly accepts certain forms of bigotry against LGBT groups.

Nonetheless, some progressive local governments—like Tokyo's Shibuya Ward—have begun to take proactive measures to support same-sex partnerships, indicating that change may be sprouting at the grassroots. Indeed, against the backdrop of complicated demographic challenges, new gender norms, growing numbers of resident foreigners, and the forces of globalization, the first decades of the new millennium convinced many Japanese—especially the young—of the need for reform in the outmoded mindsets and rigid institutions of the high-growth era. This very gradual awakening to the need for, and value of, diversity was undoubtedly one of the more positive trends in an often-demoralizing Heisei era.

Environmental Challenges

New environmental challenges confronted the Japanese people and their leaders over these decades. As an advanced nation, Japan now faced growing pressure internationally to assume greater responsibility for issues such as species conservation, waste management and reduction, and greenhouse gas emissions. More frequent environmental extremes and events like diminishing fish stocks, destructive typhoons, drenching rain belts, flooding rivers, devastating landslides, and record-setting heatwaves meant ordinary Japanese people could no longer ignore the looming crisis. As discussed in earlier chapters, thanks to concerted civic protest and litigation, in the late 1960s and 1970s, Japan reinvented itself from a polluted archipelago into a world leader in pollution reduction. While national policymaking slowed thereafter, throughout the 1970s and 1980s grassroots groups and local governments became extremely active in environmental initiatives, including recycling, organic food, and environmental protection.

Japan reemerged as a player in global environmental politics in the 1990s, to a degree in response to the country's reputation as a pollution exporter and cause of environmental degradation abroad, but also because some conservative politicians saw the environment as a relatively uncontroversial area to improve Japan's image as a voracious economic superpower snubbing its global responsibilities. In 1989, the Takeshita administration, together with the UN, convened the Tokyo Conference on the Global Environment and Human Responses toward Sustainable Development. It also announced a new package of environmental aid for developing countries, which was subsequently tripled at the UN Conference on Environment and Development (UNCED) in Brazil in 1992. This so-called green aid was aimed at helping countries solve their environmental challenges through technological innovation—especially technology provided by Japanese companies.[47]

Japan also took the lead in climate change initiatives during the 1990s. As host of the Third Conference of the Parties in 1997, Japan was instrumental in shaping the Kyoto Protocol, which operationalized the UN Framework Convention on Climate Change through commitments by industrialized countries to reduce greenhouse gas emissions. Subsequent governments, however, pulled back on these commitments, as the country failed to reach its reductions targets and vested interests weighed into environmental policymaking. The Fukushima nuclear disaster of 2011 proved to be another critical turning point as all of the country's reactors were stopped and Japan reverted to imported fossil fuels for its energy needs. Nuclear energy had been a critical element of Japan's carbon reduction strategy, so the disaster essentially pushed it in the opposite direction.

Not all was bleak for the environment during the Heisei era, however. Local governments and a burgeoning realm of environmental nongovernmental organizations (NGOs) advocated strongly for policy and social change to address the crisis. Learning from so-called transition towns in the United Kingdom, some localities in Japan began to implement transition initiatives for decarbonization at the grassroots, while prefectures like Tokyo and Saitama introduced carbon emissions trading schemes.[48] Cities like Kitakyushu—long identified with chronic industrial pollution—became models for environmental sustainability, attracting the attention of cities worldwide. At global forums like UNCED, NGOs including the Kiko Forum and the Citizens' Alliance for Saving Earth and Atmosphere advocated powerfully for substantive action on global warming and ozone depletion.[49] Japanese business also chimed in, as with the release of the Keidanren's Global Environment Charter for Japanese corporations in 1991. More recently, some of Japan's most prominent companies like Mizuho Financial Group, Softbank, Suntory Holdings, and Kyocera have joined with NGOs and other groups to establish the Japan Climate Initiative, whose stated aim is to "push for decarbonization from Japan."[50] More prosaically, in recent years, Japanese corporations (and government offices) have implemented "cool biz" initiatives, wherein employees are encouraged to wear more casual attire in the office and air conditioning thermostats are set higher in the hot months.

Of course, the energy-environment dilemma continues to confound Japanese citizens and leaders alike. While citizens may be more sensitive to the UN's Sustainable Development Goals and the urgent need to decarbonize, few are willing to pay higher prices for electricity. Faced with this dilemma, political leaders have once again begun to cautiously promote nuclear power as part of the solution in recent years. As noted earlier, public opinion—staunchly opposed to expanding nuclear power after Fukushima—also appears to be softening on the idea recently as electricity prices rise and emissions increase.[51] Given these challenges, the one certainty is that the environment will deeply shape politics and life in Japan for the foreseeable future.

The Abe Years: 2012 to 2019

Return of the LDP and Fading of the Opposition

While moves toward a more diverse, tolerant, and environmentally friendly society began to sprout during the Heisei era, high politics in Japan seemed to be stuck in a never-ending loop of LDP rule. DPJ governments had been undermined by self-inflicted wounds like the Futenma base relocation decision and political finance scandals. But the DPJ also suffered from being in government during the Triple Disaster of 2011 and the Senkaku/Diaoyu dispute with the PRC. The latter issue was very much on the minds of electors as they went to the polls for a general election in December 2012, with Prime Minister Noda facing a revitalized Abe Shinzō, who had recuperated from his illness and regained leadership of the LDP. Throughout the campaign Abe vowed that, if elected, his government would "reclaim Japan" (*Nihon o torimodosu*)—certainly from the incompetent DPJ, but also from external menaces to Japanese sovereignty like China and North Korea.

The election outcome was yet another landslide under the new electoral system, this time in favor of the LDP, which claimed 294 seats—almost tripling its 118 seats prior to the election. Conversely, the DPJ was decimated, falling from 230 seats to a mere 57. Making matters worse, seven DPJ ministers, including the chief cabinet secretary and minister of finance, were unceremoniously voted out of office. The results certainly represented a drubbing for the DPJ, but they were not evidence of an unequivocal electoral mandate for Abe and the LDP, despite the seeming landslide. The LDP and its coalition partner, the CGP, received fewer votes than the previous lower house election when they had suffered a massive defeat. In fact, the LDP was able to win with one million fewer votes overall and despite performing worse in both the SMDs and PR districts.

Several factors played into this result. First, prior to the election, the DPJ experienced internal turmoil as members left the party one after the other in opposition to Noda's support for the Trans-Pacific Partnership agreement and a hike in the consumption tax. With sixteen parties competing in the election, the DPJ's vote fragmented, opening a pathway to victory for Abe. Second, the LDP also benefited from carefully coordinated electoral cooperation with the CGP to maximize both parties' votes. And third, the significant drop in voter turnout—from 69.28 percent in 2009 to 59.32 percent in 2012—tended to favor the LDP with its strong organizational base. The same factors would help Abe in subsequent elections, making it possible for him to become Japan's longest serving prime minister without broad public support.

Following the election, the opposition was once again plunged into disrepair, with numerous phases of splits, mergers, and realignments. As in the past, opposition parties found it difficult—almost impossible—to coordinate electoral cooperation, let alone unification. The DPJ, which had always been home to great ideological extremes, finally split, with the progressive wing of the party forming the Constitutional Democratic Party (CDP) in 2017. With a coherent social democratic policy platform, the CDP grew slowly in subsequent elections, increasing from 55 seats in 2017 to 96 seats in 2021—still small compared to the LDP, but the largest opposition party in the lower house.

Abenomics

With the growing military presence of China in Northeast Asia and the ongoing threat from North Korea, Prime Minister Abe looked to transform the nation's security policy through new security frameworks and partnerships, increased defense spending, and easing of restraints on the activities of the SDF. As with his immediate predecessors, Abe continued the drive to put more power in the hands of the prime minister, notably through enhanced influence over senior bureaucratic appointments. Although more moderately expressed than in his previous term, Abe persisted with his nationalistic quest to break out of the "postwar regime." Molding positive public opinion around constitutional revision was at the core of this endeavor, but it also involved concerted efforts to silence critical voices in the media. In 2016, Abe's hawkish communications minister, Takaichi Sanae, even threatened to withdraw the licenses of "biased" television stations, while numerous high-profile television anchors critical of the government were quietly removed from their programs throughout the Abe years.[52]

But since the economy remained the primary concern for most Japanese, the realist Abe was compelled to fashion his own self-styled economic policy, known as "Abenomics." This policy revolved around Abe's so-called unbreakable "Three Arrows," an apocryphal metaphor borrowed from the samurai lord Mōri Motonari of the sixteenth century. In its initial formulation, the Three Arrows consisted of, first, monetary easing and zero or negative interest rates targeting an inflation rate of 2 percent; second, fiscal spending on public works to directly stimulate the economy; and third, structural reforms through deregulation, tax reform, and market liberalization to make the economy more open and competitive. In terms of outcomes, the inflation target of 2 percent proved elusive. Only in 2014 did Japan register inflation of 2.76 percent and, thereafter, the rate never exceeded 1 percent in the years until 2019, with negative inflation in 2016 and 2019. The second arrow of government spending was hardly new given the long (and tainted) history of LDP pork-barrel politics. What this arrow did result in, however, was a further deterioration in Japan's public finances. The third, and most difficult, arrow of structural reform was also largely unsuccessful. Regulatory hurdles for business remained prohibitively high and few effective measures were adopted to enhance the productivity declines caused by a dwindling labor force and an aging society.

Figure 7.14. Prime Minister Abe explains the "Three Arrows" of his Abenomics policy in Tokyo in June 2013. Courtesy of The Asahi Shimbun Company.

With little to show for this policy, Abe announced his "New Three Arrows" in 2015 based on, first, raising nominal GDP; second, raising the fertility rate through enhanced childcare support; and third, augmenting social security so that employees with elderly family members could continue to work. The New Three Arrows were clearly a response to popular frustrations with the neoliberal policies of the Heisei era. Abe attempted to buttress these arrows with glossy notions of "womenomics" and slogans like "creating a society in which women can shine" although, as noted earlier, many women remained in nonregular employment, the fertility rate continued to decline, the number of female managers stagnated, and Japan still ranked 116th out of 146 countries on the global gender equality index (2022).[53] Economic growth also remained sluggish throughout the Abe years, although his tenure did coincide with the second longest stretch of growth in the postwar era. After recording real GDP growth of 2.7 percent in 2013, the economy grew at less than 1 percent annually thereafter, with negative growth in 2014 and 2019.

Snubbing public opinion, Abe abandoned the DPJ promise to phase out nuclear power following the Triple Disaster, instead positioning it as a "critical source of baseload electricity" in his cabinet's Basic Energy Plan. Under Abe's energy vision, nuclear power would comprise 20 to 22 percent of Japan's energy mix by the year 2030, alongside renewables, LNG, oil, and coal. Needing thirty operational reactors to meet this goal, the Abe government began to push for plant restarts, which happened at the Sendai nuclear power plant in 2015 and the Takahama and Ikata plants in 2016. Abe also signed nuclear power agreements with Turkey and the United Arab Emirates in 2014 and India in 2017 to reinvigorate Japan's nuclear power export industry. As before, the hope was that nuclear power would partially insulate Japan from spikes in the international price of energy resources, while also helping the country meet its carbon emissions commitments.

Security and International Relations Under Abe

With the rise of a more muscular China and the continuing threat from North Korean ballistic missile testing and nuclear weapons, in the area of defense, Prime Minister Abe looked to further strengthen and enhance the security alliance with the United States through new ideas like the "Free and Open Indo-Pacific" concept and security frameworks such as the Quad, involving Australia, India, the United States, and Japan. Abe was eager to shed the low-posture Yoshida Doctrine for his own security philosophy based on "proactive pacifism," which built on earlier trends under Koizumi and others to expand the role of the SDF. The United States was highly receptive to such moves, which corresponded nicely with its vision of greater burden sharing among allies, especially in the containment of China.

Beginning in 2013, Abe set about creating the domestic framework for this security vision with several controversial pieces of legislation and cabinet decisions. In December

2013, the government passed the Law for the Protection of Specially Designated Secrets, which gave the state greater powers to restrict access to sensitive documents, provided harsher penalties for those breaching state secrets, and offered no protections to whistleblowers acting in the public interest. The law represented a significant retreat from freedom of information legislation passed in the Diet in 2001 and similar ordinances adopted by local governments nationwide. Despite protest rallies and low public support, the LDP used its numbers to push the legislation through the Diet.

The next major development came in mid-2014, when the Abe cabinet approved a change in the interpretation of the constitution to allow the exercise of collective self-defense. Under this reinterpretation, Japan would be allowed to use the SDF if the country itself or a closely-related country came under military attack and if certain conditions were met. This decision represented a fundamental reinterpretation of Japan's minimalist, self-defense security posture and became a lightning rod for later civic protest.

Following victory in the 2014 lower house election, the Abe government signed a new set of US-Japan Defense Guidelines, which expanded the requirement for Japan to provide military support for the United States in its global engagements. To support this agreement, in September 2015, the government passed or revised a handful of defense-related laws that officially allowed the SDF to engage in military actions with allies in areas other than Japan if there is a serious threat to the country. Japanese forces could now come to the aid of allies even if Japan itself is not directly under attack. Furthermore, an amendment to the Peacekeeping Operations Cooperation Law made it possible for SDF peacekeeping forces to offer protection to forces from other countries should they come under attack.

The new and amended laws drew criticism from legal scholars—including those consulted by the Abe government—as being fundamentally unconstitutional. Fierce opposition erupted both within and outside of the Diet, notably on July 14 and August 30 when upwards of 60,000 and 120,000, respectively, demonstrated around the Diet. Students, mobilizing under the banner "Students Emergency Action for Liberal Democracy" or SEALDs, played a major role in this opposition movement, actively using social media to mobilize participants and drawing on tropes from the Occupy Wall Street Movement in the United States and the Umbrella Movement in Hong Kong. Nonetheless, the LDP and CGP used their numbers to force the legislation through the Diet and the protests quickly waned.

Emboldened by this success, in a May 2017 interview in the *Yomiuri shinbun*, Abe set out his aim for revising the constitution by 2020 to coincide with the Tokyo Olympics and a "newly reborn Japan." Abe and conservatives wanted to significantly revise or even remove the war-renouncing elements of the constitution like Article 9, clarify the role of the SDF as a military, make the emperor the official

Figure 7.15. Citizens protest against the Abe government's defense-related laws outside the Diet on July 14, 2015. The signs read "We won't allow war" and "Don't destroy Article 9." Courtesy of The Asahi Shimbun Company.

head of state, and shift emphasis from civic rights to civic responsibilities. But ambivalent public opinion regarding constitutional revision meant that Abe would end his term with this deep-seated aspiration unfulfilled.

Relations with the Region

Relations with Japan's regional neighbors continued to be fragile during the Abe years, thanks to Abe's own brand of nationalism and the increasingly volatile geopolitics of Northeast Asia. Historical memory remained a lightning rod for controversy among Japan and its neighbors, particularly as the seventieth anniversary of the end of the Asia-Pacific War approached. On August 14, 2015, Chinese, Korean, and other Asian observers watched intently as the prime minister delivered his statement on live television. While careful to include much of the same language of earlier statements like Murayama's in 1995, Abe declared that the Japanese people must not be "predestined to apologize." With this hurdle cleared—albeit ambiguously—Abe met with the Chinese leader Xi Jinping in 2019 at the G20 summit in Japan. The two agreed to a summit in Japan in early 2020, indicating a possible improvement in relations. This meeting, however, would subsequently be cancelled due to the COVID-19 pandemic.

Relations with South Korea continued their tradition of volatile fluctuations. In 2015, Abe and the South Korean president, Park Geun-hye, reached a seemingly historic agreement on the "comfort women" issue. Japan agreed to pay one billion yen into a Korean foundation that would distribute funds to the surviving comfort women. In return, the South Koreans agreed that they would cease criticizing Japan about the issue, now considered to be finally resolved. Thereafter, both governments began to expand security cooperation, signing an agreement for the sharing of military intelligence in 2016. But relations began to sour again with the election of President Moon Jae-in in 2017. Moon agreed to abide by the comfort women agreement only if Abe offer a public apology—to which Abe refused, resulting in its collapse. Relations continued to deteriorate thereafter due to various irritations: a comfort women statue located near the Japanese embassy in Seoul, South Korean court verdicts against Japanese companies for wartime forced labor, South Korean naval vessels using fire control radar on SDF aircraft, and a nasty trade dispute between the two nations in 2019. Conversely, while official relations remained frosty, cultural exchanges between Japan and South Korea continued to expand through television dramas, music, cuisine, cosmetics, fashion, and tourism. All the while, transnational movements continued to pressure the Japanese government to deal with unresolved wartime issues.

Japan's relations with North Korea remained stalled under the Abe administration, much as they had been for most of the Heisei era with the brief exception of Koizumi's abductee diplomacy in the early 2000s. Throughout these years, North Korea continued to develop its missile and nuclear capabilities such that it was able to fire a ballistic missile over Japan in 2012, prompting the Japanese government to use its missile warning system for the first time. Thereafter, North Korea periodically launched missiles into the Sea of Japan and across the Japanese archipelago, encouraging prefectures like Akita in Japan's north to implement missile evacuation drills. All the while, Japan continued to push for a resolution to the abductee issue, but this too remained unresolved.

Further to the north, Japan's relations with Russia made little headway, despite Abe's continued entreaties to President Vladimir Putin for a resolution on the so-called northern territories issue. In 1993 a breakthrough looked possible when then-president Boris Yeltsin confirmed with the Japanese government that Russia would honor all earlier international agreements made by the former Soviet Union. Putin also initially promised to honor the 1956 agreement but thereafter continued to vacillate. Following Russia's invasion of Ukraine in 2022 and Japan's vocal condemnation of Putin, Russia declared Japan an "unfriendly country," even making provocative statements that Russia had legitimate claims over Hokkaidō and that it would conduct military exercises around strategically important areas, including the disputed Kuril Islands. These developments more or less eliminated any chance of a resolution to the northern territories issue during Putin's reign.

Such uncertainties and perceived threats from Japan's closest neighbors resulted in the Japanese government moving further away from the exclusively defensive principles of the Yoshida Doctrine in the years after Abe. Notably, in December 2022, the Kishida government announced an increase in Japanese defense spending from around 1 percent to 2 percent of GDP, along with revisions to key security documents. Together with Russia and North Korea, the government's national security strategy now unequivocally identified the PRC as the country's largest strategic challenge. Under the new spending, Japan would increase its preemptive strike capabilities through the development of long-range missiles and the acquisition of US-made Tomahawk cruise missiles, making it possible for the country to strike enemy bases preparing to attack Japan. Although Abe never realized his dream of constitutional revision, the evolution of national security policies and increase in defense spending moved Japan ever closer to his vision.

Prime Ministerial Power and the Detriments of Deference

Another defining feature of the Abe years was the continued concentration of power in the prime minister, coupled with various incidents exposing the abuse of this power. Following practices established under Koizumi, the Abe administration formulated all important economic policies in the Council on Economic and Fiscal Policy located in the CAO. High-ranking bureaucrats from relevant ministries involved in economic policymaking and other areas were seconded to work in either the CAO or CS. Such arrangements arguably reduced the influence of party policy specialists in LDP policy committees (i.e., PARC) in favor of the executive.

In a major revision to the National Public Service Law, the Cabinet Personnel Affairs Bureau was established in 2014 to oversee the appointment of all senior bureaucrats from the level of deputy director general upwards (roughly third from the top in the bureaucratic hierarchy). With control over these appointments, the CAO indirectly extended its influence over the career progression of all bureaucrats, arguably making them more sensitive to satisfying the demands of political leadership—especially the prime minister. Under Abe, this bureaucratic deference to political leaders intensified as bureaucrats began to engage in so-called *sontaku,* meaning to act in the interests of someone (i.e., the prime minister) without needing to be directed so.

In the latter years of his administration, Abe became embroiled in a series of scandals involving seeming favors granted by government agencies like the MOF, Ministry of Education, Culture, Sports, Science and Technology, and MHLW to Abe's friends and allies. In 2017, the media revealed that a branch of the MOF had sold land in Osaka to an associate of Abe, Kagoike Yasunori, at 14 percent of its market value. Kagoike was a rightist Abe supporter who planned to build an elementary school called the Moritomo Gakuen based on his philosophy of patriotic Japanist education. It was learned that Abe's wife had given speeches at Kagoike's kindergarten and was slated to become honorary principal of the new school. The fact that the MOF granted such a discount to an Abe associate raised suspicions. These were further heightened when it was revealed that MOF officials had ordered lower-ranking bureaucrats to alter documents concerning the sale, pushing a bureaucrat involved to suicide. Abe pledged to resign if his or his wife's involvement in the land sale could be established, but this was never shown, prompting many to describe the Moritomo affair as a classic case of bureaucratic *sontaku*. A similar scandal involving the education ministry's approval of a new veterinary school at the Okayama University of Science of the Kake Gakuen Group run by another Abe associate, Kake Kōtarō, surfaced around the same time. Finally, yet another scandal erupted in 2019 in which Abe supporters were seemingly preferentially invited to a publicly funded cherry blossom viewing party and their costs for the event partially covered from Abe's political war chest—arguably in contravention of electoral and political finance laws.

Abe's direct involvement in these scandals was never established, although they took a toll on public confidence in his government and his own health. Announcing a relapse of his medical condition, in September 2020 Abe resigned from the prime ministership, handing the reins of power to his chief cabinet secretary, Suga Yoshihide, who would be responsible for steering Japan through the early phase of the COVID-19 pandemic, including the delayed staging of the 2020 Tokyo Olympics in 2021.

Apart from some diplomatic successes, Abe's accomplishments were mixed at best. Economically, Abenomics arguably did very little for ordinary Japanese people, while his move to concentrate more power in the hands of the prime minister and cabinet appeared to promote new forms of structural corruption and coercion. So divisive a figure was Abe that, when Kishida Fumio assumed the prime ministership in October 2021, he called for greater cooperation and less division in politics and proposed a "new capitalism" based on equity and without "winners" and "losers." Nonetheless, Kishida's power depended on support from the large Abe faction.

The final chapter in Abe's contentious political career came with his shocking assassination while delivering an outdoor election speech for an LDP candidate in Nara Prefecture in July 2022. The assassin, Yamagami Tetsuya, was the disgruntled son of a member of the South Korean Unification Church—the so-called Moonies. Yamagami developed a grudge against the cult after it convinced his mother to donate the family's fortune, leaving him and his family poverty stricken. Unable to directly target church leaders, Yamagami decided to shoot Abe after seeing a congratulatory video that Abe had earlier sent to the church. After the shock of the assassination passed, it was revealed that Abe and over 180 out of the 379 LDP Diet members had connections with the Unification Church, which provided them with both campaign volunteers and voters. Stories of the church's fleecing of donations from unwitting members filled the media. Adding to the controversy, Prime Minister Kishida caused a storm of criticism when he announced that Abe would receive a state funeral costing taxpayers 1.66 billion yen. Even in death, Abe Shinzō continued to divide the Japanese. Thousands signed condolence registers and offered flowers, but just as many protested the use of public monies for the funeral.

The End of an Era: An Emperor Abdicates

In August 2016, Emperor Akihito released an unprecedented eleven-minute video announcing his desire to abdicate while still in relatively good health to ensure a smooth transition to the next emperor, his son Naruhito. Clearly alluding to the social and economic disruption leading up to Hirohito's death in 1989 (chap. 6), Akihito emphasized the great interruption caused when a sitting emperor falls ill at the end of his life. The only previous occasion Akihito directly addressed the nation was following the Triple Disaster of 2011, and no emperor had ever publicly announced his desire to abdicate. Conservatives in the LDP were hesitant about setting a precedent, agreeing only reluctantly to pass a one-time law permitting Akihito's retirement. Public opinion was overwhelmingly in favor of allowing the imperial couple to end their hectic public duties for a peaceful retirement.

Akihito was a popular emperor, untainted by the past as his father had been. He was seen very much as a "people's emperor" thanks to his public visibility and marriage to the commoner Shōda Michiko. Throughout their reign, Akihito and Michiko made a point of meeting the unfortunate and peripheralized in society, like Okinawans, victims of natural disasters, and Hansen's disease sufferers. Although somewhat restricted by his symbolic status under the constitution, throughout his reign Akihito also made efforts to express remorse to victims of Japan's previous war in Asia and the Pacific. In 1989, for example, he apologized to the Chinese premier, Li Peng, for Japan's wartime invasion of China. The following year he offered a similar expression of regret for the "unfortunate past" to the visiting South Korean president, Roh Tae-Woo. During a historic and controversial visit to China in late 1992, Akihito raised some eyebrows in Japan by unequivocally acknowledging that Japan had "inflicted great suffering on the people of China." In 2005, on the sixtieth anniversary marking the end of the Pacific War, the emperor and empress visited Saipan, which had been the site of fierce battles during the

Figure 7.16. Emperor Akihito addresses the nation on August 7, 2016, indicating his desire to abdicate. Courtesy of The Imperial Household Agency.

Asia-Pacific War. Along with visits to Japanese memorial sites, the imperial couple also made an unplanned stop to pay their respects at a memorial to Korean laborers who were forced to construct an airport on the island. Thereafter, Akihito visited memorials for the war dead in numerous countries, including Palau (2015) and the Philippines (2016). During his visit to the Philippines, Akihito once again expressed his remorse for the suffering caused to the people of the Philippines and other countries during the war.

The emperor also pushed back—albeit circumspectly—against jingoistic nationalism in the country, especially concerning Japan's Asian roots and connections. In a 2001 press conference on his birthday, the emperor expressed a sense of "kinship" with Korea, even pointing out that the mother of a Japanese emperor in the eighth century had Korean lineage.[54] Such actions ruffled the feathers of conservative nationalists, but they also revealed how—in some respects—the imperial house was thoroughly imbued with the pacifist, democratic values of postwar Japan. This was, no doubt, appropriate given that under the constitution the emperor is the "symbol of the State and of the unity of the People."[55]

Akihito's successor, his first son Naruhito, shared a similar trajectory to his father, having studied abroad (in the United Kingdom) and marrying outside the imperial family to a highly educated diplomat, Owada Masako. The new imperial couple experienced their own tribulations before assuming the throne, with Masako suffering from long-term depression, likely caused by the pressure to produce a male heir. The issue was eventually solved when Naruhito's younger brother, Fumihito, and his wife Kiko had a son in 2006. Nonetheless, an interesting debate unfolded over the possibility of changing the succession law to allow women to assume the throne. The birth of this male heir, Hisahito, ended this discussion in the short term, but it is likely to reemerge given contemporaneous debates about gender equity, inclusion, and diversity.

Naruhito ascended to the throne on May 1, 2019, marking the beginning of the new "Reiwa" era, meaning "beautiful harmony"—an admirable aspiration for a country facing much potential disruption due to precarity, rapid aging, low fertility, a declining workforce, strained public finances, rural decline, an environmental crisis, and a regional order undergoing momentous geopolitical change. Nonetheless, as noted at the outset of this chapter and as evidenced by the longer stretch of the country's postwar history, the Japanese people have consistently displayed a remarkable resilience in the face of destruction, tribulation, and disaster. They have built an advanced and complex economy and workers in many of their industries are among the most productive in the world. While state institutions certainly struggle under the weight of debt and growing social demands, Japanese medical care, education, and other social services have produced a healthy, long-lived, and cultivated populace. Finally, Japan's democratic institutions, while periodically compromised, flaunted, and abused, have survived the test of time, evidencing the commitment of the Japanese people to the fundamental values of liberal democracy written into the country's postwar constitution.

Epilogue

Whither the Postwar Era?

As described in the previous chapter, the historical narrative of this book ends in the midst of several domestic and international confluences. In May 2019, Emperor Naruhito ascended to the imperial throne following the abdication of his aging father, Akihito. The following year, 2020, marked the onset of the COVID-19 pandemic that prompted Japan—along with many other nations worldwide—to close its borders and institute widespread measures to limit the spread of the virus. People started living, working, and interacting in ways they never had before. Due to a relapse of his colitis, Prime Minister Abe resigned in late 2020 and was succeeded by his chief cabinet secretary, Suga Yoshihide. After a one-year delay due to the pandemic, in 2021, Tokyo hosted the Summer Olympics under a shield of COVID-19 countermeasures. Having overseen a relatively uneventful Olympics, Suga resigned in September 2021, handing over the prime ministership to Kishida Fumio, a long-term minister in the second Abe administration. Just as the nation was cautiously beginning to emerge from the pandemic in 2022, the assassination of former prime minister Abe while delivering an outdoor campaign speech in Nara sent shock waves around Japan and the world—as too did his expensive state funeral that riled many within Japan.

Whether or not the combination of imperial abdication, the pandemic, and the assassination signaled some kind of ending or transition is unclear and perhaps unlikely. Indeed, longer-term issues concerning demographics, government finances, and regional tensions persisted, even intensifying as the world entered a new period of instability and environmental crisis. These issues will probably be the most important in terms of historical change in the future.

Short of a satisfying and definitive finale then, it seems appropriate to complete this book with an exploration of some of the ideas historians and others have had regarding either the end of the postwar era or the conditions necessary to bring it to an end—if only as a window into the ways observers have tried to understand the significant watersheds of postwar Japan. Undoubtedly a function of its open-endedness, there is a long history of declarations of the end of the postwar era involving a colorful cast of historians, politicians, ideologues, and technocrats. As we saw, the EPA concluded in 1956 that the postwar era was finished because Japan now faced a competitive global economy without the support of its former American occupiers. In the early 1970s, Prime Minister Satō Eisaku declared that only with the return of Okinawa to Japanese sovereignty would the postwar era end—something he accomplished in 1972.

Historians likewise have proposed a variety of endings. In 1998, for example, Stephen Large and Laura Hein suggested that the postwar era finished in the early 1970s, not only because of Okinawa's return but also for economic reasons. According to Large, the Nixon Shocks and the reversion of Okinawa meant that US-Japan relations "would no longer be determined primarily by the postwar settlement dating from the Occupation years (1945–1952)."[1] Hein pointed to the First Oil Shock of 1973 that, by ending high-speed economic growth, resulted in "a new relationship" between Japan and the world economy, effectively ending "postwar Japan."[2] In a similar vein, the sociologist Yoshimi Shun'ya identifies the period from the late 1970s onward as the beginning of Japan's "post-postwar society" (*posuto-sengo shakai*). He identifies a number of significant changes at this time, such as the end of Japan's welfare state and rise of neoliberalism, the new forces of globalization, the shift from heavy industry to light industries and the service sector, the rise of nonregular employment, and a popular attraction to "fictions" versus the earlier pursuit of "dreams."[3] It is interesting, of course, that Yoshimi retains the word "postwar" in his naming of the new era beginning in the late 1970s.

Other historians have tentatively posited sometime just before or during the 1990s as the end of the postwar. Writing in the now-classic 1993 volume, *Postwar Japan as History,* Carol Gluck declared that "postwar Japan *is* history," and that "an end must be put, at long last, to *sengo.*"[4] In the same volume, Andrew Gordon asked, "Did a late postwar era, defined by the persistence of the postwar international system and the 'unfinished business' of World War II, both outside and within Japan, finally end with the close of the 1980s?"—to which he answered: "The temptation to answer yes is hard to resist."[5] Elsewhere in the early 1990s, Gluck spoke of the "post-postwar age" being "upon us" and, in 1997, she could write "as the postwar finally 'ends'."[6] As noted in this book, both the 1970s and 1990s were significant watersheds in postwar Japanese history and qualify as endings of sorts.

But what if the postwar era has yet to end? The fact that many Japanese and non-Japanese alike continue to use the term "postwar" suggests that at least some believe it has not ended. If so, what conditions would be required to produce that end? Some, like Michael Lucken, argue that the postwar era "will remain an essential chronological framework and an essential issue" until the country experiences "an event having a scope comparable to that of the Second World War."[7] Given the scale of destruction and human misery both suffered and inflicted by the Japanese during that event, one can only hope that such an ending does not eventuate. Thankfully, most historians offer less dramatic scenarios for the end of the postwar era. Writing in the first decade of the 2000s, Nakamura Masanori argued that the postwar era would finish when three international issues were resolved: the end of Japan's dependence on the United States, the resolution of the country's historical issues with Asian countries, and Japan's ascension to permanent membership on the UN Security Council while maintaining its pacifist constitution.[8] The rise of China economically and militarily coupled with an aggressive Russia in recent years, however, has made realization of the first and third of these preconditions seem highly unlikely.

Others, like Philip Seaton, only see an end to the postwar era when historical issues arising from the Asia-Pacific War are finally resolved. As Seaton explains, "Japan will have escaped its postwar when the history issue retreats from the political, popular and media arenas into the specialist arena of scholarly debate. This transition seems likely only with the passage of sufficient time and may yet take multiple generations."[9] For Paul Dunscomb the end of the postwar era hinges on both external approval and generational change. Externally, the Japanese will only be able to escape their "enduring psychological postwar" when they "can defend their legitimate interests regionally and globally, amend their Constitution to meet the needs of their democracy, conduct an autonomous foreign policy, memorialize their dead, and display patriotic pride in their nation, and when other nations *are prepared to let them do so*."[10] Generationally speaking, Dunscomb suggests that younger Japanese may eventually accept that "whatever happened in the past, the future will be different"—something which "becomes far more likely as the last of those with direct experience of these events pass from the scene."[11]

Reminiscent of Carol Gluck's 1993 proposition of "at least three *sengo*," Oguma Eiji has recently argued that we need to consider the end of the postwar era in terms of five postwars experienced since 1945.[12] In this conceptualization, some postwars may have already ended while others endure. For example, if the postwar era is understood as the material destruction after the war, then Oguma says the era ended in this sense in the late 1950s. In terms of the "destruction of international relations," the postwar did not end until relations were normalized with the PRC in 1972.[13] Territorially, Satō Eisaku declared the end of the postwar era on the reversion of Okinawa in 1972, but the persistence of territorial disputes with countries such as Russia, South Korea, and China, says Oguma, indicates an ongoing postwar era. If the period is understood in terms of "memories and traumas arising from that event," then, Oguma posits, "the era will not end until the generation that experienced the war dies out." Furthermore, "even if the generation with 'lived experience' of the war is gone, the era may persist if later generations inherit these memories."[14] Finally, if the postwar era is defined in terms of the 1947 constitution and the US-Japan Security Treaty, Oguma says that the postwar will not end until the constitution is revised or renewed and the security treaty is abrogated. Many conservatives have certainly subscribed to variations of this last perspective, like Nakasone Yasuhiro's "final settlement of the postwar" in the 1980s and Abe Shinzō's "escaping from the postwar regime" in the new millennium.[15] Oguma makes a fascinating comparison of Japan's postwar era with memory of the slave trade in the United States: just as memories of the slave trade may not recede in America until "discrimination disappears," Japan's postwar era may continue until "US military bases disappear."[16] Here Oguma comes close to the normative question of whether it is "good or bad" for Japan to remain in its "postwar" condition.[17]

Of course, it is worth reiterating that the technical challenge in determining the end of the postwar era is that, intrinsically, the period name only identifies a relatively clear starting point—unlike eras based on monarchical reigns, which have a clear end point on the death of the sovereign. As Eric Seizelet puts it, "The postwar was defined at the outset by the identification of a founding moment clearly situated in time, whereas no particular event, no objective fact, exists that would allow one to proclaim and date its ending."[18] Here postwar history faces the same lack of a precise end point as so-called contemporary history that covers roughly the same period (i.e., 1945 onward).

That being said, the notion of the "contemporary" may provide us with a hint about how Japan's postwar era will transition to something new. If contemporary history refers to the lives of people currently living, then, from a generational perspective, Japan's postwar era may begin to fade with the passing of the baby boomer generation who were born just after World War II. Just as that generation will slowly sink beneath the historical horizon, so too may Japan's postwar era—not forgotten, but duly positioned in the proximate yet unexperienced past. Over time, new challenges concerning demographics, the environment, technology, and geopolitics will also almost certainly render the overarching notion of the "postwar" obsolete. This process is no doubt well underway. As this book has shown, the richness of Japan's postwar history lies in the confluence of historical continuities with new challenges and concerns. It will be the ongoing interplay of these factors, old and new, that determines the fate of Japan's postwar era and the imagination of what follows.

NOTES

Introduction: Understanding Postwar Japan

1. Gluck, "'End' of the Postwar," p. 3.
2. Seaton, "Discourses of War and Peace," p. 327.
3. Dunscomb, *Japan Since 1945,* p. 61.
4. Gluck, "Introduction," p. xlv.
5. Gluck, "Introduction," p. xlv.
6. Gluck, "Introduction," p. xlv. See also Dunscomb, *Japan Since 1945,* pp. 61–62.
7. Gluck, "Past in the Present," p. 93.
8. Narita, *"Sengo" wa ikani katarareruka,* p. 9.
9. Green, "Periodization," p. 13; Toohey, "Cultural Logic," p. 209.
10. See, for example, Dower, *Empire and Aftermath*; Dower, *Japan in War and Peace*; Gordon, *Evolution of Labor Relations*; Gordon, *Fabricating Consumers*; Gordon, "Society and Politics," pp. 277–296; Johnson, *MITI and the Japanese Miracle*; Yamanouchi et al., eds., *Total War and Modernization.*
11. Gordon, "Society and Politics," p. 273.
12. Gordon, "Society and Politics," p. 273.
13. See Yamanouchi et al., eds., *Total War and Modernization.* For an influential discussion of the 1940s wartime system and its impact on postwar Japan, especially economically, see Noguchi, *1940nen taisei.*
14. Narita, "'Sengo shi' jojutsu," p. 220.
15. Narita, "'Sengo shi' jojutsu," p. 220.
16. Narita, "'Sengo shi' jojutsu," p. 221; Narita, *Kingendai Nihon shi,* p. 153.
17. Examples include: Handō, *Shōwa shi 1926–45*; Handō, *Shōwa shi sengohen*; Nakamura, Takafusa, *Shōwa shi 1: 1926–1945*; Nakamura, Takafusa, *Shōwa shi 2* [Note that both Handō and Nakamura's histories of the Shōwa era are divided into prewar and postwar volumes.]; Nakamura, Takafusa, *History of Shōwa Japan*; Gluck and Graubard, *Showa: The Japan of Hirohito*; Large, *Shōwa Japan.*
18. Gluck, "Introduction," p. liii.
19. Dunscomb, *Japan Since 1945,* p. 2.
20. Seaton, "Discourses of War and Peace," p. 328.
21. Seaton, "Discourses of War and Peace," p. 328.
22. Ōno and Banshō, "Hajime ni," p. 12.
23. Lucken, "Introduction," p. 3.
24. Gordon, "Conclusion," 462.
25. Green, "Periodization," pp. 14–15.

26. Green, "Periodization," pp. 14–15. For examples of how historians have subdivided the postwar era, see Gordon, "Conclusion," p. 449; Smith, Dennis B., *Japan Since 1945*; Mita, *Gendai Nihon*; Bailey, *Postwar Japan*; Allinson, *Japan's Postwar History*; Dunscomb, *Japan Since 1945*; Nakamura, Masanori, *Sengo shi*; Narita, *Sengo shi nyūmon*; Oikawa, *Mōichido yomu.*

Chapter 1: Japan Before 1945

1. See Gordon, *Labor and Imperial Democracy.*
2. Najita, *Hara Kei and the Politics of Compromise.*
3. Gordon, *Labor and Imperial Democracy,* p. 7.
4. Gordon, *Labor and Imperial Democracy,* p. 10.
5. Shōsetsu Nihon Shi Zuroku Henshū Iinkai, *Shōsetsu Nihon shi,* p. 246.
6. Shōsetsu Nihon Shi Zuroku Henshū Iinkai, *Shōsetsu Nihon shi,* p. 262.
7. Hokazono, *Nihon shi A,* p. 106.
8. Hokazono, *Nihon shi A,* p. 266.
9. Allinson, *Japan's Postwar History,* p. 6.

Chapter 2: Occupation and Recovery, 1945–1947

1. The original recording and the transcript of Hirohito's speech is available at the home page of the Japanese Imperial Household Agency, accessed October 7, 2024, https://www.kunaicho.go.jp/kunaicho/koho/taisenkankei/syusen/syusen.html. For an English translation see de Bary, Gluck, and Tiedemann, *Sources of Japanese Tradition*, pp. 1184–1185.
2. General Headquarters Supreme Commander for the Allied Powers, "SCAPIN-224."
3. Handō, *Shōwa shi sengohen,* pp. 22, 23.
4. Kajii, "Shokuryō kiki," p. 453.
5. Kajii, "Shokuryō kiki," p. 453.
6. Handō, *Shōwa shi sengohen,* p. 61.
7. Handō, *Shōwa shi sengohen,* p. 55.
8. Handō, *Shōwa shi sengohen,* p. 58
9. Handō, *Shōwa shi sengohen,* p. 59.
10. Narita, *Kingendai Nihon shi,* p. 151.
11. Hamai, "Dai-4-kō fukuin to hikiage," chap. 4, Kindle.
12. Handō, *Shōwa shi sengohen,* p. 21.
13. Narita, *Kingendai Nihon shi,* pp. 181–182.
14. Handō, *Shōwa shi sengohen,* p. 29.
15. Brands, *General vs. The President,* p. 11.
16. Acheson, "Memorandum for the President."
17. MacArthur, "Radio Broadcast to the Nation."
18. Handō, *Shōwa shi sengohen,* p. 42.
19. Fukunaga, "Dai-1-kō tennō," chap. 1, Kindle.
20. Fukunaga, "Dai-1-kō tennō," chap. 1, Kindle.
21. Kosaka, *100 Million Japanese,* p. 23.
22. Kosaka, *100 Million Japanese,* p. 23.
23. Fair, "Press Code for Japan."
24. Narita, *Kingendai Nihon shi,* p. 31.
25. Kosaka, *100 Million Japanese,* p. 34.

26. Matthews, "Politico-Military Problems in the Far East."

27. McFarland and Moore, "Basic Directive for Post-Surrender."

28. Allen, "Removal and Exclusion."

29. Akazawa, "Kōshoku tsuihō," p. 268.

30. Akazawa, "BC-kyū senpan," p. 769.

31. Takasugi, "Dai-5-kō Tōkyō saiban," chap. 5, Kindle.

32. This Rescript is available in English translation at "The World and Japan" Database: Database of Politics and International Relations," accessed October 7, 2024, https://worldjpn.net/documents/texts/docs/19460101.S1E.html.

33. MacArthur, "Incoming Classified Message."

34. MacArthur, "Incoming Classified Message."

35. Johnson, Nelson Trusler, "Secretary General."

36. Handō, *Shōwa shi sengohen,* p. 34.

37. Handō, *Shōwa shi sengohen,* p. 234.

38. Saito, *History Problem,* p. 22.

39. "Removal of Restrictions on Political, Civil, and Religious Liberties," also known as the (SCAPIN-93), October 4, 1945.

40. For the record of this meeting including the list of five major reforms, see Gaimushō, "Sōri 'Makuāsā' Kaidan."

41. Allen, "Rural Land Reform."

42. Miwa, "Zaibatsu kaitai," p. 331.

43. Miwa, "Zaibatsu kaitai," p. 332.

44. Masamura, *Zusetsu sengo shi,* p. 56.

45. Kubo, "Kyōshoku tsuihō," p. 178.

46. For the memorandum see Whitney, "Memorandum for the Supreme Commander."

47. These MacArthur notes are available online: "Three Basic Points Stated by Supreme Commander to be 'Musts' in Constitutional Revision," accessed January 20, 2023, https://www.ndl.go.jp/constitution/e/shiryo/03/072/072_002l.html.

48. Handō, *Shōwa shi sengohen,* p. 183.

49. Handō, *Shōwa shi sengohen,* p. 184.

50. Fukunaga, "Dai-1-kō tennō," chap. 1, Kindle.

51. "The Constitution of Japan," accessed January 20, 2023, https://japan.kantei.go.jp/constitution_and_government_of_japan/constitution_e.html; italics added.

52. Quoted in Narita, *Kingendai Nihon shi,* p. 165.

53. Quoted in Handō, *Shōwa shi sengohen,* p. 204.

54. Masataka, *100 million Japanese,* p. 68.

55. As quoted in "MacArthur Bans General Strike," *Sydney Morning Herald,* Saturday, February 1, 1947, 1, accessed January 20, 2023, https://trove.nla.gov.au/newspaper/article/27906152.

56. Quoted in Handō, *Shōwa shi sengohen,* p. 208.

57. Quoted in Handō, *Shōwa shi sengohen,* p. 209.

Chapter 3: The Age of Politics, 1948–1960

1. *Yomiuri shinbun,* November 15, 1951.

2. Royall, "Address by the Honorable Kenneth C. Royall."

3. NSC 13/2 was based on Kennan's report after visiting MacArthur. This report was then formalized by the State Department and approved by the National Security Council. See National Diet Library, Japan, "Report by the National Security Council on Recommendations with Respect to US Policy toward Japan (NSC 13/2)."

4. Nakamura, Masanori, *Sengo shi,* p. 61.

5. Handō, *Shōwa shi sengohen,* p. 279.

6. Gordon, *Modern History of Japan,* pp. 248–249.

7. Shōji, "Dai-10-kō Chōsen sensō to Nihon," chap. 5, Kindle.

8. Oikawa, *Mōichido yomu,* p. 62.

9. Morris-Suzuki, "Purorōgu senkyūhyaku gojūnen-dai," p. 8.

10. Handō, *Shōwa hi sengohen,* p. 300.

11. Handō, *Shōwa shi sengohen,* p. 301.

12. Kosaka, *100 Million Japanese,* p. 107.

13. Narita, *Kingendai Nihon shi,* p. 206.

14. Handō, *Shōwa shi sengohen,* p. 347.

15. For the treaty see Ministry of Foreign Affairs of Japan, "Japan-U.S. Security Treaty," accessed January 24, 2023, https://www.mofa.go.jp/region/n-america/us/q&a/ref/1.html.

16. Nishikawa, Jun, "70-nendai Ajia to Nihon," p. 37.

17. Quoted in LaFeber, *Clash,* p. 298.

18. Oikawa, *Mōichido yomu,* p. 85.

19. Smith, *Japan Since 1945,* p. 60.

20. On the developmental state see Chalmers Johnson, *MITI and the Japanese Miracle.*

21. Komiya, "Dai-17-kō gojūgonen taisei," chap. 17, Kindle.

22. Quoted in Murai, Tetsuya, "Dai-8-kō Yoshida Shigeru naikaku," ch. 8, Kindle.

23. Oikawa, *Mōichido yomu,* p. 90.

24. Kawana, "Dai-16-kō Sunagawa jiken," chap. 16, Kindle.

25. Kojima, "'Shindemoii' sonmin 700-nin."

26. Kawana, "Dai-16-kō Sunagawa jiken," chap. 16, Kindle.

27. See the section titled "Ketsugo" in Keizai Kikaku Chō, "Shōwa 31nen: Nenji keizai hōkoku."

28. Nakano, Yoshio, "Mōhaya sengo dewanai," p. 58.

29. Murakami, "Sengo Nihon ni okeru shuyō," p. 44.

30. Masamura, *Zusetsu sengo shi,* p. 220.

31. Takeda, *Kōdo seichō,* p. 85.

32. Shibagaki, *Shōwa no rekishi 9,* p. 225.

33. Amemiya, *Senryō to kaikaku,* p. 183.

34. Muchaku, *Yamabiko gakkō.*

35. Narita, *Kingendai Nihon shi,* p. 240.

36. Narita, *Kingendai Nihon shi,* p. 241.

37. Shibagaki, *Shōwa no rekishi,* pp. 261–263.

38. Shibagaki, *Shōwa no rekishi,* p. 246.

39. Shibagaki, *Shōwa no rekishi,* p. 247.

40. Nakamura, Masanori, *Sengo shi,* pp. 80–81; Gordon, *Modern History of Japan,* pp. 260–261.

41. Shibagaki, *Shōwa no rekishi,* p. 256.

Chapter 4: The Age of the Economy

1. "Mata *kowaku*-naru keisatsukan," pp. 31–35.
2. There is debate over whether de Gaulle actually made this remark. See Itō, *Ikeda Hayato to sono jidai,* p. 187.
3. Handō, *Shōwa shi sengohen,* p. 453.
4. Macrae, "Consider Japan," pp. 787–819.
5. Data drawn from Knoema, "Historical GDP Per Capita by Country."
6. Fukui, *Ima okiteiru,* chap. 4, Kindle.
7. Fukui, *Ima okiteiru,* chap. 4, Kindle.
8. Oikawa, *Mōichido yomu,* p. 137.
9. Miyamoto, *Shōwa no rekishi,* p. 107.
10. Later just over three hours and, more recently, two-and-a-half hours.
11. Miyamoto, *Shōwa no rekishi,* p. 110.
12. Smith, Dennis B., *Japan Since 1945,* p. 112.
13. Kosaka, *100 Million Japanese,* p. 220.
14. Keizai Kikaku Chō, "Shōwa 52nen nenji keizai hakusho."
15. Smith, Dennis B., *Japan Since 1945,* p. 112.
16. Nakamura, Masanori, *Sengo shi,* p. 91; Gordon, *Modern History of Japan,* p. 256.
17. *Keiretsu* also formed along supply chains and in the retail sector.
18. Bailey, *Postwar Japan,* p. 92.
19. Nihon Bōeki Kai, *Enerugī o shirō!*
20. Takeda, *Kōdo seichō,* p. 99.
21. Data from Japanese Cabinet Office public opinion surveys on national life (Kokumin Seikatsu ni kansuru Yoron Chōsa), accessed March 2, 2023, https://survey.gov-online.go.jp/index-ko.html.
22. Chiavacci, "From Class Struggle," pp. 10–11.
23. Other surveys showed a greater variability between the 1950s, 1960s, and 1970s. See Gordon, *Modern History of Japan,* p. 276.
24. The "To hell with GNP" series was later published as a book: Asahi Shinbun Keizai Bu, *Kutabare GNP.*
25. See Nakane, *Japanese Society*; Aida, *Āron shūyōjo.*
26. These statistics are sourced from Rōdō Seisaku Kenkyū-Kenshū Kikō, "Zu 2–1 rōdō sōgi."
27. Garon and Mochizuki, "Negotiating Social Contracts," pp. 145–166.
28. Gordon, *Modern History of Japan,* p. 291.
29. Nakamura, Masanori, *Sengo shi,* 88; and Kawamura, "Nenpu: Sengo Nihon," p. 122.
30. Figures drawn from Japanese government *Kokusei chōsa* (population census) for relevant years; accessed March 5, 2023, https://www.e-stat.go.jp/stat-search/files?page=1&toukei=00200521.
31. Oikawa, *Mōichido yomu,* p. 104.
32. Nōrin Suisan Shō, "Kome o meguru."
33. Yamashita, "Naze nōka no shotoku."
34. Kosaka, *100 Million Japanese,* pp. 248–249.
35. Keizai Kikaku Chō, "Shōwa 34nen neniji keizai hōkoku."
36. Takeda, *Kōdo seichō,* p. 108.
37. Takeda, *Kōdo seichō,* p. 107.
38. Naikakufu, "Tokushū 'kōtsū anzen."

39. Miyamoto, *Shōwa no rekishi,* p. 84.
40. Data for 1970 sourced from Kokuritsu Kenkō-Eiyō Kenkyūjo, "Kokumin eiyō no genjō."
41. Miyamoto, *Shōwa no rekishi,* p. 82.
42. Shutsunyūkoku Zairyū Kanri Chō, "Shutsunyūkoku kanri tōkei hyō."
43. Zaimushō Kanzei Kyoku, "Zaimushō bōeki tōkei."
44. See Japanese Government e-Stat portal, accessed March 5, 2023, https://www.e-stat.go.jp/dbview?sid=0003147040.
45. Kosaka, *100 Million Japanese,* p. 256.
46. Ishikawa and Yamaguchi, *Sengo seiji shi,* p. 109.
47. Ishikawa and Yamaguchi, *Sengo seiji shi,* p. 101.
48. Keizai Kikaku Chō, "Shōwa 42nen nenji keizai hōkoku."
49. Kosaka, *100 Million Japanese,* p. 250.
50. Miyamoto, *Shōwa no rekishi,* pp. 209–210.
51. Miyamoto, *Shōwa no rekishi,* pp. 212–213.
52. Ishimure, *Paradise in the Sea of Sorrow*; Smith and Smith, *Minamata.*
53. Ishikawa and Yamaguchi, *Sengo seiji shi,* p. 114; Narita, *Kingendai Nihon shi,* p. 322.
54. Nakamura, Masanori, *Sengo shi,* p. 122.
55. Kosaka, *100 Million Japanese,* p. 232.
56. Lynn, "Systemic Lock," p. 64.

Chapter 5: Japan, the Economic Superpower

1. Ito and Hoshi, *Japanese Economy,* p. 105.
2. "Joint Communique."
3. "Joint Communique."
4. Miyamoto, *Shōwa no rekishi,* p. 373.
5. Ishikawa and Yamaguchi, *Sengo no seiji shi,* p. 124.
6. Ishikawa and Yamaguchi, *Sengo no seiji shi,* p. 127.
7. Smith, Dennis B., *Japan Since 1945,* p. 126.
8. Miyamoto, *Shōwa no rekishi,* p. 374.
9. Miyamoto, *Shōwa no rekishi,* pp. 418–419.
10. Based on production-line workers in manufacturing industries. See Rōdōshō, "Shōwa 62nen."
11. Organisation for Economic Co-Operation and Development, *OECD Employment Outlook 1991.*
12. Bank of Japan, "Basic Discount Rate and Basic Loan Rate."
13. Miyamoto, *Shōwa no rekishi,* p. 420.
14. Nihon Jidōsha Kōgyō Kai, "Active Matrix Database System."
15. Inoue, "Heisei 24nen keizai sensasu."
16. Zaimushō Kanzei Kyoku, "Zaimushō bōeki tōkei."
17. Shigen Enerugī Chō, "Heisei 28nendo."
18. Zenkoku Chikyū Ondanka Bōshi Katsudō Suishin Sentā, "4–03 Nihon."
19. Nishina, "Jinsei hyakunen jidai."
20. Bailey, *Postwar Japan,* p. 161.
21. Narita, *Kingendai Nihon shi,* p. 379.
22. Quoted in Oguma, *Heisei shi,* pp. 37–38.

23. LeBlanc, *Bicycle Citizens.*
24. On the Japanese women's liberation movement see Shigematsu, *Scream from the Shadows.*
25. On this movement see Ruoff, "Mr. Tomino Goes to City Hall," pp. 22–33.
26. See Avenell, *Asia and Postwar Japan*; and Avenell, *Transnational Japan.*
27. See Avenell, *Transnational Japan.*
28. Yamamoto, "Han-kakuheiki," p. 102.
29. Yamamoto, "Han-kakuheiki," p. 105.
30. Fujiawara, *Nihonjin no heikinchi,* p. 32.
31. Hatakenaka, "Gurumeka," p. 71.
32. Hatakenaka, "Gurumeka," pp. 71–72.
33. Hatakenaka, "Gurumeka," p. 74.
34. Yoshimi, *Posuto sengo,* pp. 138–139.
35. Miyamoto, *Shōwa no rekishi,* p. 431.
36. Miyamoto, *Shōwa no rekishi,* p. 431.
37. Sugita, "Purorōgu," p. 5.
38. Kariya, "Purorōgu," p. 4.
39. Narita, *Kingendai Nihon shi,* p. 366.
40. Ishikawa and Yamaguchi, *Sengo seiji shi,* p. 148.
41. Ishikawa and Yamaguchi, *Sengo seiji shi,* p. 154.
42. Ito and Hoshi, *Japanese Economy,* p. 275.
43. Ishikawa and Yamaguchi, *Sengo seiji shi,* p. 155.
44. Farrell, "Japanese Foreign Direct Investment," pp. 4–5.
45. Zaimushō Kanzei Kyoku, "Zaimushō bōeki tōkei."
46. Data compiled from Zaimushō Kanzei Kyoku, "Yushutsunyū no suii."
47. Data sourced from Organisation for Economic Co-Operation and Development, "Official Development Assistance (ODA)."
48. Constantino, *Second Invasion.*
49. Data sourced from Zaimushō Kanzei Kyoku, "Yushutsunyū no suii."
50. See Balz, "Auto Makers Criticize"; and Burstein, *Yen!: Japan's New Financial Empire.*
51. Oikawa, *Mōichido yomu,* p. 163.
52. Ito and Hoshi, *Japanese Economy,* p. 577.
53. Interestingly, Morita's essays were not contained in the English translation—perhaps a reflection of Sony's significant commercial interests in the United States.
54. Tokuda, "Shinai zen'ikiteki."
55. Colombo, "Japan's Bubble Economy of the 1980s"; and Impoco, "Life After the Bubble."

Chapter 6: The 1990s

1. Nihon Keizai Shinbunsha, *Reiwa ni tsunagu,* p. 16.
2. Nihon Keizai Shinbunsha, *Reiwa ni tsunagu,* p. 14.
3. Ito and Hoshi, *Japanese Economy,* p. 145.
4. Oikawa, *Mōichido yomu,* p. 188.
5. Nakamura, Masanori, *Sengo shi,* p. 201.
6. Konoe, *Politics of Financial Markets,* pp. 119–120.
7. Nihon Keizai Shinbunsha, *Reiwa ni tsunagu,* p. 53.
8. Nihon Keizai Shinbunsha, *Reiwa ni tsunagu,* p. 18.

9. Smith, *Japan Since 1945*, p. 153.
10. Nihon Keizai Shinbunsha, *Reiwa ni tsunagu*, p. 29.
11. Nakamura, Masanori, *Sengo shi*, p. 195.
12. Midford, "China Views," p. 124.
13. Midford, "China Views," p. 124.
14. Hiraishi, "Asia Boom," pp. 27–28.
15. Kobayashi, "Sai-Ajiaka," pp. 44–46.
16. Mahathir and Ishihara, *"NO" to ieru Ajia*.
17. Funabashi, *Ajia Taiheiyō fyūjon*.
18. Chinkin, "Women's International Tribunal," pp. 335–341.
19. For this statement, see Chief Cabinet Secretary, "Issues Regarding History."
20. Nakamura, Masanori, *Sengo shi*, p. 228.
21. Murayama, "Prime Minister's Address to the Diet."
22. Nakamura, Masanori, *Sengo shi*, p. 229.
23. Nakano, Koichi, "Rightward Shift," p. 39.
24. Nicchūkan 3goku Kyōtsū Rekishi Kyōzai Iinkai, *Mirai o hiraku rekishi*.
25. Narita, *Kingendai Nihon shi*, p. 392.
26. Yoshimi, *Posuto sengo*, pp. 162–163.
27. Nihon Keizai Shinbunsha, *Reiwa ni tsunagu*, p. 251.
28. Iida, "Intānetto zen'ya," p. 148.
29. Iida, "Intānetto zen'ya," p. 150.
30. World Bank Group, "Individuals Using the Internet."
31. Yoshimi, *Heisei jidai*, pp. 158–159.
32. Galbraith, "*Evangelion* Boom," pp. 234–235.

Chapter 7: Japan in the New Millennium

1. Narita, *Kingendai Nihon shi*, p. 409.
2. Nihon Keizai Shinbunsha, *Reiwa ni tsunagu*, p. 28.
3. Onishi, "Koizumi Exits Office," p. A6.
4. Yoshimi, *Heisei jidai*, p. 102.
5. Gaunder, *Japanese Politics*, p. 64.
6. Yoshimi, *Heisei jidai*, p. 107.
7. *Asahi Shinbun*, "Shinsai no shisha 1man-5900nin."
8. Shōbōchō, *Higashi Nihon daishinsai*.
9. Fukushima Minpō, "Dēta de miru."
10. Japan Center for Economic Research, "Accident Cleanup Costs."
11. Kingston, "Tumultuous Finale," p. 332.
12. Kingston, "Tumultuous Finale," p. 332.
13. Nihon Keizai Shinbunsha, *Reiwa ni tsunagu*, p. 166.
14. See Japan Times, "Majority in Japan Backs Nuclear Power"; and Japan Times, "Poll Shows Close to 50%."
15. Nikkei Staff Writers, "Japan PM Kishida." As of September 2023, twelve reactors had been restarted, although two were offline.
16. International Atomic Energy Agency, "IAEA Committed to Monitor."
17. Katz, "Heisei Economy," p. 116.

18. McGray, "Japan's Gross National Cool," pp. 44–45.
19. McGray, "Japan's Gross National Cool," p. 47.
20. Iwabuchi, "Pop-culture Diplomacy," p. 423.
21. Suter, "Manga, National Identity," p. 317.
22. See "What is Cool Japan Fund?," https://www.cj-fund.co.jp/en/about/cjfund.html.
23. Kokudo Kōtsūshō, *Kankō hakusho,* p. 11.
24. Arai, "Nihon no kokusai," p. 20.
25. Arai, "Nihon no kokusai," p. 20.
26. Tachibana, *Nihon no keizai.*
27. Niitsu, "Nihon wa byōdō."
28. Honda, "Wakamono no konnan," p. 141.
29. Yoshimi, *Heisei jidai,* p. 152.
30. Organisation for Economic Co-operation and Development (OECD), "Poverty Rate."
31. Abe, "Hinkonritsu kara miru."
32. Recruit Co. Ltd., "Dai-37-kai."
33. Akagi, "Maruyama Masao," pp. 53–59.
34. Nihon Keizai Shinbunsha, *Reiwa ni tsunagu,* p. 180.
35. Minashita, "'Heibon to futsū'," p. 91.
36. Kokuritsu Shakai Hoshō-Jinkō Mondai Kenkyūjo, "Dai-16-kai," p. 68.
37. Katz, "Heisei Economy," pp. 123–124.
38. Sōmushō Tōkei Kyoku, "Reiwa 2nen," pp. 29–30.
39. Nihon Keizai Shinbunsha, *Reiwa ni tsunagu,* p. 270.
40. Nihon Keizai Shinbunsha, *Reiwa ni tsunagu,* p. 271.
41. After the GFC, the Japanese government began actively subsidizing hundreds of thousands of Nikkei South Americans to return home.
42. Liu-Farrer, "Japan's Immigration," p. 145.
43. Liu-Farrer, "Japan's Immigration," p. 146.
44. Tin Tin Htun, "Preserving the Status Quo," p. 176.
45. Tin Tin Htun, "Preserving the Status Quo," p. 176.
46. Tin Tin Htun, "Preserving the Status Quo," p. 167.
47. Reimann, "Japan and the Environment," p. 626.
48. Reimann, "Japan and the Environment," p. 637.
49. Avenell, *Transnational Japan,* p. 182.
50. See "Japan Climate Initiative," accessed February, 16, 2025, https://japanclimate.org/english/.
51. See "Yomiuri/Waseda University Opinion Poll: 58% 'Support' Restarting Nuclear Power Plants, 39% 'Opposed,' First Time Support and Opposition Have Reversed," accessed February, 16, 2025, https://www.yomiuri.co.jp/election/yoron-chosa/20220824-OYT1T50195/.
52. McNeill and Tanaka, "Still Half Free," p. 104.
53. Nippon.com, "Japan Ranks 116th."
54. Saaler, "Heisei Historiography," p. 291.
55. "Constitution of Japan," accessed March 7, 2023, https://japan.kantei.go.jp/constitution_and_government_of_japan/constitution_e.html.

Epilogue: Whither the Postwar Era?

1. Large, "General Introduction," p. 2.
2. Quoted in Large, "General Introduction," p. 2.
3. Yoshimi, *Posuto sengo,* p. ix.
4. Gluck, "Past in the Present," pp. 94–95; italics in the original.
5. Gordon, "Conclusion," p. 463.
6. Gluck, "Introduction," p. lvii; Gluck, "'End' of the Postwar," p. 23.
7. Lucken, "Introduction," p. 4.
8. Nakamura, Masanori, *Sengo shi,* pp. 286–288.
9. Seaton, "Discourses of War and Peace," p. 328.
10. Dunscomb, *Japan Since 1945,* p. 69; italics in the original.
11. Dunscomb, *Japan Since 1945,* p. 73.
12. Gluck, "Past in the Present," p. 93.
13. Oguma, "Postwar in the Post-Cold War," p. 347.
14. Oguma, "Postwar in the Post-Cold War," p. 347.
15. Oguma, "Postwar in the Post-Cold War," p. 347.
16. Oguma, "Postwar in the Post-Cold War," p. 360.
17. Lucken, "Introduction," p. 2.
18. Seizelet, "Postwar," p. 14.

Bibliography

Abe, Aya. "Hinkonritsu kara miru josei no jōkyō: 1985–2018." Accessed March 7, 2023. https://www.gender.go.jp/kaigi/kento/Marriage-Family/5th/pdf/3.pdf.

Abel, Jessamyn R. *Dream Super-Express: A Cultural History of the World's First Bullet Train*. Stanford, CA: Stanford University Press, 2022.

Acheson, Dean. "Memorandum for the President, Subject: Authority of the Supreme Commander for the Allied Powers," September 13, 1945. In *Foreign Relations of the United States: Diplomatic Papers, 1945, The British Commonwealth, The Far East,* vol. 6, edited by John P. Glennon, N. O. Sappington, Laurence Evans, Herbert A. Fine, John G. Reid, and Ralph R. Goodwin, document 490. Accessed January 20, 2023. https://history.state.gov/historicaldocuments/frus1945v06/d490.

Aida, Yūji. *Āron shūyōjo: Seiō hyūmanizumu no genkai.* Tokyo: Chūkō Shinsho, 1962.

Akagi, Tomohiro. "'Maruyama Masao' o hippatakitai—31sai, furītā. Kibō wa, sensō." *Ronza* 140 (2007): 53–59.

Akazawa, Shirō. "BC-Kyū senpan." In *Sengoshi daijiten zōho shinban,* edited by Sasaki Takeshi, Tsurumi Shunsuke, Tominaga Ken'ichi, Nakamura Masanori, and Masamura Kimihiro, p. 769. Tokyo: Sanseidō, 2005.

———. "Kōshoku tsuihō." In *Sengoshi daijiten zōho shinban,* edited by Sasaki Takeshi, Tsurumi Shunsuke, Tominaga Ken'ichi, Nakamura Masanori, and Masamura Kimihiro, p. 268. Tokyo: Sanseidō, 2005.

Allen, H. W. "Removal and Exclusion of Undesirable Personnel from Public Office." SCAPIN-550, January 4, 1946. Accessed January 20, 2023. https://dl.ndl.go.jp/info:ndljp/pid/9885619.

———. "Rural Land Reform." SCAPIN-411, December 9, 1945. Accessed January 20, 2023. https://dl.ndl.go.jp/info:ndljp/pid/9885478.

Allinson, Gary D. *Japan's Postwar History.* Ithaca, NY: Cornell University Press, 2004.

Amemiya, Shōichi. *Senryō to kaikaku (shirīzu Nihon kingendai shi 7).* Tokyo: Iwanami Shoten, 2008.

Arai, Naoki. "Nihon no kokusai kankō seisaku no hensen to dōkō: Korona shūsokugo no jizoku kanōna inbaundo kankō shinkō ni mukete." *Nara kenritsu daigaku kenkyū kihō* 32, no. 1 (2021): 1–40.

Asahi Shinbun. "Shinsai no shisha 1man-5900nin, 2523nin ga fumei mimoto hanmei wa 1nen de 3nin." *Asahi shinbun dejitaru,* March 9, 2022. Accessed March 7, 2023. https://www.asahi.com/articles/ASQ396J9CQ39UTIL02H.html.

Asahi Shinbun Keizai Bu. *Kutabare GNP: Kōdo keizai seichō no uchimaku.* Tokyo: Asahi Shinbunsha, 1971.

Asai, Yoshio. "1950-nendai no tokuju ni tsuite (1)." *Seijō daigaku keizai kenkyū* 158 (2002): 219–266.

Atkins, E. Taylor. *A History of Popular Culture in Japan: From the Seventeenth Century to the Present.* 2nd ed. London: Bloomsbury, 2023.

Avenell, Simon. *Asia and Postwar Japan: Deimperialization, Civic Activism, and National Identity.* Cambridge, MA: Harvard University Asia Center, 2022.

———. *Making Japanese Citizens: Civil Society and the Mythology of the* Shimin *in Postwar Japan.* Berkeley: University of California Press, 2010.

———. *Transnational Japan in the Global Environmental Movement.* Honolulu: University of Hawaiʻi Press, 2017.

———, ed. *Reconsidering Postwar Japanese History: A Handbook.* Tokyo: Japan Documents, 2023.

Bailey, David J. *Postwar Japan: 1945 to the Present.* Oxford, UK: Blackwell Publishers, 1996.

Balz, Dan. "Auto Makers Criticize Japanese Plan." *The Washington Post,* March 28, 1985. Accessed March 6, 2023. https://www.washingtonpost.com/archive/business/1985/03/28/auto-makers-criticize-jampanese-plan/ca846b0f-c8ef-4833-a6a0-ca7d35473fa8/.

Bank of Japan. "The Basic Discount Rate and Basic Loan Rate (Previously Indicated as 'Official Discount Rates')." Accessed December 8, 2022. https://www.boj.or.jp/en/statistics/boj/other/discount/discount.htm/.

Barnes, Dayna L. *Architects of Occupation: American Experts and Planning for Postwar Japan.* Ithaca, NY: Cornell University Press, 2017.

Barshay, Andrew E. *The Gods Left First: The Captivity and Repatriation of Japanese POWs in Northeast Asia, 1945–1956.* Berkeley: University of California Press, 2013.

Bix, Herbert P. *Hirohito and the Making of Modern Japan.* New York: Harper Collins Publishers, 2000.

Brands, H. W. *The General vs. The President: MacArthur and Truman at the Brink of Nuclear War.* London: Doubleday, 2016.

Brinton, Mary C. *Women and the Economic Miracle: Gender and Work in Postwar Japan.* Berkeley: University of California Press, 1993.

Bronson, Adam. *One Hundred Million Philosophers: Science of Thought and the Culture of Democracy in Postwar Japan.* Honolulu: University of Hawaiʻi Press, 2016.

Bullock, Julia. *Coeds Ruining the Nation: Women, Education, and Social Change in Postwar Japanese Media.* Ann Arbor: University of Michigan Press, 2019.

Burstein, Daniel. *Yen!: Japan's New Financial Empire and Its Threat to America.* New York: Simon and Schuster, 1988.

Cargill, Thomas F., and Takayuki Sakamoto. *Japan Since 1980.* New York: Cambridge University Press, 2008.

Chiavacci, David. "From Class Struggle to General Middle-Class Society to Divided Society: Societal Models of Inequality in Postwar Japan." *Social Science Japan Journal* 11, no. 1 (2008): 5–27.

Chief Cabinet Secretary. "Issues Regarding History: Statement by the Chief Cabinet Secretary." Accessed October 10, 2024. https://www.mofa.go.jp/a_o/rp/page25e_000343.html.

Chinkin, Christine M. "Women's International Tribunal on Japanese Military Sexual Slavery." *American Journal of International Law* 95, no. 2 (2001): 335–341.

Choi, Deokhyo. "Guest Editor's Introduction: Writing the 'Empire' Back into the History of Postwar Japan." *International Journal of Korean History* 22, no. 1 (2017): 1–10.

Colombo, Jesse. "Japan's Bubble Economy of the 1980s." *The Bubble Bubble,* June 4, 2012. Accessed March 6, 2023. https://www.thebubblebubble.com/japan-bubble/.

Constantino, Renato. *The Second Invasion: Japan and the Philippines.* Quezon City, Philippines: Karrel, 1989.

"Constitution of Japan, The." Accessed March 7, 2023. https://japan.kantei.go.jp/constitution_and_government_of_japan/constitution_e.html.

De Bary, William T., Carol Gluck, and Arthur E. Tiedemann, eds. *Sources of Japanese Tradition 1600–2000,* vol. 2. New York: Columbia University Press, 2006.

Dower, John. *Embracing Defeat: Japan in the Wake of World War II.* New York: W. W. Norton, 1999.

———. *Empire and Aftermath: Yoshida Shigeru and the Japanese Experience, 1878–1954.* Cambridge, MA: Council on East Asian Studies, Harvard University, 1979.

———. *Japan in War and Peace.* New York: The New Press, 1995.

Dunscomb, Paul E. *Japan Since 1945.* Ann Arbor, MI: Association for Asian Studies, 2014.

Esselstrom, Erik. *That Distant Country Next Door: Popular Japanese Perceptions of Mao's China.* Honolulu: University of Hawai'i Press, 2019.

Fair, Harold. "Press Code for Japan." SCAPIN-33, September 18, 1945. Accessed January 20, 2023. https://dl.ndl.go.jp/pid/9885095/1/1.

Farrell, Roger. "Japanese Foreign Direct Investment in the World Economy 1951–1997." *Pacific Economic Papers,* no. 299 (2000): 1–61. Accessed March 5, 2023. http://hdl.handle.net/1885/40701.

Field, Norma. *In the Realm of a Dying Emperor: A Portrait of Japan at Century's End.* New York: Pantheon Books, 1991.

Flath, David. *The Japanese Economy.* 4th ed. Oxford, UK: Oxford University Press, 2022.

Fujiawara, Ikurō. *Nihonjin no heikinchi: Kuwashii zukai dētā de wakariyasui! 2008.* Tokyo: Ākaibusu Shuppan, 2008.

Fukui, Shin'ichi. *Ima okiteiru koto no hontō no imi ga wakaru: Sengo Nihon shi.* Tokyo: Kōdansha, 2015. Kindle.

Fukunaga, Fumio. "Dai-1-kō tennō—Makkāsā kaidan kara shōchō tennō made." In *Shōwa shi kōgi: Sengohen (jō),* edited by Tsutsui Kiyotada, chapter 1. Tokyo: Chikuma Shinsho, 2020. Kindle.

Fukushima Minpō. "Dēta de miru higashi Nihon daishinsai—Tōden Fukushima daiichi genpatsu jiko." *Fukushima minpō.* Accessed March 7, 2023. https://www.minpo.jp/pub/sinsai_data.

Funabashi, Yōichi. *Ajia Taiheiyō fyūjon: APEC to Nihon.* Tokyo: Chūō Kōronsha, 1995.

Funabashi, Yōichi, and Barak Kushner, eds. *Examining Japan's Lost Decades.* London: Routledge, 2015.

Gaimushō. "Sōri 'Makuāsā' kaidan yōshi shō nijū, jū, jūsan, Shōwa nijūnen jūgatsu jūichinichi Shidehara shushō ni soroshi hyōmei suru 'Makuāsā' iken." Document number: A'1.0.0.2-3-4, October 11, 13, 1945. Accessed January 20, 2023. https://www.ndl.go.jp/constitution/e/shiryo/01/033shoshi.html.

Galbraith, Patrick W. "The *Evangelion* Boom: On the Explosion of Fan Markets and Lifestyles in Heisei Japan." In *Japan in the Heisei Era (1989–2019): Multidisciplinary Perspectives,* edited by Noriko Murai, Jeff Kingston, and Tina Burrett, pp. 234–244. London: Routledge, 2022.

Garon, Sheldon. *The State and Labor in Modern Japan.* Berkeley: University of California Press, 1987.

Garon, Sheldon, and Mike Mochizuki. "Negotiating Social Contracts." In *Postwar Japan as History,* edited by Andrew Gordon, pp. 145–166. Berkeley: University of California Press, 1993.

Gaunder, Alisa. *Japanese Politics and Government.* London: Routledge, 2017.

General Headquarters Supreme Commander for the Allied Powers. "SCAPIN-224 Repatriation of Non-Japanese From Japan." November 1, 1945. Accessed January 19, 2023. https://dl.ndl.go.jp/info:ndljp/pid/9885288.

George, Timothy. *Minamata: Pollution and the Struggle for Democracy in Postwar Japan.* Cambridge, MA: Harvard University Asia Center, 2000.

Gerteis, Christopher. *Mobilizing Japanese Youth: The Cold War and the Making of the Sixties Generation.* Ithaca, NY: Cornell University Press, 2021.

Gerteis, Christopher, and Timothy S. George, eds. *Japan Since 1945: From Postwar to Post-Bubble.* London: Bloomsbury, 2013.

Gluck, Carol. "The 'End' of the Postwar: Japan at the Turn of the Millennium." *Public Culture* 10, no. 1 (1997): 1–23.

———. "Introduction." In *Showa: The Japan of Hirohito,* edited by Carol Gluck and Stephen R. Graubard, pp. xi–lxii. New York: W. W. Norton, 1992.

———. "The Past in the Present." In *Postwar Japan as History,* edited by Andrew Gordon, pp. 64–95. Berkeley: University of California Press, 1993.

Gluck, Carol, and Stephen R. Graubard, eds. *Showa: The Japan of Hirohito.* New York: W. W. Norton, 1992.

Gordon, Andrew. "Conclusion." In *Postwar Japan as History,* edited by Andrew Gordon, pp. 449–464. Berkeley: University of California Press, 1993.

———. *The Evolution of Labor Relations in Japan Heavy Industry, 1853–1955.* Cambridge, MA: Harvard University Press, 1985.

———. *Fabricating Consumers: The Sewing Machine in Modern Japan.* Berkeley: University of California Press, 2012.

———. *Labor and Imperial Democracy in Prewar Japan.* Berkeley: University of California Press, 1992.

———. *A Modern History of Japan: From Tokugawa Times to the Present.* New York: Oxford University Press, 2020.

———. "Society and Politics from Transwar through Postwar Japan." In *Historical Perspectives on Contemporary East Asia,* edited by Merle Goldman and Andrew Gordon, pp. 277–296. Cambridge, MA: Harvard University Press, 2000.

———. *The Wages of Affluence: Labor and Management in Postwar Japan.* Cambridge, MA: Harvard University Press, 1998.

———, ed. *Postwar Japan as History.* Berkeley: University of California Press, 1993.

Green, William, A. "Periodization in European and World History." *Journal of World History* 3, no. 1 (1992): 13–53.

Hamai, Kazufumi. "Dai-4-kō fukuin to hikiage: Sensō shūketsu no hito no kokusai idō." In *Shōwa shi kōgi: Sengohen (jō),* edited by Tsutsui Kiyotada, chapter 4. Tokyo: Chikuma Shinsho, 2020. Kindle.

Handō, Kazutoshi. *Shōwa shi 1926–1945.* Tokyo: Heibonsha, 2009.

———. *Shōwa shi sengohen 1945–1989.* Tokyo: Heibonsha, 2009.

Hardacre, Helen, Timothy S. George, Keiko Komamura, and Franziska Seraphim, eds. *Japanese Constitutional Revisionism and Civic Activism.* Lanham, MD: Lexington Books, 2021.

Harootunian, Harry. "Japan's Long Postwar: The Trick of Memory and the Ruse of History." In *Japan After Japan: Social and Cultural Life from the Recessionary 1990s to the Present,* edited by Tomiko Yoda and Harry Harootunian, pp. 98–121. Durham, NC: Duke University Press, 2006.

Hashimoto, Akiko. *The Long Defeat: Cultural Trauma, Memory, and Identity in Japan.* New York: Oxford University Press, 2015.

Hatakenaka, Mioko. "Gurumeka, mukokusekika, soshite herushīka." In *1980nendai,* edited by Saitō Minako and Narita Ryūichi, pp. 71–76. Tokyo: Kawade Bukkusu, 2016.

Hein, Laura E. *Fueling Growth: The Energy Revolution and Economic Policy in Postwar Japan.* Cambridge, MA: Harvard University, Council on East Asian Studies, 1990.

———. *Post-Fascist Japan: Political Culture in Kamakura after the Second World War.* London: Bloomsbury Academic, 2018.

———. *Reasonable Men, Powerful Words: Political Culture and Expertise in Twentieth-Century Japan.* Berkeley: University of California Press, 2004.

Hiraishi, Naoaki. "The Asia Boom in Japanese Publishing." *Social Science Japan,* July 1994, pp. 27–28.

Hokazono, Toyochika, Okumura Norio, Takahashi Masahiro, Nakayama Tomihiro, Nunokawa Hiroshi, Matsuzawa Akira, and Morimoto Mitsunori. *Nihon shi A: Hito, kurashi, mirai.* Tokyo: Daiichi Gakushūsha, 2013.

Honda, Yuki. "Wakamono no konnan—Kyōiku no kansei." In *Heisei shi kōgi,* edited by Yoshimi Shun'ya, pp. 133–158. Tokyo: Chikuma Shobō, 2019.

Hoover, William D. *Historical Dictionary of Postwar Japan.* Lanham, MD: Rowman and Littlefield, 2019.

Hoppens, Robert. *The China Problem in Postwar Japan: Japanese National Identity and Sino-Japanese Relations.* London: Bloomsbury, 2016.

Hosaka, Masayasu. *Heisei shi.* Tokyo: Heibonsha, 2019.

Iida, Yutaka. "Intānetto zen'ya: Jōhōka no 'shokubai' toshite no toshi." In *1990nendai ron,* edited by Ōsawa Satoshi, pp. 143–155. Tokyo: Kawade Shobō Shinsha, 2017.

Impoco, Jim. "Life After the Bubble: How Japan Lost a Decade." *The New York Times,* October 19, 2008, p. WK3.

Inoue, Taku. "Heisei 24nen keizai sensasu: Katsudō chōsa no onegai." *Tōkei Today* no. 48. Accessed December 8, 2022. https://www.stat.go.jp/info/today/048.html.

International Atomic Energy Agency (IAEA). "IAEA Committed to Monitor Treated Water Discharge at Fukushima Daiichi, says Grossi in Japan," May 20, 2022. Accessed March 7, 2023. https://www.iaea.org/newscenter/news/iaea-committed-to-monitor-treated-water-discharge-at-fukushima-daiichi-says-grossi-in-japan.

Iokibe, Makoto. *The Diplomatic History of Postwar Japan.* Translated and annotated by Robert D. Eldridge. London: Routledge, 2011.

Iokibe, Makoto, and Tosh Minohara, eds. *The History of US-Japan Relations: From Perry to the Present.* Singapore: Palgrave Macmillan, 2017.

Ishikawa, Masumi, and Yamaguchi Jirō. *Sengo seiji shi.* Tokyo: Iwanami Shoten, 2021.

Ishimure, Michiko. *Paradise in the Sea of Sorrow: Our Minamata Disease.* Translated by Livia Monnet. Ann Arbor: Center for Japanese Studies, University of Michigan 2003.

Itō, Masaya. *Ikeda Hayato to sono jidai: Sei to shi no dorama.* Tokyo: Asahi Bunko, 1985.

Ito, Takatoshi, and Takeo Hoshi. *The Japanese Economy.* Cambridge, MA: The MIT Press, 2020.

Iwabuchi, Koichi. "Pop-culture Diplomacy in Japan: Soft Power, Nation Branding and the Question of 'International Cultural Exchange.'" *International Journal of Cultural Policy* 21, no. 4 (2015): 419–432.

Japan Center for Economic Research. "Accident Cleanup Costs Rising to 35–80 Trillion Yen in 40 Years," March 07, 2019. Accessed March 7, 2023. https://www.jcer.or.jp/english/accident-cleanup-costs-rising-to-35-80-trillion-yen-in-40-years.

Japan External Trade Organization. "Chokusetsu tōshi tōkei." Accessed January 11, 2023. https://www.jetro.go.jp/world/japan/stats/fdi.html.

Japan Times. "Majority in Japan Backs Nuclear Power for First Time Since Fukushima." *Japan Times,* March 28, 2022. Accessed March 7, 2023. https://www.japantimes.co.jp/news/2022/03/28/national/nuke-power-poll/.

———. "Poll Shows Close to 50% in Japan Support Restarting Some Nuclear Reactors." *Japan Times,* July 21, 2022. Accessed March 7, 2023. https://www.japantimes.co.jp/news/2022/07/21/national/japan-nuclear-politics-abe-opinion-poll/.

Jichishō Senkyobu. *Shūgiin giin senkyo, Saikō Saibansho saibankan kokumin shinsa, Sangiin giin tsūjō senkyo kekkachō.* Tokyo: Jichishō Senkyobu, 1980.

Johnson, Chalmers. *MITI and the Japanese Miracle.* Stanford, CA: Stanford University Press, 1982.

Johnson, Nelson Trusler. "The Secretary General of the Far Eastern Commission (Johnson) to the Secretary of State." FEAC/4–446, April 4, 1946. In *Foreign Relations of the United States, 1946, The Far East,* vol. 8, edited by John G. Reid and Herbert A. Fine, document 334. Accessed January 20, 2023. https://history.state.gov/historicaldocuments/frus1946v08/d334.

"Joint Communique of the Government of Japan and the Government of the People's Republic of China." Accessed March 6, 2023. https://www.mofa.go.jp/region/asia-paci/china/joint72.html.

Kaizuka, Shigeki. *Sengo Nihon kyōiku shi.* Tokyo: Hōsō Daigaku Kyōiku Shinkō Kai, 2018.

Kajii, Isoshi. "Shokuryō kiki." In *Sengoshi daijiten zōho shinban,* edited by Sasaki Takeshi, Tsurumi Shunsuke, Tominaga Ken'ichi, Nakamura Masanori, and Masamura Kimihiro, pp. 452–453. Tokyo: Sanseidō, 2005.

Kanda, Fuhito. *Shōwa no rekishi 8: Senryō to minshushugi.* Tokyo: Shōgakkan, 1989.

Kanda, Fuhito, and Kobayashi Hideo. *Zōho kanzenban Shōwa—Heisei gendai shi nenpyō.* Tokyo: Shōgakkan, 2019.

Kapur, Nick. *Japan at the Crossroads: Conflict and Compromise after Anpo.* Cambridge, MA: Harvard University Press, 2018.

Kariya, Takehiko. "Purorōgu—1990nendai: 'Miushinai no jidai' no makuake." In *Hitobito no seishin shi dai-8-kan: Baburu hōkai—1990nendai,* edited by Kariya Takehiko, pp. 1–15. Tokyo: Iwanami Shoten, 2016.

Katz, Richard. "The Heisei Economy: Explaining the Lost Decades." In *Japan in the Heisei Era (1989–2019): Multidisciplinary Perspectives,* edited by Noriko Murai, Jeff Kingston, and Tina Burrett, pp. 113–126. London: Routledge, 2022.

Kawamura, Haruhiko. "Nenpu: Sengo Nihon no chingin hendō (1945–1985)—Tōkei no jidaiteki haikei o saguru." *Jōsai daigaku daigakuin kenkyū nenpyō* 3 (1987): 119–134.

Kawana, Shinji. "Dai-16-kō Sunagawa jiken—Kichi mondai." In *Shōwa shi kōgi: Sengohen (jō),* edited by Tsutsui Kiyotada, chapter 16. Tokyo: Chikuma Shinsho, 2020. Kindle.

Keizai Kikaku Chō. "Shōwa 31nen: Nenji keizai hōkoku." Accessed January 25, 2023. https://www5.cao.go.jp/keizai3/keizaiwp/wp-je56/wp-je56-0000i1.html.

———. "Shōwa 34nen neniji keizai hōkoku: Sumiyakana keiki kaifuku to kongo no kadai." Accessed March 5, 2023. https://www5.cao.go.jp/keizai3/keizaiwp/wp-je59/wp-je59-021201.html.

———. "Shōwa 42nen nenji keizai hōkoku: Nōritsu to fukushi no kōjō." Accessed March 5, 2023. https://www5.cao.go.jp/keizai3/keizaiwp/wp-je67/wp-je67-02102.html.

———. "Shōwa 52nen nenji keizai hakusho: Antei seichō e no tekiō o susumeru Nihon keizai." Accessed March 2, 2023. https://www5.cao.go.jp/keizai3/keizaiwp/wp-je77/wp-je77-02202.html.

Kersten, Rikki. *Democracy in Postwar Japan: Maruyama Masao and the Search for Autonomy.* London: Routledge, 1996.

Kingston, Jeff. *Contemporary Japan: History, Politics, and Social Change Since the 1980s.* Malden, MA: Wiley-Blackwell, 2013.

———. *Japan.* Cambridge, UK: Polity Press, 2019.

———. *Japan in Transformation, 1945–2020.* Abingdon, Oxon: Routledge, 2021.

———. "The Tumultuous Finale: 2009–2019." In *Japan in the Heisei Era (1989–2019): Multidisciplinary Perspectives,* edited by Noriko Murai, Jeff Kingston, and Tina Burrett, pp. 328–342. London: Routledge, 2022.

Knoema. "Historical GDP Per Capita by Country, Statistics from the World Bank." Accessed March 2, 2023. https://knoema.com/jesoqmb/historical-gdp-per-capita-by-country-statistics-from-the-world-bank-1960-2018.

Kobayashi, Yōtarō. "'Sai-Ajiaka' no susume." *Foresight,* April 1991, pp. 44–46.

Kojima, Hiroyuki. "'Shindemoii' sonmin 700-nin yodōshi kesshi no suwarikomi, 70-nen-mae no tōsō." *Asahi shinbun dejitaru.* Accessed January 24, 2023. https://www.asahi.com/articles/ASQCQ6D8MQCHPISC00B.html.

Kokudo Kōtsūshō. "(3) Josei no shūgyō jōkyō no henka." Accessed December 14, 2022. https://www.mlit.go.jp/hakusyo/mlit/h24/hakusho/h25/html/n1213000.html.

———, ed. *Kankō hakusho Reiwa 2nenban.* Nikkei Insatsu, 2020.

Kokuritsu Kenkō-Eiyō Kenkyūjo. "Kokumin eiyō no genjō." Accessed December 1, 2022. https://www.nibiohn.go.jp/eiken/chosa/kokumin_eiyou/.

Kokuritsu Shakai Hoshō-Jinkō Mondai Kenkyūjo. "Dai-16-kai shussei dōkō kihon chōsa: Kekka no gaiyō." Accessed March 7, 2023. https://www.ipss.go.jp/ps-doukou/j/doukou16/JNFS16gaiyo.pdf.

———. "Jinkō tōkei shiryōshū: Hyō 10–1 kunibetsu zairyū gaikokujin jinkō: 1950–2020." Accessed January 18, 2023. https://www.ipss.go.jp/syoushika/tohkei/Popular/Popular2022.asp?chap=10.

Komiya, Hitoshi. "Dai-17-kō gojūgonen taisei no seiritsu to tenkai." In *Shōwa shi kōgi: Sengohen (jō),* edited by Tsutsui Kiyotada, chapter 17. Tokyo: Chikuma Shinsho, 2020. Kindle.

Konoe, Sara. *The Politics of Financial Markets and Regulation: The United States, Japan, and Germany.* New York: Palgrave Macmillan, 2014.

Kosaka, Masataka. *100 Million Japanese: The Postwar Experience.* Tokyo: Kodansha International, 1972.

Koschmann, J. Victor. *Revolution and Subjectivity in Postwar Japan.* Chicago: University of Chicago Press, 1996.

Kōsei Rōdōshō. *Reiwa 2nen-ban kōseirōdō hakusho: Reiwa jidai no shakai hoshō to hatarakikata o kangaeru.* Accessed December 19, 2022. https://www.mhlw.go.jp/stf/wp/hakusyo/kousei/19/backdata/01-01-01-07.html.

———. "Zuhyō 1–3-8 josei no nenrei kaikyū betsu shūgyōritsu no henka." Accessed December 14, 2022. https://www.mhlw.go.jp/stf/wp/hakusyo/kousei/19/backdata/01-01-03-08.html.

Krauss, Ellis S., and Robert J. Pekkanen. *The Rise and Fall of Japan's LDP: Political Party Organization as Historical Institutions.* Ithaca, NY: Cornell University Press, 2010.

Kubo, Yoshizō. "Kyōshoku tsuihō." In *Sengoshi daijiten zōho shinban,* edited by Sasaki Takeshi, Tsurumi Shunsuke, Tominaga Ken'ichi, Nakamura Masanori, and Masamura Kimihiro, p. 178. Tokyo: Sanseidō, 2005.

Kushner, Barak. *Men to Devils, Devils to Men: Japanese War Crimes and Chinese Justice.* Cambridge, MA: Harvard University Press, 2015.

LaFeber, Walter. *The Clash: U.S.-Japanese Relations Throughout History.* New York: W. W. Norton, 1997.

Large, Stephen S. "General Introduction." In *Shōwa Japan: Political Economic, and Social History 1926–1989,* edited by Stephen S. Large, pp. 1–27. London: Routledge, 1998.

———, ed. *Shōwa Japan: Political, Economic and Social History 1926–1989.* London: Routledge, 1998.

LeBlanc, Robin. *Bicycle Citizens: The Political World of the Japanese Housewife.* Berkeley: University of California Press, 1999.

Liu-Farrer, Gracia. "Japan's Immigration in the Heisei Era: Population, Policy, and the Ethno-Nationalist Dilemma." In *Japan in the Heisei Era (1989–2019): Multidisciplinary Perspectives,* edited by Noriko Murai, Jeff Kingston, and Tina Burrett, pp. 140–152. London: Routledge, 2022.

Lu, David. *Japan: A Documentary History Volume II—The Late Tokugawa Period to the Present.* New York: M. E. Sharpe, 1997.

Lucken, Michael. "Introduction." In *Japan's Postwar,* edited by Michael Lucken, Anne Bayard-Sakai, and Emmanuel Lozerand, translated by J. A. A. Stockwin, pp. 1–7. Oxon, UK: Routledge, 2011.

Lucken, Michael, Anne Bayard-Sakai, and Emmanuel Lozerand, eds. *Japan's Postwar.* Translated by J. A. A. Stockwin. London: Routledge, 2011.

Lynn, Hyung Gu. "Systemic Lock: The Institutionalization of History in Post-1965 South Korea–Japan Relations." *Journal of American-East Asian Relations* 9, no. 1–2 (2000): 55–84.

MacArthur, Douglas. "Incoming Classified Message From: CINCAFPAC Adv Tokyo Japan." Document number: CA-57235, January 25, 1946. Accessed January 20, 2023. https://www.ndl.go.jp/constitution/e/shiryo/03/064shoshi.html.

———. "Radio Broadcast to the Nation Following the *USS Missouri* Surrender Ceremony." American Rhetoric Online Speech Bank. Accessed January 20, 2023. https://www.americanrhetoric.com/speeches/douglasmacarthurradiojapanesesurrenderceremony.htm.

Macrae, Norman. "Consider Japan." *The Economist,* September 1, 1962, pp. 787–819.

Macrotrends. "Dollar Yen Exchange Rate (USD JPY)—Historical Chart." Accessed January 11, 2023. https://www.macrotrends.net/2550/dollar-yen-exchange-rate-historical-chart.

———. "Nikkei 22 Index—67 Year Historical Chart." Accessed January 12, 2023. https://www.macrotrends.net/2593/nikkei-225-index-historical-chart-data.

Mahathir, bin Mohamad, and Ishihara Shintarō. *"NO" to ieru Ajia: Tai-Ōbei e no Hōsaku.* Tokyo: Kōbunsha, 1994.

Maizuru Hikiage Kinenkan. "Hikiage no hajimari." Accessed December 21, 2022. https://m-hikiage-museum.jp/education/hajimari.html.

Marotti, William A. *Money, Trains, and Guillotines: Art and Revolution in 1960s Japan.* Durham, NC: Duke University Press, 2013.

Masamura, Kimihiro. *Zusetsu sengo shi.* Tokyo: Chikuma Shobō, 1993.

"Mata *Kowaku*-naru keisatsukan: Dēto mo jama-suru keishokuhō." *Shūkan myōjō* 1, no. 16 (1958): 31–35.

Matthews, H. Freeman. "Politico-Military Problems in the Far East: United States Initial Post-Defeat Policy Relating to Japan." SCAPIN-150/4, September 6, 1945. Accessed January 20, 2023. https://www.ndl.go.jp/constitution/e/shiryo/01/022/022_001r.html.

McCormack, Gavan, and Satoko Oka Norimatsu. *Resistant Islands: Okinawa Confronts Japan and the United States.* 2nd ed. Lanham, MD: Rowman & Littlefield, 2018.

McFarland, A. J., and C. J. Moore. "Basic Directive for Post-Surrender Military Government in Japan Proper." Document number: JCS-1380/15, November 3, 1945. Accessed January 20, 2023. https://www.ndl.go.jp/constitution/e/shiryo/01/036/036tx.html.

McGray, Douglas. "Japan's Gross National Cool." *Foreign Policy* 130 (2002): 44–54.

McNeill, David, and Akira Tanaka. "Still Half Free: The Japanese Media in the Heisei Era." In *Japan in the Heisei Era (1989–2019): Multidisciplinary Perspectives,* edited by Noriko Murai, Jeff Kingston, and Tina Burrett, pp. 99–110. London: Routledge, 2022.

Metzler, Mark. *Capital as Will and Imagination: Schumpeter's Guide to the Postwar Japanese Miracle.* Ithaca, NY: Cornell University Press, 2013.

Midford, Paul. "China Views the Revised US-Japan Defense Guidelines: Popping the Cork?" *International Relations of the Asia-Pacific* 4, no. 1 (2004): 113–145.

Miller, Jennifer M. *Cold War Democracy: The United States and Japan.* Cambridge, MA: Harvard University Press, 2019.

Minashita, Kiriu. "'Heibon' to 'futsū' ga kairi shita jidai." In *1990nendai ron,* edited by Ōsawa Satoshi, pp. 91–100. Tokyo: Kawade Shobō Shinsha, 2017.

Mita, Munesuke. *Gendai Nihon no kankaku to shisō.* Tokyo: Kōdansha, 1995.

Miwa, Ryōichi. "Zaibatsu kaitai." In *Sengoshi daijiten zōho shinban,* edited by Sasaki Takeshi, Tsurumi Shunsuke, Tominaga Ken'ichi, Nakamura Masanori, and Masamura Kimihiro, pp. 331–333. Tokyo: Sanseidō, 2005.

Miyamoto, Ken'ichi. *Shōwa no rekishi 10: Keizai taikoku.* Tokyo: Shōgakkan, 1994.

Morris-Suzuki, Tessa. *Borderline Japan: Foreigners and Frontier Controls in the Postwar Era.* Cambridge, UK: Cambridge University Press, 2012.

———. "Purorōgu senkyūhyaku gojūnen-dai: Sengo, kansenki, reisen, Chōsen sensō." In *Hitobito no seishin shi: Chōsen no sensō,* vol. 2, edited by Tessa Morris Suzuki, pp. 1–11. Tokyo: Iwanami Shoten, 2015.

Muchaku, Seikyō, ed. *Yamabiko gakkō: Yamagata-ken Yamamoto chūgakkō seito no seikatsu kiroku.* Tokyo: Yuri Shuppan, 1966.

Murai, Noriko, Jeff Kingston, and Tina Burrett, eds. *Japan in the Heisei Era (1989–2019): Multidisciplinary Perspectives.* London: Routledge, 2022.

Murai, Tetsuya. "Dai-8-Kō Yoshida Shigeru naikaku: Jidai de henka suru Yoshida rosen to wanman saishō." In *Shōwa shi kōgi: Sengohen (jō),* edited by Tsutsui Kiyotada, chapter 8. Tokyo: Chikuma Shinsho, 2020. Kindle.

Murakami, Masayasu. "Sengo Nihon ni okeru shuyō zōsenjo no tenkai." *Jinbun chiri* 38, no. 5 (1986): 42–58.

Murayama, Tomiichi. "Prime Minister's Address to the Diet." Accessed March 7, 2023. https://www.mofa.go.jp/announce/press/pm/murayama/address9506.html.

Nagao, Nishikawa, Ōno Mitsuaki, and Banshō Ken'ichi, eds. *Sengo shi saikō: "Rekishi no sakeme" o toraeru.* Tokyo: Heibonsha, 2014.

Naikakufu. "Tokushū 'kōtsū anzen taisaku no ayumi—Kōtsū jiko nonai shakai o mezashite." Accessed December 1, 2022. https://www8.cao.go.jp/koutu/taisaku/r01kou_haku/zenbun/genkyo/feature/feature_02_2.html.

Naikakufu, Danjo Kyōdō Sankaku Kyoku. "Dai-1-setsu kyōiku o meguru jōkyō." Accessed January 6, 2023. https://www.gender.go.jp/about_danjo/whitepaper/h29/zentai/html/honpen/b1_s05_01.html.

Naikakufu Keizai Shakai Sōgō Kenkyūjo. "Keiki tōkei, shōhi dōkō chōsa, tōkeihyō ichiran." Accessed January 10, 2023. https://www.esri.cao.go.jp/jp/stat/shouhi/shouhi.html.

———. "Kokumin keizai keisan (GDP tōkei)." Accessed January 4, 2022. https://www.esri.cao.go.jp/jp/sna/menu.html.

Najita, Tetsuo. *Hara Kei and the Politics of Compromise, 1905–1915.* Cambridge, MA: Harvard University Press, 2013.

Nakamura, Masanori. *Sengo shi.* Tokyo: Iwanami Shoten, 2005.

Nakamura, Takafusa. *A History of Shōwa Japan 1926–1989,* translated by Edwin Whenmouth. Tokyo: University of Tokyo Press, 1998.

———. *Shōwa shi 1: 1926–1945.* Tokyo: Tōyō Keizai Shinpōsha, 1993.

———. *Shōwa shi 2: 1945–1989.* Tokyo: Tōyō Keizai Shinpōsha, 1993.

Nakane, Chie. *Japanese Society.* Berkeley: University of California Press, 1970.

Nakano, Koichi. "The Rightward Shift of Japanese Politics." In *Japan in the Heisei Era (1989–2019): Multidisciplinary Perspectives,* edited by Noriko Murai, Jeff Kingston, and Tina Burrett, pp. 33–43. London: Routledge, 2022.

Nakano, Yoshio. "Mōhaya sengo dewanai." *Bungei shunjū* 413 (2009): 56–66.

Narita, Ryūichi. *Kingendai Nihon shi to no taiwa: Senchū—sengo—genzaihen.* Tokyo: Shūeisha, 2019.

———. "'Sengo shi' jojutsu o megutte (kōenroku)." *Hiroshima heiwa kenkyūjo bukkretto* 6 (2019): 197–226.

———. *Sengo shi nyūmon.* Tokyo: Kawade Shobō Shinsha, 2015.

———. *"Sengo" wa ikani katarareruka.* Tokyo: Kawade Shobō Shinsha, 2016.

National Diet Library, Japan. "Report by the National Security Council on Recommendations with Respect to US Policy toward Japan (NSC 13/2)," October 7, 1948. Accessed January 23, 2023. https://www.ndl.go.jp/modern/e/img_r/M008/M008-002r.html.

Nicchūkan 3goku Kyōtsū Rekishi Kyōzai Iinkai. *Mirai o hiraku rekishi: Nihon—Chūgoku—Kankoku kyōdō henshū Higashi Ajia 3goku no kingendai shi.* Tokyo: Kōbunken, 2006.

Nihon Bōeki Kai. *Enerugī o shirō!* Accessed March 2, 2023. https://www.jftc.or.jp/kids/energy/section2/blue.html.

Nihon Jidōsha Kōgyō Kai (JAMA). "Active Matrix Database System." Accessed December 8, 2022. https://jamaserv.jama.or.jp/newdb/.

Nihon Keizai Shinbunsha, ed. *Reiwa ni tsunagu Heisei no 30nen: Tōsui to nekkyō no daishō to sono saki no kibō.* Tokyo: Nihon Keizai Shinbun Shuppansha, 2019.

Niitsu, Naoko. "Nihon wa byōdō na shakai? Fubyōdō ni naritsutsuaru? Jini keisū kara kangaeru." *e's Inc,* April 24, 2017. Accessed March 7, 2023. https://www.es-inc.jp/graphs/2017/grh_id008991.html.

Nikkei Staff Writers. "Japan PM Kishida Orders New Nuclear Power Plant Construction." *Nikkei Asia,* August 24, 2022. Accessed March 7, 2023. https://asia.nikkei.com/Politics/Japan-PM-Kishida-orders-new-nuclear-power-plant-construction.

Nippon.com. "Japan Ranks 116th in 2022 Global Gender Gap Report," July 15, 2022. Accessed March 7, 2023. https://www.nippon.com/en/japan-data/h01385/.

Nishikawa, Jun. "70-nendai Ajia to Nihon no sentaku." *Nihon no shōrai* 1 (1972): 28–47.

Nishikawa, Katsumi. "Rōdō kumiai." In *Sengoshi daijiten zōho shinban,* edited by Sasaki Takeshi, Tsurumi Shunsuke, Tominaga Ken'ichi, Nakamura Masanori, and Masamura Kimihiro, p. 950. Tokyo: Sanseidō, 2005.

Nishina, Kōichi. "'Jinsei hyakunen jidai' o kenshō suru." *Mizuho jōhō sōken repōto* 18 (2019): 1–9. Accessed March 6, 2023. https://www.mizuho-rt.co.jp/publication/report/2019/mhir18_life_01.html.

Noguchi, Yukio. *1940nen taisei (zōhanban): Saraba senji keizai.* Tokyo: Tōyō Keizai Shinpōsha, 2010.

Nōrin Suisan Shō. "Kome o meguru kankei shiryō." Accessed March 5, 2023. https://www.maff.go.jp/j/council/seisaku/syokuryo/171130/.

O'Bryan, Scott. *The Growth Idea: Purpose and Prosperity in Postwar Japan.* Honolulu: University of Hawai'i Press, 2009.

Ogawa, Akihiro. *Lifelong Learning in Neoliberal Japan: Risk, Community, and Knowledge.* Albany: State University of New York Press, 2015.

Oguma, Eiji. *Heisei shi (kanzenban).* Tokyo: Kawade Shobō Shinsho, 2019.

———. *"Minshu" to "aikoku": Sengo Nihon no nashonarizumu to kōkyōsei.* Tokyo: Shin'yōsha, 2002.

———. "Postwar in the Post-Cold War: Postwar in the Heisei Era." In *Reconsidering Postwar Japanese History: A Handbook,* edited by Simon Avenell, pp. 345–362. Tokyo: Japan Documents, 2023.

Ogura Kazuo. "A Call for a New Concept of Asia." *Japan Echo* 20, no. 3 (1993): 37–44.

Oikawa, Yoshinobu. *Mōichido yomu Yamakawa Nihon sengoshi.* Tokyo: Yamakawa Shuppansha, 2016.

Onishi, Norimitsu. "Koizumi Exits Office as He Arrived: Defiant on War Shrine." *New York Times,* August 16, 2006, p. A6.

Ono, Hiroshi. "Sengo Nihon no jidōsha sangyō no hatten." *Keizaigaku kenkyū* 45, no. 1 (1995): 68–76.

Ōno, Mitsuaki, and Banshō Ken'ichi. "Hajime ni." In *Sengo shi saikō: "Rekishi no sakeme" o toraeru,* edited by Nishikawa Nagao, Ōno Mitsuaki, and Banshō Ken'ichi, pp. 9–24. Tokyo: Heibonsha, 2014.

Organisation for Economic Co-Operation and Development (OECD). *OECD Employment Outlook 1991.* Paris, France: OECD Publishing. Accessed December 8, 2022. https://www.oecd.org/els/employmentoutlook-previouseditions.htm.

———. "Official Development Assistance (ODA)." Accessed March 6, 2023. https://www.oecd.org/dac/financing-sustainable-development/development-finance-standards/official-development-assistance.htm.

———. "Poverty Rate." Accessed March 7, 2023. https://data.oecd.org/inequality/poverty-rate.htm.

Partner, Simon. *Assembled in Japan: Electrical Goods and the Making of the Japanese Consumer.* Berkeley: University of California Press, 2000.

Pekkanen, Robert J., and Saadia M. Pekkanen. *The Oxford Handbook of Japanese Politics.* New York: Oxford University Press, 2022.

Pyle, Kenneth B. "The Making of Postwar Japan: A Speculative Essay." *Journal of Japanese Studies* 46, no. 1 (2020): 113–143.

Recruit Co. Ltd. "Dai-37-kai wākusu daisotsu kyūjin bairitsu chōsa (2021nen sotsu)." Accessed March 7, 2023. https://www.recruit.co.jp/newsroom/2020/0806_18778.html.

Reimann, Kim. "Japan and the Environment." In *The Oxford Handbook of Japanese Politics,* edited by Robert J. Pekkanen and Saadia M. Pekkanen, pp. 621–642. New York: Oxford University Press, 2020.

Rekishigaku Kenkyū Kai, ed. *Sengo Nihon shi.* 5 vols. Tokyo: Aoki Shoten, 1961–1962.

Rōdō Seisaku Kenkyū-Kenshū Kikō. "Hayawakari gurafu de miru chōki rōdō tōkei, II rdōryoku, shūgyō, koyō—Zu 8 koyō keitai-betsu koyōshasū." Accessed October 14, 2024. https://www.jil.go.jp/kokunai/statistics/timeseries/index.html.

———. "Zu 2–1 rōdō sōgi." Accessed March 5, 2023. https://www.jil.go.jp/kokunai/statistics/timeseries/html/g0702_01.html.

Rōdōshō. "Shōwa 62nen rōdō keizai no bunseki." Accessed December 8, 2022. https://www.mhlw.go.jp/toukei_hakusho/hakusho/roudou/1987/.

Royall, Kenneth C. "Address by the Honorable Kenneth C. Royall, Secretary of the Army, before the Commonwealth Club of San Francisco, 6th January, 1948." *Current Notes on International Affairs* 19, no. 5 (1948): 284–288. Accessed January 23, 2023. http://nla.gov.au/nla.obj-1182178028.

Ruoff, Kenneth J. *Japan's Imperial House in the Postwar Era, 1945–2019.* Cambridge, MA: Harvard University Asia Center, 2020.

———. "Mr. Tomino Goes to City Hall: Grass-roots Democracy in Zushi City, Japan." *Bulletin of Concerned Asian Scholars* 25, no. 3 (1993): 22–33.

Saaler, Sven. "Heisei Historiography: Academic History and Public Commemoration in Japan, 1990–2020." In *Japan in the Heisei Era (1989–2019): Multidisciplinary Perspectives,* edited by Noriko Murai, Jeff Kingston, and Tina Burrett, pp. 287–298. London: Routledge, 2022.

Saito, Hiro. *The History Problem: The Politics of War Commemoration in East Asia.* Honolulu: University of Hawai'i Press, 2017.

Samuels, Richard J. *3.11: Disaster and Change in Japan.* Ithaca, NY: Cornell University Press, 2013.

———. *The Business of the Japanese State: Energy Markets in Comparative and Historical Perspective.* Ithaca, NY: Cornell University Press, 1987.

Sasaki, Takeshi, Tsurumi Shunsuke, Tominaga Ken'ichi, Nakamura Masanori, and Masamura Kimihiro, eds. *Sengoshi daijiten zōho shinban.* Tokyo: Sanseidō, 2005.

Seaton, Philip A. "Discourses of War and Peace during Japan's 'Postwar.'" In *Reconsidering Postwar Japanese History: A Handbook,* edited by Simon Avenell, pp. 327–344. Tokyo: Japan Documents, 2023.

———. *Japan's Contested War Memories: The "Memory Rifts" in Historical Consciousness of World War II.* London: Routledge, 2007.

Seizelet, Eric. "The Postwar as Political Paradigm." In *Japan's Postwar,* edited by Michael Lucken, Anne Bayard-Sakai, and Emmanuel Lozerand, translated by J. A. A. Stockwin, pp. 11–33. Oxon, UK: Routledge, 2011.

Seraphim, Franziska. *War Memory and Social Politics in Japan, 1945–2005.* Cambridge, MA: Harvard University Press, 2006.

Shibagaki, Kazuo. *Shōwa no rekishi 9: Kōwa kara kōdo seichō e.* Tokyo: Shogakkan, 1994.

Shigematsu, Setsu. *Scream from the Shadows: The Women's Liberation Movement in Japan.* Minneapolis: University of Minnesota Press, 2012.

Shigen Enerugī Chō. "Heisei 28nendo enerugī ni kansuru nenji hōkoku (enerugī hakusho 2017)." Accessed December 8, 2022. https://www.enecho.meti.go.jp/about/whitepaper/2017html/2-1-1.html.

Shōbōchō. *Higashi Nihon daishinsai kirokushū.* Tokyo: Shōbōchō, 2013. Accessed March 7, 2023. https://www.fdma.go.jp/disaster/higashinihon/post.html.

Shōji, Jun'ichirō. "Dai-10-kō Chōsen sensō to Nihon." In *Shōwa shi kōgi: Sengohen (jō),* edited by Tsutsui Kiyotada, chap. 16. Tokyo: Chikuma Shinsho, 2020. Kindle.

Shōsetsu Nihon Shi Zuroku Henshū Iinkai. *Shōsetsu Nihon shi zuroku.* 6th edition. Tokyo: Yamakawa Shuppansha, 2013.

Shutsunyūkoku Zairyū Kanri Chō. "Shutsunyūkoku kanri tōkei hyō." Accessed December 2, 2022. https://www.moj.go.jp/isa/policies/statistics/toukei_ichiran_nyukan.html.

Siniawer, Eiko Maruko. *Waste: Consuming Postwar Japan.* Ithaca, NY: Cornell University Press, 2018.

Smith, Dennis B. *Japan Since 1945: The Rise of an Economic Superpower.* New York: St. Martin's Press, 1995.

Smith, Eugene W., and Aileen M. Smith. *Minamata: The Story of the Poisoning of a City, and of the People Who Choose to Carry the Burden of Courage.* New York: Holt, Rinehart, and Winston, 1975.

Sōmushō. *Jōhō tsūshin hakusho Heisei 29nen-ban*. Accessed December 19, 2022. https://www.soumu.go.jp/johotsusintokei/whitepaper/ja/h29/html/nc135230.html.

Sōmushō Tōkei Kyoku. "III henka suru sangyō—Shokugyō kōzō." Accessed January 6, 2023. https://www.stat.go.jp/data/kokusei/2005/sokuhou/03.htm.

———. "Dai-rokujūgo-kai Nihon tōkei nenkan Heisei-28-nen." Accessed January 12, 2023. https://www.stat.go.jp/data/nenkan/65nenkan/20.html.

———. "Reiwa 2nen kokusei chōsa: Jinkōtō kihon shūkei kekka—Kekka no gaiyō," November 30, 2021. Accessed March 7, 2023. https://www.stat.go.jp/data/kokusei/2020/kekka/pdf/outline_01.pdf.

———. "Rōdō kumiai shuruibetsu rōdō kumiai sū, rōdō kumiaiin sū oyobi suitei soshikiritsu no suii." Accessed January 20, 2023. https://www.e-stat.go.jp/stat-search/files?tclass=000001018508.

Sugimoto, Yoshio. *An Introduction to Japanese Society*. 5th ed. New York: Cambridge University Press, 2020.

Sugita, Atsushi. "Purorōgu—1980nendai: 'Min'eika' to shōhi shakai no kage de." In *Hitobito no seishin shi dai-7-kan: Shūen suru shōwa—1980nendai*, edited by Sugita Atsushi, pp. 1–11. Tokyo: Iwanami Shoten, 2016.

Suter, Rebecca. "Manga, National Identity and Internationalization in Postwar Japan." In *Reconsidering Postwar Japanese History: A Handbook*, edited by Simon Avenell, pp. 307–323. Tokyo: Japan Documents, 2023.

Tachibana, Toshiaki. *Nihon no keizai kakusa: Shotoku to shisan kara kangaeru*. Tokyo: Iwanami Shoten, 1998.

Takasugi, Yōhei. "Dai-5-Kō Tōkyō saiban: Hikoku Tōjō Hideki no kēsu kara." In *Shōwa shi kōgi: Sengohen (jō)*, edited by Tsutsui Kiyotada, chapter 5. Tokyo: Chikuma Shinsho, 2020. Kindle.

Takeda, Haruhito. *Kōdo seichō—Shirīzu Nihon kindai shi 8*. Tokyo: Iwanami Shoten, 2008.

Takemae, Eiji. *Inside GHQ: The Allied Occupation of Japan and Its Legacy*. Translated by Robert Ricketts and Sebastian Swann. New York: Continuum, 2002.

Takenaka, Akiko. *Yasukuni Shrine: History, Memory, and Japan's Unending Postwar*. Honolulu: University of Hawai'i Press, 2015.

Tamanoi, Mariko Asano. *Memory Maps: The State and Manchuria in Postwar Japan*. Honolulu: University of Hawai'i Press, 2009.

Tin Tin Htun. "Preserving the Status Quo: Japan's Laws and Policies on Ethnic and Sexual Minorities." In *Japan in the Heisei Era (1989–2019): Multidisciplinary Perspectives*, edited by Noriko Murai, Jeff Kingston, and Tina Burrett, pp. 166–179. London: Routledge, 2022.

Tokuda Ryūhei. "Shinai zen'ikiteki ni hirogaru shōgyōchi no anteiteki chika jōshō kichō! Sabupuraimu rōn mondai ga motarasu purasu men." *Sūji de miru keizai—Osaka no potensharu sono11*, no. 80. Accessed March 6, 2023. https://www.sansokan.jp/tyousa/archive/toukei/suji/suji_80-1.html.

Toohey, Peter. "The Cultural Logic of Historical Periodization." In *Handbook of Historical Sociology*, edited by Gerard Delanty and Engin F. Isin, pp. 209–219. London: Sage, 2003.

Totani, Yuma. *The Tokyo War Crimes Trial: The Pursuit of Justice in the Wake of World War II.* Cambridge, MA: Harvard University Press, 2008.

Trend Economics. "Japan General Government Gross Debt to GDP." Accessed January 12, 2023. https://tradingeconomics.com/japan/government-debt-to-gdp.

Tsutsui, William M., ed. *A Companion to Japanese History.* Malden, MA: Blackwell Publishing, 2007.

Vogel, Ezra F. *Japan as Number 1: Lessons for America.* New York: Harper Colophon, 1980.

Walker, Brett L. *Toxic Archipelago: A History of Industrial Disease in Japan.* Seattle: University of Washington Press, 2010.

Watt, Lori. *When Empire Comes Home: Repatriation and Reintegration in Postwar Japan.* Cambridge, MA: Harvard University Asia Center, 2010.

Whitney, Courtney. "Memorandum for the Supreme Commander: Constitutional Reform." February 1, 1946. Accessed January 20, 2023. https://www.ndl.go.jp/constitution/e/shiryo/03/069shoshi.html.

Winkler, Christian G. *The Quest for Japan's New Constitution: An Analysis of Visions and Constitutional Reform Proposals 1980–2009.* New York: Routledge, 2013.

World Bank Group. "Individuals Using the Internet (% of Population)—Japan, United States." Accessed March 7, 2023. https://data.worldbank.org/indicator/IT.NET.USER.ZS?locations=JP-US&most_recent_value_desc=true.

Yamamoto, Akihiro. "Han-kakuheiki kara han-genpatsu e: 'Watashitachi' ni yoru 'kakkoii' undō." In *1980nendai,* edited by Saitō Minako and Narita Ryūichi, pp. 95–109. Tokyo: Kawade Bukkusu, 2016.

Yamanouchi, Yasushi, J. Victor Koschmann, and Ryuichi Narita, eds. *Total War and Modernization.* Ithaca, NY: Cornell University East Asia Program, 1998.

Yamashita, Kazuhito. "Naze nōka no shotoku dake hoshō shinakereba naranainoka?" Special Report, Research Institute of Economy, Trade, and Industry. Accessed December 1, 2022. https://www.rieti.go.jp/jp/special/special_report/065.html.

Yanbe, Yukio. *Nihon keizai 30nen shi: Baburu kara Abenomikusu made.* Tokyo: Iwanami Shoten, 2019.

Yasutomi, Kunio. "Nihon tekkōgyō no sengo hensei to sono seikaku." *Tōhoku keizai* 72 (1982): 25–68.

Yoshikawa, Hiroshi, and Miyakawa Shūko. "Sangyō kōzō no henka to sengo Nihon no keizai seichō." *RIETI Discussion Paper Series,* 09-J-024. Accessed January 16, 2023. https://www.rieti.go.jp/jp/publications/summary/09090001.html.

Yoshiki, Tsuneo. "Sengo kenzō ōgata tankā gijutsu kaihatsu no keitōka to shiryō chōsa." In *Kokuritsu kagaku hakubutsukan gijutsu no keitōka chōsa hōkoku,* vol. 4, edited by Kokuritsu Kagaku Hakubutsukan Sangyō Gijutsu Shi Shiryō Jōhō Sentā, pp. 135–177. Tokyo: Kokuritsu Kagaku Hakubutsukan, 2004.

Yoshimi, Shun'ya. *Heisei jidai.* Tokyo: Iwanami Shoten, 2019.

———. *Posuto sengo shakai (shirīzu Nihon kingendai Shi 9).* Tokyo: Iwanami Shoten, 2009.

Zaimushō. "Zaisei ni kansuru shiryō: Ippan kaikei zeishū, saishutsu sōgaku oyobi kōsai hakkōgaku no suii." Accessed December 13, 2022. https://www.mof.go.jp/tax_policy/summary/condition/a02.htm.

Zaimushō Kanzei Kyoku. "Yushutsunyū no suii (chiiki [kuni] betsu-shuyō shōhin betsu): Yushutsunyū no suii (chiiki [kuni] betsu)." Accessed March 6, 2023. https://www.customs.go.jp/toukei/suii/html/time.htm.

———. "Zaimushō bōeki tōkei nenbetsu yushutsunyū sōgaku (kakuteichi)." Accessed December 2, 2022. https://www.customs.go.jp/toukei/suii/html/nenbet.htm.

Zenkoku Chikyū Ondanka Bōshi Katsudō Suishin Sentā. "4–03 Nihon no nisankatansō haishutsuryō no suii (1990–2020nendo)." Accessed December 14, 2022. https://www.jccca.org/download/65455.

Index

Page numbers in **boldface** refer to illustrations.

ABOUT THE AUTHOR

SIMON AVENELL is professor in the School of Culture, History, and Language at the Australian National University.